Eighth Edition

Notary Signing Agent Training Course

Notary Signing Agent Training Course

The Most Complete and Helpful
Self-Education Program for Notary Signing Agents

EIGHTH EDITION

NATIONAL NOTARY ASSOCIATION

Published by:

National Notary Association
9350 De Soto Avenue
Chatsworth, CA 91311-4926
(818) 739-4000
Fax: (818) 700-0920
Website: www.NationalNotary.org
Email: nna@nationalnotary.org

All names, addresses, phone numbers and identification used as examples in this text are purely fictitious. Any similarity to any person living or dead or to any actual addresses, phone numbers or identification is unintended and coincidental.

The information in this Course is correct and current at the time of its publication. This information is provided to aid comprehension of Notary Signing Agent practices and procedures and should not be construed as legal advice. Please consult an attorney for inquiries relating to legal matters.

Eighth Edition © 2012
First Edition © 2002

ISBN: 1-59767-075-8

Table of Contents

List of Loan Documents vii

Preface: Your New Opportunity. xi

Introduction: About this Course. 1

Chapter 1: The Notary Signing Agent's Role 5

Chapter 2: Ensuring Customer Privacy 21

Chapter 3: TILA, RESPA and the PATRIOT Act 37

Chapter 4: Preparing for Loan Signings 59

Chapter 5: Presenting Loan Documents 103

Chapter 6: Closing Out the Assignment 279

Chapter 7: Notary Signing Agent Responsibility 307

Appendix 1: Answers for Chapter Test Questions. 331

Appendix 2: Questions for Further Learning. 333

Appendix 3: Why Notary Signing Agents Must Be
Background Screened 335

Glossary of Important Terms 347

Course Index 365

About the NNA®: The National Notary Association 373

List of Loan Documents

3-Year Prepayment Penalty Addendum to Note 266
Acknowledgment of Receipt of Appraisal Report 200
Acknowledgment of Receipt of Good Faith Estimate
and Truth in Lending Act Disclosures 162
Addendums to Note 263–267
Addendum to Adjustable-Rate Note 263–264
Addendum to Closing Instructions 150–151
Address Certification 193
Adjustable-Rate Rider 248–249
Affiliated Business Arrangement Disclosure 247
Affordable Merit Rate Addendum to Note 265
Allonge 170
Appraisal Disclosure 198
Automated Valuation Model Notice 201–202
Balloon Rider 250–251
Biweekly Payment Rider 252–253
Borrower's Certification & Authorization 163
Buyer's Final Closing Statement 143

California Domestic Partnership Addendum
to Uniform Residential Loan Application 231
California Finance Lenders Law Statement of Loan. 197
California Impound Account Statement and Election Form. 189
Certificate of Loans to One Borrower 194
Comparison of Sample Mortgage Features:
Typical Mortgage Transaction. 206–208
Compliance Agreement. 211
Condominium Rider 185–187
Consumer Credit Score Disclosure. 203–204
Customer Identification Verification. 233
Customer's Statement of Non-Rescission 269
Deed of Trust (Mortgage) 171–184
Demand/Payoff Statement. 268
Disclosure Concerning the Charging of Per Diem Interest
on California Residential Mortgage Loans 230
Document Correction Agreement 212
Escrow Waiver Agreement (Tax Only). 190
False Statement/Employment/Occupancy Form
Borrowers Certification. 215
Federal Equal Credit Opportunity Act Notice. 227
FNMA 1009 Affidavit. 259
General Closing Instructions 147
Good Faith Estimate of Settlement Charges 152–154
Good Faith Estimate Providers of Services. 155
Hardship 165
Hazard Insurance Authorization and Requirements 195
Hazard Insurance Disclosure. 196
HOEPA/HMDA Required Information 229
Housing Financial Discrimination Act Fair Lending Notice 228
HUD (U.S Department of Housing and Urban Development)
Settlement Statement 144–146
Impound Authorization. 188

Initial Escrow Account Disclosure Statement .192
IRS Form 4506-T (Request for Copy of Transcript of Tax Return) . . 223–224
IRS Form 8821 (Tax Information Authorization). 254–257
IRS Form W-9 (Request for Taxpayer Identification Number
and Certification) 219–222
Itemization of Amount Financed 166
Limited Power of Attorney 213–214
Loan Modification Agreement 270–271
Mortgage: see Deed of Trust. 171–184
Mortgagor's Affidavit. 260–261
Name Affidavit 210
Note. 167–169
Notice Concerning the Furnishing of Negative Information
to Consumer Reporting Agency 205
Notice of Assignment, Sale or Transfer of Servicing Rights 226
Notice of Right to Cancel 258
Notice of Right to Copy of Appraisal. 199
Occupancy Affidavit 218
Occupancy and Financial Status Affidavit 216–217
Payment Letter to Borrower 164
Privacy Policy Disclosure 236–238
Real Estate Tax Bill Certification (Not Titled). 191
Request for Change to Flood Certification 235
Request for Change to Insurance Policy 234
Riders to Security Instrument 185–187, 248–253
Servicing Disclosure Statement 225
Signature Affidavit & AKA Statement 209
Specific Closing Instructions 148–149
Statement of Information 262
Tax Information Sheet 232
Timely Payment Rewards Addendum to Note 267
Truth in Lending Disclosure Statement 161
Uniform Residential Loan Application 156–160

PREFACE

Your New Opportunity

Discovery consists of seeing what everybody has seen and thinking what nobody has thought.

Those are the words of Albert von Szent-Györgyi, the Hungarian-born American biochemist who, during experiments on cell respiration, succeeded in isolating a reducing agent from oranges and lemons. He named this substance ascorbic acid, but we all know it as vitamin C. We owe a debt of gratitude to Szent-Györgyi for his pioneering work, which has contributed in no small part to the healthy lives we lead.

In the innovative spirit of Szent-Györgyi, the National Notary Association (NNA®) has been a forerunner in creating training for a relatively new vocation for Notaries Public: the Notary Signing Agent.

In years past, it was common for a homebuyer to travel to the office of an escrow agent or title company to sign loan papers and conduct the settlement. Due to a number of factors, however, a market has been created for Notaries Public to travel to a borrower's home or office to coordinate the loan signing, notarize any applicable instruments and return the documents to the closing agent for processing.

With this business opportunity for Notaries comes the need to acquire new skills, training and certification. You are to be commended for seeking out this instruction by obtaining the NNA®'s *Notary Signing Agent Training Course*. By doing so, you have shown that you are a conscientious Notary Signing Agent or Notary Signing Agent-to-be who is eager to excel in this exciting field.

The *Notary Signing Agent Training Course* was developed by the NNA® to prepare you to take the Notary Signing Agent Certification Examination. In your preparation you will gain an understanding of the varied considerations that affect loan document signings and will receive an explanation of all the important aspects of lawful, prudent and ethical signing agent practice. This book will serve as an invaluable reference throughout your loan document signing career.

Whether you are a longtime Notary Signing Agent or about to embark on your first loan signing, I am confident the *Notary Signing Agent Training Course* will provide you with new insights and understanding. Your improved comprehension of signing agent practices and procedures will result in greater proficiency and profitability as a professional Notary Signing Agent.

Milton G. Valera
Chairman
National Notary Association

INTRODUCTION

About this Course

The primary purpose of the *Notary Signing Agent Training Course* is to prepare the learner to complete the Notary Signing Agent Certification Examination, which assesses the candidate's mastery of the proper procedures for conducting a loan document signing. For complete details about the Examination, including prerequisites and instructions for taking it, please contact the NNA®.

In addition to passing the Notary Signing Agent Certification Examination, candidates for certification must undergo a background screening. The background screening is applicable for all parties in the chain of a mortgage loan finance transaction with responsibilities for or access to private customer financial information. In recognition of both the valuable skills they have attained and their readiness to safeguard customer privacy, those who successfully pass the Examination and a background screening earn the designation, NNA® Certified and Background Screened Notary Signing Agent.

The *Notary Signing Agent Training Course* teaches new and experienced Notary Signing Agents the relevant principles and practices of acting as a Notary Signing Agent within the context of loan document signings. The *Course* also provides the information necessary to handle properly and confidently the many documents that appear in loan document packages, both those that require notarization and those that do not.

Each of this *Course*'s seven chapters includes footnotes, which provide additional references that can deepen understanding of the concepts appearing throughout the chapters. All chapters conclude with several "Test Yourself" questions, which reinforce each chapter's important concepts. At the end of the *Course*, there are three appendices. Appendix 1 gives the answers to the self-test questions at the end of each chapter, Appendix 2 contains supplemental questions to promote further learning and Appendix 3 provides a detailed analysis of why Notary Signing Agents must be background screened and includes the text of the relevant federal laws. Finally, the appendices are followed by a glossary of important terms for Notary Signing Agents and the index.

By providing all these resources for Notary Signing Agents, this *Course* will serve as a valuable professional reference for years to come.

The *Notary Signing Agent Training Course* is the most comprehensive and practical self-education tool ever developed for Notary Signing Agents. The *Course* reflects the NNA®'s half-century of experience educating and serving Notaries Public. Since its founding in 1957 by Raymond C. Rothman and throughout its subsequent stewardship by current chairman Milton G. Valera, the NNA® has educated, trained and supported hundreds of thousands of Notaries throughout the United States.

While the *Notary Signing Agent Training Course* serves as a comprehensive guide to learning and understanding how to perform loan document signings, it is not intended to take the place of an attorney or state official in interpreting specific notarial laws and regulations. It must be complemented by careful study of other state-specific materials, often provided to Notaries by a commissioning official.

By completing the *Notary Signing Agent Training Course* and successfully passing the Examination and background screening, students demonstrate an uncommon degree of professional dedication. As knowledgeable and trustworthy public servants, *Course* graduates are ready to perform the vital and challenging role of official impartial witness in loan document signings with legal, technical and ethical correctness.

CHAPTER 1

The Notary Signing Agent's Role

INTRODUCTION

Before the early 1990s, the Notary Signing Agent was largely an unknown occupation. The concept of having a specialized impartial witness visit one's home or business to oversee and expedite the process of signing loan documents had not yet emerged as a widespread need. Certainly, there were mobile Notaries who advertised their willingness to travel "anywhere at any time" to serve those who were unable to leave their homes. It nonetheless was taken as a given that borrowers would have to travel to the offices of a lender, escrow company or title firm in order to complete a loan.

However, innovations in technology, greater competition in the lending market, a new corporate preference for outsourcing and consumers' expectations about customer service have altered the lending picture across the nation. One of these alterations is the expectation that the borrower always must travel to the lender.

In addition, the computer's penetration into every corner of American business has propelled loan processing into "fast mode." Speed in approving and closing a loan now offers a competitive advantage. To expedite loan processing, fax machines, emails and overnight-delivery services allow Notary Signing Agents to operate swiftly and effectively in the field, often a continent away from a lender's home office.

PRECURSORS OF THE NOTARY SIGNING AGENT

Many of the precursors of today's Notary Signing Agents were far from respectable. Often they were sales representatives with a direct financial interest in closing deals by securing a client's signature. High pressure and low deception were too often common practices among these sales closers.[1]

Decades ago, the function of a Notary Signing Agent was typically assumed by a sales agent or broker. Such people often catered to clients by traveling to their homes. This was as much a tactic for disarming the clients and putting them at ease as it was for making the process more convenient for them.

The closing and the sale were the overriding priority of the forerunners of today's Notary Signing Agent, because they were motivated by personal interest above all else. Matters such as avoiding undue influence or ensuring the signer understood the terms of the document were of little or no concern. Any notarizations required in a transaction were often performed out of the presence of the client.

What was missing was an honest and impartial third party to guarantee the integrity of each transaction and thereby protect the interests of all involved. Today, with the advent of the Notary Signing Agent, a lender has the option of foregoing a face-to-face meeting with a borrower in favor of relying on a trusted third party to obtain the needed signatures, perform the requisite notarizations and return all documents to the lender in a timely fashion.

[1] The deceptive tactics of these individuals were so widespread and virtually institutionalized that unscrupulous closers were colorfully categorized by the techniques they used to con clients into signing documents against their interest: the Folder, the Stacker, the Holder. These unscrupulous techniques were described in "Hitting Homes," a cover feature in *The National Notary*, May 1987, pp. 10-11.

WHAT IS A NOTARY SIGNING AGENT?

A Notary Signing Agent is an independent contractor who is hired and compensated by a closing agent[2] to coordinate and oversee the appointment at which loan documents are signed by a borrower. The Agent receives or reproduces documents for a loan signing appointment, ensures that documents are properly executed by a borrower, notarizes one or more documents in the package and returns the completed documents to the closing agent for processing.

A Notary Signing Agent is not the employee of the closing agent — usually a lender or title company — but is in business independently. Typically, the Notary Signing Agent contracts with the lender or with a title or escrow company in the transaction to perform the signing. Even when the Agent is hired by a signing service (a middleman, hired by the lender, title company or escrow firm, who enlists Notary Signing Agents to conduct loan signings), the Agent will act as an independent agent.

That the Notary Signing Agent is an independent contractor also means that the Agent is responsible for paying income taxes on the profits of the Agent's business, by filing an IRS Form 1040 Schedule C ("Profit or Loss from Business") along with a personal tax return each year. As an independent contractor, the Notary Signing Agent is also responsible for paying self-employment taxes.[3]

The definition highlights five chief duties of a Notary Signing Agent:

1. **To coordinate and oversee the appointment at which loan documents are signed by a borrower:** A Notary Signing Agent will either set or confirm the appointment with a borrower and make any necessary arrangements, such as reminding the borrower to present valid identification and produce any items (pay stubs, proof of insurance, a check for closing costs, etc.) required for the closing.

[2] A closing agent is an individual or firm that represents a buyer and handles the closing of the loan and the legal transfer of title and ownership from the seller to the buyer. The closing agent is also referred to as a settlement agent. Usually the loan closing is conducted by title companies, escrow companies or attorneys.

[3] See Chapter 6, "Closing Out the Assignment," for further information.

2. **To receive or reproduce documents for the signing appointment and to carry the documents to the appointment:** In years past, documents were sent to the Notary Signing Agent via overnight courier and received on the day of the appointment. Increasingly, however, lenders and closing agents today are transmitting documents to the Notary Signing Agent electronically (called e-documents or "e-docs"). For an additional fee, the Agent then downloads the documents and prints both signing and borrower's copies. Irrespective of how the documents are transmitted, lenders rely on the Notary Signing Agent to receive and safely bring the documents to the signing.[4] Borrowers appreciate that the Agent comes to their home or office to conduct the signing.

3. **To ensure that real estate loan documents are properly executed:** The Notary Signing Agent fulfills an important role in the real estate loan and refinancing process. A real estate loan is among the most important transactions a person will ever execute. Much is riding on the proper execution of these documents: the opportunity of home ownership for a first-time buyer, a lower interest rate and lower monthly payments for a mortgagee, a loan sale for the lender and a closing transaction for the title or escrow company. The Notary Signing Agent is the critical link in making the loan closing happen.

4. **To ensure that the documents requiring notarization are properly notarized:** The number and type of documents requiring notarization differ by lender and loan program. However, in order to notarize the security instrument, any affidavits and perhaps a power of attorney document, the Notary Signing Agent must hold a valid Notary commission.

5. **To return the documents for processing:** It is the Notary Signing Agent's responsibility to ensure that the properly executed and

[4] See Chapter 4, "Preparing for Loan Signings," where the benefits of this courier service are discussed more fully.

notarized documents are delivered or express-mailed by deadline to the company responsible for conducting the loan closing.

Finally, the definition of Notary Signing Agent clarifies that it is the contracting company that compensates the Agent for performing all services related to the loan signing. It is important to note that the Notary Signing Agent is not paid directly by the borrower. The contracting company typically pays the Agent an industry standard flat fee per signing for all services the Agent performs in connection with the signing.

Technically, the fee which the Agent receives is not a Notary fee that is governed by state Notary fee laws. In a strictly notarial transaction, the person for whom notarial services are performed pays the Notary directly. Even though one or more documents in the loan package may be notarized, the Agent is not being paid by the borrower for these notarizations. Rather, the Agent is being paid for the full range of services he or she provides to the contracting company, one of which is to notarize documents in the loan package.

THE HOME LOAN PROCESS

The term Notary Signing Agent originally was coined to distinguish this role from that of other participants in the loan process. Besides the Notary Signing Agent, there are three other major parties to this process, and each has its own unique role.

1. **The borrower** initiates the loan by contacting the lender and applying for the loan.

2. **The lender** processes the loan, contacts the closing agent and funds the loan.

3. **The closing agent,** an independent third party authorized by the lender, performs the closing duties on the loan and acts as an implementer for the borrowers. It is usually the closing agent who

hires the Notary Signing Agent, either directly or indirectly through a signing service.

The Borrower

In a purchase transaction, the loan process starts when a prospective homebuyer looks for a home. The buyer typically secures the services of a real estate agent, who scans the Multiple Listing Service (MLS) for a home that will meet the buyer's needs and be within the buyer's price range. In most instances, the buyer already will have applied and been preapproved for a loan.

In a refinance transaction, a homeowner decides to refinance an existing mortgage. In a secondary finance transaction, the homeowner decides to take out a second loan on the property.

The Lender

Once a homebuyer finds a home, the buyer works with the real estate agent to secure a loan. In the case of a refinance or second mortgage, the homeowner shops for a loan. After a lender has been selected, the borrower applies for a loan by providing personal financial information in a face-to-face or phone interview or through an online submission. The information the borrower provides will be entered into the Uniform Residential Loan Application (Fannie Mae 1003) (pages 156–160).

The lender will review the loan application and may request additional information from the borrower, such as verification, disclosure or authorization forms to substantiate employment, bank account information and identity.

During the loan-approval phase, the lender will order a number of other items to supplement the borrower's application:

1. **A copy of the borrower's most recent credit report:** The credit report is used to verify the borrower's credit status.

2. **A preliminary title report on the subject property:** A title search is a detailed examination of the property records. These records include deeds, court filings, property and name indexes and many other documents. The purpose of the search is to verify the seller's right to transfer ownership and to discover any claims, liens, defects or other matters affecting the property.

3. **An appraisal of the subject property:** The appraisal, which is conducted by a qualified appraiser with the necessary education, training and experience, will determine the value of the home based upon comparable homes in the immediate neighborhood. The appraised value is the home's fair market value and is based on the appraiser's analysis of the property.

Based on the complete application package, the lender may approve the loan either as submitted or with conditions. A loan approved as submitted means the loan is accepted based upon the information provided. If the loan is approved with conditions, further information is necessary to obtain approval. Here, the lender will work with the borrower to obtain any further requirements, such as explanatory letters or copies of investment documents, divorce papers or additional verifications that may clarify the borrower's qualifications for the loan.

The Closing Agent

When the lender has approved the borrower's loan, the closing agent enters the process. The closing agent is a title or escrow company representative or an attorney who is responsible for the paperwork and general logistics in completing the transaction. The closing agent draws the documents, collects and disburses funds, obtains the signatures of the borrowers and submits the title documents for recording.

In the past, the borrower would travel to an escrow office to sign loan documents, but life today makes this increasingly impractical. The inconvenience of signing documents at an escrow office was one factor that helped to start the Notary Signing Agent industry. By sending a Notary Signing Agent to conduct the signing portion of the transaction in the borrower's home at a time that is convenient to the borrower and having the Agent return the documents to the title company via overnight carrier, the closing agent can ensure that the loan process moves forward to a timely closing. Since signing service costs are typically added into the borrower's costs, the lender does not normally object to a signing being conducted at a borrower's office or home.

Following any right of rescission period,[5] the closing of escrow occurs. The closing agent will receive the loan documents, signed, dated and notarized as necessary, and will then finalize preparations for the closing. These include the following:

1. Calculating the various prorations, charges and adjustments, such as interest on an old loan, interest on the new loan, money for impound accounts for taxes and insurance, etc.

2. Making sure all funds are deposited

3. Providing the borrower with a settlement statement showing all of the costs involved in the loan

4. Ordering the title examination and survey

5. Providing the mortgage lender with a title insurance commitment

6. Ensuring the seller can convey marketable title

7. Ensuring all parties are paid after the loan is funded

8. Recording applicable documents (deeds, powers of attorney, etc.)

[5] For refinance loans, federal law gives a borrower a three-day cooling off period before the loan closes. The borrower can cancel, or rescind, the loan at any time up until midnight of the third day of this three-day period.

Does the Notary Signing Agent "Close" the Loan?

With the Notary Signing Agent being enlisted to facilitate the signing portion of the transaction, a question has arisen that is asked by Notary Signing Agents and some closing agents: Does the Notary Signing Agent actually close the loan? Notary Signing Agents ask this question when they come across documents in a loan package requiring the signature of the settlement (closing) agent and wonder whether they must sign in this space. An example of one such document, a Property Tax Information Certificate appearing below, contains a signature line for the settlement agent.

PROPERTY TAX INFORMATION CERTIFICATE
(This form must be typed)

Borrower/s: ROBERT L. CLARKSON AND VERONICA M. CLARKSON

Property Address: 9089 WICOPEE AVENUE, LOS ANGELES, CALIFORNIA 90041-2526
Legal Description: THAT PORTION OF LOT 89 OF THE MYERS TRACT, IN THE CITY OF LOS ANGELES, COUNTY OF LOS ANGELES, STATE OF CALIFORNIA AS PER MAP
Tax Authority Record Owner: ____________
(Use name current billing will be issued in)

Notification to Closing Agent: **Obtain and pay tax bills due at the time of this certification as well as bills due within the next sixty (60) days.**

Tax Authority		Tax Information	
County		Improved ___ Unimproved ___ Tax Estimated	
Payable to		Annual Tax	
Address		Monthly Escrow Amount	
City	State	Date Taxes Last Paid	
Phone # ( )	Zip	Billing Cycle	
Tax ID/Account #		Date Next Taxes Due	
City		Improved ___ Unimproved ___ Tax Estimated	
Payable to		Annual Tax	
Address		Monthly Escrow Amount	
City	State	Date Taxes Last Paid	
Phone # ( )	Zip	Billing Cycle	
Tax ID/Account #		Date Next Taxes Due	

"Annual Tax" amounts specified above are based upon the improved value of the Property (and without exemption/s if the exemption/s will no longer apply). If the property is new construction or subject to an exemption that will no longer apply, please indicate taxes are estimates. Attach copies of all paid tax certificates and/or tax receipts.

I hereby certify that all of the above is complete and accurate to the best of my knowledge.

Settlement Agent Signature ____________ Date____________

Settlement Agent Phone # ( ) ____________

In rare instances, closing agents have asked Notary Signing Agents to sign wherever the signature line for the settlement agent occurs. The confusion seems to stem from the time when the loan signing portion of the transaction was performed during a closing appointment with an escrow agent. For most people, this signing appointment still signifies the closing. However, with Notary Signing Agents taking on the signing portion of the transaction, the signing no longer signifies a closing. The loan closes after the loan documents are signed and returned to the title company for processing.

Even a refinance or second mortgage signed in an escrow office is not legally considered a closing, since the borrower has three days to cancel the loan and the conditions of the loan still can be modified. The true closing does not occur until the three-day right of rescission period has elapsed and the funds are disbursed.

For those purchase transactions in which property is conveyed without a loan, there is typically no rescission period and the signing usually takes place at the closing table: When the documents are signed, the deal is sealed and the disbursement of funds is completed. Notary Signing Agents primarily handle refinance loans, second mortgages and equity lines of credit. These are transactions where no property is being transferred or conveyed. The Notary Signing Agent's duties are limited to obtaining the signatures on the documents, notarizing the title documents and other forms requiring notarization and returning the documents to the title company or lender quickly.

These Notary Signing Agent functions do not comprise the typical closing functions performed by the closing agent, which include the following:

1. Drawing documents

2. Disbursing funds

3. Providing abstraction of the title

4. Ensuring the title documents are properly recorded

These duties are performed outside the loan signing by a licensed closing agent or attorney. Therefore, a Notary Signing Agent is not a closing agent and does not, properly speaking, close the loan. In places where the signature line for the settlement agent appears, the Notary Signing Agent should not sign and should leave it for the escrow officer to complete.

Attorney-Only, Licensure and Restrictive States

Despite the apparent differences between the duties of a true closing agent and those of a Notary Signing Agent, some states view the part of the loan document signing that is handled by the Notary Signing Agent as part of the closing and thus classify the Agent as a closing agent.

In some of those states, only qualified attorneys are allowed to serve as closing agents. In many cases, such attorney-only requirements relate solely to documents that convey or transfer property, and not to home equity or refinancing papers. The states potentially involved include, but are not necessarily limited to, Delaware, Georgia, Massachusetts, South Carolina, Vermont and West Virginia.

On the other hand, some of the states that view the Notary Signing Agent as a type of closing agent require anyone who handles closings to obtain some type of license. For example, in Maryland and Indiana a person must be a licensed title insurance producer in order to work in accordance with state laws. In Virginia, a Notary Signing Agent who handles funds at a closing must be licensed as a settlement agent.

Finally, in the state of Texas, certain loan signings may not be performed in the homes of signers. The Texas Constitution states that a homestead is protected from a forced sale for the payment of debt for an extension of credit, unless such extension of credit is closed at the offices of the lender, an attorney at law or a title company. Closings performed at locations other than these may be subject to homestead protection (preventing a forced sale of the homestead). Therefore, many lenders have instructed Notaries not to acknowledge a borrower's signature at other locations (such as the borrower's home).

Notary Signing Agent Opportunity

Given that the Notary Signing Agent plays a critical role in the home loan process, there is a great opportunity now for Notary Signing Agents and those who would like to begin a career in this field. What are the past and current market conditions that have created a demand for such services?

1. **The Gramm-Leach-Bliley Act (GLBA) of 1999** contributed to significant growth in the Notary Signing Agent industry by eliminating legal barriers to affiliations among banks and other financial service companies. The GLBA allows banks, insurance companies, securities firms and other financial services companies to enter one another's business specialties. Through implementation of the GLBA, Congress allows for the application of more dynamic and creative business strategies, which have resulted in greater financial activity. The GLBA has led to more loan closings in the home loan industry, which has translated into greater demand for Notary Signing Agents to ensure that loan documents are properly executed.

2. **Historically low interest rates** have created a massive amount of business in the loan industry. Lower rates make it possible for many first-time buyers to enter the market, since their anticipated monthly mortgage payments are lower than in any recent time. These same low interest rates also generated a refinancing boom in the early 2000s, allowing existing homeowners to refinance their current mortgages, consolidate debt and better plan for major expenses, such as college and retirement. Today's interest rates remain at an all-time low.

3. **An outsourcing trend** in the real estate loan industry, which reflects a larger national trend, is another market factor fueling the growth of the loan signing business. To keep up with the volume in the prior refinancing boom, closing agents conducted fewer and

fewer in-house loan signings and relied instead on Notary Signing Agents to handle the signing portion of loan transactions.

4. **Notary Signing Agents provide a valuable service** to closing agents, who have discovered that using Notary Signing Agents can increase their volume of loan closings and reduce settlement costs.

5. **Notary Signing Agents offer convenience** to borrowers. In a highly personal and sensitive transaction, such as a home purchase, a borrower is likely to be more comfortable executing loan documents in the privacy of his or her own home or office rather than in a closing agent's office. The borrower does not have to take time off from work, fight traffic or juggle conflicting commitments. The Notary Signing Agent provides a valuable service by going to the borrower to execute the loan documents instead of the borrower disrupting work or weekend to travel to a title or escrow office.

Notary Signing Agent Transactions

What types of loan transactions require the services of a Notary Signing Agent? In the early phases of the Notary Signing Agent's remarkable ascendance, Agents almost exclusively handled transactions involving the refinancing of existing mortgages. While the refinance transaction is without a doubt the bread and butter of the Notary Signing Agent's repertoire, as the Notary Signing Agent career field has developed and matured, Agents are regularly enlisted to handle one or more of the following types of transactions:

1. **Home Equity Lines of Credit (HELOC):** A HELOC is a revolving line of credit for a maximum draw, rather than a fixed dollar amount. HELOCs are designed to finance a wide array of financial needs, including remodeling, home improvement, debt consolidation and college tuition. In most cases, a HELOC is secured by the property as collateral and becomes a second lien on the title.

2. **Sale or purchase transactions:** Notary Signing Agents occasionally may be asked to supervise the execution of papers for a sale or purchase of real property. In a sale or purchase transaction, the Notary Signing Agent may handle the signing for the seller, the buyer or both.

3. **Reverse (Home Equity Conversion) mortgages:** These innovative new loans are for qualifying seniors age 62 or older, who either own their own homes or have sufficient equity to tap. In a reverse mortgage, seniors do not make payments on a typical loan; rather, the lender makes payments to the borrower in the form of a lump sum payout, a line of credit or regular monthly payments (hence the term "reverse"). Repayment by the senior is postponed as long as the senior lives in the home. The loan is settled from the proceeds of the sale of the home.

4. **Commercial loans:** A commercial loan involves a financial transaction for real property involving a business, corporation, partnership or other legal entity.

5. **Construction loans:** Consumers wanting to build their own homes must obtain a construction loan. Construction loans are typically temporary in nature: Once the building of the home is complete, the borrower obtains a traditional mortgage loan to pay off the construction loan (a construction-only loan) or the construction loan is converted into a traditional mortgage (a construction-to-permanent loan).

THE NOTARY SIGNING AGENT AS NOTARY PUBLIC

In executing a loan signing, a Notary Signing Agent fulfills a second important role: that of a Notary Public. A Notary Public is a government officer and public servant who serves as an impartial witness in taking acknowledgments, administering oaths and affirmations and performing other acts authorized by law.

Notaries exist to facilitate the workings of commerce and law by lending credibility to certain sensitive signed documents. When a document is notarized, the public can be assured that its signer is not an impostor, and any contracting parties can be assured that the document they have signed — and no other — will have full force and effect.

Certain documents affecting title to real property that Notary Signing Agents handle must be acknowledged before a Notary as a condition for recording in the official land records. In addition, there are various affidavits and other documents in the closing documents for a mortgage loan that must be notarized. For this reason, any person who handles mortgage loan document signings must of necessity be a Notary Public. ■

CHAPTER 1 TEST

True/False Questions

1. The Notary Signing Agent is also the settlement or closing agent in the transaction.

2. A Notary Signing Agent is hired as an independent contractor.

3. Notary Signing Agents draw the documents, collect and disburse funds, obtain the signatures of the borrowers and submit the title documents for recording.

Multiple Choice Questions

(Choose the Best Answer)

1. Which of the following factors helped to expand the Notary Signing Agent business?
   a) The passage of the GLBA
   b) The outsourcing of loan signings
   c) The convenience Agents offer borrowers
   d) All of the above

2. The term Notary Signing Agent was coined for which of the following reasons?
   a) To distinguish the new role from that of other participants in the loan process
   b) To increase opportunities to make money
   c) To heighten the status of the Notary in business commerce
   d) None of the above

3. The Uniform Residential Loan Application is also known as which of the following?
   a) Fannie Mae 1015
   c) Fannie Mae 1003
   b) Fannie Mae 1005
   d) None of the above

See page 331 for correct responses.

CHAPTER 2

Ensuring Customer Privacy

NOTARY SIGNING AGENT RESPONSIBILITY

As Notaries Public first and foremost, Notary Signing Agents fulfill the critical role of official impartial witness to the execution of home loan finance papers. They must perform all required notarial acts with precision and skill, carefully following the Notary laws of their respective states. When state laws and official rules for notarization are silent or lacking, Agents must follow all widely adopted Notary best practices and standards as espoused in *The Notary Public Code of Professional Responsibility*. Such statutory deficiencies will vary from state to state. The effectiveness or shortcomings of a state's Notary laws, regulations and official directives will dictate the degree to which a Notary will depend upon the *Code* to inform and guide his or her conduct.

However, there is at least one important standard of conduct that is universally absent from state Notary codes and regulations, and Notaries of all states will be united in reliance upon the *Code* for a best practice recommendation. Consider the *Code*'s Guiding Principle IX:

> The Notary shall respect the privacy of each signer and not divulge or use personal or proprietary information disclosed during the execution of a notarial act for other than an official purpose.

Guiding Principle IX is premised upon the notion that, in notarizing documents, a Notary may be privy to a client's personal information. The *Code* stresses that, as a public official of the state, the Notary must respect the privacy rights of those served and, especially when sensitive matters are involved, must be proactive in protecting this information. In Chapter 4, Agents will be encouraged to review all loan documents in advance of a scheduled loan signing as part of the Agent's preparation. As will be explained later, briefly skimming the documents to see which ones must be notarized, signed, initialed and/or dated will ensure that the Agent performs a thorough and efficient signing in the least amount of time. But perusing the documents in preparation for an appointment also inevitably exposes an Agent to myriad personal financial details about the borrower. A Notary Signing Agent not only must be trusted to impartially witness the transaction; the Agent also must be trusted to protect the personal financial information to which he or she is exposed.

Therefore, it is absolutely essential that Notary Signing Agents understand and pledge to abide by the standards of professional and ethical practice of Guiding Principle IX of *The Notary Public Code of Professional Responsibility.*

GRAMM-LEACH-BLILEY FINANCIAL SERVICES MODERNIZATION ACT

Recent developments in the lending and title insurance industries have only confirmed what *The Notary Public Code of Professional Responsibility* previously advanced. The Gramm-Leach-Bliley Financial Services Modernization Act (GLBA) of 1999, mentioned in Chapter 1 as an impetus to the professional opportunity now enjoyed by Notary Signing Agents, brought with it an important professional responsibility as well.[1]

[1] See Appendix 3 for the relevant excerpts of the GLBA.

The GLBA protects the privacy of consumer information held by financial institutions and requires companies to give consumers privacy notices that explain the institutions' information sharing practices. The GLBA also provides consumers with the right to limit some sharing of their information.

Section 6801 of the GLBA requires the relevant Agencies[2] to establish standards relating to the safety and security of customer records and information for the financial institutions that are subject to their respective jurisdictions. The standards that have been issued to implement the GLBA customer information privacy provisions, known as the Interagency Guidelines,[3] were published in the *Federal Register* on February 1, 2001.[4]

The three objectives of the Interagency Guidelines are as follows:

1. Ensure the security and confidentiality of customer information

2. Protect against any anticipated threats or hazards to the security or integrity of such information

3. Protect against unauthorized access to or use of such information that could possibly harm any customer

The Interagency Guidelines require all financial institutions governed under the GLBA to implement a comprehensive information security program (Guidelines, Sec. II.A. and Sec. III.C.1.). The GLBA applies to almost any business that is involved in providing financial products or services to consumers, including mortgage lenders, lending institutions and mortgage brokers.

---

[2] The "Agencies" in this case are the Office of the Comptroller of the Currency (Department of the Treasury), the Board of Governors of the Federal Reserve System, the Federal Deposit Insurance Corporation, the Office of Thrift Supervision (Department of the Treasury), the National Credit Union Administration, the Securities and Exchange Commission and the Federal Trade Commission.

[3] See Appendix 3 for the full text of the Interagency Guidelines.

[4] Office of the Federal Register, National Archives and Records Administration, *Federal Register*, Vol. 66, No. 22 (February 1, 2001). All volumes of the *Federal Register* from 1994 to the present also may be found in electronic form on the website of the U.S. Government Printing Office (GPO), http://www.gpoaccess.gov/fr.

The Interagency Guidelines require financial institutions to exercise due diligence in selecting service providers (Guidelines, Sec. III.D.1.). Financial institutions in turn must require their service providers to implement the measures needed to meet the Interagency Guidelines (Guidelines, Sec. III.D.2.). The Interagency Guidelines define a service provider as "any person or entity that maintains, processes, or otherwise is permitted access to customer information through its provision of services directly to [entities over which OTS has authority]" (Guidelines, Sec. I.C.2.d. [and Sec. I.A.]). Under this definition, service providers include title companies and signing services.

The Preamble to the Interagency Guidelines specifies that, as part of its due diligence in selecting service providers, "a financial institution must determine that the service provider has adequate controls to ensure that the subservicer will protect the customer information in a way that meets the objectives of these Guidelines."[5] The Interagency Guidelines define a subservicer as "any person who has access to an institution's customer information through its provision of services to the service provider."[6] Under this definition, subservicers include Notary Signing Agents hired by title companies and signing services.

In short, since Notary Signing Agents qualify as subservicers, the Interagency Guidelines require Notary Signing Agents to protect the personal and sensitive customer information that is found in loan document packages for every mortgage finance loan transaction. This chapter will present practical steps Agents must take to preserve the confidentiality of customer information before, during and after the loan signing appointment.

Beyond ensuring that subservicers protect customer information, financial institutions must consider and adopt as needed an additional security measure that is of particular relevance to Notary Signing Agents. This is the requirement for "employee background checks for employees with responsibilities for or access to customer information" (Guidelines,

---

[5] *Federal Register*, Vol. 66, No. 22 (February 1, 2001), p. 8624, also available on the website of the GPO, http://frwebgate.access.gpo.gov/cgi-bin/getdoc.cgi?dbname=2001_register&docid=01-1114-filed.pdf.

[6] *Federal Register*, Vol. 66, No. 22 (February 1, 2001), p. 8619 n. 8. See previous note for URL.

Sec. III.C.1.e.). Why Notary Signing Agents must undergo background checks is discussed in detail in Appendix 3.

FAIR AND ACCURATE CREDIT TRANSACTIONS ACT

Subsequent to the publication of the final Interagency Guidelines and in response to issuing rules in connection with section 216 of the Fair and Accurate Credit Transactions (FACT) Act of 2003, the Agencies published a proposal to amend the GLBA Interagency Guidelines. The resulting rulemaking for the FACT Act added a fourth objective to the GLBA Interagency Guidelines, which requires a financial institution to "develop, implement and maintain, as part of its information security program, appropriate measures to properly dispose of customer information and consumer information in accordance with each of the requirements in this paragraph III."[7]

This fourth objective has implications for Notary Signing Agents in at least two areas:

1. **Disposal of any digital or "e-doc" computer files temporarily saved on the Agent's computer system:** In a digital or e-document loan signing, an Agent receives the loan documents electronically and prints them out to take to the signing appointment. Since the documents are instantaneously transmitted to the Agent via email or are housed on the lender's secure Web server for access by the Agent for printing, the delay of receiving the documents via overnight courier is eliminated, and Agents can receive same-day assignments. Careful and prudent Agents print the e-documents directly from an email or a Web server, eliminating the need for the loan documents to be saved on the Agent's computer. However, in instances when the files containing the loan documents must be downloaded to the Agent's computer before they can be printed, the Agent must take precautions to permanently delete these files after printing the documents.

[7] *Federal Register*, Vol. 69, No. 248 (December 28, 2004), p. 77618, also available on the website of the GPO, http://edocket.access.gpo.gov/2004/pdf/04-27962.pdf.

2. **Proper handling of personal identifying information stored in Notary journals:** All applicable state laws, administrative and best practices, and rules governing retention and disposition of Notary journals must be followed when the Notary Signing Agent resigns his or her commission or retires from being a Notary.

GRAMM-LEACH-BLILEY AND FACT ACT COMPLIANCE

As part of a Notary Signing Agent's preparation for a loan signing appointment, the Agent must take all necessary steps and precautions to comply with GLBA and FACT Act requirements and thereby to protect the personal financial information appearing in the loan documents. A comprehensive list of precautions Agents should take to secure customer information follows. The list covers steps Agents should take both at all times and specifically before, during and after the loan signing appointment. Steps for securing e-documents and electronic communications also are provided.

At All Times

1. Once the Notary Signing Agent receives loan documents, the Agent is responsible for them until he or she returns them to the contracting company. Agents should keep loan documents in a safe, secure and locked location at all times.

2. Notary Signing Agents should never leave loan documents unattended in their car. If an Agent must temporarily store loan documents in a vehicle, then the Agent should keep them in a locked briefcase or box in the vehicle's locked trunk. Loan documents should never be stored in a car overnight or for protracted periods of time.

3. If the Notary Signing Agent has a vehicle without an enclosed trunk (e.g., a hatchback or truck), then the Agent should install a trunk

tarp, cargo cover or tonneau cover to provide more security for temporary storage of loan documents.

4. Notary Signing Agents should never leave loan documents in public places such as on a grocery store or bank counter or in a copy shop, a restaurant or another borrower's home.

5. Notary Signing Agents should never leave originals or copies of loan documents in fax or copy machines, whether personal or public.

6. Notary Signing Agents should never allow others to handle or read a borrower's loan documents or leave them in a place where they might be perused by anyone other than the borrower.

7. Notary Signing Agents should never discuss details of an appointment with family members, friends or coworkers.

8. Notary Signing Agents should protect their Notary journal from theft. Agents should always keep their journal in a locked or secure place when it is not in use, and they should securely archive all completed Notary journals.

9. Notary Signing Agents must follow all state laws and rules governing retention and disposition of Notary journals at the end of their Notary commission or career as a Notary.

10. If at any point in the assignment loan documents are compromised, the Notary Signing Agent should immediately contact the contracting company to report the incident and receive any follow-up procedures and instructions. If necessary, the Agent should contact local law enforcement to report stolen documents.

Before the Signing Appointment

1. When contacting a borrower by phone, the Notary Signing Agent should ask for the person by his or her full name. The Agent should verify that he or she is talking to the borrower before revealing any confidential information. If the borrower is not available when the Agent calls, then the Agent should ask when he or she may call again or if there is an alternate number where the borrower can be reached.

2. If the Notary Signing Agent must leave a voicemail message, the Agent should not include any personal information. The Agent should leave only his or her contact information and a general message about the appointment.

3. Whenever possible, the Notary Signing Agent should receive a physical shipment of loan documents from the courier in person. If the Agent is not present when the shipment arrives, an unauthorized person could intercept the package and open it.

4. If the Notary Signing Agent is unable to receive a physical shipment of loan documents personally, then he or she should arrange a secure location in which to receive loan documents from the courier. For example, the Agent may use a locked container near his or her front door or rent a mail delivery box at a mail service office.

5. Once the Notary Signing Agent receives a physical shipment of loan documents, he or she should make sure that the seals on the packages are not broken. The Agent should promptly report to the contracting company any packages received with broken seals. Agents should keep in mind that packages may be battered and damaged due to handling, but this is not necessarily evidence of tampering.

6. When the Notary Signing Agent is copying the loan documents, the Agent should never let the originals or copies out of his or her sight.

During the Signing Appointment

1. Notary Signing Agents should not bring the loan documents from a previous or upcoming appointment into the location of the current appointment. The Agent should store such loan documents in a locked box or case at home, at the Agent's office or in the trunk of the Agent's car.

2. The Notary Signing Agent should never leave loan documents unattended during a signing and should never allow anyone other than the borrower (or authorized signer) to view the loan documents.

3. The Notary Signing Agent must positively identify all signers before they sign or view the loan documents.

4. The Notary Signing Agent should always use a privacy guard or protector with the Notary journal to shield from view by the current signer the personal information of previous signers.

5. In order to protect themselves from allegations of mishandling personal identifying information, Notary Signing Agents should review the signed loan documents and seal the return package in the presence of the borrower at the signing table if at all possible. Before sealing the package, Agents should make sure that there are no missed signatures, dates, initials, seal impressions or notarial certificates.

6. The Notary Signing Agent should place any check for closing costs or other items to be returned with the signed loan documents in a special envelope, mark it clearly and securely attach it to the loan documents before placing everything in the shipping envelope.

7. The Notary Signing Agent must be sure to use the correct shipping envelope (e.g., a FedEx envelope for a FedEx shipment). The Agent should be particularly careful when handling several sets of loan documents that must be shipped back after a day's appointments. The Agent should verify that the label or air bill matches the envelope and that he or she has attached the correct shipping label or air bill.

8. When it is not possible to seal the return package in front of the borrower (as when the Agent must fax certain loan documents after the appointment), the Notary Signing Agent should place all loan documents in an envelope in a locking briefcase or messenger bag until he or she can seal the envelope and send the package.

After the Signing Appointment

1. The Notary Signing Agent should return loan documents to the contracting company as soon as possible after the assignment. If the signing takes place during the day, the Agent should send the loan documents by the close of the business day. For an evening signing, the Agent should send the loan documents as soon as possible the following morning.

2. Notary Signing Agents should never delegate the responsibility of returning completed and signed loan documents to another person. Agents should always return the loan documents themselves.

3. The Notary Signing Agent should make sure the shipping envelope is completely sealed before handing it to a courier or putting it in a drop box.

4. Notary Signing Agents should return loan documents by the most secure method available. In order of priority, Agents may: (1) drop off the package at an authorized shipping center; (2) schedule

a pick-up at the Agent's home or office when he or she will be personally present to deliver the package; or (3) drop the package into a drop box.

5. When dropping off a package of loan documents at an authorized shipping center, the Notary Signing Agent should personally hand the package to a person at the counter and obtain a receipt with a tracking number. The Agent should never leave the package on the counter or hand it off without obtaining a receipt.

6. If the Notary Signing Agent has scheduled a home pick-up with an overnight courier, the Agent should never leave the package unsecured on his or her porch but should hand it to the courier in person.

7. When a courier arrives for a pick-up, the Notary Signing Agent should be sure that the courier scans all packages before leaving.

8. The Notary Signing Agent should keep a record of the shipper's tracking number for each returned set of loan documents. Some Agents record the tracking number in their Notary journals.

9. If the Notary Signing Agent deposits loan documents in a drop box, the Agent must be sure to use the correct drop box (e.g., a FedEx box for FedEx shipments). The Agent should keep a record of the exact location of the box and the date and time that he or she dropped off the package. Again, some Agents record this information in their Notary journals.

10. The Notary Signing Agent should never retain copies of any loan documents. A detailed journal entry is a sufficient record.

11. The Notary Signing Agent should shred any printed copies of loan documents that were not used for the signing in a cross-cut

shredder. The Agent should never throw loan documents in the trash until they have been shredded.

E-Documents and Electronic Communications

1. If the Notary Signing Agent will receive loan documents electronically, the Agent should make sure that his or her computer is equipped with security software such as a firewall and virus protection.

2. Notary Signing Agents should apply the strongest possible level of encryption to their home- or office-based wireless routers and networks. Agents should set the security level on wireless routers to allow only the computers and devices specifically authorized in their network.

3. The Notary Signing Agent should establish individual user accounts on his or her computer(s). Even if an Agent is the only user of a laptop, strong login credentials are critical if the laptop is ever lost or stolen.

4. Notary Signing Agents should never permit others to access their computer. Agents should never share with any other person, including family members, their login credentials for the computer or for an email account where e-documents may be delivered.

5. Notary Signing Agents should make sure that emails and e-documents received on their computer are not accessible by any other person, including family members. Agents should never permit anyone to download and/or print loan documents for them.

6. The Notary Signing Agent should encrypt email communications to the contracting company or borrower if these communications contain confidential information.

7. The Notary Signing Agent should never forward emails containing e-documents or other confidential borrower information to anyone, and especially not to third parties.

8. The Notary Signing Agent should never use a hotspot or a public computer to access loan-related emails.

9. When printing loan documents, Notary Signing Agents should not leave e-document files open or visible on their computer screen.

10. The Notary Signing Agent should never download and print e-documents from public networks (at Starbucks, for example) or unsecured computers, even if the loan documents are retrieved remotely.

11. Whenever possible, Notary Signing Agents should print e-documents directly from an email or website associated with the loan documents, and then immediately delete the email containing the link or e-documents. Unless Agents have no other choice, they should never save e-document files on any computer they may be using.

12. After the Notary Signing Agent finishes an assignment, the Agent should delete all emails containing personal information from his or her computer and all text messages from his or her cell phone.

13. After the Notary Signing Agent finishes an assignment, the Agent should delete any emails to which e-documents are attached or that contain a link to and/or login credentials for a Web server from which the e-documents were printed.

14. If Notary Signing Agents had to save e-documents on their computer, then after they finish an assignment, Agents should completely delete the files, including deleting them from their computer's Trash or Recycle Bin.

15. Since cell phones may be lost or stolen, the Notary Signing Agent should set a locking password on his or her phone to prevent unauthorized persons from accessing emails, text messages and contact lists.

16. Notary Signing Agents should consider purchasing for their cell phone software that uses GPS or another technology to locate a lost or stolen phone and remotely lock or wipe it. ■

CHAPTER 2 TEST

True/False Questions

1. The Interagency Guidelines, establishing standards for safeguarding customer information, require financial institutions to implement an information security program.

2. The GLBA provides consumers with the right to limit sharing of their information.

Multiple Choice Questions

(Choose the Best Answer)

1. The Gramm-Leach-Bliley Act protects the privacy of consumer information held by which of the following?
   a) Educational institutions
   b) Financial institutions
   c) Consumer organizations
   d) Both b and c

2. Objectives of the Interagency Guidelines include which of the following?
   a) Ensuring security and confidentiality of consumer information
   b) Protecting against any anticipated threats or hazards to the security or integrity of consumer information
   c) Protecting against unauthorized access to or use of consumer information in ways that could possibly harm any consumer
   d) All of the above

See page 331 for correct responses.

CHAPTER 3

TILA, RESPA and the PATRIOT Act

The Gramm-Leach-Bliley Financial Services Modernization Act (GLBA) discussed in the previous chapter is not the only federal law affecting Notary Signing Agents. Agents have also felt the impact of two additional federal laws in documents related to their practice: the Truth in Lending Act (TILA) and the Real Estate Settlement Procedures Act (RESPA). Both of these longstanding laws require certain standard written disclosures to be provided to borrowers during a home loan transaction.

In addition, since October of 2003, Notary Signing Agents have regularly come across another document pointing to a fourth law that impacts mortgage finance transactions and real property closings: the Uniting and Strengthening America by Providing Appropriate Tools Required to Intercept and Obstruct Terrorism Act (USA PATRIOT Act) of 2001.

TRUTH IN LENDING ACT

The federal Truth in Lending Act (TILA) was enacted in 1968 to fulfill the following stated purpose:

> The Congress finds that economic stabilization would be enhanced and [that] the competition among the various financial institutions and other firms engaged in the extension of consumer credit would be strengthened by the informed use of credit. The informed use of credit results from an awareness of the cost thereof by consumers. It is the purpose of this subchapter to assure a meaningful disclosure of credit terms so that the consumer will be able to compare more readily the various credit terms available to him and avoid the uninformed use of credit, and to protect the consumer against inaccurate and unfair credit billing and credit card practices.[1]

The TILA is intended to ensure that credit terms are disclosed in a meaningful way so that consumers can comparison shop for loans among competing lenders. Before the enactment of the TILA, consumers in the market for a loan encountered widely divergent and non-uniform credit terms and rates. These terms and rates were seldom presented in a format that made comparison of loans and lenders possible, let alone understandable. The single defining achievement of the TILA was to require all lenders to use the same credit terminology and expressions of rates.

Regulation Z

Like many federal laws, the TILA requires the overseeing regulatory agency — the Board of Governors of the Federal Reserve System — to publish rules to implement the Act.[2] The regulations implementing the TILA are known as Regulation Z.[3]

Regulation Z was published soon after the TILA was enacted by Congress. Since the nature of consumer credit is constantly evolving, the regulation has been revised on numerous occasions to keep pace with the times. Some of the more prominent revisions to the regulation that affect home mortgage loans include the following:

1. Enactment of the Truth in Lending Simplification and Reform Act of 1980

[1] 15 USC § 1601(a).
[2] 15 USC §§ 1602(b) and 1604(a).
[3] Code of Federal Regulations (CFR), Section 226, hereafter referred to as Regulation Z.

2. Rate limitations for home-secured loans as set forth in section 1204 of the Competitive Equality Banking Act of 1987, requiring disclosures for adjustable-rate mortgage (ARM) loans

3. Disclosure of key terms at the time of loan application as set forth in the Home Equity Loan Consumer Protection Act of 1988

4. New disclosure requirements and limitations on certain higher-cost, closed-end mortgage loans and reverse mortgage transactions under the Home Ownership and Equity Protection Act of 1994

5. Amendments to the 1995 Truth in Lending Act

6. Simplification of adjustable-rate mortgage disclosures brought about by the Economic Growth and Regulatory Paperwork Reduction Act of 1996[4]

One final official document of interest to Notary Signing Agents who wish to understand this important law is the official staff commentary to Regulation Z, published by the Federal Reserve Board.[5] This document guides Board staff in providing interpretations on the many Regulation Z provisions. Of particular importance to Notary Signing Agents is the interpretation of "business day" as it applies to the three-day right of rescission rule for certain mortgage loan transactions. At a later point we will discuss this official interpretation in more detail.

---

[4] Division of Consumer and Community Affairs, Federal Reserve Board, "Regulation Z (Truth in Lending)," in *Consumer Compliance Handbook* (Washington, DC: Board of Governors of the Federal Reserve System, 2010), http://www.federalreserve.gov/boarddocs/supmanual/cch/til.pdf. Regulation Z also may be found in a more searchable electronic form on the website of the Federal Deposit Insurance Corporation (FDIC): for the entire text, http://www.fdic.gov/regulations/laws/rules/6500-1400.html#fdic6500part226tilregz; for the updates effective July 1, 2010, http://www.fdic.gov/regulations/laws/rules/6500-1360.html#fdic6500part226tilregznew.

[5] Division of Consumer and Community Affairs, Federal Reserve Board, "Supplement I to Part 226 [of Regulation Z] – Official Staff Interpretations," http://www.fdic.gov/regulations/laws/rules/6500-1360.html#fdic6500supplement1topart226new. This commentary includes the updated sections that became effective July 1, 2010.

Our consideration of TILA provisions will focus on three main areas that relate specifically to the mortgage lending process and that affect the practice of Notary Signing Agents:

1. Early and Final Regulation Z Disclosure Requirements
2. Disclosure Requirements for ARM Loans
3. Right of Rescission

Early and Final Regulation Z Disclosure Requirements

The TILA requires lenders to make certain disclosures on loans subject to the Real Estate Settlement Procedures Act (RESPA) within three business days after receipt of a written application. This early disclosure statement is partially based on the initial information provided by the consumer. The Truth in Lending Disclosure Statement (page 161), a document with which Notary Signing Agents are quite familiar, is the form on which these disclosures are made. The disclosure statement must be in a specific format and include the following information:[6]

1. Name and address of creditor
2. Amount financed
3. Itemization of amount financed
4. Finance charge
5. Annual percentage rate (APR)
6. Variable-rate information

[6] The only disclosure on this list that is not included in the Truth in Lending Disclosure Statement is the Itemization of Amount Financed, which is a separate form (see page 166).

7. Payment schedule

8. Total of payments

9. Demand feature

10. Total sales price

11. Prepayment policy

12. Late payment policy

13. Security interest

14. Insurance requirements

15. Certain security interest charges

16. Contract reference

17. Assumption policy

18. Required deposit information

In addition to the initial Truth in Lending Disclosure Statement that the borrower must receive within three days of submitting a loan application, the borrower must receive a final disclosure statement from the lender. This final Truth in Lending Disclosure Statement is in the closing package of documents executed at the signing appointment with the Notary Signing Agent.

Disclosure Requirements for ARM Loans

One of the most important terms defined by the TILA is the annual percentage rate, or APR. The APR is "a measure of the cost of credit, expressed as a yearly rate, that relates the amount and timing of value received by the consumer to the amount and timing of payments made."[7] Since the actual interest rate on a loan does not include the fees comprising the cost of credit, the TILA created this new term, which factors these costs into one simplified rate for the purposes of aiding consumers in comparing rates between lenders. The Truth in Lending Disclosure Statement (page 161) that is included in every residential finance transaction prominently displays the APR for that loan.

The concept behind the APR was simple enough: to give consumers a rate they can use to comparison shop for loans among competing lenders. However, any experienced Notary Signing Agent can attest that the APR is the term least understood by borrowers at a loan signing and is regularly confused with the actual interest rate for the loan appearing on the Note. There is perhaps no single question raised more often by borrowers at a loan signing than, "Why is the annual percentage rate greater than the interest rate I was quoted for my loan?"[8]

With traditional fixed-rate loans, the APR will not change over the life of the loan. However, the APR on an ARM loan can change. Therefore, the TILA specifies additional disclosure requirements for fluctuating variable-rate mortgages.

According to the TILA, if the APR on a loan secured by the consumer's principal dwelling may increase after consummation and if the term of the loan exceeds one year, then additional adjustable-rate mortgage disclosures must be provided. One of these is a loan program disclosure for each variable-rate program in which the consumer expresses an interest. Depending upon the lender and the particular type of ARM loan, Notary Signing Agents will encounter loan program disclosures in loan packages.

Right of Rescission

While the APR represents the Notary Signing Agent's single most frequent point of contact to the TILA, the right of rescission rule is a close second.

---

[7] Regulation Z § 226.22(a).

[8] In an attempt to explain the annual percentage rate associated with a home loan, some lenders now include a Lender APR Worksheet in their loan document package. This worksheet lists the loan amount, total prepaid finance charges, amount financed, total interest and total mortgage insurance (if applicable) and computes the APR for the loan.

When a consumer's principal dwelling is used as security for a residential mortgage finance loan, the TILA right of rescission rule often applies. In short, the rule allows each consumer whose ownership of the property is pledged as security to cancel the loan within three business days. Lenders are required to deliver two copies of the Notice of Right to Cancel to each consumer entitled to rescind.[9] This notice must identify the start and termination dates of the rescission period, clearly disclose that the consumer's principal dwelling is being used to secure the loan and specifically state how the consumer can rescind the transaction by contacting the lender at the designated address of the lender's place of business.

The word consumer has been carefully used in this context. In a majority of loans involving two persons — a husband and wife, for example — both will appear as co-borrowers on the loan application. That is, each co-borrower's income, employment and other factors were considered in determining loan approval. Both would be provided with the opportunity to rescind the loan.

However, in many loans, Notary Signing Agents will discover that there is only one borrower but that the borrower's spouse must be present at the signing appointment to sign the Notice of Right to Cancel. In these cases, if the non-borrower spouse (consumer) has an ownership interest in the home that secures the loan, then the non-borrower spouse also will be provided with the opportunity to rescind the loan.

In order to exercise the right to rescind, the consumer must notify the lender of the rescission by mail, telegram or other means of written communication — not infrequently, by fax.[10] Notice is considered effective when mailed, faxed, filed for telegraphic transmission or sent by other means. The consumer may exercise the right to rescind until midnight of the third business day following consummation of the transaction, delivery of the Notice of Right to Cancel or delivery of all material disclosures, whichever occurs last. When more than one consumer in a transaction has the right to rescind, one consumer's act to rescind is effective for all consumers in the transaction.

---

[9] Regulation Z § 226(b)(1).
[10] Regulation Z § 226.23(a)(2).

Prior to the loan closing, the consumer may modify or waive the right to rescind if the consumer determines that the extension of credit is needed to meet a bona fide personal financial emergency.[11]

Not all home loan transactions have a rescission option. Regulation Z Section 226.23 lists the following transaction types to which the right to rescind does not apply:

1. A residential mortgage transaction, in which a borrower purchases a home as a principal residence[12]

2. A refinancing or consolidation by the same creditor of an extension of credit already secured by the consumer's principal dwelling[13]

3. A transaction in which a state agency is a creditor

4. An advance, other than an initial advance, in a series of advances or in a series of single-payment obligations that is treated as a single transaction under Sec. 226.17(c)(6), if the notice required by paragraph (b) of this section and all material disclosures have been given to the consumer

5. A renewal of optional insurance premiums that is not considered a refinancing under Sec. 226.20(a)(5)

The right to rescind also does not apply to loans used to finance vacation homes, investment properties or a private business.

While these exemptions are numerous, most refinance and home equity line of credit (HELOC) transactions Notary Signing Agents handle have a rescission option. As part of the Agent's preparation for a signing,

[11] Regulation Z § 226(e).

[12] Regulation Z § 226.2(a)(24) defines a residential mortgage transaction as "a transaction in which a mortgage, deed of trust, purchase money security interest arising under an installment sales contract or equivalent consensual security interest is created or retained in the consumer's principal dwelling to finance the acquisition or initial construction of that dwelling."

[13] The right of rescission does apply to the extent the new amount financed exceeds the unpaid principal balance, any earned unpaid finance charge on the existing debt and amounts attributed solely to the costs of the refinancing or consolidation.

the Agent should review all documents in the loan package to see if a Notice of Right to Cancel is present. If one is not present, the transaction may fall under one of the above-mentioned exceptions, and the Agent should not represent to the borrower that he or she has a right to rescind. To be certain that this is in fact the case, the Agent should contact the contracting company or the title company closing the loan to verify whether the transaction has a rescission option.

Whether a loan transaction has a rescission option could affect how the loan signing is conducted. Loan signing appointments for transactions without a right to rescind could conceivably take longer to execute, since the borrower could be more cautious or deliberate in considering the documents before signing. On the other hand, a signing appointment for a simple refinance loan with a rescission option might take considerably less time, because the borrower knows he or she has three days to carefully review the documents before the transaction is final.

We now turn our attention to the important subject of calculating the rescission period dates. Notary Signing Agents are expected to know how to calculate the commencement and termination dates and to enter the dates into the applicable spaces or guide the borrowers in doing so.

The TILA gives borrowers three business days to rescind, beginning with the first business day following the date of signing and ending at midnight on the third business day. Every day is a business day except Sundays and federal holidays. Saturday counts as a business day, even if the lender's office is closed on Saturdays.

The federal holidays that do not count as a business day are New Year's Day, Martin Luther King Jr. Day, Presidents' Day, Memorial Day, Independence Day, Labor Day, Columbus Day, Veterans Day, Thanksgiving Day and Christmas Day.

The greatest challenge Agents encounter in calculating the rescission period dates arises when one of these holidays falls on a weekend. For example, if Independence Day falls on a Saturday, many Agents have wondered whether the date the holiday is observed by government and business offices should be considered a legal holiday for the purpose of calculating the rescission date. This is a common point of confusion not only for Notary Signing Agents but also for many experienced professionals in the mortgage lending industry as well.

The official staff commentary on Regulation Z introduced earlier in this chapter contains an important official interpretation on this very point. In the actual law itself,[14] four of the 10 federal holidays listed are date-specific: New Year's Day (January 1), Independence Day (July 4), Veterans Day (November 11) and Christmas Day (December 25). The other six holidays affected in rescission period calculations do not have a specific date assigned. For example, Martin Luther King Jr. Day is observed on the third Monday in January and Labor Day on the first Monday in September.

In the recently revised commentary on Regulation Z, the Federal Reserve Board issued an important official interpretation of the term "business day" in relation to the four date-specific holidays. According to the commentary, the only date that counts when computing the rescission period is the date of the actual holiday itself.[15] Using the previous example of Independence Day falling on a Saturday, the Monday following would count as a business day for rescission period calculations, even if the holiday is nationally observed on Monday, with government office closures, etc.

Therefore, Notary Signing Agents can no longer assume that, if banks, the post office and other state and federal government offices are closed on a weekday in observance of a holiday falling on a weekend, the day of observance would not count as one of the three business days.

REAL ESTATE SETTLEMENT PROCEDURES ACT

The federal Real Estate Settlement Procedures Act (RESPA) was enacted in 1974 to fulfill the following stated purpose:

> SEC. 2. (a) The Congress finds that significant reforms in the real estate settlement process are needed to insure that consumers throughout the Nation are provided with greater and more timely information on the nature and costs of the settlement process and are protected from unnecessarily high settlement charges caused by certain abusive practices

[14] 5 USC § 6103(a).

[15] "Supplement I to Part 226 [of Regulation Z] – Official Staff Interpretations," Sec. 226.2 – Definitions and Rules of Construction, 2(a)(6) Business day.

> that have developed in some areas of the country. The Congress also finds that it has been over two years since the Secretary of Housing and Urban Development and the Administrator of Veterans' Affairs submitted their joint report to the Congress on "Mortgage Settlement Costs" and that the time has come for the recommendations for Federal legislative action made in that report to be implemented.
>
> (b) It is the purpose of this Act to effect certain changes in the settlement process for residential real estate that will result —
>
> (1) in more effective advance disclosure to home buyers and sellers of settlement costs;
>
> (2) in the elimination of kickbacks or referral fees that tend to increase unnecessarily the costs of certain settlement services;
>
> (3) in a reduction in the amounts home buyers are required to place in escrow accounts established to insure the payment of real estate taxes and insurance; and
>
> (4) in significant reform and modernization of local recordkeeping of land title information.[16]

The RESPA, like the TILA, is a federal consumer protection statute aimed at helping consumers become better shoppers for settlement services and at eliminating kickbacks and referral fees that increase the costs of certain settlement services.

The RESPA covers federally related loans secured with a mortgage placed on a one- to four-family residential property. These include most purchase loans, assumptions, refinances, property improvement loans and equity lines of credit. The U.S. Department of Housing and Urban Development (HUD) Office of RESPA and Interstate Land Sales is responsible for enforcing the RESPA.

The following discussion will center on the sections of the RESPA of most immediate concern and interest to Notary Signing Agents.

Key RESPA Provisions

At a loan closing, borrowers routinely sign documents explicitly stating that they can select any service provider they choose.[17] In practice, however, consumers rarely undertake the time-consuming task

[16] 12 USC § 2601.

[17] See the sample Affiliated Business Arrangement Disclosure Notice (page 247), which contains the following paragraph: "You are not required to use ABC Title Security Agency of Arizona as a condition for settlement of your loan on the subject property. You are free to check with other settlement service providers to determine that you are receiving the best services and the best rate for these services."

of price shopping for title insurance, escrow services, appraisals, closing companies … or even Notary Signing Agents. Rather, they accept the recommendation of a real estate agent, mortgage broker, mortgage banker or loan agent to utilize those companies with which that professional regularly conducts business.

Consequently, settlement service providers have marketed their services more to industry players who can influence consumers and not to consumers directly. Over the years, many professional relationships forged between real estate agents and brokers, lenders, mortgage brokers and settlement service providers have been based upon arrangements involving fee splits, kickbacks or other compensation in exchange for referrals.

Section 8 of the RESPA prohibits this type of compensation for referrals. Violators may be fined up to $10,000, imprisoned up to one year or both. In addition, they are civilly liable to the person charged for the settlement service up to three times the amount actually paid for the service.[18]

Section 9 of the RESPA prohibits a seller from requiring the home buyer to use a particular title insurance company as a condition of sale.[19]

Section 10 of the RESPA sets limits on the amounts that a lender may require a borrower to put into an escrow or impound account for purposes of paying property taxes, premiums for hazard and mortgage insurance and other charges.[20] The Initial Escrow Account Disclosure Statement (page 192) is routinely included in loan document packages and is a document that discloses the impounds for the upcoming year.

RESPA Disclosures

Many of the disclosures appearing in a typical set of loan document packages are required by the RESPA. While Notary Signing Agents may be most familiar with the disclosures provided at closing, the RESPA actually requires a series of disclosures to be made available to consumers at four distinct stages: at the time of loan application, before settlement, at settlement and after settlement.

[18] 12 USC §§ 2607(a), 2607(b) and 2607(d). Since Notary Signing Agents provide a form of settlement services, they are subject to RESPA and are liable for any penalties incurred for violating RESPA provisions.

[19] 12 USC § 2608.

[20] 12 USC § 2609(a)(2).

At the time of loan application, a special information booklet which includes consumer information concerning various real estate settlement services (for purchase transactions only), an initial Good Faith Estimate of settlement charges (pages 152–154) and a Servicing Disclosure Statement (page 225) must be provided to the borrower.

Before settlement or closing occurs, the RESPA requires an Affiliated Business Arrangement Disclosure (page 247) and a HUD-1 Settlement Statement (pages 144–146) to be provided to the borrower.

At settlement, the HUD-1 Settlement Statement and the Initial Escrow Account Disclosure Statement (page 192) must be provided to borrowers.

After settlement, the Annual Escrow Statement and the Servicing Disclosure Statement must be provided to borrowers.

RESPA Reform

On November 17, 2008, HUD published its final rule for reforming the RESPA.[21] The most substantive changes, including those of most interest to Notary Signing Agents, became effective on January 1, 2010. The changes relevant to Notary Signing Agents are as follows:

1. **Closing Script:** On March 14, 2008, HUD published a proposed rule for public comment that contained certain changes to the RESPA. One of the more controversial proposals was the idea of a closing script: an addendum to the HUD-1/1A that would have compared the loan terms and settlement charges estimated on the GFE to the actual final charges on the HUD-1/1A and described in detail the terms for the specific mortgage loan. The settlement agent or other person conducting the closing would have been required to read the addendum aloud to the borrower and explain any discrepancies between the settlement costs reported on the GFE and HUD-1/1A.

   HUD proposed the closing script as a means to give borrowers a clearer understanding of loan terms and settlement costs.

[21] At the time of printing, the final RESPA rule was viewable online and available for download on the website of the U.S. Department of Housing and Urban Development (HUD), http://www.hud.gov/offices/hsg/ramh/res/finalrule.pdf. This document is a reprint of *Federal Register*, Vol. 73, No. 222 (November 17, 2008), pp. 68204–68288, also available on the website of the GPO, http://edocket.access.gpo.gov/2008/pdf/E8-27070.pdf .

The NNA® and many Notary Signing Agents opposed the closing script on the grounds that, as Notaries Public, Agents are not allowed to explain loan terms and settlement costs to the borrower. Bowing to wide industry opposition, HUD removed the closing script provision from the final rule but determined instead to incorporate the information from the closing script into page 3 of the new HUD-1 and page 2 of the new HUD-1A Settlement Statements without requiring settlement agents, closing attorneys or Notary Signing Agents to read and explain the information.

2. **Good Faith Estimate of Settlement Charges:** The Good Faith Estimate form, or GFE, has been completely redesigned by HUD. For all loans originated after January 1, 2010, use of the new form[22] is mandatory.

   Notary Signing Agents will recognize the GFE as one of the many standard forms routinely appearing in closing document packages.

   The new GFE is a three-page standardized form that all lenders must use. Page 1 of the GFE contains a summary of important loan terms and the total of estimated closing costs for the loan. These costs are broken out in more detail on page 2 of the form. Page 3 provides a diagram explaining the three "buckets" of settlement charges,[23] a "tradeoff table" that allows the borrower to consider the exact same loan with lower settlement costs or a lower interest rate and a "shopping chart" that enables the borrower to comparison shop the loan reported on the GFE against loans from other lenders.

   Significantly, Notary Signing Agents will notice that the new GFE does not have lines for borrower signatures. Instead of asking borrowers to sign the GFE itself, lenders likely will require a borrower to sign and date an additional document in which the lender discloses

---

[22] At the time of printing, the new GFE was viewable online and available for download on the HUD website, http://www.hud.gov/offices/hsg/ramh/res/gfestimate.pdf. A copy of the form also may be found on pages 152–154 of this Course.

[23] The three "buckets" are: (1) charges reported on the GFE that cannot change on the HUD-1/1A; (2) charges reported on the GFE that cannot increase by more than 10% in total on the HUD-1/1A; and (3) charges that can change.

that the borrower has received a GFE for the loan and the borrower acknowledges having received a GFE from the lender.

3. **HUD-1/1A Settlement Statement:** The changes to the HUD-1[24] and HUD-1A[25] Settlement Statements are also noteworthy. Page 1 of the HUD-1 is mostly unchanged from previous versions. However, page 2 of the HUD-1 and page 1 of the HUD-1A have been modified to allow consumers to directly compare the fees identified on the GFE with the fees reported at closing. Each closing cost identified on a line of the HUD-1/1A is mapped to its corresponding line on the GFE, and the HUD-1/1A uses the same terminology as the GFE to identify fees.

   Notary Signing Agents will notice another change to the new HUD-1/1A. Line 1106, which was previously labeled "Notary Fee" and used by closing agents to list the fee paid for the services of a Notary Signing Agent or mobile Notary, has been redesignated. The new forms do not contain any individual line for reporting Notary fees. In its *New RESPA Rule FAQs*, HUD explains that fees for the services of a Notary or Notary Signing Agent are to be lumped in with the fees for "Title services and lender's title insurance" appearing on line 1101.[26]

   Page 3 of the HUD-1 and page 2 of the HUD-1A contain the most substantive changes. Charts summarize the fees reported on the GFE and the HUD-1/1A in each of the three "tolerance buckets." The final section of HUD-1/1A, "Loan Terms," incorporates much of the information from the closing script in the proposed rule but, as indicated earlier, no longer must be read aloud or explained to the borrower at the loan signing appointment.

[24] At the time of printing, the new HUD-1 was viewable online and available for download on the HUD website, http://www.hud.gov/offices/hsg/ramh/res/hud1.pdf. A copy of the form also may be found on pages 144–146 of this Course.

[25] The HUD-1A is an optional settlement statement for use in transactions without sellers. At the time of printing, the new HUD-1A was viewable online and available for download on the HUD website, http://www.hud.gov/offices/hsg/ramh/res/hud1-a.pdf.

[26] At the time of printing, the *New RESPA Rule FAQs* were viewable online and available for download on the HUD website, http://www.hud.gov/offices/hsg/ramh/res/resparulefaqs.pdf. See page 47 of that document for questions related to Notary and Notary Signing Agent fees.

Even though Notary Signing Agents are no longer required to read or explain the closing script information, borrowers may ask Agents to explain the information anyway. The settlement services industry as a whole has been bracing to address a number of anticipated questions on some of the more technical aspects of the new RESPA rule, such as the closing-costs tolerance buckets, lumped fees and the reporting of yield spread premiums. Undoubtedly, Notary Signing Agents will be asked questions on these and other technical matters.

Readers are encouraged to review the discussion in Chapter 4 of this Course for assistance on how to handle borrower questions and, at the closing table, be prepared to contact the mortgage broker, lender or closing agent involved in the transaction in case the borrower seeks an answer to a question that Notary Signing Agents cannot provide.

USA PATRIOT ACT

On September 11, 2001, our nation changed forever.

In response to the acts of terrorism on our nation's soil, President George W. Bush signed into law the USA PATRIOT Act on October 26, 2001. The PATRIOT Act, which was aimed at fighting terrorism in the United States and abroad, added sweeping new changes to U.S. law, including amendments to the nation's bank secrecy laws.

The section of the PATRIOT Act which most affects Notary Signing Agents is Section 326. Section 326 requires the Secretary of the Department of the Treasury to prescribe regulations "setting forth the minimum standards for financial institutions and their customers regarding the identity of the customer that shall apply in connection with the opening of an account at a financial institution."[27] At a minimum, these regulations must require all financial institutions to implement procedures for verifying the identity of any person seeking to open an account, maintaining records of the information used to verify a person's identity and consulting lists

[27] 31 USC § 5318(1)(1).

of known or suspected terrorists or terrorist organizations provided to the financial institution by any government agency to determine whether a person seeking to open an account appears on any such list.[28]

Customer Identification Program

In the regulations implementing Section 326,[29] the major focus of the final rule for financial institutions was the requirement that they establish a Customer Identification Program, or CIP, for identifying new account holders.

According to CIP regulations, every qualifying financial institution must have a written procedure for establishing the true identity of its customers. The regulations require financial institutions to conduct a risk assessment to determine whether their business practices meet minimally acceptable compliance standards. The regulations do not impose specific methods, policies or business rules to achieve these objectives but leave it up to the individual institution to develop its own program.

The regulations also require institutions to implement procedures for collecting standard information such as a customer's name, address, date of birth and taxpayer identification number (for U.S. citizens, typically a Social Security number, and for non-U.S. citizens, a similar number from a government-issued document).

The definition of a financial institution is actually quite broad and encompasses a wide range of institutions.[30] Under the law, "persons involved in real estate closings and settlements" qualify as a financial institution. This is where Notary Signing Agents enter the picture, because Notary Signing Agents often contract with settlement service companies to provide loan signing services. In addition, a number of the entities defined as financial institutions provide mortgage loans or settlement services and thus could need Notary Signing Agents to conduct the signings for these loans.

The process for applying for a loan today is markedly different from the past. Applicants submit applications and receive approval for loans over

[28] 31 USC § 5318(1)(2).
[29] *Federal Register*, Vol. 68, No. 90 (May 9, 2003), passim, also available on the website of the GPO, http://www.access.gpo.gov/su_docs/fedreg/a030509c.html.
[30] 31 USC §§ 5312(a)(2) and (c)(1).

the Internet or on the phone. Applicants often do not have a face-to-face encounter with any person representing the lender or closing company until the actual closing appointment when loan documents are signed. This presents a challenge for financial institutions in implementing their CIPs.

In carrying out their risk assessment, lenders, banks, savings and loan institutions, credit unions, mortgage brokers and other lending institutions providing home loans did not have to think long to determine that the most effective, most cost-conscious and least intrusive method for obtaining new customer identifying information was to employ Notary Signing Agents to complete this task at the loan signing appointment.

Positively identifying the signer is the hallmark of the Notary Public office. In the typical loan signing, a Notary Signing Agent must positively identify the borrower to execute the acknowledgment on a mortgage or deed of trust. Asking Agents to complete a Customer Identification Verification form containing the borrower's identification information, as shown on the ID cards presented, seemed to be the logical solution for complying with CIP regulations in cases where the borrower never personally appears before a representative of the financial institution.

On October 1, 2003, Notary Signing Agents began informing the NNA® that these PATRIOT Act CIP forms were appearing in loan document packages, and the Agents raised a number of questions about these forms. Among the comments and questions were the following:

1. What exactly is the PATRIOT Act? The current section of this Course is intended to answer that question.

2. Is the Notary Signing Agent or the borrower responsible for completing and signing the CIP form? The Agent completes, signs and dates the form.

3. Does the CIP form need to be notarized? No: The Agent signs and dates the form as a Signing Agent — not as a Notary Public — without completing a notarial certificate or affixing an official seal.

4. By completing the form, is the Notary Signing Agent subject to questioning or search regarding terrorist investigations? The borrower is subject to search of government lists of known and suspected terrorists and terrorist groups, not the Notary Signing Agent.

Since that day, it has become almost second nature that Notary Signing Agents will complete a form on behalf of the lender certifying that the Agent properly identified the borrower at the signing appointment.

Summary

The Notary Signing Agent has two distinct roles: that of Signing Agent and that of Notary Public. The duties of each are shaped by laws that Agents must learn. Historically, Notaries have almost exclusively concerned themselves with mastering state Notary statutes, since the Notary Public office is regulated by the individual states. However, with the advent of the professional career field of Notary Signing Agent, Agents now work within the mortgage finance and settlement services industries and must become familiar with federal laws which regulate these industries.

The primary federal laws regulating Notary Signing Agents are the Truth in Lending Act (TILA) of 1968, the Real Estate Settlement Procedures Act (RESPA) of 1974 and the Uniting and Strengthening America by Providing Appropriate Tools Required to Intercept and Obstruct Terrorism Act (USA PATRIOT Act) of 2001. In the case of the TILA and PATRIOT Act, Agents must also become familiar with regulations and official interpretations of these regulations that are published by the regulating agency. ■

CHAPTER 3 TEST

True/False Questions

1. The Truth in Lending Act (TILA) requires all lenders to use the same credit terminology and expression of rates.

2. According to the TILA right of rescission rule, borrowers whose mortgage is for the purchase of a principle residence are guaranteed three days to cancel the loan.

3. The Real Estate Settlement Protection Act (RESPA) gives consumers an opportunity to select their settlement service providers.

4. The Affiliated Business Arrangement Disclosure is required by the federal TILA.

5. If New Year's Day falls on a Saturday, the following Monday is counted as one of the three business days in a right of rescission period.

Multiple Choice Questions

(Choose the Best Answer)

1. The RESPA is a federal consumer protection act aimed at helping consumers avoid the increased cost of settlement services due to which of the following?
   a) Kickbacks and referral fees between real estate agents, brokers and other settlement providers
   b) High interest rates
   c) Inflation
   d) All of the above

2. Violators of the RESPA kickback prohibition may be fined, imprisoned or both. How much is the maximum fine?
   a) $1,000
   b) $100,000
   c) $10,000
   d) None of the above

3. The USA PATRIOT Act was enacted to fight terrorism in what part of the world?
   a) In the United States and abroad
   b) In the United States
   c) In New York
   d) In the Middle East

See page 331 for correct responses.

CHAPTER 4

Preparing for Loan Signings

BUSINESS TOOLS

One of the great benefits of entering the Notary Signing Agent business is that it requires a relatively small initial investment. A person wishing to become a Notary Signing Agent likely already possesses many of the tools necessary to conduct an effective loan signing business. If the person is already a Notary Public, then the initial investment is even less. Eight essential tools are needed to start.

Cell Phone

In the loan signing business, a cell phone is indispensable. Since the main way Notary Signing Agents get assignments is by phone, an Agent must be able to receive calls anywhere at any time.

Appointment-setters in lender, title and signing service offices seeking Notary Signing Agents first will call tried and true Agents who have performed successfully for them in the past. If an experienced Agent is not available, they will look at their list of Agents in a given area and begin with the first Agent on the list. If an Agent is unavailable or the

Agent's voicemail picks up the call, the scheduler will call the next Agent on the list. The first Agent who answers the call gets the appointment.

Fax Machine

A fax machine is another essential piece of equipment. Companies scheduling assignments often rely on fax machines to send pertinent forms to the Notary Signing Agent. Lenders and title companies may use the fax to send last-minute documents for a loan signing appointment or may ask the Notary Signing Agent to fax back certain documents after they have been signed. Submitting assignment completion invoices by fax to signing services is also common. Fortunately, fax machines are relatively inexpensive to purchase these days.

Another way to fax is by computer. Most computers sold today come equipped with a fax modem that will enable the Notary Signing Agent to send and receive faxes. However, to fax back hard copies of documents or invoices that are not computer files, using a scanner is necessary to capture or digitize the document before sending it. Scanners cost about as much as standard fax machines.

While scanning and faxing documents through a personal computer is convenient and may allay the cost of purchasing a dedicated fax machine, Notary Signing Agents should not scan and fax documents that contain personal identifying or financial information of borrowers (see Chapter 2, "Ensuring Customer Privacy").

Another option is to use a Web-based fax service.[1] For a monthly fee, the Notary Signing Agent can obtain a fax number and the ability to receive a fax as an email attachment. When a company sends a faxed assignment sheet to a subscriber's number, the fax is processed and emailed to the subscriber as an attached file. When a subscriber wishes to send a fax, he or she sends the file directly from a desktop application such as Microsoft® Word. The fax is processed and delivered to the recipient like a normal incoming fax.

[1] eFax (http://www.efax.com) is one such service.

Notarial Supplies

New Notary Signing Agents who are already Notaries will likely own the tools and supplies necessary to begin. Essential supplies include a Notary journal and seal, pads of "loose" notarial certificates, an inkless thumbprinting device (required for Notaries in California when notarizing most deeds, deeds of trust and powers of attorney, and for Notaries in Illinois when notarizing certain documents of conveyance that transfer the title to residential real property) and a Notary bond (for Notaries in jurisdictions requiring a surety protection for the public). Additionally, errors and omissions insurance is recommended to provide financial protection to the Notary Signing Agent in the event of innocent mistakes. However, a Notary's errors and omissions insurance will not cover mistakes made on loan documents that did not require notarization.

Office Tools

A few inexpensive office supplies can help the Notary Signing Agent efficiently perform signing services. Since many title companies require documents to be signed with similar pens, providing black or blue ballpoint pens is a good idea. The Notary Signing Agent may consider purchasing promotional pens, printed with the Agent's contact information, and handing them out at signing appointments.

Post-it® notes or Redi-Tag® flags are handy for marking where the borrower must sign and/or initial documents.

A small stapler or paper clips may be used for securing to the closing statement a cashier's check for closing costs, a W-2 form or other stipulations. Binder clips may be used to keep all the pages in a loan package in one place before and after the signing.

Mileage Log

A mileage log should be purchased to record vehicle mileage for income tax purposes.[2]

[2] The Internal Revenue Service requires clear and sufficient documentation of all business-related expenses. See Chapter 6, "Closing Out the Assignment," for a discussion of relevant tax issues.

Notary Signing Agent Log

A recordkeeping system for maintaining business records of loan signing appointments, such as the NNA®'s Notary Signing Agent Log, may be used to keep appointment, invoice and tax-related records.

Appointment Book, Personal Data Assistant (PDA) or Smartphone

For recording appointments and contact information, an appointment book is essential. Using a PDA to keep a calendar of appointments can help, because it allows an Agent to review and set appointments in the field. Later, the PDA can be connected to a computer to synchronize the appointments made in the field with a master calendar. In addition, other useful software applications may be installed on a PDA for mobile use. Newer smartphones — cell phones with PDA capabilities — can also be used to manage appointments in the same way a PDA can.

Laser Printer

Since Notary Signing Agents receive nearly all loan document packages electronically,[3] a laser printer with the capability to print legal-sized documents will be needed to print out the originals and the borrower's copies of the loan documents.[4] Notary Signing Agents should purchase a black and white printer capable of printing a large volume of documents as quickly as possible. While Agents use all of the major brands of printers available in the market, some printers are more suitable for printing loan documents than others. Agents in the market for a new printer should purchase a printer with the following minimum specifications:

[3] To receive emailed or digital documents, the Notary Signing Agent informs the agency providing the assignment that he or she is able to receive such documents. The Notary Signing Agent is directed to a website to download software, such as Adobe® Reader®, to read and print the files. While capability to receive emailed documents is not a requirement with most lenders, Agents with this capability are paid an extra fee (often $25 or more) to provide the copies and essentially serve as the courier for the loan documents.

[4] Use of a laser printer is preferred over an inkjet printer, since the ink from an inkjet printer is less permanent and may smudge. The Notary Signing Agent should inquire whether lenders will accept documents printed on an inkjet printer. In addition, laser printers have become more affordable, and toner costs might be significantly less than ink cartridges for an inkjet printer.

1. A print speed as fast as can be afforded (usually measured in pages per minute)

2. Dual trays for handling both letter and legal size paper automatically (since many loan documents in a typical set of documents are printed on both letter and legal size paper)

3. The ability to add additional printer memory (which enables loan document packages to be processed faster by the printer)

4. A recommended monthly printing volume of at least 5,000 pages for part-time Agents (which converts to about 33 complete sets of loan documents per month, at 150 pages per set of both original and borrower's copies) and up to 10,000 if the Agent performs loan signings full time

Laser Printer Paper and Toner

Notary Signing Agents should keep on hand a sufficient stock of letter and legal size laser printer paper and toner cartridges to facilitate the printing of large quantities of loan documents.

MARKETING NOTARY SIGNING AGENT SERVICES

Potential Clients

In order to receive an assignment, the Notary Signing Agent must market his or her services to potential clients. The Agent has two general options when it comes to selecting the companies with which to do business. The Agent either may enlist with a service that brokers loan signing appointments or may solicit companies that provide direct work: title companies, lenders, mortgage brokers, mortgage bankers, banks, savings and loans and real estate offices that initiate the loan signing appointments. In general, while direct work will pay more than signing services, Agents may obtain a more steady stream of assignments by contracting with signing services.

A general description of the companies that broker or initiate loan signing appointments, and the factors a Notary Signing Agent should consider when marketing services to each type of company, follows.

Signing Services

A signing service is a middleman that establishes accounts with large lenders and title companies to provide Notary Signing Agents for loan signings. Signing services provide the "one-stop shop" to large lenders who wish to delegate the responsibility of contacting Agents to perform loan signings regionally or nationwide, coordinate appointments and ensure the documents' timely delivery.

A lender or title company will pay the signing service a flat fee to cover the signing. The signing service enlists and then dispatches a Notary Signing Agent in a borrower's immediate locale to conduct the signing and pays the Agent a flat fee for the signing.

1. Application Procedure

Prospective Notary Signing Agents seeking assignments through a signing service typically contact a signing service by phone or by visiting a website and submitting an application. The application will ask for standard contact information, a priority phone number (the number the agency calls first), information about the Agent's employment, legal residency and areas of service (typically by city or county) and times when the Agent is available to conduct signings. Some signing services ask the Agent to provide proof of automobile insurance, answer questions related to prior felony or misdemeanor convictions and list any additional languages the Agent speaks.

The signing service will ask the Notary Signing Agent to provide Notary commission information, including the name in which the Agent's Notary commission is issued, commission identification number (if applicable), commission expiration date, county where the Agent is qualified, proof of Notary bonding (if applicable) and errors and omissions insurance policy information (if applicable).

As an additional requirement, signing services may ask the Notary Signing Agent to affix an impression of his or her Notary seal on the application. The NNA® recommends that the Agent deny the request, since use of a Notary seal for purposes other than for performing notarial acts is an unwise practice, if not directly prohibited by law.

Signing services will ask prospective Notary Signing Agents to complete and sign IRS Form W-9. This form, also found in most loan packages, is required for the signing service to verify the Agent's Social Security number for issuing a 1099-MISC ("Miscellaneous Income") form at the end of the year.[5] In some instances, the signing service may ask the Agent to include a photocopy of his or her Social Security card.

For identification purposes and verification that the Agent's driving privileges are valid, a signing service often will request a photocopy of a driver's license.

Signing services also will ask the Agent to describe any relevant industry experience or training in executing loan documents that he or she may have had.

2. Independent Contractor's Agreement

Every signing service will require the Notary Signing Agent to sign an independent contractor's agreement. The provisions of this agreement vary by signing service and should be carefully read and considered. The independent contractor's agreement will typically outline the contractor's general responsibilities in confirming appointments, returning documents quickly, following all state laws in the performance of notarial acts, refusing to perform notarizations when state laws are not followed, maintaining records of all assignments, keeping his or her Notary commission current and keeping information obtained during loan signings confidential.

The agreement will clarify that the Notary Signing Agent is not an employee of the signing service and that the Agent is an independent contractor. In these clauses, signing services may advise the Agent that, as an independent contractor, he or she is responsible for setting a working

[5] For more information on the 1099-MISC, see pages 291–292 of this Course.

schedule, obtaining training, providing the necessary equipment to conduct signings, incurring all related travel expenses in performing signings, submitting invoices for payment and filing taxes. Agreements also may affirm the Agent's right to contract with other companies and that the Agent's services will be used only on an "as needed" basis.

The agreement also will discuss the signing service's fee and payment schedule. Often the standard loan signing fee will cover a maximum mileage radius from the Notary Signing Agent's home or office and will state the conditions under which an Agent may request additional compensation for mileage expenses outside of this radius. Agreements will clarify when payment for services rendered may be expected.

The most important element in the contractor's agreement from the signing service's perspective is the noncompetition clause. In general, a noncompetition clause prohibits a Notary Signing Agent from engaging in unfair competition practices. Since a signing service typically provides a lender or title company contact with each assignment, a noncompetition clause may prohibit an Agent from directly or indirectly soliciting business from that lender or title company. Noncompetition clauses protect the signing service's relations with its clientele.

Since a particular independent contractor's agreement may not foresee every possible provision the Notary Signing Agent considers important, the Agent may wish to clarify the particular agency's policies on several additional matters:

1. If the assignment requires the Notary Signing Agent to oversee the signing of first and second mortgage papers at the same signing, there will be two sets of papers to execute. The Notary Signing Agent should ensure that the agreement clearly states that the Agent will be paid for executing two sets of documents and lists the fee for executing the second set of papers. Typically the fee for the second set of papers will be lower than the first, since the Agent has already traveled to the location to meet with the borrower.

2. In some loans, the lender may ask that multiple copies of the Note and security instrument (Deed of Trust or Mortgage) be executed. The duplicate is typically stamped, "True and Certified Copy." In essence, the lender is asking that duplicate originals of these documents be signed and, if necessary, notarized. The Notary Signing Agent should inquire whether additional compensation for duplicate originals is provided.

3. Notary Signing Agents should ensure that the contractor's agreement includes the standard fee for printing out the original loan documents (the set the borrower signs) and the borrower's copies (the set the borrower keeps). When two loans are involved, the fee for printing the second set of documents, if it differs from the first fee, should also be stated.

4. If the agreement does not mention a maximum range of travel for the standard fee, the Notary Signing Agent may ask that a range be included and that the signing service be willing to negotiate an additional fee for assignments outside of the maximum mileage range.

5. If the independent contractor's agreement does not have a clause on missed appointments, the Notary Signing Agent should seek clarification on whether he or she will be paid when the borrower fails to make an appointment.

6. The Notary Signing Agent also should clarify the agency's policy when one spouse misses the appointment. Will the Agent be compensated with an additional fee for scheduling a return appointment to obtain and notarize the signature of the absent spouse? Reputable signing services realize that missed appointments require an investment of time and are typically willing to compensate Agents for making a second trip.

7. Notary Signing Agents should review and clarify what the signing service's fee policy is in cases where the Agent makes the trip to the borrower's home but the borrower refuses to sign the documents.

8. Since a signing may stop because a borrower cannot present adequate proof of identity[6] or display adequate awareness or willingness to enter into the transaction, the Notary Signing Agent should seek clarification of the signing service's payment policy in such cases.

9. For signings where the Notary Signing Agent makes the trip to the borrower's home but the signing does not proceed as scheduled because of a missed appointment, refused signing or inability to prove the borrower's identity, awareness or willingness, the Agent should ensure that the independent contractor's agreement contains a provision outlining the additional fee paid to the Agent for rescheduling these appointments. The above-mentioned reasons are not the only reasons an appointment may be rescheduled. A lender may discover after a completed signing that it failed to include a particular document in the loan package that was needed to close the loan. Because of this omission, the documents may need to be redrawn and a second signing appointment scheduled. Or, a Notary Signing Agent may complete an assignment and return the documents as required, but the documents might not reach the title company on time to close the loan or may be lost in transit. For these and other possible situations where a return trip must be scheduled, the Notary Signing Agent should carefully read the contractor's agreement to clarify the signing service's fee policy.

[6] The Notary Signing Agent can avoid identification problems if the Agent has checked prior to the appointment that the borrower possesses an acceptable ID card or, in the absence of an ID card, can be identified by credible witnesses. For this and other steps the Notary Signing Agent should take to prepare the borrower for the signing appointment, see pages 75–78 of this Course.

10. Most contractor's agreements will clearly state that the Notary Signing Agent is responsible for incurring all expenses related to the signing. Typically, the Notary Signing Agent bears the cost of ordinary phone, fax and vehicle expenses for all signings the Agent performs. However, in a given assignment, the Notary Signing Agent may incur expenses that are above and beyond what the Agent would normally be expected to bear. For example, a signing held in a downtown Manhattan high-rise office building may require the Notary Signing Agent to pay downtown parking rates, or the title company may ask the Notary Signing Agent to fax an usually high number of documents before the signed documents are sent off via overnight delivery so that the title company can get a head start on processing the papers.

The contractor's agreement should include provisions for reimbursing these and other expenses, or it should be modified to include such provisions if they do not exist.

3. Benefits to Enlisting with Signing Services

While some Notary Signing Agents may bypass the signing services in hope of earning higher fees with companies providing direct work, many Agents will discover several distinct advantages to enlisting with signing services:

1. Working with the signing services can provide a steady stream of assignments, especially in the major cities.

   The volume that Notary Signing Agents receive from doing business with signing services is the same benefit the signing services reap from securing accounts with the major lenders. Like the Notary Signing Agent, a signing service may be willing to take a lower fee to ensure a greater number of assignments.

2. Signing services make the assignments that Notary Signing Agents otherwise would have to make for themselves. Once an Agent proves that he or she is a good performer, the Agent can expect the signing service to call with assignments whenever they are in the Agent's area. The Agent may just have to wait near the phone for assignments. Cultivating a good working relationship with a few signing services that provide steady assignments may especially suit Notary Signing Agents who are less inclined or available to directly market their services.

   Even though the fee paid by signing services brokering assignments is less than that paid by companies providing direct work, an Agent should keep in mind that there is a cost to marketing one's services as a Notary Signing Agent. The lower fee paid to the Agent by a signing service reflects the fact that the Agent is spared this cost.

3. The reputable signing services typically have fair, and at times generous, payment policies for missed appointments, refused signings and other situations where return appointments must be scheduled. These signing services view the Notary Signing Agent as their most valuable resource and compensate their Agents well to maintain a positive working relationship.

   In addition, reputable signing services often will pay the Notary Signing Agent for a signing whether or not the transaction actually closes. In contrast, lenders and title companies are paid for their services only if a transaction closes, so Notary Signing Agents working directly with lenders and title companies may not receive payment for transactions that do not close.

   These benefits come at a cost. The signing service pays the Notary Signing Agent a fee which is typically less than half of what the Agent would be paid if he or she received the assignment directly from a lender or title company. This broker fee covers the signing service's operating expenses and all the extras paid out to Notary Signing

Agents in the form of payments for missed appointments, refused and rescheduled signings, extra mileage and additional expenses.

4. Signing services provide the new Notary Signing Agent with the best opportunity to gain experience conducting loan document signings. Not only do Agents who work directly with lenders and title companies face competition from other Notary Signing Agents seeking the same work, but also lenders and title companies typically contract with the more experienced Agents who have demonstrated expertise in all types of loan transactions.

   This is not to say, however, that signing services tolerate the mistakes of inexperienced Agents. On the contrary, most independent contractor's agreements state that the Notary Signing Agent bears the costs of all return visits to a borrower to collect signatures and initials that were missed at the signing appointment.

   In fact, some lenders even have instituted measures to track the effectiveness of their signing services. Under one such system, every error an Agent makes at a signing costs the signing service 10-15 points. If 50 points are accumulated in a given week, the signing service loses the lender's business for one week. For accumulating 100 points, one month's worth of business is docked, which for some agencies is over $30,000 per month. For accumulating 150 points in one week, the company loses the lender's account altogether. Signing services thus cannot afford inexperienced Notary Signing Agents' mistakes when these errors can jeopardize important accounts.

   Many signing services have instituted similar systems to rate the performance of Notary Signing Agents.

Direct Work

While enlisting with a document signing service is one way to obtain signing assignments, it is not the only way. Many Notary Signing Agents will want to eliminate the middleman and solicit business from the companies that can provide direct assignments and higher fees.

1. Companies Providing Direct Work

Notary Signing Agents who directly market their services can solicit business from a number of different types of companies in the industry.

At times, lenders will make the decision to coordinate their own signing appointments, particularly if the lender is a smaller, regional institution.

Closing companies typically work in-house for a lender to coordinate signing appointments, draw closing documents and disburse funds. Closing companies work for one or perhaps two large lenders and do not typically perform title work.

Escrow and title companies are very similar to closing companies, but they usually work for many lenders all across the country. Many also perform title work. Escrow companies handle all types of loans.

A mortgage broker is an independent real estate financing professional who specializes in the origination of residential and commercial mortgages. It is estimated that mortgage brokers originate more than 55 percent of home loans each year.[7] After a home loan closes, the mortgage broker collects a fee from the borrower for the services he or she provides.

Mortgage banking companies originate mortgages exclusively for resale in the secondary mortgage market and frequently provide direct assignments for Notary Signing Agents.

Notary Signing Agents directly marketing their services should also approach local banks and savings and loans, which lend money for home loans and need Agents to help with loan signings.

In states where attorneys serve as closing agents, direct work assignments may be obtained through attorneys wanting to sublet this portion of the closing process. Notary Signing Agents should be aware that some states may require closing attorneys to supervise the persons conducting the loan signing appointments.

[7] Statistic provided by the National Association of Mortgage Brokers (http://www.namb.org/namb/Default.asp).

2. Benefits of Taking Direct Work

There are several advantages to working with lenders, title companies and other companies providing direct assignments:

1. Taking on direct work eliminates the broker in the transaction, so the Notary Signing Agent receives the full fee for the signing. Many lenders and title companies pay Agents taking on direct work the identical fee they pay to a signing service. Receiving higher fees raises the Agent's bottom line and reduces the number of signings necessary to make a profit.

2. When an Agent works directly with a lender or title company, he or she may have greater access to a loan or closing agent than an Agent who receives the assignment from a signing service. In direct work assignments, every party depends upon the closing to be paid, so loan and closing agents rely more on Notary Signing Agents to complete jobs quickly and efficiently. Because of this, Agents may find that loan and closing agents are more willing to take after-hours phone calls to resolve any lingering signing issues.

3. When an Agent works closely with a lender or specific contact person, the Agent begins to understand the business policies of that company or contact. Knowing these policies provides a certain level of comfort and almost always reduces the number of variables that could potentially cause problems with a signing. Conversely, Agents who obtain assignments through signing services must work with many different lenders and closing agents, all of whom have their own styles and policies.

RECEIVING ASSIGNMENTS

Once the Notary Signing Agent has marketed his or her services to prospective clients (whether signing services or companies providing direct work), the Agent can receive assignments. A client will call to present the assignment. In many instances, the assignment date and time will have been prearranged by either the signing service or lender, and the client will ask the Agent if he or she can take the appointment at the stated time.

Prearranged appointment times may be set at the request of the lender or borrower. The lender may prefer to set an appointment time during normal business hours to ensure that the borrower's loan agent is available to answer questions about the signing. Or, if the deadline for a loan is imminent, the lender may require the signing to take place no later than mid-afternoon so that the Notary Signing Agent will have enough time at the end of the appointment to ship the documents for a next-day arrival to the closing agent.

With many assignments, however, only the signing date is set. For example, the client may call and say, "I have a signing for you that must be signed either tomorrow or Friday. Can you take it?" In these instances, the client gives the Notary Signing Agent the responsibility to contact the borrower to set the time for the appointment. During the initial phone call in which the Notary Signing Agent accepts the assignment, the client will clarify that e-documents will be sent to the Agent or, if a physical package of documents is to be shipped, to whom the documents will be sent. It is customary for the Notary Signing Agent to receive the documents.

Whether documents are sent electronically or physically, the lender assigns the Notary Signing Agent the responsibility of carrying the documents for a number of reasons:

1. Having the Notary Signing Agent carry the documents to the appointment unburdens the borrower and frees him or her to just sign the documents.

2. The lender assigns the Notary Signing Agent the task of delivering the documents to the courier service after the signing because the lender wants to ensure that the documents are shipped back in a timely manner. If the documents are not returned in an expeditious

manner, the lender would prefer that the Notary Signing Agent, not the borrower, shoulder the responsibility.

3. Lenders often want to be sure documents are not altered prior to the signing appointment. In many cases, unauthorized changes to the Note or the Deed of Trust or Mortgage may cause extra complications or delays and may even prevent recordation of the documents when the loan is set to fund.

4. Lenders prefer that an impartial third-party witness carry the documents to and from the appointment to ensure the transaction is completed properly.[8]

Once the Notary Signing Agent accepts the assignment, most signing services will provide the Agent with the details of the assignment, including the borrower's name and contact information, the date and time of the signing, the name of the contact at the lender or title company, the loan or escrow number and the address where the documents will be sent.

SETTING THE APPOINTMENT

Having accepted the assignment, the Notary Signing Agent should immediately call the borrower to set or confirm the appointment. Most signing services will request a return confirmation from the Notary Signing Agent that the borrower was contacted and the appointment confirmed as soon as possible, but usually not later than a couple of hours after the Agent accepts the assignment.

The initial contact with the borrower is crucial; it is not just for confirming the appointment time and place. The Notary Signing Agent may use this initial contact to manage the signing from start to finish. Many of the potential pitfalls that can complicate or halt a signing may be overcome by preparing the borrower in advance of the signing.

[8] In this respect, the Notary Signing Agent is uniquely qualified to provide this important level of assurance. See Chapter 1, "The Notary Signing Agent's Role," for a more complete discussion of the Notary's function as impartial witness.

After confirming the time and place of the appointment, the Notary Signing Agent should discuss the following matters that will ensure the appointment proceeds smoothly.

Proper ID

The Notary Signing Agent should remind the borrower to bring proper identification for the documents that must be notarized. In states with laws that prescribe the ID cards a Notary may accept, the Agent should inform the borrower exactly what is needed. In California, for example, the Agent would tell the borrower that a current California driver's license or nondriver's ID card, U.S. passport, driver's license or nondriver's ID from another U.S. state, foreign passport, U.S. military ID, driver's license from Mexico or Canada, or government employee ID (issued by an agency or office of the state of California or by an agency or office of a California city, county or city and county) is required. If the borrower does not have one of these IDs, then one or two credible witnesses may be used.[9] By reminding the borrower about the ID requirement, the Notary Signing Agent is doing the single most important thing that can be done to manage the signing efficiently. Nothing could be worse than for an Agent to show up at an appointment, only to find out that the borrower does not possess a state-approved ID card or that the borrower's driver's license has expired.

Notary Signing Agents should attempt to avert ID problems before the appointment. When discussing the ID requirement during the phone call in which the signing appointment is confirmed, there is time to fix the situation if a problem arises. If, for example, the Agent discovers during the initial phone call that the borrower is an elderly homeowner who is signing papers in a reverse mortgage transaction,[10] no longer drives and does not possess another ID card that meets his state's requirements, the Agent

[9] A credible witness is an individual who personally knows the document signer and takes an oath or affirmation to confirm the identity of the signer. In California, a single credible witness may be used if the witness is personally known by the Notary and presents a state-approved ID card. Alternatively, two credible witnesses who are not personally known by the Notary and who present state-approved ID may be used.

[10] A reverse mortgage, also known as a home equity conversion mortgage or a rising debt, falling equity mortgage, is a loan for persons older than 62 that does not require repayment as long as the borrower makes the home his or her principal residence.

can give the elderly borrower enough time to line up one or two credible witnesses to satisfy the identification requirement. If the borrower will be using an ID card, the Agent should ask for the exact spelling of the name on the card, to be sure it matches the name on the loan documents.[11]

Borrower Stipulations

During the initial phone contact, a second way the Notary Signing Agent can prepare the borrower for the signing is to inform the borrower of any stipulations the borrower must meet to close the loan. A stipulation is any requirement the borrower must bring to the signing appointment. For example, a lender may ask the borrower to produce a W-2 form, pay stub or proof of hazard insurance as a condition to close the loan. In addition, the lender or closing agent may require the Notary Signing Agent to pick up a check from the borrower for closing costs and include the check with the signed papers the Agent returns. In situations where the Notary Signing Agent is aware of any borrower stipulations when he or she accepts the assignment, it is best to inform the borrower of these stipulations when the initial phone call is made.

However, the Notary Signing Agent is typically unaware of any borrower stipulations until receiving and reviewing the loan documents on the day of the signing. Some lenders include specific Notary Signing Agent instructions that advise the Agent to halt the signing if the borrower does not produce the stipulations. When the Notary Signing Agent learns of borrower stipulations by reviewing the documents or lender instructions, the Notary Signing Agent should immediately inform the borrower of these stipulations.

Agents operating in the states of Utah and Virginia should generally avoid handling checks for closing costs, since insurance regulators in these states have informed the NNA® that an escrow agent license is required to do so.

[11] For information on handling name discrepancies, see page 95 of this Course.

Notary Signing Agent Role and Limitations

Because Notary Signing Agents cannot explain document terms and conditions, the initial phone call can be used to briefly inform the borrower of the Notary Signing Agent's role and limitations in the transaction. The Agent can inform the borrower that if he or she has questions about the loan, these questions should be addressed to the lender before the appointment.

Borrower Receives Loan Documents

In the instances when the documents are shipped directly to the borrower, the Notary Signing Agent should ask the borrower to review the packet with a couple of concerns in mind:

1. The borrower should look for any documents in the package that must be completed by the borrower. For example, there is a form in many sets of loan documents called the Statement of Information that asks the borrower to provide residence, employment and marital status information going back 10 years. Asking the borrower to complete this form in advance can save time at the appointment and prevent the Notary Signing Agent from having to wait for the borrower to dig through personal files for the information to complete the form.

2. The borrower should review the documents to ensure that all names are spelled correctly and that the documents have the correct dates.

3. The Agent can remind the borrower to contact the lender for any questions related to certain documents before the appointment.

REVIEWING THE DOCUMENTS

Loan documents are typically delivered to Notary Signing Agents electronically. The documents will arrive in the Agent's inbox or the Agent will log on to the lender's website to access and print the documents.

Once the documents have been printed, the Notary Signing Agent should review the documents. The Agent should look for the following:

Specific Lender Instructions

Lenders may provide a summary sheet at the front of the package that will guide the Agent through the signing. The instructions also may note the stipulated items the borrower must return to the closing agent along with the signed documents. The instructions may ask the Agent to complete a form with the Agent's contact and Notary commission information. If the timing of the loan is critical, the lender also may ask the Agent to fax certain signed and notarized documents to the office before they are shipped.

Number of Documents to Be Notarized

The Notary Signing Agent should check to see how many documents in the package must be notarized. This review will help the Agent remember at the signing which documents must be notarized and may prevent the Agent from forgetting to notarize a document. Making a list of notarized documents on a Post-it and affixing the list to the inside of the Agent's Notary journal will expedite the process of recording journal entries at the beginning of the signing.

Basic Loan Terms and Conditions

The Notary Signing Agent should briefly skim the Instructions to Escrow, the HUD-1 Settlement Statement, the Borrower's Closing Statement, the Note and any other document in the package to become familiar with the terms and conditions of the loan. The Agent does this not to answer questions or provide advice to the borrower but to direct the borrower to documents in the package that may provide answers to the borrower's questions.[12] The Notary Signing Agent may find it helpful

[12] The Notary Signing Agent would be violating the prohibition against the unauthorized practice of law if the Agent answered a borrower's specific questions about the loan or provided unauthorized advice. To review the prohibition against providing unauthorized legal advice as a Notary, see Chapter 7, "Notary Signing Agent Responsibility." For a full discussion of the questions a Notary Signing Agent may and may not answer in a loan signing context, see Chapter 5, "Presenting Loan Documents."

to complete the Loan Signing Prep Sheet, pictured on pages 80–81, which the Agent may use to identify the various documents that appear in the package and the forms which must be notarized.

Loan Signing Prep Sheet

CONTACT INFORMATION

Name(s) of Borrower(s) ______________________ Home Phone ______________

Signing Appointment Date/Time ______________________ Business Phone ______________

Address ______________________ Phone (other)______________

Directions ____

____

____

____

Docs sent to ☐ Signing Agent ☐ Borrower Date Received __________ Borrower Copy? ☐ Yes ☐ No

Assignment Contact ______________________ Office Phone ______________

______________________ After Hours Phone ______________

DOCUMENT INFORMATION

Two Right to Cancel Forms? ☐ Yes ☐ No Rescission Period Ends ______________

Number of Documents to be Notarized __________ Number of Signatures to be Notarized __________

List Documents to be Notarized

1 ______________ 6 ______________

2 ______________ 7 ______________

3 ______________ 8 ______________

4 ______________ 9 ______________

5 ______________ 10 ______________

CHECK DOCUMENTS INCLUDED IN LOAN PACKAGE

☐ Addendum to Residential Loan Application
☐ Address Certification
☐ Affidavit Death of Spouse
☐ Affidavit of Continuous Marriage
☐ Affidavit of Death of Joint Tenant
☐ Affidavit of Death of Spouse Survivorship
☐ Affidavit of No Debts/Liens
☐ Affidavit of Payment of Taxes
☐ Affidavit of Settlement Agent
☐ Affidavit to Affirm Conveyance
☐ Affiliated Business Arrangement Disclosure
☐ Aggregate Analysis Trial Balance
☐ Aggregate Escrow Accounting Disclosure
☐ Agreement for the Arbitration of Disputes
☐ Appraisal Disclosure
☐ Assignment — General Request for Special Notice
☐ Assignment of Ownership Documents
☐ Assignment of Proprietary Lease
☐ Authorization to Reverify
☐ Automatic Drafting Authorization
☐ Billing Rights
☐ Borrower Credit Program Disclosure
☐ Borrower's Affidavit
☐ Borrower's Certification and Authorization
☐ Borrower's Disbursement Authorization
☐ Borrower's Income Certification
☐ Certificate of Loans to One Borrower
☐ Certificate of Trust
☐ Certification of Trust
☐ Claim of Lien
☐ Commitment Letter
☐ Compliance Agreement

continued on reverse side

Document Dates

The Notary Signing Agent should also check the dates on certain loan documents. For a signing taking place the same day, the date on the

CHECK DOCUMENTS INCLUDED IN LOAN PACKAGE

- ☐ Consumer Credit Score Disclosure Conditions
- ☐ Corporate Quitclaim Deed
- ☐ Corporation Assignment Deed of Trust
- ☐ Deceased Joint Tenancy Affidavit
- ☐ Declaration of Abandonment of Declared Homestead
- ☐ Deed of Trust (or Mortgage)
- ☐ Errors and Omissions Correction Agreement
- ☐ Escrow Waiver
- ☐ Estoppel Affidavit (By Individual Giving Deed-In-Lieu of Foreclosure) — Full Reconveyance
- ☐ Fair Lending Notice
- ☐ False Statement/Employment/Occupancy Form
- ☐ Federal Equal Credit Opportunity Act Notice
- ☐ Fire Insurance Authorization
- ☐ First Payment Letter
- ☐ Flood Insurance Authorization
- ☐ FNMA 1009 Affidavit
- ☐ Good Faith Addendum
- ☐ Good Faith Estimate of Settlement Charges
- ☐ Grant Deed
- ☐ Hardship Letter
- ☐ Hazard Insurance Authorization
- ☐ Home Equity Line of Credit and Promissory Note
- ☐ Homestead Declaration
- ☐ Homestead Waiver
- ☐ HUD-1 Addendum
- ☐ HUD-1 Settlement Statement
- ☐ Impound Authorization
- ☐ Initial Escrow Account Disclosure
- ☐ Instructions to Escrow (Closing Instructions)
- ☐ Insurance Information Sheet
- ☐ Inter Vivos Revocable Trust as Borrower Acknowledgment
- ☐ Inter Vivos Revocable Trust Rider
- ☐ Interest Rate and Loan Fee Policy
- ☐ Interspousal Transfer Grant Deed
- ☐ Interspousal Transfer Grant Deed Community Property with Right of Survivorship
- ☐ IRS 4506 Request
- ☐ IRS 8821 Tax Information Authorization
- ☐ IRS Form 8821
- ☐ IRS W-9 Form
- ☐ Itemization of Finance Charges
- ☐ Joint Tenancy Grant Deed
- ☐ Lead Paint Disclosure
- ☐ Limited Power of Attorney
- ☐ Loan Conditions
- ☐ Loan Disbursement Summary
- ☐ Long Form All-Inclusive Deed of Trust and Assignment of Rents
- ☐ Long Form Deed of Trust and Assignment of Rents
- ☐ Long Form Security — Land Contract
- ☐ Mortgage Broker Fee Disclosure
- ☐ Mortgagor's Affidavit for Master Home Equity Loan Policy and Certificate Program (Oath)
- ☐ Nearest Living Relative
- ☐ Non-Impound Notice
- ☐ Note
- ☐ Notice of Applicant to Receive Copy of Appraisal
- ☐ Notice of Right to Cancel
- ☐ Notice of Termination of "Right of First Refusal"
- ☐ Occupancy Affidavit
- ☐ Occupancy Affidavit and Financial Disclosure Status Conditions
- ☐ Overnight Fee Statement
- ☐ Partial Reconveyance
- ☐ Payoff Statement
- ☐ Privacy Policy (Optional)
- ☐ Property Locator
- ☐ Provider of Service Schedule
- ☐ Quitclaim Deed
- ☐ Release of Claim of Mechanics Lien
- ☐ Request and Authorization for Lender's Loss Payable Endorsement
- ☐ Request for Loss Payable Endorsement
- ☐ Request for Notice
- ☐ Revocation of Power of Attorney
- ☐ Riders to Deed of Trust (specify Rider below)
  - ____________________
  - ____________________
  - ____________________
- ☐ Section 255 Affidavit
- ☐ Security Instrument Cover Sheet
- ☐ Short Form Deed of Trust and Assignment of Rents (Individual)
- ☐ Signature Affidavit
- ☐ Signature Statement Acceptance of Terms and Conditions
- ☐ Special Power of Attorney as to Real Property
- ☐ Specific Release of Lien
- ☐ State Application Disclosure
- ☐ Statement of Information
- ☐ Subordination Agreement — Existing Deed of Trust to Additional Advance
- ☐ Subordination Agreement — Lease to Deed of Trust
- ☐ Subordination Agreement (Form A) — Existing Deed of Trust to New Deed of Trust
- ☐ Subordination Agreement (Form B) — New Deed of Trust to New Deed of Trust
- ☐ Substitution of Trustee
- ☐ Substitution of Trustee and Full Reconveyance
- ☐ Terms of Your Loan
- ☐ Transfer of Servicing Disclosure
- ☐ Trust Certification
- ☐ Truth in Lending Disclosure
- ☐ Uniform Residential Loan Application
- ☐ Verification of Important Loan Information
- ☐ Warranty Deed

Other

- ☐ ____________________
- ☐ ____________________
- ☐ ____________________
- ☐ ____________________
- ☐ ____________________
- ☐ ____________________
- ☐ ____________________

Note and the Deed of Trust or Mortgage, for example, either must match the date the borrower actually signs the documents or must precede the signature date. Under no circumstances may the date on which a document is signed or notarized precede the date on the document itself.

While checking the document dates, the Agent can determine if the documents are date-sensitive. Documents that are date-sensitive must be signed on the day they are dated. If the documents must be signed on the date indicated, it is important that the Agent know this and remind the borrower that a rescheduled appointment will make it necessary for the lender to redraw the documents, causing a delay in the closing. Sometimes the closing instructions state if the documents are date-sensitive.

Signatures, Initials and Dates

Reviewing the documents in advance of the appointment also alerts the Notary Signing Agent to those documents that require signatures, initials and dates. Agents soon discover that some documents in a loan package need only be signed. Others need to be signed and dated, others must be initialed and still others must be initialed on all pages and signed on the last page.

Since an initial on a document is as important as a signature, the Notary Signing Agent must take the time to scan the documents for all spaces requiring initials. Many standard loan documents require initials, including the Note, the Deed of Trust or Mortgage, the Uniform Residential Loan Application and various tax forms. The Agent soon will become familiar with these and other documents requiring initials. In addition, a lender may add an "Initial Here" stamp opposite a provision or date that must be initialed, as on the Notice of Right to Cancel, where the lender wishes to emphasize when the three-day right of rescission ends.[13] Spaces for initials can be difficult to spot. The Agent may wish to flag these documents with a Post-it so that the initial spaces are not overlooked.

In certain situations, the lender may already have flagged signature, initial and notarization spaces with Redi-Tags, although such circumstances are rare. It is even rarer for the lender to mark these spaces with a highlighter. The Notary Signing Agent should never use a highlighter to mark these spaces when they have not been marked already. Use of Post-its or Redi-Tags is preferred.

[13] The Notice of Right to Cancel informs the borrower that he or she has until midnight of the third business day following the date the documents are signed to cancel the loan.

Notice of Right to Cancel

On refinance loans that require a three-day right of rescission option, the Notice of Right to Cancel will appear in the loan package. In the initial review of the loan package, the Notary Signing Agent will want to know if the important dates on the Notice of Right to Cancel have been calculated. If the dates have not been calculated, then the lender expects the Agent to calculate and enter the dates.[14]

Borrower Stipulations

As has been mentioned, the Notary Signing Agent will want to be informed of any specific stipulations the borrower must meet for the loan to close.

Documents Printed Back to Back

In most loan packages that are physically printed and shipped, the documents are printed on one side only. However, occasionally a package will be printed on both sides of the paper. Since this print format is somewhat unusual, the potential for missing a signature or initial on documents printed this way is greater than if the documents are printed on one side only.

Borrower's Copies

When the documents are physically shipped to the Notary Signing Agent, the Agent should review the package in advance to see if there is a borrower's set of documents. Lender policies on providing a borrower's set vary. Many will include copies of all documents, while other lenders will provide the copies only after the originals have been signed and returned for processing.

When the borrower's set is not provided, it is a good business practice to make copies and provide them to the borrower at the appointment. The Notary Signing Agent should clarify with the company that provided the assignment whether the company will reimburse the Agent for making the copies.

[14] See Chapter 5, "Presenting Loan Documents," for instructions on how to calculate the three-day right of rescission date on the Notice of Right to Cancel.

At minimum, the Notary Signing Agent should provide copies of the following documents if a borrower's set is not included with the originals:

1. HUD-1 Settlement Statement

2. Truth in Lending Disclosure Statement

3. Two copies of the Notice of Right to Cancel for each borrower unless both borrowers signed one form[15]

4. Note

5. Borrower's First Payment Information, if in the loan package

When providing copies, the Notary Signing Agent should write a note to the lender or title company that the borrower's copies were not provided in the initial shipment and add the note to the return package containing the completed and signed originals.

Return Shipping Instructions

The Notary Signing Agent should check the assignment information to confirm that instructions for return shipping have been provided. This information typically includes the address of the lender or closing agent and either a preprinted air bill or an account number to charge for the return shipment. Agents will have to obtain quantities of return packaging materials and blank air bills from the major shipping companies. Most lenders include return packaging materials when physically shipping loan documents to Notary Signing Agents in order to expedite the return of the signed documents.

Finally, when reviewing the loan documents in preparation for the signing, the Notary Signing Agent always should keep the documents

[15] Federal disclosure laws require that the borrower receive copies of the HUD-1 Settlement Statement, the Truth in Lending Disclosure Statement and the Notice of Right to Cancel.

[16] Lender, closing agent and IRS forms are typically grouped together in sets of loan documents. In most cases, the Note and the Deed of Trust or Mortgage will be grouped together.

in the order received. After working with various lenders and title companies, the Agent will soon discover that there is a common sequential order in which documents in loan packages appear,[16] and it is best to not rearrange the documents in any way. The Agent should adopt the mindset that his or her job is to make life as easy as possible for the closing agent in the transaction.

EXECUTING THE LOAN SIGNING

After the Notary Signing Agent has made all preparations for the signing appointment, it is time to execute the actual signing.

The Agent should carefully plan for travel to the borrower's home or residence to ensure that he or she arrives on time (see Chapter 7, "Notary Signing Agent Responsibility").

Arranging the Workspace

Once the Notary Signing Agent arrives at the location of the signing appointment and makes introductions, the borrower or borrowers will lead the Agent to the table where documents will be signed.

The table where the signing is conducted is critical to ensuring a successful signing. A few simple pointers for arranging the workspace can make the signing proceed smoothly:

1. The Notary Signing Agent should request a clear table with sufficient room to pass the documents. If the Agent discovers that the table is cluttered, the Agent should politely ask that the table be cleared of all objects so nothing gets misplaced. It is also best if the table is free from any linens or tablecloths, as these items can make it difficult to sign and pass documents around the table.

2. All food and beverages should be kept clear of the documents. Many Agents make it a policy to decline an offer of a beverage for this reason.

3. The Notary Signing Agent should set up the table for the signing in a way that creates an efficient signing and document workflow. One method is to visualize the table as a clock, as illustrated above.

As the example illustrates, the Notary Signing Agent sits at the 6 o'clock position of the table. For one-borrower signings, the borrower sits at 9 o'clock; for two-borrower signings, the borrowers sit at 8 o'clock and 10 o'clock, respectively. Positioning the borrowers accordingly will let the borrowers talk freely about matters as the documents are routed without having to speak and pass documents to each other from opposite sides of the table. When one borrower is more passive in the signing process, it works best if that borrower signs the documents second. In these instances, the first signing borrower can instruct and lead the second borrower through the signing process.

The documents are routed clockwise and the signed documents are placed at 3 o'clock. Once a document is signed, it is placed outside the reach of the borrowers so that they can focus their full attention on the next document that comes down the line.

Document Dates

In general, loan documents contain three dates with which Notary Signing Agents must be familiar:

1. **The document date**, located at the top of most documents (e.g., the Note, the Deed of Trust or Mortgage)

2. **The signing date**, when the borrower actually signs the loan documents (usually indicated by a blank line opposite each signature line, sometimes with the word "Date" underneath it)

3. **The date of notarization**, when the Notary Signing Agent notarizes the signature on a document (always typed or written on the notarial certificate)

Keeping these three types of dates in mind is important, because there are a number of date-related issues that cause confusion for Notary Signing Agents within the context of a loan document signing. These issues are discussed on the following pages.

1. Document and Signing Dates Do Not Match

When the date preprinted on the documents does not reflect the actual date the documents will be signed (as written on a date line by the borrower opposite his or her signature), the Notary Signing Agent should never change the date unless he or she has been specifically directed to do so by the client or the lender. Changing the date could void the transaction or cause problems when the recordable documents reach the county recorder's office.

Many lenders may allow the documents to be signed on any date on or after the date preprinted on the document. Just because the Note and the Deed of Trust or Mortgage are dated with yesterday's date does not mean they cannot be signed today. In most instances, this is perfectly acceptable.

[17] See Chapter 7, "Notary Signing Agent Responsibility," for the criminal and other legal ramifications of postdating documents.

2. Postdated Documents

Occasionally, Notary Signing Agents may encounter loan documents that bear a date that is in the future. Under no circumstances may the signatures and notarial certificates on such documents be dated to match that future date rather than dated on the actual date of signature and notarization. This is known as *postdating*.[17] Postdated documents are a problem that the Agent must resolve before proceeding with the signing.

1. The Notary Signing Agent should attempt to contact the lender or client who assigned the signing appointment. If the lender or client can be reached, this person will provide the Agent with the necessary instructions on how to proceed with the signing. Depending upon how date-sensitive the transaction is, the typical options are either to reschedule the appointment for the date the documents will be valid or to postpone the signing and redraw the documents.

2. If the Notary Signing Agent cannot reach the lender or client, the Agent should leave a message stating that, since the documents are postdated, the appointment will be rescheduled for the date when the documents will be valid.

3. The Agent should contact the borrower and reschedule the appointment for the date when the documents will be valid.

3. Backdated Documents

The following scenario raises a red flag: Documents contain a prior date, the transaction is date-sensitive and the Notary Signing Agent is asked to enter the prior date as the date of signing and notarization rather than entering the actual date on which the documents are signed and notarized. This is known as *backdating*.

[18] The Note provides the evidence that a debt has been incurred on the property, while the Deed of Trust or Mortgage secures the debt against the property. See Chapter 5, "Presenting Loan Documents," for descriptions of the Note, Deed of Trust and Mortgage.

This scenario — the opposite of the preceding one — also puts the Notary Signing Agent at risk. In essence, the client is asking the Agent to backdate the documents to save the transaction.

4. Mismatched Dates on the Note and Security Instrument

It is important that the Note and the Deed of Trust or Mortgage contain the same document dates.[18] Problems may occur if the dates do not match. If a signing proceeds when the Note and the Deed of Trust or Mortgage contain differing dates, the lender might face difficulty finding a buyer for the loan when the lender offers the loan for sale in the secondary market.[19] If the dates on the Note and the Deed of Trust or Mortgage are mismatched, then the Notary Signing Agent should call the lender or client and obtain information on how to proceed. If the Agent were instructed to correct the error, usually the date on the Note and not the Deed of Trust or Mortgage would be changed to avoid making a correction to a recordable document.

It should be noted that the borrower typically is not required to enter the date he or she actually signed the security instrument (the Deed of Trust or Mortgage). The date of notarization provides the evidence of when the borrower executed or acknowledged executing the document.

5. Date Format Conventions

The format the borrower uses to record the date of signing should always remain consistent throughout the documents. If a certain convention is begun (e.g., 8/1/12), then the Notary Signing Agent should ask the borrower to use the same convention when entering dates into the other documents the borrower signs (avoiding switches to 8-1-12 or 08/01/2012 or August 1, 2012, for example).

[19] The originating lender often sells a home loan to another investor after the loan has funded. This practice is called selling the loan on the secondary market.

6. Borrower Dates the Documents

The Notary Signing Agent should never date the documents for the borrower to ensure the correct dates are entered. Since the handwriting of the Agent and borrower will differ, the transaction could be voided and investigated for fraud. In addition, the differing handwriting could prevent the loan from being sold in the secondary market. The best practice is for the Agent simply to make sure the borrower uses the same dating convention consistently throughout the documents.

7. Dates on the Notice of Right to Cancel

If the lender has not entered the proper dates into the Notice of Right to Cancel, the Notary Signing Agent must calculate the dates and have the borrower enter the dates into the proper places in the form.

The Agent should ensure that the borrower enters the proper dates into the borrower's copies of the Notice of Right to Cancel as well. There was an actual court case where the dates were not entered into the form and the borrower cancelled the loan a year later. The courts upheld the borrower's right to cancel because the borrower's copy was not properly completed at the time of the signing.

Signatures

The documents are typically drawn with the name information provided by the borrower on the initial application. The borrower must sign all documents exactly as typed and must sign the same name even on the documents where the name is not typed under the signature line.

For example:

John D. Smith	*John Smith*	*John David Smith*
John D. Smith	**John D. Smith**	**John D. Smith**
(Correct)	(Wrong: Undersigned)	(Wrong: Oversigned)

Some borrowers sign their name with an entirely unrecognizable signature. This should not pose a problem provided the signature is the way the borrower usually signs his or her name.

A Notary Signing Agent may discover that a borrower must sign documents for a property held in a trust and that the signature line contains the borrower's typed name with the title "Trustee" following it. The most common methods of signing as a trustee are as follows:

John D. Smith, Trustee for the Smith Family Trust UDT 8/1/2012;[20] or
John D. Smith, Trustee

The Notary Signing Agent should check with the lender to determine which method the lender prefers. If the documents do not specify a signing method and the Agent cannot reach the lender for instructions, the borrower may use the most comfortable method, provided that, at the minimum, the second of the two options just shown is followed.

Initials

On documents where the borrower must sign with initials, the borrower should use the same number of initials used in signing his or her signature, followed by a suffix, if applicable.

For example, for John David Smith, Jr.:

Initial: *JDS, Jr*	Initial: *JS*
(Correct)	(Wrong: Undersigned)

Following any specific preference dictated by the lender, when a borrower initials a document in the capacity of trustee, the borrower may initial as follows:

JDS, TTee or *JDS, TT* = John D. Smith, Trustee

[20]In this signature format, "UDT" stands for "under declatation of trust," and the date is that of the trust instrument in which the trustee was named.

Making Corrections

In situations where the lender has misspelled a borrower's name, entered an incorrect property address or typed in an inaccurate document date, the Notary Signing Agent should contact the client to verify that corrections may be made to the documents prior to making any actual corrections.

Provided that corrections may be made, the best practice for correcting a mistake is to draw a single line through the mistake with a pen, print the correction above, below or to the side of the mistake, and have all borrowers initial the correction.

For example:

John D. Smith

John ~~R.~~ Smith

D JDS

Signings by Proxy

Most lenders and title officers prefer that the borrowers themselves execute the loan documents whenever possible. There are occasions, however, when the borrower may not be able to complete the transaction, and an attorney in fact appears instead to sign the papers in the borrower's absence, a procedure called a signing by proxy.

For a person to sign as attorney in fact, a legal document known as a power of attorney must first have been executed. The power of attorney requires the principal signer to name the attorney in fact who will become the principal's authorized representative and to indicate the circumstances under which the attorney in fact may sign. Powers of attorney may be general or limited. A general power of attorney gives the attorney in fact authority to sign for the principal in any transaction where the principal's signature is required. A limited (or special) power of attorney, in contrast, authorizes the attorney in fact to sign for the principal only for a specified purpose or transaction as outlined in the power of attorney.

When the Notary Signing Agent learns that an attorney in fact will be executing the documents or when, unbeknownst to the Agent, an attorney in fact shows up at an appointment to sign for a borrower, the Agent should immediately contact the lender or contracting client company to obtain specific instructions for executing the loan signing. If the documents have not been drawn for signature by the attorney in fact, then the lender may ask that the Notary Signing Agent reschedule the appointment for a time when the borrower can be present or may redraw the documents for signature by the attorney in fact.

If, however, the Notary Signing Agent arrives at the signing, the borrower informs the Agent that he intends to sign for his spouse as her duly authorized attorney in fact and the lender cannot be reached, then the Agent can proceed with the appointment as scheduled as long as the following conditions are satisfied:

1. The original or a certified copy of the original power of attorney document is presented to prove a person has authority to sign, and a copy is sent back to the lender or escrow company with the signed documents.

2. The power of attorney document authorizes the attorney in fact to sign for the principal. If the power of attorney document specifically permits the attorney in fact to sign for the principal in the loan transaction or if it is general (the attorney in fact may sign in all circumstances), then the signing may proceed.

3. The Notary Signing Agent does not have direct knowledge that the signing procedure is improper or a substantive suspicion about the procedure or person posing as attorney in fact.

Under the circumstances presented, the Agent may proceed for the following reasons:

1. The Notary Signing Agent's primary objective is to complete the loan signing. If the lender does not permit the attorney in fact to

sign, then the documents would have to be redrawn anyway and the appointment rescheduled for a time when the borrower could sign the documents.

2. If the lender permits the attorney in fact to sign, the Notary Signing Agent has saved the additional expense of redrawing the documents and a delay in closing the loan.

3. If the Agent decides not to proceed with the signing and the lender would have accepted the signature of the attorney in fact, then the Agent could possibly be held liable for any expenses incurred that are caused by the delay, because it was the Agent's decision to halt the signing.

1. Signature as Attorney in Fact

When an attorney in fact signs loan documents for a principal signer, the attorney in fact should sign the documents as follows:

Sam P. Davis by John D. Smith as his attorney in fact, or *John D. Smith, attorney in fact for Sam P. Davis, principal*

2. Initials as Attorney in Fact

When an attorney in fact initials loan documents, the attorney in fact should initial the documents as follows:

SPD by JDS = Sam P. Davis by John D. Smith as his attorney in fact

STEPS IN THE LOAN SIGNING PROCESS

The following section presents a checklist of steps for conducting a signing from start to finish.

Request the Borrower's ID Card

During the initial phone contact, the Notary Signing Agent has previously spoken with the borrower about the need to bring a state-approved ID card to the signing appointment and has asked the borrower to give the Agent the exact spelling of the name on the ID so the Agent can compare that name to the name in which the documents are drafted. The Agent now must check the ID card itself to make sure the name on the documents matches the name on the card. If there is a discrepancy in how the names appear, the name on the ID may be more but not less than the name on the document. Therefore, if the signer's ID card shows a middle name, then the document may include the middle initial or omit the middle name all together. However, the first and last names must match those on the ID. Discovering a discrepancy at this late stage is disconcerting and may cause the signing to halt unless one or two credible witnesses may be summoned who can positively identify the borrower.

An actual story which represents what can happen emphasizes this point. A Notary Signing Agent received a same-day call late in the day to conduct a signing appointment. After the Agent received the documents by email, the Agent noticed that the documents were drafted in the name Susan B. Williams. The Agent called the borrower to check on her ID card and ask what name appeared on her driver's license. The borrower replied that the license was issued in her name, B. Susan Williams. The Agent then told the borrower that he needed to make a couple of calls. The Agent called the title company — a well-known and reputable company — and was counseled to proceed with the signing even though the names on the ID card and documents did not match. The Agent then called the lender, who also counseled the Agent to proceed with the signing.

In the end, the Notary Signing Agent, a California Notary Public, did not follow the advice of the title company and lender and required the borrower to enlist two close acquaintances as credible witnesses who could identify the borrower in the name B. Susan Williams. Fortunately, with less than two hours' notice, the two witnesses were summoned and the signing appointment was salvaged.

Present Borrower's Copies

The Notary Signing Agent should show the borrower the borrower's set of documents and place them out of reach until the end of the signing. It is best to place the copies out of the way during the signing so the copies are not confused with the originals.

Obtain Stipulations

The Notary Signing Agent should obtain any borrower stipulations and collect any funds required at the signing. The Agent can check the HUD-1 Settlement Statement and Instructions to Escrow to look for any required stipulations.

Record Journal Entries

The Notary Signing Agent should complete the journal entries for the documents requiring notarization early on in the signing process and before any documents are signed.

Present Key Documents First

This next point is entirely optional, but many Notary Signing Agents have found it effective to present and sign certain documents first. By presenting certain documents early in the signing, the Agent can attempt to resolve potential problems at the earliest possible point or, if necessary, can halt the signing early on when it is evident that the borrower does not wish to continue with the signing. In preparation for the signing, the Agent may flag the following four documents with a Post-it or Redi-Tag:

1. **HUD-1:** The HUD-1 Settlement Statement contains all the closing costs. At the signing, no matter is of greater concern to a borrower than the closing costs. By clarifying the closing costs first, the Notary averts a potential area of contention and a possible reason for the borrower to halt the signing.

2. **Note:** If the Note contains incorrect terms (rate, amount, prepayment penalty, balloon payment, etc.), then it may present a problem that cannot be remedied. Since some lenders will not accept changes to the Note, it is best to look at this early on. The Agent would not want to get halfway into a signing and discover a problem with the Note that would cause the signing to halt. If there is a problem with the Note, the Agent should contact the lender or escrow agent to obtain specific instructions.

3. **Notice of Right to Cancel:** By signing this form at the outset, the borrower may be less inclined to refuse signing other documents, since he or she will know about the three-day right to rescind the loan.

4. **Deed of Trust or Mortgage:** The Notary Signing Agent should have the borrower check the spelling of names, property address and vesting[21] on the security instrument.

Sign the Remaining Documents

After presenting and signing these documents first, the Notary Signing Agent should return the HUD-1 Settlement Statement, the Note, the Notice of Right to Cancel and the Deed of Trust or Mortgage to their proper sequence in the packet. The remaining documents in the packet may be signed in the order they appear.

Take Notes

A very helpful service Notary Signing Agents can provide for the borrower and lender is to take notes during the signing.

The Agent may take notes and jot down questions the borrower can discuss with the lender. Borrowers appreciate this service for at least two reasons: First, it shows that the Agent is providing an excellent service by

[21] Vesting refers to how a borrower takes title. Depending upon the state or jurisdiction, vesting options include joint tenancy, tenancy in common, community property, community property with right of survivorship, as trustee of a trust, as a corporation or partnership, as separate property or as a DBA.

listening to and recording their concerns. Second, borrowers can relax during the signing when they know that no issues of concern about the signing have been forgotten.

Taking notes for the lender is equally valuable. The Agent may note, for example, that a borrower would not sign a document until a thorough explanation of the document's purpose was provided or that the signer will ship via overnight delivery a W-2 form or other stipulated document that he or she may have forgotten to bring to the signing.

WRAP-UP PROCEDURES

At this point the signing appointment is almost completed. There are a few finishing steps the Notary Signing Agent should complete before leaving the borrower's home.

Review the Documents

The Agent should ask the borrower for a minute to review all documents for missed signatures, initials and dates. Since return visits are at the Notary Signing Agent's expense, the Agent should take as much time as necessary to ensure that all signatures, initials and dates have been collected. If pages in the packet are printed back-to-back, the Agent should be especially careful when double-checking the documents.

Secure Borrower Stipulations

The Notary Signing Agent should staple the borrower's stipulations (W-2, pay stubs, insurance policy, check, etc.) to the settlement statement.

WHEN THE BORROWER WILL NOT SIGN

In the majority of cases, signing appointments will proceed without complications. Occasionally, however, the Notary Signing Agent may encounter a borrower who does not want to complete a signing. It is always the borrower's prerogative to proceed with or stop the signing process.

A borrower may halt a signing for any number of reasons. Aside from the borrower experiencing the proverbial cold feet, other reasons for a borrower to halt a signing may include a failure to adequately understand a document, a belief that the terms of the loan have been changed, mistakes on the Uniform Residential Loan Application about the borrower's income, assets and debts, etc.

What can a Notary Signing Agent do when faced with a borrower who wishes to stop a signing?

Contact the Lender or Closing Agent

For specific questions related to document terms and conditions, the Agent should attempt to reach the borrower's loan officer or closing agent. During daytime signings, this will most always be possible.

Avoid Duress

The Notary Signing Agent should never haggle with the borrower over a decision to stop a signing. Any pressure the Agent exerts could be interpreted as duress by the borrower.

Never Leave Documents

If the signing appointment does stop, the Notary Signing Agent should collect all the documents and leave. Most lenders also ask that the borrower's copies be collected as well.

Call the Assigning Company

Once the Notary Signing Agent has left the borrower's home, the Agent should contact the company that provided the assignment to receive instructions for disposing of the documents. If the documents are date-sensitive, the lender may want the Agent to retain the documents for a rescheduled appointment in case the borrower's questions can be answered quickly. Alternatively, the lender may ask the Agent to return the documents via next-day delivery. ■

CHAPTER 4 TEST

True/False Questions

1. Lenders prefer to send documents to the Notary Signing Agent because of the Agent's role as impartial witness in the transaction.

2. If the documents are sent to the borrower, the Notary Signing Agent should ask the borrower to review the documents for the correct spelling of all names.

3. A Deed of Trust or Mortgage may not be notarized if the document date is before the actual date of signing.

4. The "secondary market" is a term that refers to the market for the buying and selling of existing mortgages.

Multiple Choice Questions

(Choose the Best Answer)

1. Which of the following documents is best to have signed at the beginning of the signing?
   a) The HUD-1 Settlement Statement
   b) The Itemization of Amount Financed
   c) The Good Faith Estimate of settlement charges
   d) The Borrower's Certification & Authorization

2. If the lender has not entered the proper dates into the Notice of Right to Cancel, the Notary Signing Agent must calculate the dates and then do what?
   a) Have the borrower enter the dates into the proper places
   b) Enter the dates into the proper places him- or herself
   c) Leave the spaces open so the lender can fill in the proper dates
   d) None of the above

3. Which of the following is not considered a business day for the purpose of calculating a rescission period date?
   a) Sunday
   b) Saturday
   c) Veterans Day
   d) Both a and c

See page 331 for correct responses.

CHAPTER 5

Presenting Loan Documents

INTRODUCTION

Knowledge of Documents Essential

Aside from knowing state Notary laws and how to notarize documents according to accepted standards of Notary Public practice, knowledge of the various loan documents themselves is the next most critical area of expertise for Notary Signing Agents.

To minimize mistakes that postpone closings, lenders and closing agents require Notary Signing Agents to possess experience with loan documents.

Besides security instruments and the relatively few other documents that are notarized, there are numerous additional documents in a loan package that must be signed, dated and initialed. The client expects the Notary Signing Agent to be familiar with them.

When receiving an assignment from a client, it is not uncommon for a Notary Signing Agent to hear the client ask something like, "Have you ever handled a signing involving a Chase loan?" The client wants to know if that Agent has experience handling a signing for a particular lender, since procedures and documents for that lender may differ from the procedures and documents the Agent has encountered with other lenders.

To obtain assignments, Notary Signing Agents therefore must demonstrate a familiarity with a wide range of documents that may be included in a loan signing. The broader the Agent's experience with these documents and the more experience an Agent has in conducting signings for many different lenders, the more confidence a client will have in providing the Agent with assignments.

A Notary Signing Agent's specific knowledge of loan documents also benefits the borrower. A borrower is often overwhelmed by the sheer number of documents in a typical loan transaction. A Notary Signing Agent's familiarity with the documents can help put the borrower at ease in what is for many a tension-laden process.

Notary Signing Agents May Not Explain Documents

The Notary Signing Agent's familiarity with the various types of loan documents does not mean, however, that the Agent may help the borrower by explaining the documents.

1. Identifying Documents Proper

In a previous chapter, reference was made to the importance of avoiding the unauthorized practice of law as a Notary Public. The Notary must steer clear of the potential hazards of exceeding the proper boundaries of the Notary's role as an impartial witness.[1] The same temptation faces the Notary Signing Agent. The temptation to exceed the parameters of the Notary Signing Agent's role by explaining documents and providing unauthorized advice is a real danger that must be avoided.

What information can the Notary Signing Agent give to a borrower without stepping over the line into the domain of licensed attorneys? What must the Agent avoid saying?

To steer clear of providing unauthorized legal advice, the Notary Signing Agent may identify, but not explain, documents. An Agent may guide the

[1] The unauthorized practice of law by a Notary is discussed in further detail in Chapter 7, "Notary Signing Agent Responsibility."

borrower to a particular document that addresses the borrower's question. However, the Agent must stop short of answering the borrower's question and must insist that the borrower read the document to find the answer.

An example will help to clarify the principle. During a signing appointment, a borrower inquires about the prepayment policy for his particular loan, a common occurrence most Notary Signing Agents encounter.

The temptation for the informed Notary Signing Agent is to provide an answer to this specific question. Yet, prepayment policies differ by lender and loan. Furthermore, prepayment clauses are written in precise and often complex legal language that requires an individual with the proper training to interpret. For these reasons, the Notary Signing Agent should not answer the question.

However, while declining to answer the question itself, the experienced Agent may suggest that the borrower refer to a particular document containing the prepayment provisions.[2] The Agent pulls the document from its placement in the package for the borrower to consider.

The trained and experienced Notary Signing Agent may respond to most common questions by identifying a particular document that provides the needed information. The borrower may ask, "Where can I find the interest rate for my loan?" to which the Agent may reply, "Look at your Note." To the borrower's question, "Where can I find out if I will owe funds at closing?" the Agent may respond, "Look at your HUD-1 Settlement Statement."

In addition to identifying the document that may contain the answer to the borrower's question, the Notary Signing Agent also may provide a general description of a document's function, as long as the explanation steers clear of providing specific advice. For example, when the Truth in Lending Disclosure Statement[3] is presented for signing, the borrower may look at the annual percentage rate on the form and mistake it for the interest rate on the loan. The borrower may express alarm that the annual percentage rate for the loan is higher than the interest rate and ask why.

[2] The Note and the Truth in Lending Disclosure Statement outline the prepayment provisions for the loan.

[3] The Truth in Lending Disclosure Statement is specifically discussed later in this chapter.

The Agent may explain that the annual percentage rate appearing in the Truth in Lending Disclosure Statement is typically higher than the interest rate, since it includes all the fees associated with the loan and calculates these fees over the life of the loan as a percentage rate. The Agent may further explain that federal law requires lenders to disclose an annual percentage rate so borrowers may comparison shop among competing lenders and loan programs. In describing the purpose of the Truth in Lending Disclosure Statement and its annual percentage rate, the Agent may not, however, explain the specific fees that make up the annual percentage rate or how the rate is calculated in the borrower's particular case.

The Notary Signing Agent must stop short of providing answers to questions that go beyond the limited scope of identifying and providing general descriptions of documents. When a borrower asks, "What am I promising by signing this Arbitration Rider?" the Notary Signing Agent must refer the borrower to the lender or loan broker who can interpret and explain the provisions of the Arbitration Rider. Another type of question the Notary Signing Agent must avoid answering is, "When is my loan going to close?" If the closing date is not clearly stated in a particular document that the Notary Signing Agent can identify to the borrower, then the Agent must refuse to answer.

A Notary Signing Agent must refuse to answer any "why" question. During the point in a signing when the borrower is reviewing the closing costs for the loan on the HUD-1 Settlement Statement, the borrower may discover an amount for a loan origination fee. Up to this point, the borrower may have been under the impression that an origination fee was not to be charged and may ask why the fee was imposed. As is the case with other questions the Notary Signing Agent may not safely answer, the only recourse in this situation is to refer the borrower to the loan officer.

2. Answering Specific Questions Improper

Research suggests that there are certain questions borrowers frequently ask at loan signings. If the Notary Signing Agent cannot direct a borrower to a specific document for the answer to any of the following twenty questions, then the Notary Signing Agent would do well to refer the borrower to the loan officer or closing agent handling the loan.

1. When is my loan going to close?

2. What is the APR (Annual Percentage Rate)?

3. Why is the APR higher than the interest rate I was quoted?

4. What am I agreeing to do by signing the Correction Agreement: Limited Power of Attorney?

5. Does my loan have a prepayment penalty?

6. When does my adjustable rate reset?

7. What is the interest rate on my loan?

8. Does my monthly payment include impounds for property taxes and insurance?

9. Can you confirm that my loan has a fixed and not an adjustable interest rate?

10. How much cash back will I receive after closing?

11. I was told I have a “zero fees loan”; why are fees for closing costs appearing on the closing statement?

12. What is the “estimated refundable pad” expense appearing on the closing statement?

13. What is the "tax service" fee on the closing statement? (The preceding three questions are representative of those a borrower may ask regarding any fee on the closing statement that the borrower does not understand.)

14. Why am I signing two Deeds of Trust/Mortgages and Notes (in a reverse mortgage transaction)?

15. How does my name appear on title to the property?

16. Why are my closing costs so high?

17. Why do I have to sign a W-9 form?

18. Am I being charged points on the loan?

19. Why am I being charged interest on my old loan and the new loan at the same time?

20. Why does this credit card balance appear on my loan application when I paid this off?

3. Avoiding the Temptation to Explain Documents

Why do Notary Signing Agents answer questions they shouldn't? While the allure of explaining documents can be subtle, the reasons range from selfless to self-serving. The reasons include the following:

1. **To provide superior service:** A Notary Signing Agent who improperly explains documents to a borrower is often motivated by a desire to be helpful. The Agent certainly does not intend to harm a borrower with improper or inaccurate information.

2. **To receive high marks:** An Agent may believe that he or she will be perceived as knowledgeable, proficient and professional and

that the borrower will provide a positive evaluation of the Agent's services to the contracting company.

3. **To expedite the signing:** Agents who explain documents may do so simply to keep the signing moving to completion. If the Agent has a signing appointment immediately following the current appointment, he or she may feel pressured to answer a question so as not to be late for the next customer.

4. **To close the loan:** The most overtly selfish reason for an Agent to succumb to the temptation of explaining a document is the hope that the borrower may be motivated to consummate the transaction and the loan will close as scheduled. This may be especially true if the Agent's fee is contingent upon the closing.

There is never a good reason to explain documents. An Agent who refuses to answer a borrower's specific questions about the transaction is being helpful in the best sense of the term. No matter how well the Agent executed the other aspects of the loan signing, the Agent's reputation will suffer if the contracting company learns that the Agent provided unauthorized advice to a borrower.

Scheduling appointments with ample time between will remove any pressure to answer a question and speed up the signing.

Finally, while some pay arrangements in the settlement services industry are contingent upon the closing, a Notary Signing Agent must never compromise the impartiality and objectivity expected of professional Notary Signing Agents.

In light of the prohibitions against offering unauthorized legal advice and answering specific questions, the Notary Signing Agent should inform the borrower during the appointment-setting contact and again at the beginning of the signing appointment that the Agent cannot answer specific legal and financial questions about the loan. The Notary Signing Agent should tell the borrower that the Agent is not acquainted with the borrower's loan and is not authorized to answer questions about it. The Agent should inform the borrower to direct all such questions to the lender prior to the appointment.

4. Notary Signing Agent Pledge of Ethical Practice

In an effort to help Notary Signing Agents explain their role and limitations to borrowers, the NNA® has created the Notary Signing Agent Pledge of Ethical Practice. Agents may find it helpful to provide borrowers with a copy of the Pledge at the beginning of the loan signing appointment. The Pledge reads as follows:

> I am not an attorney and therefore, by law, I cannot explain or interpret the contents of any document for you, instruct you on how to complete a document or direct you on the advisability of signing a particular document. By doing so I would be engaging in the unauthorized practice of law, and could face legal penalties that include the possibility of incarceration.
>
> Any important questions about your document should be addressed to the lender, title company or an attorney.

Business card and desktop display templates containing the Pledge are available as a free download to members of the NNA®'s Notary Signing Agent Section at www.NationalNotary.org.

LOAN DOCUMENT REVIEW

A description of 57 loan documents will be presented in the pages that follow. These documents comprise an actual set of documents produced for a loan signing. Notary Signing Agents will soon discover that some of these documents will appear at every signing the Agent conducts. Following the document descriptions, the documents themselves are presented.

Following the presentation of this sample set of documents are 16 additional documents that Notary Signing Agents encounter frequently. For example, a Notice of Right to Cancel is presented in this second section because the complete set of sample loan documents presented earlier in the chapter was for a purchase transaction and did not contain this common form. Samples of these additional documents appear following their descriptions.

Any Notary Signing Agent certainly will encounter more than the 73 different documents described and illustrated in these pages. Since the different types of loan documents that an Agent might see are virtually unlimited, three lists of additional loan and real property documents follow at the conclusion of the chapter. These documents are categorized under three headings: documents executed by signatures and/or initials, documents typically notarized and documents requiring information the borrower must provide.

A few words about the documents themselves:

1. The documents illustrated in the following pages are representative of documents found in a loan package, but the actual documents that a Notary Signing Agent encounters in the field may look different than they do here. Each lender creates its own forms. Even such standard documents as IRS tax forms may look slightly different in actual loan packages.

2. While certain forms appear in virtually every package, there are many possible combinations. While every attempt has been made to discuss the most common documents, the reader may discover that there are forms not discussed here that appear repeatedly.

3. The reader will notice that there are documents in the sample loan package that appear to overlap each other. For example, there is an Occupancy Affidavit, an Occupancy and Financial Status Affidavit and a False Statement/Employment/Occupancy Form Borrowers Certification. In each of these documents, the borrower must certify his or her occupancy intentions with respect to the subject property. Similarly, there is a Document Correction Agreement, a Compliance Agreement and a Limited Power of Attorney in the sample set that in various ways provide a means for correcting errors in the documents after the closing. There is both a Signature Affidavit & AKA Statement and a Name Affidavit in the package as well.

Why are there three substantially similar occupancy forms, three separate documents for securing the borrower's assistance in correcting documents and two comparable name affidavits when perhaps one would do?

There are a number of reasons why these variations appear. There may be subtleties within the documents themselves that account for the differences. A federal and state law may impose a requirement for a lender to disclose certain information to a mortgage loan applicant, generating separate forms. A good example is the Housing Financial Discrimination Act of 1977 Fair Lending Notice (page 228), which is required by California law, and the Federal Equal Credit Opportunity Act Notice (page 227), which is required by federal law.

Furthermore, three different entities are involved in a typical loan transaction: the broker or originating lender, the closing agent and the secondary purchaser or servicer. Each party has compliance issues and requirements for retaining original documents as a record of the transaction. This fact alone may account for the presence of seemingly redundant forms.

4. In addition to containing documents required under federal laws such as the Real Estate Settlement Procedures and Truth in Lending Acts, the sample set of loan documents contains forms required under the laws of the state of California. The state-specific forms presented in the sample set may not conform to documents required in other states.

5. The documents in the sample set have been presented with certain similar forms grouped together (e.g., forms related to occupancy, appraisal, escrow, impound). The actual order of documents in packages encountered in the field may be substantially different.

6. The sample documents are for training purposes only. They are not to be used as models or blank forms for any actual transaction.

Buyer's Final Closing Statement (Page 143)

1. The Buyer's Final Closing Statement is a closing statement separate from and supplemental to the HUD-1 Settlement Statement used in certain parts of the U.S. for listing the actual settlement costs associated with the transaction.

2. The form illustrated on page 143 is the final closing statement; at the loan signing appointment, an estimated closing statement will be presented to the buyer (or borrower in a refinance transaction). The closing agent will mail the final statement to the buyer or borrower after the transaction closes.

3. Since the sample loan document package illustrated in this chapter was for a purchase transaction, a separate Seller's Final Closing Statement was provided to the seller listing the seller's costs for the transaction. This document was omitted from the sample set of documents.

4. In a refinance transaction, this form will be renamed as Borrower's Final Closing Statement.

HUD (U.S Department of Housing and Urban Development) Settlement Statement (Pages 144–146)

1. In the HUD-1 Settlement Statement, the lender itemizes the actual closing services provided and fees charged to the borrower.

2. The fully completed HUD-1 Settlement Statement generally must be delivered or mailed to the borrower at or before the settlement. The RESPA allows the borrower to ask to see the settlement statement one day before the closing. The settlement agent must provide the borrower with a completed settlement statement based on information known to the agent at that time. In cases where there is no settlement meeting, the escrow agent will mail the statement after closing.

3. If the lender did not provide an instruction sheet for the Notary Signing Agent's use, Cash From/To Borrower (line 303) is where the Agent would check to see if the borrower must bring in funds for closing. The lender may ask the Agent to collect these funds at the signing appointment.

4. Effective January 1, 2010, pages 2-3 of the HUD-1 Settlement Statement have been modified in an attempt to help buyers and borrowers better understand the closing costs and loan terms for the particular loan they have obtained.

   a. Individual lines representing closing costs on page 2 are linked to the corresponding lines of the Good Faith Estimate of settlement charges (pages 152–154), so buyers and borrowers have a point of reference to the final closing costs charged compared with the estimated costs provided earlier in the transaction.

   b. Charts on page 3 summarize the closing costs into three categories and the material terms of the buyer's or borrower's loan.

5. The HUD-IA form is an alternate form to the HUD-1 Settlement Statement that is often used in transactions without sellers, such as a refinance or home equity line of credit transaction.

General Closing Instructions (Page 147)

1. The General Closing Instructions provide the lender's general requirements (conditions) to the settlement agent for the closing of a single-family residential mortgage transaction.

2. The General Closing Instructions provide the lender's conditions for executing and correcting documents, using a Power of Attorney and handling transactions with a rescission period.

3. Another condition stipulated in the General Closing Instructions is the lender's requirement that the buyer or borrower must provide proof of hazard insurance on the subject property. Item 3 under Hazard Insurance stipulates how the loss payee/mortgagee clause on the insurance policy must read. Since the loan in the sample documents appearing in this chapter has been assigned to a new servicer, the Request for Change to Insurance Policy and the Request for Change to Flood Certification (pages 234 and 235) contain the new information for this loss payee/mortgagee clause.

4. The General Closing Instructions are not signed by the buyer or borrower; they are signed by the closing agent.

Specific Closing Instructions (Pages 148–149)

1. The Specific Closing Instructions provide the detailed closing stipulations and requirements for a specific residential mortgage transaction.

2. The Specific Closing Instructions list many of the loan documents appearing in the loan package. Not all documents presented in the sample set of documents are listed in the Specific Closing Instructions. Nevertheless, a Notary Signing Agent may peruse these instructions to determine if a particular document, such as a Notice of Right to Cancel, is included in the documents.

3. The Specific Closing Instructions also list the terms for the loan, an estimate of closing costs, the party responsible for paying the costs and any impounds.

4. The buyer or borrower must sign the form to acknowledge having read the Specific Closing Instructions.

Addendum to Closing Instructions (Pages 150–151)

1. The Addendum to Closing Instructions lists other conditions from the lender to the closing agent that are not a part of the general or specific instructions but that must be satisfied prior to disbursement of the loan and close of escrow.

2. For example, a verbal verification of employment (VOE) must be made to confirm that the borrower is still employed in his or her current job, a critical stipulation necessary to assure the lender to proceed with funding.

3. A second Addendum to Closing Instructions lists additional estimated settlement fees not appearing in the Specific Closing Instructions.

4. The closing agent signs both addenda.

Good Faith Estimate of Settlement Charges (Pages 152–154)

1. The Good Faith Estimate of settlement charges (GFE) is a standardized 3-page form, required under the Real Estate Settlement Procedures Act (RESPA), that provides an estimate of settlement charges for a loan.

2. Effective January 1, 2010, the GFE now contains a summary of loan terms as well as tables and charts that are designed to assist a borrower in understanding the loan being applied for and in comparison shopping the loans of other lenders.

3. A lender must provide a GFE to a loan applicant within three business days of his or her application for the loan. If there are substantive changes in the loan transaction after the initial GFE is supplied (for example, when the loan amount changes), then a new GFE must be issued.

4. The new GFE form does not contain signature lines for the borrower, but many lenders will include another document in the loan package disclosing that the GFE has been provided and asking the borrower to acknowledge receiving the GFE (see Acknowledgment of Receipt of Good Faith Estimate and Truth in Lending Act Disclosures, page 162). If a subsequent GFE is issued, another document disclosing that the subsequent GFE has been provided may be included.

Good Faith Estimate Providers of Services (Page 155)

1. In the Good Faith Estimate Providers of Services, a lender informs the borrower of the names of alternate settlement services providers the borrower may select in order to shop for settlement services for a loan.

Uniform Residential Loan Application (Pages 156–160)

1. Known as the 1003, the Uniform Residential Loan Application is a typed version of the loan application, containing information the borrower provided to initiate the loan.

2. The Uniform Residential Loan Application contains the contact information for the lender, which is helpful in case the lender must be contacted during office hours.

3. At the bottom of each page there is a space for the borrower's initials, and on page 3 there is a space for the borrower's signature.

4. Pages 4 and 5 are for extended information that would not fit into the body of the application. The borrower must sign these pages.

Truth in Lending Disclosure Statement (Page 161)

1. The Truth in Lending Disclosure Statement is a form required by the federal Truth in Lending Act (TILA).

2. The Truth in Lending Disclosure Statement contains the following information:

   a. The annual percentage rate (APR): The APR is the cost of the loan in percentage terms and includes private mortgage insurance and prepaid finance charges (loan discount, origination fees, prepaid interest and other credit costs). The APR is calculated by spreading these charges over the life of the loan, resulting in a higher rate than the interest rate shown on the Note.

   b. Finance charges: The finance charge is the sum of all charges imposed by the lenders as an incident to the extension of credit. 15 USC § 1605 defines a finance charge and specifies the types of costs that are included and excluded.

   c. The amount financed: The amount financed is the borrower's loan amount.

   d. Total payments: The total amount of payments is the sum the borrower will have paid after he or she has made all minimum required scheduled payments, including principal, interest, prepaid finance charges and mortgage insurance.

   e. Payment schedule: The payment schedule is the breakdown of the borrower's monthly payments and includes principal and interest. Depending on circumstance, the payment schedule may also include applicable property taxes and hazard insurance, if these amounts are impounded.

   f. Prepayment penalties, if any: A prepayment penalty is an additional fee imposed by a lender upon a borrower for paying a loan off early.

g. Assumption option, if allowed: Assumption in a residential mortgage transaction refers to a subsequent buyer of the home taking on the remaining obligation of the seller's loan on its original terms.

Acknowledgment of Receipt of Good Faith Estimate and Truth in Lending Act Disclosures (Page 162)

1. Under the Real Estate Settlement and Procedures and Truth in Lending Acts, lenders and closing agents are required to provide the borrower with certain disclosures.

2. The borrower signs this document to acknowledge having received a copy of the Good Faith Estimate of settlement charges (pages 152–154) and a copy of all disclosures required under the Truth in Lending Act (TILA). TILA disclosures include the Truth in Lending Disclosure Statement (page 161) and the Notice of Right to Cancel (page 258).

Borrower's Certification & Authorization (Page 163)

1. By signing the Borrower's Certification & Authorization, a borrower certifies that the information contained in the borrower's loan application is true and complete, without misrepresentation or omission of important facts.

2. The borrower also authorizes the lender to release loan-specific information to an investor looking to purchase the loan in the secondary market. Information provided to the investor could include the borrower's employment history and income, bank account balances and credit history and copies of the borrower's income tax returns.

Payment Letter to Borrower (Page 164)

1. In the Payment Letter to Borrower, the lender informs the borrower what the borrower's monthly payment for the loan will be. This

document breaks down the costs for principal and interest, for property taxes and for fire, flood and mortgage insurance (when applicable).

2. The document also informs the borrower where to make payments for the loan.

Hardship (Page 165)

1. In the Hardship, the borrower states that he or she understands that the first payment on the loan is due within 30 days of the closing of the loan and that this will not create any financial hardship.

2. While the Hardship appears in the sample set of documents for a purchase transaction, it is also seen with second mortgages and, in particular, debt consolidation loans.

Itemization of Amount Financed (Page 166)

1. Another Truth in Lending Act (TILA) disclosure, the Itemization of Amount Financed, itemizes finance and prepaid finance charges paid by the borrower. The sample form shows two columns, the one on the left for the fees that are financed and the one on the right for the fees that are prepaid.

2. The fees listed on the form have corresponding HUD-1 reference numbers that appear on the HUD-1 Settlement Statement (pages 144–146).

Note (Pages 167–169)

1. The Note is the written evidence of indebtedness and the borrower's promise to repay.

2. The Note includes the following information:

   a. Loan amount

b. Interest rate

c. Payment amount

d. First payment due date

e. Prepayment stipulations

f. Late charge terms and conditions, including default

3. Each Note executed in a mortgage finance transaction will be accompanied by a security instrument (Mortgage or Deed of Trust). In a reverse mortgage loan, there will be two Notes and two security instruments. The Note is held in conjunction with the Deed of Trust or Mortgage (pages 171–184), which provides the security for the Note.

Allonge (Page 170)

1. The Allonge is an attachment to a legal document — in this case the Note — that is used to insert language or signatures when the original document does not have sufficient space for the inserted material or signatures.

2. Since the loan in the sample documents has been assigned to a new servicer (see Notice of Assignment, Sale or Transfer of Servicing Rights, page 226), the Allonge provides the place for the endorsement of the originating lender's funding manager to pay the principal balance on the Note to the new servicer.

3. The Allonge is not signed by the buyer or borrower.

Deed of Trust (Mortgage) (Pages 171–184)

1. The Deed of Trust (Mortgage) is a security instrument whereby real property is pledged as security for a debt.

2. A Mortgage differs from a Deed of Trust primarily in the way that foreclosure proceedings are handled. In states that use the Mortgage, foreclosure proceedings are governed by state law and handled through the state's legal system.[4]

3. States that use the Deed of Trust include Arizona, Alaska, California, Colorado, District of Columbia, Georgia,[5] Idaho, Mississippi, Missouri, Montana, Nebraska, Nevada, North Carolina, Oregon, Tennessee, Texas, Utah, Washington and West Virginia.

4. States that use the Mortgage include Alabama, Connecticut, Delaware, Florida, Guam, Hawaii, Illinois, Indiana, Iowa, Kansas, Louisiana, Maine, Massachusetts, Michigan, Minnesota, New Hampshire, New Jersey, New Mexico, New York, North Dakota, Ohio, Oklahoma, Pennsylvania, Puerto Rico, Rhode Island, South Carolina, South Dakota, Vermont, Wisconsin and Wyoming.

5. Arkansas, Kentucky, Maryland and Virginia use both.

6. The Deed of Trust (Mortgage) contains the following information:

   a. Account number

   b. Date

   c. Name of trustor (borrower)

   d. Name of beneficiary (lender)

   e. State of incorporation

   f. Address of lender

---

[4] States that use the Mortgage are called judicial states.
[5] Georgia uses a Security Deed.

g. Principal loan balance

h. Legal description of property

i. Property address

j. Linkage to Note

7. A Mortgage and a Deed of Trust serve the same function. A Mortgage is simpler, as it involves only the borrower and the lender. As its name implies, a Deed of Trust also involves a trust relationship. It works as follows:

   a. A trustor or mortgagor (the borrower) who signs a Deed of Trust receives title to the property but conveys the title to a neutral third party called a trustee or mortgagee (a title company).

   b. The trustee holds the title to the property for the borrower and the beneficiary (the lender) until the loan is fully paid.

   c. When the borrower pays off the loan, the trustee transfers the property title back to the borrower.

8. Note: The sample set of loan documents presented in the following pages does not contain a sample of a Mortgage.

Condominium Rider (Pages 185–187)

1. It is sometimes necessary to add or delete provisions to the Deed of Trust (Mortgage) to acknowledge special provisions that apply to certain loans. The additions or deletions are included in a rider to the security instrument. In the sample set of loan documents, a Condominium Rider amends and supplements the covenants and agreements in the Deed of Trust (Mortgage).

2. If a rider is included in the loan package, it will be referred to in the applicable section of the Deed of Trust (Mortgage).

Impound Authorization (Page 188)

1. By signing the Impound Authorization, a borrower authorizes the lender to collect and manage that portion of the borrower's monthly payments allocated for taxes, insurance and other items as they become due.

2. The sample Impound Authorization states that impounds are required on all conventional loans with a principal amount that exceeds 80% of the sales price or appraised value, whichever is lower. An impound account may also be required in certain other circumstances.

3. The Impound Authorization contains checkboxes to indicate whether or not impounds are required by the lender in the current transaction.

4. The Impound Authorization also contains checkboxes to indicate whether or not the borrower wishes to set up an impound account. If both boxes are blank, then the borrower should check the box that best represents the borrower's choice.

California Impound Account Statement and Election Form (Page 189)

1. As required by California law, a lender must inform the borrower that the borrower is required to pay property taxes, hazard insurance premiums and other applicable charges related to the property along with regular monthly payments, that an escrow account is required when the principal balance of the loan is less than 90% of the purchase price or appraised value and that the lender can establish an escrow account if the borrower is not otherwise required to have one and the borrower so chooses.

2. As with the Impound Authorization previously discussed, the borrower must elect whether to establish an escrow account or to pay property taxes, insurance and other related property costs directly.

Escrow Waiver Agreement (Tax Only) (Page 190)

1. In the Escrow Waiver Agreement, a lender agrees to waive collection of property tax escrows under certain conditions disclosed in the agreement. The disclosure is provided in loan document packages when the borrower's principal loan amount exceeds 80% of the sales price or appraised value.

2. By signing the Escrow Waiver Agreement, the borrower acknowledges having received a copy of the document but does not elect whether or not to establish an escrow or impound account for the payment of property taxes.

Real Estate Tax Bill Certification (Not Titled) (Page 191)

1. This document, which does not have a title, is signed by the borrower to acknowledge that in the event the lender pays impounds for property taxes and insurance and the property is in a "homeowner area" — an area in which property tax bills are forwarded directly to the homeowner, rather than to the lender — the homeowner will promptly forward any tax bill received to the address included in the document.

2. The borrower agrees to pay any late fees charged to the lender for a late payment when the late payment was the result of the homeowner's failure to promptly forward the tax bill.

Initial Escrow Account Disclosure Statement (Page 192)

1. The Initial Escrow Account Disclosure Statement is required under the Real Estate Settlement Procedures Act (RESPA).

2. The Initial Escrow Account Disclosure Statement presents the activity in an escrow or impound account in the coming year. An escrow or impound account is a special account into which are deposited the funds for taxes and insurance premiums that are paid as part of the monthly mortgage payment. When the taxes and insurance premiums become due, escrow pays these amounts from the account.

3. The disclosure breaks down the monthly payment into the following:

   a. PI (principal and interest)

   b. TI (taxes and insurance), which go into the escrow account

4. In the sample Initial Escrow Account Disclosure Statement, the amounts paid into the escrow account for county taxes and hazard insurance are indicated. The chart summarizes the anticipated activity in the account over the course of the upcoming year. It shows the initial deposit, anticipated amounts deposited into the account each month, total scheduled payments, account "cushion" and running escrow account balance.

Address Certification (Page 193)

1. In the Address Certification, the closing agent certifies the accuracy of the complete street and mailing address for the property that is the subject of the loan.

2. The borrower is not required to sign the Address Certification.

Certificate of Loans to One Borrower (Page 194)

1. In the Certificate of Loans to One Borrower, a borrower certifies and represents to the originating lender the total of all loans applied for or made in connection with the loan transaction.

2. The purpose of this document is for the borrower to disclose under penalty of perjury any other loans to the lender. Any additional loans procured by the borrower could be reason for the lender to refuse to approve the borrower's loan.

Hazard Insurance Authorization and Requirements (Page 195)

1. In the Hazard Insurance Authorization and Requirements, the lender outlines the policies and minimum requirements for a hazard insurance policy that must be provided to cover the subject property.

2. After the Hazard Insurance Authorization and Requirements is signed and returned with the other documents in the loan package, the document will be submitted to the borrower's insurance agent, who will provide the necessary coverage.

Hazard Insurance Disclosure (Page 196)

1. The purpose of the Hazard Insurance Disclosure is for a lender to disclose to the borrower that the amount of required hazard insurance coverage for the property is in excess of the replacement value of the improvements on the property.

2. The Hazard Insurance Disclosure is another state-specific disclosure required under the California Civil Code.

California Finance Lenders Law Statement of Loan (Page 197)

1. In the California Finance Lenders Law Statement of Loan, a lender discloses to the borrower certain particulars of the loan transaction required under the California Finance Code Sections 22337-22338.

2. The disclosures include the lender's license number, the name, address and license of any mortgage broker involved in the

transaction, the basic terms of the loan, whether the loan is a purchase or refinance loan and a notification that advance payments on the loan are permitted.

Appraisal Disclosure and Notice of Right to Copy of Appraisal (Pages 198 and 199)

1. Under Section 202.14 of Regulation B, which implements the federal Fair Lending Act, banks and lenders must provide to a credit applicant, within 30 days of receipt of a written request, a copy of the appraisal report used in connection with an application for credit secured by a lien on a dwelling.

2. In order to receive a copy of the appraisal report, a borrower must provide a written request to the lender no later than 90 days after the lender has provided notice of action taken on the application.

Acknowledgment of Receipt of Appraisal Report (Page 200)

1. In the Acknowledgment of Receipt of Appraisal Report, the borrower indicates that he or she understands that a copy of the appraisal report concerning the value of the property securing the loan will be provided no less than three days prior to the closing of the loan, according to the terms of the Home Valuation Code of Conduct (HVCC).

2. The HVCC is a professional code developed by Freddie Mac, the Federal Housing Finance Agency, and the New York State Attorney General, which aims to enhance the independence and accuracy of the appraisal process and provide added protections to homebuyers, investors and the housing market. Effective May 1, 2009, Freddie Mac will no longer purchase mortgages from sellers who do not adopt the HVCC, and sellers/servicers must represent and warrant that the appraisal report is obtained in a manner consistent with the code.

Automated Valuation Model Notice (Pages 201–202)

1. An automated valuation model is a computer-generated report used by lending institutions to estimate property values. An automated valuation model report is not an appraisal. An appraisal is performed by a trained and certified appraiser, who inspects the property and evaluates its value based upon a comparable market analysis of similar properties in the immediate area that have recently sold.

2. In the Automated Valuation Model Notice, the lender informs the borrower that an automated valuation model result was used in connection with the borrower's application for credit and that the borrower may receive a copy of this model result by mailing a written request to the lender within 90 days of the lender providing notice of the action taken on the loan application.

Consumer Credit Score Disclosure (Pages 203–204)

1. The Consumer Credit Score Disclosure is a form required under both the federal Fair Credit Reporting Act and the California Civil Code.

2. In the Consumer Credit Score Disclosure, the lender cites both laws and requires the borrower to acknowledge receipt of this disclosure.

3. Page 2 of the Consumer Credit Score Disclosure cites the credit scores obtained from the major consumer reporting agencies.

Notice Concerning the Furnishing of Negative Information to Consumer Reporting Agency (Page 205)

1. Under the Fair Credit Reporting Act, a creditor who reports negative information about a credit applicant to a consumer reporting agency must disclose to the applicant that the negative information was furnished. By signing the Notice Concerning the Furnishing of Negative Information to Consumer Reporting Agency, the borrower acknowledges receipt of a copy of that disclosure.

2. In the Notice Concerning the Furnishing of Negative Information to Consumer Reporting Agency, the lender states that late payments, missed payments or other defaults may be reflected in a credit report and subsequently shared with credit bureaus.

Comparison of Sample Mortgage Features: Typical Mortgage Transaction (Pages 206–208)

1. As required under the California Financial Code and California Code of Regulations, a lender must disclose to a borrower sample loan payment and balance scenarios for nontraditional mortgage loans, such as adjustable-rate mortgages and interest-only loans, when a borrower has applied for a nontraditional mortgage loan.

2. Following the Comparison of Sample Mortgage Features: Typical Mortgage Transactions is a 2-page Instructional Guide for Comparison of Sample Mortgage Features: Typical Mortgage Transactions, which explains the information in the Comparison of Sample Mortgage Features: Typical Mortgage Transactions.

Signature Affidavit & AKA Statement and Name Affidavit (Pages 209 and 210)

1. In the Signature Affidavit & AKA Statement, a borrower discloses any other names under which he or she is known and writes signatures for each name.

2. The Signature Affidavit & AKA Statement ensures signature verification and uniformity on all documentation. If a document requires the borrower to sign in a different name, the Signature Affidavit & AKA Statement validates that name and corresponding signature.

3. The Signature Affidavit & AKA Statement routinely is notarized. Both acknowledgment and jurat formats exist. However, variations of the Signature Affidavit & AKA Statement exist which are simply

signed without the need for notarization, despite the fact that its title (Affidavit) suggests that it should be notarized.[6]

4. In the sample document, the name under the Signature Affidavit is the borrower's primary or full legal name. The alternative names listed under the AKA Statement have appeared in credit reports, land title records and other sources. The borrower must sign a sample signature for each name.

5. Like the Signature Affidavit & AKA Statement, the Name Affidavit requires the borrower to certify that he or she is also known by any other names listed in the Name Affidavit. The version of the Name Affidavit appearing in the sample set of documents must be signed and sworn to before a Notary (that is, it must be notarized with a jurat).

6. Unlike the Signature Affidavit & AKA Statement, the Name Affidavit does not require the borrower to sign each name variation with a separate signature.

Compliance Agreement (Page 211)

1. By signing the Compliance Agreement, the borrower agrees to cooperate with the lender or lender's agent in correcting any loan documents containing clerical errors after the loan closes. If an error is discovered in one of the forms after the closing, the borrower agrees to rectify the error.

2. Accurate information in the loan package is crucial to closing the loan or selling it later. The Compliance Agreement is executed in consideration of the lender disbursing funds for the closing of the

[6] Curiously, this and other loan documents with the term "affidavit" in the title routinely call for notarization with an acknowledgment or do not require notarization at all. An affidavit technically is defined as a written statement made under oath or affirmation before an officer authorized to administer oaths. Based on that definition, affidavits traditionally have been notarized with a jurat. However, the Notary Signing Agent should notarize any so-called "affidavit" with an acknowledgment if preprinted acknowledgment wording appears on the document.

loan and to enable the lender to sell, convey or market the loan in the secondary market.

3. The sample Compliance Agreement routinely is notarized. Both acknowledgment and jurat formats exist, as well as versions that do not require notarization.

4. Unlike the Document Correction Agreement appearing in the sample set of documents (page 212), the Compliance Agreement covers the correction of clerical errors in the documents.

5. Unlike the Limited Power of Attorney appearing in the sample set of documents (pages 213–214), the Compliance Agreement means the borrower agrees to comply in making corrections to the documents instead of appointing an agent of the lender to do so.

Document Correction Agreement (Page 212)

1. By signing the Document Correction Agreement, a borrower agrees to execute, acknowledge, initial or deliver any document necessary to replace a lost, misplaced, misstated or inaccurate document to the lender within 10 days after receipt of the lender's written request and agrees to be liable to the lender for any loss or damage that the lender reasonably suffers on account of the failure.

2. Furthermore, by signing the Document Correction Agreement, a borrower agrees to pay any additional amount or fee which was previously disclosed to the borrower but which was not collected for any reason at closing.

Limited Power of Attorney (Pages 213–214)

1. By signing the Limited Power of Attorney, a borrower authorizes the lender or its assignees to act as attorney in fact for the borrower in matters as defined in the document.

2. In the Limited Power of Attorney appearing in the sample set of documents, the borrower specifically authorizes the lender to correct typographical or clerical errors as to the names of the parties, legal description, county or street address of the property and the date of any document.

3. The borrower does not authorize the lender to make changes or corrections to the interest rate stated in the deed of trust or promissory note, the amount of principal indebtedness or the amount of consideration on any conveyance deed that is a part of the transaction.

4. The Limited Power of Attorney must be notarized. The notarial act required on this particular sample document is an acknowledgment.

5. The Limited Power of Attorney differs from the Compliance Agreement (page 211). In the former, the borrower appoints an agent to make the corrections; in the latter, the borrower him- or herself agrees to comply in fixing any typographical or clerical errors.

False Statement/Employment/Occupancy Form Borrowers Certification (Page 215)

1. In the False Statement/Employment/Occupancy Form Borrowers Certification, a lender warns a borrower that it is a federal crime, punishable by fine, imprisonment or both, to knowingly make any false statements in connection with an application for a conventional mortgage. Furthermore, the lender warns the borrower that federal law provides severe penalties for failing to move into the property within 90 days or for committing fraud or making misrepresentations for the purpose of influencing the issuance of any guaranty or insurance or the making of any loan by the Administrator of Veterans Affairs.

2. In particular, by signing the False Statement/Employment/Occupancy Form Borrowers Certification, a borrower makes the following representations:

   a. The borrower is currently employed with the same employer as disclosed on the loan application.

   b. All debts and obligations as stated in the loan application were fully disclosed and there have been no new debts or credit obligations incurred from the date of making application.

   c. No monies have been borrowed nor debt incurred to obtain or cover the closing costs or the down payment for the loan.

   d. The borrower intends either to occupy the property as his or her home or not to occupy the property because it is an investment property.

   e. The condition of the property exists now as it did when the appraisal report was issued.

3. This form requires the borrower to be placed under oath, but no notarial certificate is provided for the Notary Signing Agent to complete, sign and seal. A Notary Signing Agent should check with the closing agent to determine whether or not a loose notarial certificate must be completed, signed, sealed and attached by the Agent.

Occupancy and Financial Status Affidavit (Pages 216–217)

1. In the Occupancy and Financial Status Affidavit, a buyer makes certain declarations related to the buyer's occupancy of the property that is the subject of the mortgage loan and to his or her financial condition. These declarations must be made under

oath before a Notary Public or other officer authorized to take acknowledgments and administer oaths.

2. There are three possible occupancy options in the sample Occupancy and Financial Status Affidavit. The first option is selected as applicable in this particular case. Quite often the form is left blank, and the borrower must choose which of the three options specifically applies. This is important from a notarization standpoint, since many states prohibit notarization of a document that contains a blank space.[7]

3. In the Occupancy and Financial Status Affidavit, the buyer also declares that the buyer's financial condition has not substantially changed since submitting the loan application.

4. The Occupancy and Financial Status Affidavit is used as a condition to obtain a loan, with federal fines and other penalties resulting from the buyer misrepresenting his or her true occupancy intention and financial condition.

5. The Occupancy and Financial Status Affidavit routinely is notarized, but, depending upon the lender, the form may be notarized with a jurat (as it is here) or an acknowledgment. Variations of the Occupancy Affidavit and Financial Status exist that do not call for notarization at all, such as the Occupancy Affidavit which follows below.

Occupancy Affidavit (Page 218)

1. The Occupancy Affidavit is the third form in the sample set of documents in which a borrower makes certifications about his or her occupancy intentions.

[7] Laws in some states and prudent notarial practice dictate that documents must be complete — that is, must contain no blank spaces — before they can be notarized.

2. The Occupancy Affidavit states, "Please mark with an 'X' the applicable property type for which this mortgage is being obtained and sign below to indicate compliance with the Lender's occupancy requirements." If the borrower intends to occupy the property as his or her primary residence, the lender offers a particular loan and interest rate to the borrower. The borrower would not qualify for the loan and interest rate if he or she intended to occupy the property as a second home.

IRS Form W-9 (Request for Taxpayer Identification Number and Certification) (Pages 219–222)

1. Each year, the mortgage company will report to the IRS the interest the borrower paid on the mortgage during the previous tax year.

2. The W-9 verifies the borrower's Social Security number.

IRS Form 4506-T (Request for Copy of Transcript of Tax Return) (Pages 223–224)

1. Loans are periodically and randomly chosen for audit to ensure that a borrower did not commit fraud by providing falsified tax returns or information in obtaining the loan.

   a. The Request for Copy of Transcript of Tax Return is sent to the IRS to request a copy of the borrower's tax return for auditing purposes.

   b. The IRS Form 4506-T is rarely used and is kept in the borrower's file.

2. The borrower should check the accuracy of all the information on the form before signing it.

3. Currently there is a $57.00 fee for transcripts of tax forms for each period requested, but the fee is not paid until the form is used. The

borrower does not pay the fee if the loan file is audited; the fee is paid by the entity requesting the borrower's tax forms.

4. In a husband-wife transaction, there is usually a form for each spouse to sign. The borrower's spouse also must sign the form.

Servicing Disclosure Statement (Page 225)

1. In the Servicing Disclosure Statement, another RESPA form, the lender informs the borrower of the lender's intent to sell the loan in the secondary market.

2. In the sample Servicing Disclosure Statement, the lender has checked the box to indicate that it does not service mortgage loans and that it intends to assign, sell or transfer the servicing of the loan before the first payment is due.

3. The form appearing in the sample document package does not require a borrower's signature.

Notice of Assignment, Sale or Transfer of Servicing Rights (Page 226)

1. In the Notice of Assignment, Sale or Transfer of Servicing Rights, a lender notifies a borrower that the servicing of the borrower's mortgage loan is being assigned, sold or transferred to a loan servicing company.

2. The Notice of Assignment, Sale or Transfer of Servicing Rights contains the name and contact information of the loan servicer and the date that the new loan servicer will begin accepting payments.

3. The Notice of Assignment, Sale or Transfer of Servicing Rights also contains a disclosure required under the RESPA that, during the 60-day period following the effective date of the transfer of loan

servicing, a loan payment received by the previous servicer on or before its normal due date cannot be regarded as late by the new servicer solely because it was sent to the previous servicer.

4. The borrower must sign the form to acknowledge having been informed of the new servicing provider for the loan.

Federal Equal Credit Opportunity Act Notice (Page 227)

1. In the Federal Equal Credit Opportunity Act Notice, the lender advises the borrower that federal law prohibits creditors from discriminating against credit applicants.

2. The Federal Equal Credit Opportunity Act Notice complements the Housing Financial Discrimination Act of 1977 Fair Lending Notice, the California-specific disclosure informing the borrower that discrimination is prohibited under state law, which is described below.

Housing Financial Discrimination Act of 1977 Fair Lending Notice (Page 228)

1. State and federal laws prohibit financial institutions from discriminating in their lending policies, and loan packages often contain one or more antidiscrimination disclosure forms for a borrower to sign.

2. The particular Housing Financial Discrimination Act of 1977 Fair Lending Notice shown contains disclosures from the state of California Housing Financial Discrimination Act, also known as the Holden Act.

HOEPA/HMDA Required Information (Page 229)

1. The HOEPA/HMDA Required Information identifies lender reporting requirements under two federal laws, the Home Owner's Equity Protection Act (HOEPA) and the Home Mortgage

Disclosure Act (HMDA). The HOEPA, enacted in 1994, imposes substantive limitations and additional disclosures on certain types of home mortgage loans with rates or fees above a certain percentage or amount. The HMDA, enacted in 1975, requires financial institutions to maintain and annually disclose data about home purchases, home purchase pre-approvals, home improvement applications and refinance applications involving typical residential and multifamily homes.

2. The servicer for the loan requires the correspondent lender to report certain information about the loan as a condition for funding. A correspondent lender is a mortgage broker that originates and closes the loan in its own company name, funds the loan from its own source of funds and then immediately sells the loan to a sponsoring lender.

Disclosure Concerning the Charging of Per Diem Interest on California Residential Mortgage Loans (Page 230)

1. Under California law, a lender may begin charging interest on a mortgage loan at the Note rate up to one day prior to disbursement of loan proceeds. If loan proceeds are disbursed on a Monday or on the day immediately following a bank holiday, interest may begin to accrue on the business day immediately preceding the day of disbursement, resulting in the borrower having to pay additional interest charges beyond the minimum one-day period allowed under the law.

2. In the Disclosure Concerning the Charging of Per Diem Interest on California Residential Mortgage Loans, a borrower may choose when disbursement of loan proceeds may be made. By marking the first checkbox, the borrower essentially states that he or she does not want to pay more than the minimum one day's interest

charges allowed under the law. By selecting the second checkbox, the borrower agrees to incur additional interest charges for multiple days prior to disbursement.

California Domestic Partnership Addendum to Uniform Residential Loan Application (Page 231)

1. Under California law, persons registered as domestic partners have the same rights, protections, benefits and duties as marriage partners. Thus, as is the case in a marriage, a non-borrowing domestic partner will be presumed to have a community property interest in the real property of the borrowing domestic partner that will secure repayment of the loan, regardless of whether the non-borrowing partner holds, or will hold, legal title to the property.

2. Non-borrowing domestic partners must sign the security instrument (Deed of Trust or Mortgage) that secures repayment of the loan.

3. In the California Domestic Partnership Addendum to Uniform Residential Loan Application, the borrower represents whether or not he or she is involved in a domestic partnership in California or any other jurisdiction and matters related thereto.

Tax Information Sheet (Page 232)

1. In the Tax Information Sheet, the lender informs the closing agent that all tax bills are due within the 30-day period following the closing of the loan.

2. In the sample, the closing agent completes and signs the bottom of the form.

Customer Identification Verification (Page 233)

1. In the Customer Identification Verification, the Notary Signing Agent documents the identifying information from a borrower's ID card to help lenders, title offices and escrow companies comply with

regulations implementing the Uniting and Strengthening America by Providing Appropriate Tools Required to Intercept and Obstruct Terrorism Act (USA PATRIOT Act) of 2001.

2. The PATRIOT Act requires all financial institutions to establish a Customer Identification Program (CIP) for all new account holders. The information supplied in the Customer Identification Verification is used to determine whether the borrower's name appears on a list of known or suspected terrorists who have engaged in terrorist acts against the United States.

3. The Customer Identification Verification must include the signature, date and title of the person completing the form. Notary Signing Agents may enter the title Signing Agent in the relevant space on this form but should not use the title Notary Public.

Request for Change to Insurance Policy and Request for Change to Flood Certification (Pages 234 and 235)

1. The context for the Request for Change to Insurance Policy and the Request for Change to Flood Certification is the Hazard Insurance Authorization and Requirements (page 195) and the General Closing Instructions (page 147). The former lays out the lender's minimum requirements for hazard and flood insurance that the borrower must hold on the property. The latter contains a specific instruction about how the payee/mortgagee clause on the insurance policy must read. The name and address of the originating lender is stated as well as the loan number of the transaction.

2. In the Request for Change to Insurance Policy and the Request for Change to Flood Certification, the originating lender asks the insurer to correct the mortgagee clause with the name and contact information of the new servicer for the loan and to send the corrected endorsement to the new servicer.

Privacy Policy Disclosure (Page 236–238)

1. In keeping with federal requirements under the Gramm-Leach-Bliley Financial Modernization Act (GLBA), lenders must provide customers with a privacy policy disclosure at the time of establishing a customer relationship and not less than annually during the continuation of such relationship.[8]

2. The privacy disclosure must inform customers about the lender's policies and practices with respect to disclosing nonpublic personal information of both current and former customers, both to the lender's affiliates and to nonaffiliated third parties, and the lender's policies and practices with respect to protecting the nonpublic personal information of both current and former customers. The precise information to be included in the privacy policy is set forth in 5 USC § 6803 and any subsequent rules issued to implement the GLBA.

3. Many privacy disclosures appearing in a package of loan documents do not require a signature, but some (including the Privacy Policy included in the sample set of documents) provide the borrower with an option to "opt out": an opportunity for the borrower to tell the lender not to disclose nonpublic personal information to a nonaffiliated third party. If an opt-out option exists, then Agents should bring this to the attention of the borrower at the signing and ask the borrower to complete the form.

[8] 5 USC § 6803.

Southern Escrow Company

1001 Main Street
Los Angeles, CA 90025
(310) 321-9876 Fax (310) 321-9875

Escrow No. ML-09876 Closing Date: February 19, 2010
Reference: 8624 Oaklawn Avenue #13
Canoga Park, CA 91304

BUYER'S FINAL CLOSING STATEMENT

BORROWER: RICHARD WILLIAM ROGERS

	DEBITS	CREDITS
Purchase Price		
Contract Sales Price	**252,500.00**	
Receipts		
Deposit		56,346.0
New Loan		
Principal Loan Amount to Tristar Financial Corp.		202,000.00
Appraisal Fee to Ron Martin Appraisals (POC) $375.00	375.00	
Appraisal Fee to B&K Appraisal (2nd Appraisal)		
Appraisal Review Fee to Autologic	40.00	
HOA Cert to Condo Certs $90.00		
Daily Interest Charges from 2/18/10 to 3/1/10 @ $28.36/Day To Tristar Financial Corp.	311.96	
Hazard Insurance Reserve 3 Months @ $44.83/Month To Tristar Financial Corp.	134.49	
County Property Taxes 2 Months @ $268.75/Month To Tristar Financial Corp.	537.50	
Aggregate Accounting Adjustment to Tristar Financial Corp.		44.83
Sales Commission		
Credit from Selling Agent RE/MAX OLSON & Associates		1,000.00
Prorations	695.00	
Proration of HOA Dues $300/Mo. For 2/19/10 to 3/1/10	120.00	
County Taxes (Paid) 1401.6400/6 Mos. 2/19/10 to 7/1/10	1,027.87	
Escrow Fees		
Escrow Fee	705.00	
Loan Tie-In Fee (Buyer's Discount of $90)	160.00	
Document Preparation and Archive Fee	185.00	
Electronic Documents Download Plus Copy of Docs	100.00	
Messenger Fee	12.00	
Recording Fees		
Recording Deed of Trust	73.00	
Recording Grant Deed	22.00	
Title Charges		
Lender's Coverage to First Title Co.	416.00	
Endorsement 100.13/8.1	50.00	
Sub-Escrow Fee	70.00	
Additional Settlement Fees		
Service Fee (Selling) to RE/MAX OLSON & Associates	300.00	
Service Fee (Selling) to RE/MAX OLSON & Associates	75.00	
Condominium Insurance for 1 Year to Mercury Casualty	592.00	
March HOA Dues to Oak Creek HOA	300.00	
Proceeds or Balance Due		
Borrower Refund	1,284.01	
Balance Due		0.00
Totals:	**$259,390.83**	**$259,390.83**

OMB Approval No. 2502-0265

A. Settlement Statement (HUD-1)

B. Type of Loan

1. ☐ FHA 2. ☐ RHS 3. ☒ Conv. Unins. 4. ☐ VA 5. ☐ Conv. Ins.	6. File Number: ML-09876	7. Loan Number: 200911000	8. Mortgage Insurance Case Number:

C. Note: This form is furnished to give you a statement of actual settlement costs. Amounts paid to and by the settlement agent are shown. Items marked "(p.o.c.)" were paid outside the closing; they are shown here for informational purposes and are not included in the totals.

D. Name & Address of Borrower:	E. Name & Address of Seller:	F. Name & Address of Lender:
RICHARD WILLIAM ROGERS 4098 LARWIN AVENUE LOS ANGELES, CA 90032	WALTER AND GERRI SINGLETARY 9087 VIA PRINCESSA SANTA CLARITA, CA 91351	TRISTAR FINANCIAL CORP. 1000 MAIN STREET LOS ANGELES, CA 90025
G. Property Location: 8624 OAKLAWN AVENUE, #13 CANOGA PARK, CA 91304	H. Settlement Agent: SOUTHERN ESCROW Place of Settlement: 1001 MAIN STREET, LOS ANGELES, CA	I. Settlement Date: 02/19/2010

J. Summary of Borrower's Transaction

100. Gross Amount Due from Borrower	
101. Contract sales price	$252,500.00
102. Personal property	
103. Settlement charges to borrower (line 1400)	$4,414.12
104.	
105.	
Adjustment for items paid by seller in advance	
106. City/town taxes (Paid) to	
107. County taxes (Paid) 2/19/10 to 7/01/10	$1,027.87
108. Assessments (Paid) to	
109. Proration of HOA Dues 2/19/10 to 3/01/10	$120.00
110.	
111.	
112.	
120. Gross Amount Due from Borrower	$258,061.99
200. Amount Paid by or in Behalf of Borrower	
201. Deposit or earnest money	$56,346.00
202. Principal amount of new loan(s)	$202,000.00
203. Existing loan(s) taken subject to	
204. Credit from Selling Agent	$1,000.00
205.	
206.	
207.	
208.	
209.	
Adjustments for items unpaid by seller	
210. City/town taxes to	
211. County taxes to	
212. Assessments to	
213.	
214.	
215.	
216.	
217.	
218.	
219.	
220. Total Paid by/for Borrower	$259346.00
300. Cash at Settlement from/to Borrower	
301. Gross amount due from borrower (line 120)	$258,061.99
302. Less amounts paid by/for borrower (line 220)	($259,346.00)
303. Cash ☐ **From** ☒ **To Borrower**	$1,284.01

K. Summary of Seller's Transaction

400. Gross Amount Due to Seller	
401. Contract sales price	
402. Personal property	
403.	
404.	
405.	
Adjustment for items paid by seller in advance	
406. City/town taxes to	
407. County taxes to	
408. Assessments to	
409.	
410.	
411.	
412.	
420. Gross Amount Due to Seller	$0.00
500. Reductions In Amount Due to seller	
501. Excess deposit (see instructions)	
502. Settlement charges to seller (line 1400)	$0.00
503. Existing loan(s) taken subject to	
504. Payoff of first mortgage loan	
505. Payoff of second mortgage loan	
506.	
507.	
508.	
509.	
Adjustments for items unpaid by seller	
510. City/town taxes to	
511. County taxes to	
512. Assessments to	
513.	
514.	
515.	
516.	
517.	
518.	
519.	
520. Total Reduction Amount Due Seller	$0.00
600. Cash at Settlement to/from Seller	
601. Gross amount due to seller (line 420)	
602. Less reductions in amounts due seller (line 520)	( )
603. Cash ☐ **To** ☒ **From Seller**	$0.00

The Public Reporting Burden for this collection of information is estimated at 35 minutes per response for collecting, reviewing, and reporting the data. This agency may not collect this information, and you are not required to complete this form, unless it displays a currently valid OMB control number. No confidentiality is assured; this disclosure is mandatory. This is designed to provide the parties to a RESPA covered transaction with information during the settlement process.

Previous edition are obsolete | Page 1 of 3 | HUD-1

L. Settlement Charges

700. Total Real Estate Broker Fees			Paid From Borrower's Funds at Settlement	Paid From Seller's Funds at Settlement
Division of commission (line 700) as follows :				
701. $ to				
702. $ to				
703. Commission paid at settlement				
704. Service Fee (Selling) to RE/MAX OLSON & ASSOCIATES			$375.00	
800. Items Payable in Connection with Loan				
801. Our origination charge to Tristar Financial Corp.	$ 40.00	(from GFE #1)		
802. Your credit or charge (points) for the specific interest rate chosen	$	(from GFE #2)		
803. Your adjusted origination charges		(from GFE #A)	$40.00	
804. Appraisal fee to B&K Appraisal		(from GFE #3)	$375.00	
805. Credit report to		(from GFE #3)		
806. Tax service to		(from GFE #3)		
807. Flood certification to		(from GFE #3)		
808.				
809.				
810.				
811.				
900. Items Required by Lender to be Paid in Advance				
901. Daily interest charges from 2/18/10 to 3/1/10 @ $ 28.36 /day		(from GFE #10)	$311.96	
902. Mortgage insurance premium for months to		(from GFE #3)		
903. Homeowner's insurance for years to		(from GFE #11)		
904.				
1000. Reserves Deposited with Lender				
1001. Initial deposit for your escrow account		(from GFE #9)	$627.16	
1002. Homeowner's insurance Reserve 3 months @ $ 44.83 per month	$ 134.49			
1003. Mortgage insurance months @ $ per month	$			
1004. Property Taxes 2 months @ $ 268.75 per month	$ 537.50			
1005. months @ $ per month	$			
1006. months @ $ per month	$			
1007. Aggregate Adjustment	-$ -44.83			
1100. Title Charges				
1101. Title services and lender's title insurance		(from GFE #4)	$1,698.00	
1102. Settlement or closing fee Southern Escrow	$ 705.00			
1103. Owner's title insurance		(from GFE #5)		
1104. Lender's title insurance First Title Co.	$ 466.00			
1105. Lender's title policy limit $ 202,000.00				
1106. Owner's title policy limit $ 252,500.00				
1107. Agent's portion of the total title insurance premium to First Title Co.	$ 1,255.70			
1108. Underwriter's portion of the total title insurance premium to Old Republic Title Co.	$ 137.30			
1109. Sub-Escrow Fee to First Title Co.			$70.00	
1110.				
1111.				
1200. Government Recording and Transfer Charges				
1201. Government recording charges		(from GFE #7)	$95.00	
1202. Deed $ 22.00 Mortgage $ 73.00 Release $				
1203. Transfer taxes		(from GFE #8)		
1204. City/County tax/stamps Deed $ Mortgage $				
1205. State tax/stamps Deed $ Mortgage $				
1206.				
1300. Additional Settlement Charges				
1301. Required services that you can shop for		(from GFE #6)		
1302. HOA Transfer Fee to POC	$ 175.00			
1303. HOA Dues Feb. (Seller) to OAK CREEK HOA	$ 300.00			
1304. March HOA dues to OAK CREEK			$300.00	
1305. Condominium Insurance 1 Year to Mercury Casualty Company			$592.00	
1400. Total Settlement Charges (enter on lines 103, Section J and 502, Section K)			$4,414.12	

Previous edition are obsolete Page 2 of 3 HUD-1

Comparison of Good Faith Estimate (GFE) and HUD-1 Charrges		Good Faith Estimate	HUD-1
Charges That Cannot Increase	**HUD-1 Line Number**		
Our origination charge	# 801	$0.00	$40.00
Your credit or charge (points) for the specific interest rate chosen	# 802	$0.00	
Your adjusted origination charges	# 803	$0.00	$40.00
Transfer taxes	# 1203	$0.00	

Charges That In Total Cannot Increase More Than 10%		Good Faith Estimate	HUD-1
Government recording charges	# 1201	$115.00	$95.00
	#		
	#		
	#		
	#		
	#		
	#		
	#		
	Total		
	Increase between GFE and HUD-1 Charges	$ or	%

Charges That Can Change		Good Faith Estimate	HUD-1
Initial deposit for your escrow account	# 1001	$0.00	$627.16
Daily interest charges $ 28.36 /day	# 901	$0.00	$311.96
Homeowner's insurance	# 903		
	#		
	#		
	#		

Loan Terms

Your initial loan amount is	$ 202,000.00
Your loan term is	30 years
Your initial interest rate is	5.125 %
Your initial monthly amount owed for principal, interest, and any mortgage insurance is	$ 1,099.86 includes ☒ Principal ☒ Interest ☐ Mortgage Insurance
Can your interest rate rise?	☒ No ☐ Yes, it can rise to a maximum of %. The first change will be on and can change again every after . Every change date, your interest rate can increase or decrease by %. Over the life of the loan, your interest rate is guaranteed to never be **lower** than % or **higher** than %.
Even if you make payments on time, can your loan balance rise?	☒ No ☐ Yes, it can rise to a maximum of $
Even if you make payments on time, can your monthly amount owed for principal, interest, and mortgage insurance rise?	☒ No ☐ Yes, the first increase can be on and the monthly amount owed can rise to $. The maximum it can ever rise to is $.
Does your loan have a prepayment penalty?	☒ No ☐ Yes, your maximum prepayment penalty is $
Does your loan have a balloon payment?	☒ No ☐ Yes, you have a balloon payment of $ due in years on .
Total monthly amount owed including escrow account payments	☐ You do not have a monthly escrow payment for items, such as property taxes and homeowner's insurance. You must pay these items directly yourself. ☒ You have an additional monthly escrow payment of $ 1,413.44 that results in a total initial monthly amount owed of $. This includes principal, interest, any mortagage insurance and any items checked below: ☒ Property taxes ☒ Homeowner's insurance ☐ Flood insurance ☐ ☐ ☐

Note: If you have any questions about the Settlement Charges and Loan Terms listed on this form, please contact your lender.

Previous edition are obsolete Page 3 of 3 HUD-1

FROM: TRISTAR FINANCIAL CORP.
1000 MAIN STREET
LOS ANGELES, CALIFORNIA 90025
Phone: (310)321-4567
Fax: (310)321-4568

TO: SOUTHERN ESCROW
1001 MAIN STREET
LOS ANGELES, CALIFORNIA 90024
Phone: (310)321-9876

ATTN: MARY LEE

RE: Borrower(s): RICHARD WILLIAM ROGERS

Property Address: 8624 OAKLAWN AVENUE, NO. 13 (CANOGA PARK AREA), LOS ANGELES, CALIFORNIA 91304

Document Date: FEBRUARY 12, 2010
Closing Date: FEBRUARY 17, 2010
Disbursement: FEBRUARY 17, 2010
Case No.:
Loan No.: 200911000
App. No.:
Order No.: 2a-1000001
Escrow No.: ML-09876

GENERAL CLOSING INSTRUCTIONS

Do not close or fund this loan unless **ALL** conditions in these closing instructions and any supplemental closing instructions have been satisfied. The total consideration in this transaction except for our loan proceeds and approved secondary financing must pass to you in the form of cash. Do not close or fund this loan if you have knowledge of a concurrent or subsequent transaction which would transfer the subject property.

You must follow these instructions exactly. These closing instructions can only be modified with our advance written approval. You shall be deemed to have accepted and to be bound by these closing instructions if you fail to notify us in writing to the contrary within 48 hours of your receipt hereof or if you disburse any funds to or for the account of the Borrower(s).

All documents with the exception of those to be recorded (Security Instrument, Riders, Corporation Assignment(s), Grant Deed, Quit Claim, Power of Attorney, etc.) must be returned to our office within 72 HOURS of the signing. Please return certified copies of those documents that are to be recorded. Failure to comply with these instructions may delay funding.

EXECUTION OF DOCUMENTS:

1. Each Borrower must sign all documents exactly as his or her name appears on the blank line provided for his or her signature. All signatures must be witnessed if required or customary. All signature acknowledgements must be executed by a person authorized to take acknowledgements in the state of closing.
2. Any correction to loan documents must be approved in writing by us in advance. **No white-out permitted.** Approved deletion should be made by marking a single line through the language being deleted. All additions and deletions must be initialed by all borrowers.
3. All Powers of Attorney must be provided to and approved by us in advance. If approved, the Power of Attorney must be recorded in the same county(ies) in which the Security Instrument is recorded, a certified copy provided to us.

RESCISSION:

1. If the transaction is subject to rescission, provide **each** Borrower and **each** person having any ownership interest in the security property with **two (2) copies** of the completed Notice of Right to Cancel. The Notice of Right to Cancel must be properly completed (including all dates) and each borrower and person given two notices must execute an acknowledgement of receipt. Your failure to properly complete and provide the Notices of Right to Cancel to each person entitled to receive them will delay this closing.
2. No Borrower or other person having an ownership interest in the Security Property may modify or waive his or her right to rescind without our prior written consent.
3. If any Borrower or other person having an ownership interest in the security property indicates that he or she wishes to cancel this transaction, contact us immediately for further instructions.

SURVEYS:

1. A valid survey dated within 90 days of closing is required in areas where surveys are customary.
2. The survey must contain all relevant and customary information and certifications and the legal description, lot size and street must agree with the appraisal and closing documents.

HAZARD INSURANCE:

1. The Borrower(s) must provide satisfactory evidence of hazard insurance coverage and flood insurance coverage if the Property is located in a special flood hazard area.
2. Dwelling coverage must be equal to the lesser of the loan amount or the full replacement value of the property improvements, and must extend for either a term of at least one (1) year after the closing date for purchase transactions or six (6) months after the closing date for refinance transactions.
3. Loss payee/mortgagee clause to read: TRISTAR FINANCIAL CORP.,
ITS SUCCESSORS AND/OR ASSIGNS
1000 MAIN STREET
LOS ANGELES, CALIFORNIA 90025
Loan Number: 200911000

ACKNOWLEDGED AND AGREED:

Settlement Agent
MARY LEE

FROM: TRISTAR FINANCIAL CORP.
1000 MAIN STREET
LOS ANGELES, CALIFORNIA 90025
Phone:(310)321-4567
FAX:(310)321-4568

TO: SOUTHERN ESCROW
1001 MAIN STREET
LOS ANGELES, CALIFORNIA 90025
Phone: (310)321-9876
ATTN: MARY LEE

RE: Borrower(s): RICHARD WILLIAM ROGERS

Property Address: 8624 OAKLAWN AVENUE,
NO. 13 (CANOGA PARK AREA)
LOS ANGELES, CALIFORNIA 91304

Document Date: FEBRUARY 12, 2010
Closing Date: FEBRUARY 17, 2010
Disbursement: FEBRUARY 17, 2010
Case No.:
Loan No.: 200911000
App. No.:
Order No.: 2a-1000001
Escrow No.: ML-09876

SPECIFIC CLOSING INSTRUCTIONS

LOAN DOCUMENTS:

We enclose the following documents necessary to complete the above referenced loan transaction:

(X) Note	(X) Allonge to Note	(X) Worksheets
(X) Deed of Trust	(X) Truth-in-Lending	(X) Loan Application
(X) Condominium Rider	(X) Payment Letter	(X) Patriot Act
(X) Transfer of Servicing	(X) Initial Escrow Acct. Disc. Stmt.	(X) Borrowers Cert.
(X) Itemization of amt fin.		(X) 4506T
(X) Impound Auth.	(X) Fair Lending Notice	

Deliver one (1) copy of all loan documents to the Borrower(s); deliver one (1) copy of the Federal Truth-In-Lending Disclosure Statement to **each** Borrower.

LOAN TERMS:

Loan Amount: 202,000.00
Initial Advance:
Sales Price: 252,500.00
Term (Months): 360
Interest Rate: 5.125
Initial Payment: 1,099.86
First Payment Date: APRIL 1, 2010
Last Payment Date: MARCH 1, 2040

ARM Loan: ( ) Yes (X) No
Index:
Margin:
Periodic Rate Cap:
Lifetime Rate Cap:
Lifetime Rate Floor:
Interest Change Date:
Payment Change Date:
Loan Purpose: PURCHASE

PAYOFF REQUIREMENTS:

It is a condition to the funding of this loan that the following payoffs be made through this closing. Indicate payoffs on the HUD-1 Settlement Statement or provide other satisfactory evidence of payoff:

CONDITIONS TO BE SATISFIED PRIOR TO DISBURSEMENT OF LOAN PROCEEDS:

REAL ESTATE COMMISSIONS FOR SUBJECT PROPERTY MAY NOT EXCEED 8%
UNDERWRITER TO REVIEW HUD AND CASH TO CLOSE
ADDED 2-11-10, VERIFY TRANSFER OF FUNDS FROM EQUIVEST TO WELLS FARGO..
SEE ATTACHED ADDENDUM TO CLOSING INSTRUCTIONS

WE ARE TO BE AT NO EXPENSE IN THIS TRANSACTION

TITLE INSURANCE REQUIREMENTS:

You are authorized to use funds for the account of the Borrowers and to record all instruments when you comply with the following:

1. THIS LOAN MUST RECORD IN 1ST LIEN POSITION ON OR PRIOR TO THE DISBURSEMENT DATE NOTED ABOVE. PROVIDE DUPLICATE ORIGINALS OF THE ALTA TITLE POLICY.
2. Vesting to read: RICHARD WILLIAM ROGERS, AN UNMARRIED MAN
3. Title Policy must contain the following endorsements (or their equivalents): 8.1, 100, 116, 115.1, 100.13, 116.2
4. ALTA Title Policy must be free from liens, encumbrances, easements, encroachments and other title matters except (i) the lien of our loan in the amount of our loan on the property described herein showing the Instrument or Document Number and the date of recording of the Security Instrument; (ii) general, specific, state, county, city, school or other taxes and assessments not yet due or payable: (PAY TAXES CURRENT FOR 2009/2010) ; (iii) other items as permitted by us; and (iv) the following items as shown on the preliminary title report, commitment, binder or equivalent dated JANUARY 15, 2010: 1-9

SECONDARY FINANCING:

Secondary financing in the amount of $ NONE has been approved.

Page 1 of 2

ESTIMATE OF FEES AND COSTS:

ITEM	AMOUNT	POC	PAID BY
LOAN ORIGINATION FEE to: TRISTAR FINANCIAL CO	$2,020.00		Borrower
LOAN DISCOUNT POINTS to: TRISTAR FINANCIAL CO	$0.00		Borrower
RECORDING MORTGAGE FEE to: FIRST TITLE CO	$115.00		Borrower
TIE IN FEE to: SOUTHERN ESCROW	$250.00		Borrower
APPRAISAL FEE to: B & K APPRAISAL SERVICES, I	$375.00	$375.00	Borrower
APPRAISAL FEE to: B & K APPRAISAL SERVICES, I	$375.00		Borrower
ESCROW FEE to: SOUTHERN ESCROW	$705.00		Borrower
LENDER'S TITLE INSURANCE FEE to: FIRST TITLE	$416.00		Borrower
TITLE ENDORSEMENT FEE to: FIRST TITLE CO	$50.00		Borrower
SUB ESCROW FEE to: FIRST TITLE COMPANY	$70.00		Borrower
APPRAISAL REVIEW FEE to: B & K APPRAISAL SERV	$40.00		Borrower
HOA FEE to: FIRST TITLE COMPANY	$90.00	$90.00	Borrower
PROCESSING FEE to: TRISTAR FINANCIAL CORP.	$495.00		Borrower
UNDERWRITING FEE to: TRISTAR FINANCIAL CORP.	$795.00		Borrower
OWNER'S TITLE INSURANCE FEE to: FIRST TITLE	$587.21		Other
TRANSFER TAX to: FIRST TITLE COMPANY	$1,414.00		Other
ELECTRONIC DELIVERY to: SOUTHERN ESCROW	$100.00		Borrower
COURIER FEE to: SOUTHERN ESCROW	$60.00		Borrower
INSURANCE CERT to: FIRST TITLE COMPANY	$125.00		Borrower
WIRE FEE to: FIRST TITLE COMPANY	$45.00		Borrower
COUNTY PROPERTY TAX to: FIRST TITLE COMPANY	$1,082.38		Borrower
HOA DUES to: FIRST TITLE COMPANY	$190.00		Borrower
HO6 to: FIRST TITLE COMPANY	$538.00		Borrower

Subtotal of Estimated Fees and Costs: $ 9,657.59

PER DIEM INTEREST: SEE ATTACHED ADDENDUM

From: 02/17/10 (Anticipated Closing Date) To: 03/01/10

12 days at $ 28.36 per day Subtotal of Per Diem Interest: $ 340.32

IMPOUNDS/ESCROWS:

Impound/escrow checks should be made payable to and sent to us together with the original final HUD-1 Settlement Statement.

HAZARD INSURANCE	3	month(s) at $ 44.83	per month = $	134.49
COUNTY TAX	2	month(s) at $ 268.75	per month = $	537.50
		month(s) at $	per month = $	
		month(s) at $	per month = $	
		month(s) at $	per month = $	
		month(s) at $	per month = $	

Aggregate Escrow Adjustment: $ -44.83

Impound Subtotal: $ 627.16
Mortgage Ins. Premium: $
TOTAL OF FEES AND COSTS: $ 10,625.07

HUD-1 SETTLEMENT STATEMENT:

The **final** HUD-1 Settlement Statement must be completed at settlement and must accurately reflect all receipts and disbursements indicated in these closing instructions and any amended closing instructions subsequent hereto. If any changes to fees occur documents may need to be re-drawn and re-signed. Fax a certified copy of the final HUD-1 Settlement Statement to TRISTAR FINANCIAL CORP. @ (310)321-4567
Attention: Quality Assurance. Send the original final HUD-1 Settlement Statement to us at the following address within 24 hours of settlement: TRISTAR FINANCIAL CORP., 1000 MAIN STREET, LOS ANGELES, CALIFORNIA 90025, Phone:(310)321-4567 FAX:(310)321-4568

ADDITIONAL INFORMATION: BORROWER MUST SIGN AND DATE THESE CLOSING INSTRUCTIONS.

If for any reason this loan does not close within 48 hours of your receipt of funds, immediately return all documents to Lender and wire all funds only to: TRISTAR FINANCIAL CORP.
1000 MAIN STREET, LOS ANGELES, CALIFORNIA 90025

If you have any questions regarding any of these instructions, please contact TRISTAR FINANCIAL CORP. at (310)321-4567 .

BORROWER ACKNOWLEDGMENT: I/We have read and acknowledged receipt of these Closing Instructions.

Borrower RICHARD WILLIAM ROGERS Date   Borrower Date

Borrower Date   Borrower Date

Borrower Date   Borrower Date

ACKNOWLEDGED AND AGREED:

Settlement Agent Date
MARY LEE

Page 2 of 2

FROM: TRISTAR FINANCIAL CORP.
1000 MAIN STREET
LOS ANGELES, CALIFORNIA 90025
Phone:(310)321-4567
FAX:(310)321-4568

TO: SOUTHERN ESCROW
1001 MAIN STREET
LOS ANGELES, CALIFORNIA 90025
Phone: (310)321-9876
Fax: (310)321-9875
ATTN: MARY LEE

RE: Borrower(s): RICHARD WILLIAM ROGERS

Property Address: 8624 OAKLAWN AVENUE, NO. 13 (CANOGA PARK AREA), LOS ANGELES, CALIFORNIA 91304

Document Date: FEBRUARY 12, 2010
Closing Date: FEBRUARY 17, 2010
Disbursement Date: FEBRUARY 17, 2010
Case No.:
Loan No.: 200911000
App. No.:
Order No.: 2a-1000000
Escrow No.: ML-09876

ADDENDUM TO CLOSING INSTRUCTIONS

(Additional conditions to be satisfied prior to disbursement of loan proceeds)

ADDED 2-11-10, VERIFY ALL FUNDS USED TO CLOSE ESCROW, INCLUDING ESCROW DEPOSIT $7200.00

EVIDENCE OF RECEIPT OF THE GIFT FUNDS INTO ESCROW (COPY OF CHECK AND ESCROW DEPOSIT RECEIPT) OR BORROWER'S BANK ACCOUNT (COPY OF CHECK AND DEPOSIT RECEIPT) UTR

VERBAL VOE COMPLETED BY LENDER NO SOONER THAN 2 DAYS PRIOR TO FUNDING

TELEPHONE CONFIRMATION OF EMPLOYMENT INCLUDING DATE OF EMPLOYMENT

SELLER CREDIT NOT TO EXCEED $5800

APPRAISER TO ANSWER QUESTION RE: ENVIROMENTAL CONDITIONS, ON PAGE 1, SHOULD BE YES OR NO

CERTIFICATE OF MASTER HOA INSURANCE AND H06 COVERAGE

MASTER IN THE FILE, NEED H06 *

FINAL TYPED, SIGNED, AND DATED LOAN APPLICATION FNMA 1003

NAME AFFIDAVIT

CLOSING PROTECTION LETTER

ACKNOWLEDGED AND AGREED:

Settlement Agent   Date
MARY LEE

FROM: TRISTAR FINANCIAL CORP. 1000 MAIN STREET LOS ANGELES, CALIFORNIA 90025 Phone:(310)321-4567 FAX:(310)321-4568	Document Date: FEBRUARY 12, 2010
TO: SOUTHERN ESCROW 1001 MAIN STREET LOS ANGELES, CALIFORNIA 90025 Phone:(310)321-9876 Fax:(310)321-9875	Closing Date: FEBRUARY 17, 2010 Disbursement Date: FEBRUARY 17, 2010 Case No.:
ATTN: MARY LEE	Loan No.: 200911000 App. No.:
RE: Borrower(s): RICHARD WILLIAM ROGERS	Order No.: 2a-100001
Property Address: 8624 OAKLAWN AVENUE, NO. 13 (CANOGA PARK AREA) LOS ANGELES, CALIFORNIA 91304	Escrow No.: LM-09876

ADDENDUM TO CLOSING INSTRUCTIONS

(Additional costs and fees)

ESTIMATE OF FEES AND COSTS

ITEM	AMOUNT	POC	PAID BY
DOCUMENT PREPARATION to: FIRST TITLE CO.	185.00		Borrower

ACKNOWLEDGED AND AGREED:

Settlement Agent   Date
MARY LEE

ADDENDUM TO CLOSING INSTRUCTIONS

OMB Approval No. 2502-0265

Good Faith Estimate (GFE)

Name of Originator Tristar Financial Corp	Borrower Richard William Rogers
Originator Address 1000 Main Street Los Angeles, CA 90025	Property Address 8624 Oaklawn Avenue, 13 Los Angeles (Canoga Park area), CA 91304
Originator Phone Number (310) 321-4567	
Originator Email mortgagebroker@tristarfin.com	Date of GFE 1/20/2010

Purpose

This GFE gives you an estimate of your settlement charges and loan terms if you are approved for this loan. For more information, see HUD's *Special Information Booklet* on settlement charges, your *Truth-in-Lending Disclosures*, and other consumer information at www.hud.gov/respa. If you decide you would like to proceed with this loan, contact us.

Shopping for your loan

Only you can shop for the best loan for you. Compare this GFE with other loan offers, so you can find the best loan. Use the shopping chart on page 3 to compare all the offers you receive.

Important dates

1. The interest rate for this GFE is available through 1/20/2010 1:23 pm. After this time, the interest rate, some of your loan Origination Charges, and the monthly payment shown below can change until you lock your interest rate.
2. This estimate for all other settlement charges is available through 2/1/2010.
3. After you lock your interest rate, you must go to settlement within ☐ days (your rate lock period) to receive the locked interest rate.
4. You must lock the interest rate at least ☐ days before settlement.

Summary of your loan

Your initial loan amount is	$ 202,000.00
Your loan term is	30 years
Your initial interest rate is	5.125 %
Your initial monthly amount owed for principal, interest, and any mortgage insurance is	$ 1, 099.86 per month
Can your interest rate rise?	☒ No ☐ Yes, it can rise to a maximum of %. The first change will be in .
Even if you make payments on time, can your loan balance rise?	☒ No ☐ Yes, it can rise to a maximum of $
Even if you make payments on time, can your monthly amount owed for principal, interest, and any mortgage insurance rise?	☒ No ☐ Yes, the first increase can be in and the monthly amount owed can rise to $. The maximum it can ever rise to is $.
Does your loan have a prepayment penalty?	☒ No ☐ Yes, your maximum prepayment penalty is $.
Does your loan have a balloon payment?	☒ No ☐ Yes, you have a balloon payment of $ due in years.

Escrow account information

Some lenders require an escrow account to hold funds for paying property taxes or other property-related charges in addition to your monthly amount owed of $ 1,099.86.
Do we require you to have an escrow account for your loan?
☐ No, you do not have an escrow account. You must pay these charges directly when due.
☒ Yes, you have an escrow account. It may or may not cover all of these charges. Ask us.

Summary of your settlement charges

A	Your Adjusted Origination Charges *(See page 2.)*	$ 3,310.00
B	Your Charges for All Other Settlement Services *(See page 2.)*	$ 7,086.33
A + B	Total Estimated Settlement Charges	$ 10,396.33

Good Faith Estimate (HUD-GFE) 1

Understanding your estimated settlement charges

Your Adjusted Origination Charges	
1. **Our origination charge** This charge is for getting this loan for you.	$3,310.00
2. **Your credit or charge (points) for the specific interest rate chosen** ☐ The credit or charge for the interest rate of [ ] % is included in "Our origination charge." (See item 1 above.) ☐ You receive a credit of $[ ] for this interest rate of [ ] %. This credit **reduces** your settlement charges. ☐ You pay a charge of $[ ] for this interest rate of [ ] %. This charge (points) **increases** your total settlement charges. The tradeoff table on page 3 shows that you can change your total settlement charges by choosing a different interest rate for this loan.	$0.00
A Your Adjusted Origination Charges	$ 3,310.00

Some of these charges can change at settlement. See the top of page 3 for more information.

Your Charges for All Other Settlement Services	
3. **Required services that we select** These charges are for services we require to complete your settlement. We will choose the providers of these services. *Service* — *Charge* Re-Appraisal Fee — $375.00 Appraisal and Appraisal Review Fee — $415.00 HOA Cert — $90.00	$880.00
4. **Title services and lender's title insurance** This charge includes the services of a title or settlement agent, for example, and title insurance to protect the lender, if required.	$2,475.00
5. **Owner's title insurance** You may purchase an owner's title insurance policy to protect your interest in the property.	$587.21
6. **Required services that you can shop for** These charges are for other services that are required to complete your settlement. We can identify providers of these services or you can shop for them yourself. Our estimates for providing these services are below. *Service* — *Charge* Association Transfer Fee — $75.00	$75.00
7. **Government recording charges** These charges are for state and local fees to record your loan and title documents.	$115.00
8. **Transfer taxes** These charges are for state and local fees on mortgages and home sales.	$1,414.00
9. **Initial deposit for your escrow account** This charge is held in an escrow account to pay future recurring charges on your property and includes ☒ all property taxes, ☐ all insurance, and ☒ other [HO6 Insurance].	$636.16
10. **Daily interest charges** This charge is for the daily interest on your loan from the day of your settlement until the first day of the next month or the first day of your normal mortgage payment cycle. This amount is $[28.36] per day for [11] days (if your settlement is [2/12/2010]).	$311.96
11. **Homeowner's insurance** This charge is for the insurance you must buy for the property to protect from a loss, such as fire. *Policy* — *Charge* HO6 Insurance — $592.00	$592.00
B Your Charges for All Other Settlement Services	$ 7,086.33
A + B Total Estimated Settlement Charges	$ 10,396.33

Good Faith Estimate (HUD-GFE) 2

Instructions

Understanding which charges can change at settlement

This GFE estimates your settlement charges. At your settlement, you will receive a HUD-1, a form that lists your actual costs. Compare the charges on the HUD-1 with the charges on this GFE. Charges can change if you select your own provider and do not use the companies we identify. (See below for details.)

These charges **cannot increase** at settlement:	The total of these charges **can increase up to 10%** at settlement:	These charges **can change** at settlement:
▪ Our origination charge ▪ Your credit or charge (points) for the specific interest rate chosen *(after you lock in your interest rate)* ▪ Your adjusted origination charges *(after you lock in your interest rate)* ▪ Transfer taxes	▪ Required services that we select ▪ Title services and lender's title insurance *(if we select them or you use companies we identify)* ▪ Owner's title insurance *(if you use companies we identify)* ▪ Required services that you can shop for *(if you use companies we identify)* ▪ Government recording charges	▪ Required services that you can shop for *(if you do not use companies we identify)* ▪ Title services and lender's title insurance *(if you do not use companies we identify)* ▪ Owner's title insurance *(if you do not use companies we identify)* ▪ Initial deposit for your escrow account ▪ Daily interest charges ▪ Homeowner's insurance

Using the tradeoff table

In this GFE, we offered you this loan with a particular interest rate and estimated settlement charges. However:

- If you want to choose this same loan with **lower settlement charges,** then you will have a **higher interest rate.**
- If you want to choose this same loan with a **lower interest rate,** then you will have **higher settlement charges.**

If you would like to choose an available option, you must ask us for a new GFE.

Loan originators have the option to complete this table. Please ask for additional information if the table is not completed.

	The loan in this GFE	The same loan with lower settlement charges	The same loan with a lower interest rate
Your initial loan amount	$ 202,000.00	$ 202,000.00	$ 202,000.00
Your initial interest rate[1]	5.125 %	%	%
Your initial monthly amount owed	$ 1,099.86	$	$
Change in the monthly amount owed from this GFE	No change	You will pay $ **more** every month	You will pay $ **less** every month
Change in the amount you will pay at settlement with this interest rate	No change	Your settlement charges will be **reduced** by $	Your settlement charges will **increase** by $
How much your total estimated settlement charges will be	$ 10,396.33	$	$

[1] *For an adjustable rate loan, the comparisons above are for the initial interest rate before adjustments are made.*

Using the shopping chart

Use this chart to compare GFEs from different loan originators. Fill in the information by using a different column for each GFE you receive. By comparing loan offers, you can shop for the best loan.

	This loan	Loan 2	Loan 3	Loan 4
Loan originator name				
Initial loan amount	$202,000.00			
Loan term	30 years			
Initial interest rate	5.125%			
Initial monthly amount owed	$1,099.86			
Rate lock period				
Can interest rate rise?	No			
Can loan balance rise?	No			
Can monthly amount owed rise?	No			
Prepayment penalty?	No			
Balloon payment?	No			
Total Estimated Settlement Charges	$10,396.33			

If your loan is sold in the future

Some lenders may sell your loan after settlement. Any fees lenders receive in the future cannot change the loan you receive or the charges you paid at settlement.

Good Faith Estimate (HUD-GFE) 3

GOOD FAITH ESTIMATE PROVIDERS OF SERVICES

Loan Number: 200911000
Borrower Name(s): Richard William Rogers

SERVICES FOR WHICH YOU MAY SHOP
Listed below are service providers from which you may choose if you do not have one of your own. The estimates on the Good Faith Estimate are based on the charges we typically incur for these services.

SERVICE		PROVIDER 1	PROVIDER 2
Escrow Services	Company:	West Side Escrow	West L.A. Escrow
	Address:	2000 Oak Street Los Angeles, CA 90025	3000 Maple Street Los Angeles, CA 90025
	Phone:	310-987-5432	310-765-0967
Title Services	Company:	Elite Title Co.	Integrity Title Co.
	Address:	4000 Pine Street	5000 Fir Street
	Phone:	Los Angeles, CA 90025	Los Angeles, CA 90025
Pest Control Services	Company:	Best Pest Co.	West L.A. Pest Control
	Address:	6000 Cedar St.	7000 Birch Street
	Phone	Los Angeles, CA 90025	Los Angeles, CA 90025
	Company:		
	Address:		
	Phone:		
	Company:		
	Address:		
	Phone:		
	Company:		
	Address:		
	Phone:		
	Company:		
	Address:		
	Phone:		
	Company:		
	Address:		
	Phone:		

I/We hereby acknowledge receipt of this Good Faith Estimate Providers of Services list.

Borrower: RICHARD WILLIAM ROGERS Date

Uniform Residential Loan Application

This application is designed to be completed by the applicant(s) with the Lender's assistance. Applicants should complete this form as "Borrower" or "Co-Borrower," as applicable. Co-Borrower information must also be provided (and the appropriate box checked) when ☐ the income or assets of a person other than the "Borrower" (including the Borrower's spouse) will be used as a basis for loan qualification or ☐ the income or assets of the Borrower's spouse or other person who has community property rights pursuant to state law will not be used as a basis for loan qualification, but his or her liabilities must be considered because the spouse or other person has community property rights pursuant to applicable law and Borrower resides in a community property state, the security property is located in a community property state, or the Borrower is relying on other property located in a community property state as a basis for repayment of the loan.

If this is an application for joint credit, Borrower and Co-Borrower each agree that we intend to apply for joint credit (sign below):

Borrower ____________________ Co-Borrower ____________________

I. TYPE OF MORTGAGE AND TERMS OF LOAN

Mortgage Applied for: ☐ VA ☒ Conventional ☐ Other (explain): ☐ FHA ☐ USDA/Rural Housing Service	Agency Case Number	Lender Case Number 200911000

Amount	Interest Rate	No. of Months	Amortization Type:
$202,000.00	5.125 %	360	☒ Fixed Rate ☐ GPM ☐ Other (explain): ☐ ARM (type):

II. PROPERTY INFORMATION AND PURPOSE OF LOAN

Subject Property Address (street, city, state, & ZIP): 8624 OAKLAWN AVENUE, NO. 13 (CANOGA PARK AREA), LOS ANGELES, CALIFORNIA 91304 — No. of Units: 1

Legal Description of Subject Property (attach description if necessary): SEE ATTACHED EXHIBIT "A" — Year Built: 1990

Purpose of Loan: ☒ Purchase ☐ Refinance ☐ Construction ☐ Construction-Permanent ☐ Other (explain):

Property will be: ☒ Primary Residence ☐ Secondary Residence ☐ Investment

Complete this line if construction or construction-permanent loan.

Year Lot Acquired	Original Cost	Amount Existing Liens	(a) Present Value of Lot	(b) Cost of Improvements	Total (a+b)
	$	$	$	$.00	$.00

Complete this line if this is a refinance loan.

Year Acquired	Original Cost	Amount Existing Liens	Purpose of Refinance	Describe Improvements ☐ made ☐ to be made
	$	$		Cost: $

Title will be held in what Name(s): RICHARD WILLIAM ROGERS, An Unmarried Man

Manner in which Title will be held: An Unmarried Man

Estate will be held in: ☒ Fee Simple ☐ Leasehold (show expiration date)

Source of Down Payment, Settlement Charges, and/or Subordinate Financing (explain): Savings

III. BORROWER INFORMATION

Borrower	Co-Borrower
Borrower's Name (include Jr. or Sr. if applicable): RICHARD WILLIAM ROGERS	Co-Borrower's Name (include Jr. or Sr. if applicable):
Social Security Number: 000-00-0000; Home Phone (incl. area code): (818)739-2468; DOB (MM/DD/YYYY): 03/22/1956; Yrs. School: 19	Social Security Number; Home Phone (incl. area code); DOB (MM/DD/YYYY); Yrs. School
☐ Married ☒ Unmarried (include single, divorced, widowed) ☐ Separated; Dependents (not listed by Co-Borrower) no. 0 ages	☐ Married ☐ Unmarried (include single, divorced, widowed) ☐ Separated; Dependents (not listed by Borrower) no. ages
Present Address (street, city, state, ZIP) ☐ Own ☒ Rent 10 No. Yrs.: 8720 DE SOTO AVENUE, LOS ANGELES, CA 91311	Present Address (street, city, state, ZIP) ☐ Own ☐ Rent ____ No. Yrs.
Mailing Address, if different from Present Address: 8624 Oaklawn Avenue, No. 13, Canoga Park, CA 91304	Mailing Address, if different from Present Address

If residing at present address for less than two years, complete the following:

Borrower	Co-Borrower
Former Address (street, city, state, ZIP) ☐ Own ☐ Rent ____ No. Yrs.	Former Address (street, city, state, ZIP) ☐ Own ☐ Rent ____ No. Yrs.

IV. EMPLOYMENT INFORMATION

Borrower		Co-Borrower	
Name & Address of Employer ☐ Self Employed: Acme Services, Inc. 9350 De Soto Avenue, Chatsworth, CA 91311	Yrs. on this job: 9 yrs 4 mos; Yrs. employed in this line of work/profession: 9 yrs 4 mos	Name & Address of Employer ☐ Self Employed	Yrs. on this job; Yrs. employed in this line of work/profession
Position/Title/Type of Business: Foreman	Business Phone (incl. area code): (818)739-0000	Position/Title/Type of Business	Business Phone (incl. area code)

If employed in current position for less than two years or if currently employed in more than one position, complete the following:

Borrower		Co-Borrower	
Name & Address of Employer ☐ Self Employed	Dates (from - to); Monthly Income $	Name & Address of Employer ☐ Self Employed	Dates (from - to); Monthly Income $
Position/Title/Type of Business	Business Phone (incl. area code)	Position/Title/Type of Business	Business Phone (incl. area code)
Name & Address of Employer ☐ Self Employed	Dates (from - to); Monthly Income $	Name & Address of Employer ☐ Self Employed	Dates (from - to); Monthly Income $
Position/Title/Type of Business	Business Phone (incl. area code)	Position/Title/Type of Business	Business Phone (incl. area code)

Fannie Mae Form 1003 7/05
Freddie Mac Form 65 7/05

Page 1

Borrower: ________

V. MONTHLY INCOME AND COMBINED HOUSING EXPENSE INFORMATION

Gross Monthly Income	Borrower	Co-Borrower	Total	Combined Monthly Housing Expense	Present	Proposed
Base Empl. Income*	$ 7,100.00	$	$ 7,100.00	Rent	$ 1,000.00	
Overtime				First Mortgage (P&I)		$ 1,099.86
Bonuses				Other Financing (P&I)		
Commissions				Hazard Insurance		44.83
Dividends/Interest				Real Estate Taxes		268.75
Net Rental Income				Mortgage Insurance		
Other (before completing, see the notice in "describe other income," below)				Homeowner Assn. Dues		300.00
				Other:		
Total	$ 7,100.00	$	$ 7,100.00	Total	$ 1,000.00	$ 1,713.44

* **Self Employed Borrower(s) may be required to provide additional documentation such as tax returns and financial statements.**

Describe Other Income ***Notice:*** **Alimony, child support, or separate maintenance income need not be revealed if the Borrower (B) or Co-Borrower (C) does not choose to have it considered for repaying this loan.**

B/C		Monthly Amount
		$

VI. ASSETS AND LIABILITIES

This Statement and any applicable supporting schedules may be completed jointly by both married and unmarried Co-Borrowers if their assets and liabilities are sufficiently joined so that the Statement can be meaningfully and fairly presented on a combined basis; otherwise, separate Statements and Schedules are required. If the Co-Borrower section was completed about a non-applicant spouse or other person, this Statement and supporting schedules must be completed about that spouse or other person also.

Completed ☐ Jointly ☒ Not Jointly

ASSETS Description	Cash or Market Value
Cash deposit toward purchase held by:	$
List checking and savings accounts below	
Name and address of Bank, S&L, or Credit Union COMMUNITY FIRST BANK	
Acct. no. 0000000000	$ 14,0000.00
Name and address of Bank, S&L, or Credit Union COMMUNITY CREDIT UNION	
Acct. no. 000000000	$ 5,000.00
Name and address of Bank, S&L, or Credit Union	
Acct. no.	$
Name and address of Bank, S&L, or Credit Union	
Acct. no.	$
Stocks & Bonds (Company name/number & description)	$
Life Insurance net cash value Face amount: $	$
Subtotal Liquid Assets	$ 19,000.00
Real estate owned (enter market value from schedule of real estate owned)	$
Vested interest in retirement fund	$ 150,000.00
Net worth of business(es) owned (attach financial statement)	$
Automobiles owned (make and year)	$
Other Assets (itemize) GIFTS TOTAL	$ 25,000.00
Total Assets a.	$ 194,000.00

Liabilities and Pledged Assets. List the creditor's name, address and account number for all outstanding debts, including automobile loans, revolving charge accounts, real estate loans, alimony, child support, stock pledges, etc. Use continuation sheet, if necessary. Indicate by (*) those liabilities which will be satisfied upon sale of real estate owned or upon refinancing of the subject property.

LIABILITIES	Monthly Payment & Months Left to Pay	Unpaid Balance
Name and address of Company FUNDING ONE AUTO FINAN	$ Payment/Months 256.00 24	$ 7,649.00
Acct. no. 000000000000000000		
Name and address of Company Chase	$ Payment/Months 10.00 R	$ 259.00
Acct. no. 000000******0000		
Name and address of Company	$ Payment/Months	$
Acct. no.		
Name and address of Company	$ Payment/Months	$
Acct. no.		
Name and address of Company	$ Payment/Months	$
Acct. no.		
Name and address of Company	$ Payment/Months	$
Acct. no.		
Alimony/Child Support/Separate Maintenance Payments Owed to:	$	
Job-Related Expense (child care, union dues, etc.)	$	
Total Monthly Payments	$ 266.00	
Net Worth (a minus b) ► $ 186,092.00	**Total Liabilities b.**	$ 7,908.00

Fannie Mae Form 1003 7/05
Freddie Mac Form 65 7/05 Borrower: ________ Page 2

VI. ASSETS AND LIABILITIES (cont'd)

Schedule of Real Estate Owned (If additional properties are owned, use continuation sheet.)

Property Address (enter S if sold, PS if pending sale or R if rental being held for income)		Type of Property	Present Market Value	Amount of Mortgages & Liens	Gross Rental Income	Mortgage Payments	Insurance, Maintenance, Taxes & Misc.	Net Rental Income
			$	$	$	$	$	$
			$	$	$	$	$	$

List any additional names under which credit has previously been received and indicate appropriate creditor name(s) and account number(s):

Alternate Name	Creditor Name	Account Number

VII. DETAILS OF TRANSACTION

a.	Purchase price	$ 252,500.00
b.	Alterations, improvements, repairs	
c.	Land (if acquired separately)	
d.	Refinance (incl. debts to be paid off)	.00
e.	Estimated prepaid items	2,587.86
f.	Estimated closing costs	8,037.21
g.	PMI, MIP, Funding Fee	
h.	Discount (if Borrower will pay)	
i.	Total costs (add items a through h)	263,125.07
j.	Subordinate financing	.00
k.	Borrower's closing costs paid by Seller	.00
l.	Other Credits (explain) OTHER OTHER CC paid by Broker, Lender, and Other	3,400.00 587.21 1,414.00 2,001.21
m.	Loan amount (exclude PMI, MIP, Funding Fee financed)	202,000.00
n.	PMI, MIP, Funding Fee financed	
o.	Loan amount (add m & n)	202,000.00
p.	Cash from/to Borrower (subtract j, k, l & o from i)	53,722.65

VIII. DECLARATIONS

If you answer "Yes" to any questions a through i, please use continuation sheet for explanation.

		Borrower Yes	Borrower No	Co-Borrower Yes	Co-Borrower No
a.	Are there any outstanding judgments against you?	☐	☒	☐	☐
b.	Have you been declared bankrupt within the past 7 years?	☐	☒	☐	☐
c.	Have you had property foreclosed upon or given title or deed in lieu thereof in the last 7 years?	☐	☒	☐	☐
d.	Are you a party to a lawsuit?	☐	☒	☐	☐
e.	Have you directly or indirectly been obligated on any loan which resulted in foreclosure, transfer of title in lieu of foreclosure, or judgment? (This would include such loans as home mortgage loans, SBA loans, home improvement loans, educational loans, manufactured (mobile) home loans, any mortgage, financial obligation, bond, or loan guarantee. If "Yes," provide details, including date, name and address of Lender, FHA or VA case number, if any, and reasons for the action.)	☐	☒	☐	☐
f.	Are you presently delinquent or in default on any Federal debt or any other loan, mortgage, financial obligation, bond, or loan guarantee? If "Yes," give details as described in the preceding question.	☐	☒	☐	☐
g.	Are you obligated to pay alimony, child support, or separate maintenance?	☐	☒	☐	☐
h.	Is any part of the down payment borrowed?	☐	☒	☐	☐
i.	Are you a co-maker or endorser on a note?	☐	☒	☐	☐
j.	Are you a U.S. citizen?	☒	☐	☐	☐
k.	Are you a permanent resident alien?	☐	☒	☐	☐
l.	**Do you intend to occupy the property as your primary residence?** If "Yes," complete question m below.	☒	☐	☐	☐
m.	Have you had an ownership interest in a property in the last three years?	☐	☒	☐	☐
	(1) What type of property did you own - principal residence (PR), second home (SH), or investment property (IP)?				
	(2) How did you hold title to the home - solely by yourself (S), jointly with your spouse (SP), or jointly with another person (O)?				

IX. ACKNOWLEDGEMENT AND AGREEMENT

Each of the undersigned specifically represents to Lender and to Lender's actual or potential agents, brokers, processors, attorneys, insurers, servicers, successors and assigns and agrees and acknowledges that: (1) the information provided in this application is true and correct as of the date set forth opposite my signature and that any intentional or negligent misrepresentation of this information contained in this application may result in civil liability, including monetary damages, to any person who may suffer any loss due to reliance upon any misrepresentation that I have made on this application, and/or in criminal penalties including, but not limited to, fine or imprisonment or both under the provisions of Title 18 United States Code, Sec. 1001, et. seq.; (2) the loan requested pursuant to this application (the "Loan") will be secured by a mortgage or deed of trust on the property described in this application; (3) the property will not be used for any illegal or prohibited purpose or use; (4) all statements made in this application are made for the purpose of obtaining a residential mortgage loan; (5) the property will be occupied as indicated in this application; (6) the Lender, its servicers, successors or assigns may retain the original and/or an electronic record of this application, whether or not the Loan is approved; (7) the Lender and its agents, brokers, insurers, servicers, successors, and assigns may continuously rely on the information contained in the application, and I am obligated to amend and/or supplement the information provided in this application if any of the material facts that I have represented herein should change prior to closing of the Loan; (8) in the event that my payments on the Loan become delinquent, the Lender, its servicers, successors or assigns may, in addition to any other rights and remedies that it may have relating to such delinquency, report my name and account information to one or more consumer reporting agencies; (9) ownership of the Loan and/or administration of the Loan account may be transferred with such notice as may be required by law; (10) neither Lender nor its agents, brokers, insurers, servicers, successors, or assigns has made any representation or warranty, express or implied, to me regarding the property or the condition or value of the property; and (11) my transmission of this application as an "electronic record" containing my "electronic signature," as those terms are defined in applicable federal and/or state laws (excluding audio and video recordings), or my facsimile transmission of this application containing a facsimile of my signature, shall be as effective, enforceable and valid as if a paper version of this application were delivered containing my original written signature.

Acknowledgement. Each of the undersigned hereby acknowledges that any owner of the Loan, its servicers, successors and assigns, may verify or reverify any information contained in this application or obtain any information or data relating to the Loan, for any legitimate business purpose through any source, including a source named in this application or a consumer reporting agency.

Borrower's Signature	Date	Co-Borrower's Signature	Date
X		X	

X. INFORMATION FOR GOVERNMENT MONITORING PURPOSES

The following information is requested by the Federal Government for certain types of loans related to dwelling in order to monitor the lender's compliance with equal credit opportunity, fair housing and home mortgage disclosure laws. You are not required to furnish this information, but are encouraged to do so. The law provides that a lender may not discriminate either on the basis of this information, or on whether you choose to furnish it. If you furnish the information, please provide both ethnicity and race. For race, you may check more than one designation. If you do not furnish ethnicity, race, or sex, under Federal regulations, this lender is required to note the information on the basis of visual observation and surname if you have made this application in person. If you do not wish to furnish the information, please check the box below. (Lender must review the above material to assure that the disclosures satisfy all requirements to which the lender is subject under applicable state law for the particular type of loan applied for.)

BORROWER ☐ I do not wish to furnish this information	CO-BORROWER ☐ I do not wish to furnish this information
Ethnicity: ☐ Hispanic or Latino ☒ Not Hispanic or Latino	**Ethnicity:** ☐ Hispanic or Latino ☐ Not Hispanic or Latino
Race: ☐ American Indian or Alaska Native ☐ Asian ☐ Black or African American ☐ Native Hawaiian or Other Pacific Islander ☒ White	**Race:** ☐ American Indian or Alaska Native ☐ Asian ☐ Black or African American ☐ Native Hawaiian or Other Pacific Islander ☐ White
Sex: ☐ Female ☒ Male	**Sex:** ☐ Female ☐ Male

To be Completed by Interviewer	Interviewer's Name (print or type)	Name and Address of Interviewer's Employer
This application was taken by:	Brad Donnelly	TRISTAR FINANCIAL CORP.
☐ Face-to-face interview	Interviewer's Signature / Date: 01/20/10	1000 MAIN STREET,
☐ Mail ☐ Telephone	Interviewer's Phone Number (incl. area code)	LOS ANGELES, CA 90025
☒ Internet	(310) 321-4567	

Fannie Mae Form 1003 7/05
Freddie Mac Form 65 7/05

Borrower: ________

Page 3

CONTINUATION SHEET/RESIDENTIAL LOAN APPLICATION

Use this continuation sheet if you need more space to complete the Residential Loan Application. Mark **B** for Borrower or **C** for Co-Borrower	Borrower: RICHARD WILLIAM ROGERS	Agency Case Number:
	Co-Borrower:	Lender Case Number: 200911000

Additional Names under which credit has been received

Alternate Name	Creditor Name	Account Number

I/We fully understand that it is a Federal crime punishable by fine or imprisonment, or both, to knowingly make any false statements concerning any of the above facts as applicable under the provisions of Title 18, United States Code, Section 1001, et seq.

Borrower's Signature	Date	Co-Borrower's Signature	Date
X		X	

Fannie Mae Form 1003 7/05
Freddie Mac Form 65 7/05

Page 4

Continuation Sheet / Residential Loan Application

Use this continuation sheet if you need more space to complete the Residential Loan Application. Mark B for Borrower or C for Co-Borrower	Borrower: RICHARD WILLIAM ROGERS Co-Borrower:	Agency Case Number: Lender Case Number: 200911000

VI. ASSETS AND LIABILITIES

Schedule of Real Estate Owned

Property Address (enter S if sold, PS if pending sale or R if rental being held for income)		Type of Property	Present Market Value	Amount of Mortgages & Liens	Gross Rental Income	Mortgage Payments	Insurance, Maintenance, Taxes & Misc.	Net Rental Income

I/We fully understand that it is a Federal crime punishable by fine or imprisonment, or both, to knowingly make any false statements concerning any of the above facts as applicable under the provisions of Title 18, United States Code, Section 1001, et seq.

Borrower's Signature	Date	Co-Borrower's Signature	Date
X		X	

Fannie Mae Form 1003
Freddie Mac Form 65

Page 5

FEDERAL TRUTH-IN-LENDING DISCLOSURE STATEMENT

(THIS IS NEITHER A CONTRACT NOR A COMMITMENT TO LEND)

Loan Number: 200911000 Date: FEBRUARY 12, 2010
Creditor: TRISTAR FINANCIAL CORP.
Address: 1000 MAIN STREET, LOS ANGELES, CALIFORNIA 90025

Borrower(s): RICHARD WILLIAM ROGERS

Address: 8624 OAKLAWN AVENUE, NO. 13 (CANOGA PARK AREA), LOS ANGELES, CALIFORNIA 91304

Disclosures marked with an "x" are applicable:

ANNUAL PERCENTAGE RATE The cost of your credit as a yearly rate	**FINANCE CHARGE** The dollar amount the credit will cost you.	**Amount Financed** The amount of credit provided to you or on your behalf.	**Total of Payments** The amount you will have paid after you have made all payments as scheduled.	☐ **Total Sale Price** The total cost of your purchase on credit including your down-payment of $
5.343 %	$198,833.15	$197,119.68	$395,952.83	$

PAYMENTS: Your payment schedule will be:

Number of Payments	Amount of Payment **	When Payments Are Due	Number of Payments	Amount of Payment **	When Payments Are Due	Number of Payments	Amount of Payment **	When Payments Are Due
		Monthly Beginning			Monthly Beginning			Monthly Beginning
359	1,099.86	04/01/10						
1	1,103.09	03/01/40						

☐ **DEMAND FEATURE:** This obligation has a demand feature.

☐ **VARIABLE RATE FEATURE:** Your loan contains a variable rate feature. Disclosures about the variable rate feature have been provided to you earlier.

PROPERTY INSURANCE: You may obtain fire and other hazard insurance from anyone you want that is acceptable to the Creditor.
NO OBLIGATION: You are not required to complete this agreement merely because you have received these disclosures or signed a loan application.
SECURITY: You are giving a security interest in: 8624 OAKLAWN AVENUE, NO. 13 (CANOGA PARK AREA), LOS ANGELES, CALIFORNIA 91304
☒ The goods or property being purchased ☐ Real property you already own.
FILING FEES: $ 115.00
LATE CHARGE: If payment is more than 15 days late, you will be charged 6.000 % of the payment.
PREPAYMENT: If you pay off early, you
☐ may ☒ will not have to pay a penalty.
☐ may ☒ will not be entitled to a refund of part of the finance charge.
ASSUMPTION: Someone buying your property
☐ may ☐ may, subject to conditions ☒ may not assume the remainder of your loan on the original terms.
See your contract documents for any additional information about nonpayment, default, any required repayment in full before the scheduled date and prepayment refunds and penalties.
☒ "e" means an estimate ☐ all dates and numerical disclosures except the late payment disclosures are estimates.

Each of the undersigned acknowledge receipt of a complete copy of this disclosure. The disclosure does not constitute a contract or a commitment to lend.

Applicant RICHARD WILLIAM ROGERS Date Applicant Date

Applicant Date Applicant Date

Loan Number: 200911000

ACKNOWLEDGMENT OF RECEIPT OF GOOD FAITH ESTIMATE AND TRUTH IN LENDING ACT DISCLOSURES

Lender: TRISTAR FINANCIAL CORP.

Borrower(s): RICHARD WILLIAM ROGERS

Property Address: 8624 OAKLAWN AVENUE, NO. 13 (CANOGA PARK AREA), LOS ANGELES, CALIFORNIA 91304

The undersigned ("you" or "your") hereby acknowledge receipt of a "good faith estimate" of the charges which you are likely to incur at the settlement of your loan as provided pursuant to the Real Estate Settlement Procedures Act of 1974, as amended (12 U.S.C.A. 2601 et seq.), and all applicable disclosures required by the Truth in Lending Act, as amended (15 U.S.C.A. 1601 et seq.).

Borrower RICHARD WILLIAM ROGERS Date

Borrower Date

Borrower Date

Borrower Date

Borrower Date

Borrower Date

Loan Number: 200911000

BORROWER'S CERTIFICATION & AUTHORIZATION

Certification

The undersigned certify the following:

1. I/We have applied for a mortgage loan from TRISTAR FINANCIAL CORP. ("Lender").

In applying for the loan, I/we completed a loan application containing various information on the purpose of the loan, the amount and source of the downpayment, employment and income information, and assets and liabilities. I/We certify that all of the information is true and complete. I/We made no misrepresentations in the loan application or other documents, nor did I/we omit any pertinent information.

2. I/We understand and agree that Lender reserves the right to change the mortgage loan review process to a full documentation program. This may include verifying the information provided on the application with the employer and/or the financial institution.

3. I/We fully understand that it is a Federal crime punishable by fine or imprisonment, or both, to knowingly make any false statements when applying for this mortgage, as applicable under the provisions of Title 18, United States Code, Section 1014.

Authorization to Release Information

To Whom It May Concern:

1. I/We have applied for a mortgage loan from Lender. As part of the application process, Lender and the mortgage guaranty insurer (if any), may verify information contained in my/our loan application and in other documents required in connection with the loan, either before the loan is closed or as part of its quality control program.

2. I/We authorize you to provide to Lender and to any investor to whom you may sell my mortgage, and to the mortgage guaranty insurer (if any), any and all information and documentation that they request. Such information includes, but is not limited to, employment history and income; bank, money market, and similar account balances; credit history; and copies of income tax returns.

3. Lender or any investor that purchases the mortgage, or the mortgage guaranty insurer (if any), may address this authorization to any party named in the loan application.

4. A copy of this authorization may be accepted as an original.

5. Your prompt reply to Lender, the investor that purchased the mortgage, or the mortgage guaranty insurer (if any) is appreciated.

6. Mortgage guaranty insurer (if any):
   N/A

Right of Financial Privacy Act of 1978 Notice- The Department of Housing and Urban Development (HUD) and the Department of Veterans Affairs (VA) have the right to access financial information held by a financial institution in determining whether to qualify a prospective applicant under their respective loan programs. If you are applying for HUD or VA loan, your financial records will be made available to the requesting government agency without further notice to or authorization from you; such financial information will not be disclosed or released outside the requesting agency except as required or permitted by law. Prior to the time that your financial records are disclosed, you may revoke this authorization at any time; however, your refusal to provide the information may cause your application to be delayed or rejected. If you believe that your financial records have been disclosed improperly, you may have legal rights under the Right to Financial Privacy Act of 1978 (12 USC 3400 **et seq**.).

Borrower RICHARD WILLIAM ROGERS	Date	000-00-0000 Social Security Number
Borrower	Date	Social Security Number
Borrower	Date	Social Security Number
Borrower	Date	Social Security Number
Borrower	Date	Social Security Number
Borrower	Date	Social Security Number

PAYMENT LETTER TO BORROWER

FROM: TRISTAR FINANCIAL CORP.
1000 MAIN STREET
LOS ANGELES, CALIFORNIA 90025

RE: Loan Number: 200911000
Property Address: 8624 OAKLAWN AVENUE, NO. 13 (CANOGA PARK AREA),
LOS ANGELES, CALIFORNIA 91304

TO: RICHARD WILLIAM ROGERS
8624 OAKLAWN AVENUE, NO. 13 (CANOGA PARK AREA)
LOS ANGELES, CALIFORNIA 91304

Dear Borrower:

The monthly payments on the above referred to loan are to begin on APRIL 1, 2010, and will continue monthly until MARCH 1, 2040.

Your monthly payment will consist of the following:

PRINCIPAL AND INTEREST	$ 1,099.86
MMI/PMI INSURANCE	
RESERVE FOR TAXES	
RESERVE FOR INSURANCE	44.83
RESERVE FOR FLOOD INSURANCE	
COUNTY TAX	268.75
TOTAL MONTHLY PAYMENTS	$ 1,413.44

You are to make your payments to:
TRISTAR FINANCIAL CORPORATION
1000 MAIN STREET
LOS ANGELES, CALIFORNIA 90025

Any correspondence, or calls, in reference to your loan, please refer to the above loan number.

Copy received and acknowledged.

Date: ______________________ ______________________
RICHARD WILLIAM ROGERS

____

____

____

____

____

80-649-1362

HARDSHIP

Loan Number: 200911000

Re: Borrower(s): RICHARD WILLIAM ROGERS

Property Address: 8624 OAKLAWN AVENUE, NO. 13 (CANOGA PARK AREA), LOS ANGELES, CALIFORNIA 91304

I/WE, THE UNDERSIGNED BORROWER(S) UNDERSTAND AND ACKNOWLEDGE THAT MY/OUR FIRST MORTGAGE PAYMENT FOR THIS LOAN ON THE ABOVE REFERENCED PROPERTY IS DUE WITHIN THIRTY (30) DAYS OF LOAN CLOSING. THIS WILL NOT CREATE ANY FINANCIAL HARDSHIP TO ME/US.

______________________	______________________
Borrower RICHARD WILLIAM ROGERS	Borrower
______________________ Borrower	______________________ Borrower
______________________ Borrower	______________________ Borrower

Lender: TRISTAR FINANCIAL CORP.
1000 MAIN STREET
LOS ANGELES, CALIFORNIA 90025

Re: RICHARD WILLIAM ROGERS
8624 OAKLAWN AVENUE, NO. 13 (CANOGA PARK AREA)
LOS ANGELES, CALIFORNIA 91304

Date: FEBRUARY 12, 2010
Loan Number: 200911000

Ref HUD-1 Statement	ITEMIZATION OF AMOUNT FINANCED		
	▪ Amount given to you directly		$
	▪ Amount paid on your account		
1001	Insurance Reserves	134.49	
1004	Tax Reserves		
	Other Reserves	537.50	
1009	Aggregate Adjustment	-44.83	
	▪ Amount paid to others on your behalf:		
803	Appraisal Fee to: B & K APPRAISAL SERVICES, INC.	375.00	(375.00 POC/B)
804	Credit Reporting Fee		
903	Hazard Insurance Premium		
809	Document Preparation Fee to: FIRST TITLE COMPANY	185.00	
1106	Notary Fee		
1108	Title Ins. Premium		
1201	Recording Fee		
	RECORDING MORTGAGE FEE to: FIRST TITLE COMPANY	115.00	
	APPRAISAL FEE to: B & K APPRAISAL SERVICES, INC.	375.00	
	LENDER'S TITLE INSURANCE FEE to: FIRST TITLE COMPANY	416.00	
	TITLE ENDORSEMENT FEE to: FIRST TITLE COMPANY	50.00	
	APPRAISAL REVIEW FEE to: B & K APPRAISAL SERVICES, INC.	40.00	
	HOA FEE to: FIRST TITLE COMPANY	90.00	(90.00 POC/B)
	INSURANCE CERT to: FIRST TITLE COMPANY	125.00	
	COUNTY PROPERTY TAX to: FIRST TITLE COMPANY	1,082.38	
	HOA DUES to: FIRST TITLE COMPANY	190.00	
	HO6 to: FIRST TITLE COMPANY	538.00	
	Loan Proceeds to: SOUTHERN ESCROW		$193,376.14
	▪ AMOUNT FINANCED		$ 197,119.68
	▪ Prepaid Finance Charge		$ 4,880.32

▪ Loan Amount $ 202,000.00

	▪ Itemization of Prepaid Finance Charge:	
801	Loan Origination Fee to: TRISTAR FINANCIAL	$ 2,020.00
802	Loan Discount Fee to: TRISTAR FINANCIAL	.00
806	Tax Service Fee	
	Prepaid Interest (12 days)	
901	@ 5.125% per annum	340.32
902	Mtge. Ins. Premium	
1002	Mtge. Ins. Reserves	
808	Origination Fee	
	TIE IN FEE to: SOUTHERN ESCROW	250.00
	ESCROW FEE to: SOUTHERN ESCROW	705.00
	SUB ESCROW FEE to: FIRST TITLE COMPANY	70.00
	PROCESSING FEE to: TRISTAR FINANCIAL CORP.	495.00
	UNDERWRITING FEE to: TRISTAR FINANCIAL CORP.	795.00
	ELECTRONIC DELIVERY to: SOUTHERN ESCROW	100.00
	COURIER FEE to: SOUTHERN ESCROW	60.00
	WIRE FEE to: FIRST TITLE COMPANY	45.00
	Total Prepaid Finance Charge	$ 4,880.32

This form does not cover all items you will be required to pay in cash at settlement, for example, deposits in escrow for real estate taxes and insurance may be different. You may wish to inquire as to the amounts of such other items. You may be required to pay other additional amounts to be settled.

☐ All disclosures are estimates

The undersigned acknowledge receiving and reading a completed copy of this disclosure.

(Borrower) RICHARD WILLIAM ROGERS (Date) (Borrower) (Date)

(Borrower) (Date) (Borrower) (Date)

(Borrower) (Date) (Borrower) (Date)

NOTE

MIN: 1000000-0200911000-7 Loan Number: 200911000

FEBRUARY 12, 2010 LOS ANGELES CALIFORNIA
[Date] [City] [State]

8624 OAKLAWN AVENUE, NO. 13 (CANOGA PARK AREA), LOS ANGELES, CALIFORNIA 91304
[Property Address]

1. BORROWER'S PROMISE TO PAY

In return for a loan that I have received, I promise to pay U.S. $ 202,000.00 (this amount is called "Principal"), plus interest, to the order of the Lender. The Lender is TRISTAR FINANCIAL CORP., A CALIFORNIA CORPORATION .

I will make all payments under this Note in the form of cash, check or money order.

I understand that the Lender may transfer this Note. The Lender or anyone who takes this Note by transfer and who is entitled to receive payments under this Note is called the "Note Holder."

2. INTEREST

Interest will be charged on unpaid principal until the full amount of Principal has been paid. I will pay interest at a yearly rate of 5.125 %.

The interest rate required by this Section 2 is the rate I will pay both before and after any default described in Section 6(B) of this Note.

3. PAYMENTS

(A) Time and Place of Payments

I will pay principal and interest by making a payment every month.

I will make my monthly payment on the 1st day of each month beginning on APRIL 1 , 2010 . I will make these payments every month until I have paid all of the principal and interest and any other charges described below that I may owe under this Note. Each monthly payment will be applied as of its scheduled due date and will be applied to interest before Principal. If, on MARCH 1, 2040 , I still owe amounts under this Note, I will pay those amounts in full on that date, which is called the "Maturity Date."

I will make my monthly payments at 1000 MAIN STREET, LOS ANGELES, CALIFORNIA 90025 or at a different place if required by the Note Holder.

(B) Amount of Monthly Payments

My monthly payment will be in the amount of U.S. $ 1,099.86 .

4. BORROWER'S RIGHT TO PREPAY

I have the right to make payments of Principal at any time before they are due. A payment of Principal only is known as a "Prepayment." When I make a Prepayment, I will tell the Note Holder in writing that I am doing so. I may not designate a payment as a Prepayment if I have not made all the monthly payments due under the Note.

I may make a full Prepayment or partial Prepayments without paying a Prepayment charge. The Note Holder will use my Prepayments to reduce the amount of Principal that I owe under this Note. However, the Note Holder may apply my Prepayment to the accrued and unpaid interest on the Prepayment amount, before applying my Prepayment to reduce the Principal amount of the Note. If I make a partial Prepayment, there will be no changes in the due date or in the amount of my monthly payment unless the Note Holder agrees in writing to those changes.

5. LOAN CHARGES

If a law, which applies to this loan and which sets maximum loan charges, is finally interpreted so that the interest or other loan charges collected or to be collected in connection with this loan exceed the permitted limits, then: (a) any such loan charge shall be reduced by the amount necessary to reduce the charge to the permitted limit;

MULTISTATE FIXED RATE NOTE--Single Family
Fannie Mae/Freddie Mac UNIFORM INSTRUMENT
Form 3200 1/01 Page 1 of 3

and (b) any sums already collected from me which exceeded permitted limits will be refunded to me. The Note Holder may choose to make this refund by reducing the Principal I owe under this Note or by making a direct payment to me. If a refund reduces Principal, the reduction will be treated as a partial Prepayment.

6. BORROWER'S FAILURE TO PAY AS REQUIRED

(A) Late Charge for Overdue Payments

If the Note Holder has not received the full amount of any monthly payment by the end of 15 calendar days after the date it is due, I will pay a late charge to the Note Holder. The amount of the charge will be 6.000 % of my overdue payment of principal and interest. I will pay this late charge promptly but only once on each late payment.

(B) Default

If I do not pay the full amount of each monthly payment on the date it is due, I will be in default.

(C) Notice of Default

If I am in default, the Note Holder may send me a written notice telling me that if I do not pay the overdue amount by a certain date, the Note Holder may require me to pay immediately the full amount of Principal which has not been paid and all the interest that I owe on that amount. That date must be at least 30 days after the date on which the notice is mailed to me or delivered by other means.

(D) No Waiver By Note Holder

Even if, at a time when I am in default, the Note Holder does not require me to pay immediately in full as described above, the Note Holder will still have the right to do so if I am in default at a later time.

(E) Payment of Note Holder's Costs and Expenses

If the Note Holder has required me to pay immediately in full as described above, the Note Holder will have the right to be paid back by me for all of its costs and expenses in enforcing this Note to the extent not prohibited by applicable law. Those expenses include, for example, reasonable attorneys' fees.

7. GIVING OF NOTICES

Unless applicable law requires a different method, any notice that must be given to me under this Note will be given by delivering it or by mailing it by first class mail to me at the Property Address above or at a different address if I give the Note Holder a notice of my different address.

Any notice that must be given to the Note Holder under this Note will be given by delivering it or by mailing it by first class mail to the Note Holder at the address stated in Section 3(A) above or at a different address if I am given a notice of that different address.

8. OBLIGATIONS OF PERSONS UNDER THIS NOTE

If more than one person signs this Note, each person is fully and personally obligated to keep all of the promises made in this Note, including the promise to pay the full amount owed. Any person who is a guarantor, surety or endorser of this Note is also obligated to do these things. Any person who takes over these obligations, including the obligations of a guarantor, surety or endorser of this Note, is also obligated to keep all of the promises made in this Note. The Note Holder may enforce its rights under this Note against each person individually or against all of us together. This means that any one of us may be required to pay all of the amounts owed under this Note.

9. WAIVERS

I and any other person who has obligations under this Note waive the rights of Presentment and Notice of Dishonor. "Presentment" means the right to require the Note Holder to demand payment of amounts due. "Notice of Dishonor" means the right to require the Note Holder to give notice to other persons that amounts due have not been paid.

10. UNIFORM SECURED NOTE

This Note is a uniform instrument with limited variations in some jurisdictions. In addition to the protections given to the Note Holder under this Note, a Mortgage, Deed of Trust, or Security Deed (the "Security Instrument"), dated the same date as this Note, protects the Note Holder from possible losses which might result if I do not keep

MULTISTATE FIXED RATE NOTE--Single Family
Fannie Mae/Freddie Mac UNIFORM INSTRUMENT
Form 3200 1/01 Page 2 of 3

the promises which I make in this Note. That Security Instrument describes how and under what conditions I may be required to make immediate payment in full of all amounts I owe under this Note. Some of those conditions are described as follows:

If all or any part of the Property or any Interest in the Property is sold or transferred (or if Borrower is not a natural person and a beneficial interest in Borrower is sold or transferred) without Lender's prior written consent, Lender may require immediate payment in full of all sums secured by this Security Instrument. However, this option shall not be exercised by Lender if such exercise is prohibited by Applicable Law.

If Lender exercises this option, Lender shall give Borrower notice of acceleration. The notice shall provide a period of not less than 30 days from the date the notice is given in accordance with Section 15 within which Borrower must pay all sums secured by this Security Instrument. If Borrower fails to pay these sums prior to the expiration of this period, Lender may invoke any remedies permitted by this Security Instrument without further notice or demand on Borrower.

WITNESS THE HAND(S) AND SEAL(S) OF THE UNDERSIGNED.

______________________ (Seal) RICHARD WILLIAM ROGERS -Borrower	______________________ (Seal) -Borrower
______________________ (Seal) -Borrower	______________________ (Seal) -Borrower
______________________ (Seal) -Borrower	______________________ (Seal) -Borrower

[Sign Original Only]

MULTISTATE FIXED RATE NOTE--Single Family
Fannie Mae/Freddie Mac UNIFORM INSTRUMENT
Form 3200 1/01 Page 3 of 3

ALLONGE

Loan Number: 200911000

Loan Date: FEBRUARY 12, 2010

Borrower(s): RICHARD WILLIAM ROGERS

Property Address: 8624 OAKLAWN AVENUE, NO. 13 (CANOGA PARK AREA), LOS ANGELES, CALIFORNIA 91304

Principal Balance: $202,000.00

PAY TO THE ORDER OF

JPMORGAN CHASE BANK, N.A.

Without Recourse

Company Name: TRISTAR FINANCIAL CORP.

By: ______________________ FUNDING MANAGER
(Title)

FRANCES KLEIMAN

Recording Requested By:
TRISTAR FINANCIAL CORP.

And After Recording Return To:
TRISTAR FINANCIAL CORP.
1000 MAIN STREET
LOS ANGELES, CALIFORNIA 90025
Loan Number: 200911000

[Space Above This Line For Recording Data]

DEED OF TRUST

MIN: 1000000-0200911000-7

DEFINITIONS

Words used in multiple sections of this document are defined below and other words are defined in Sections 3, 11, 13, 18, 20 and 21. Certain rules regarding the usage of words used in this document are also provided in Section 16.

(A) "Security Instrument" means this document, which is dated FEBRUARY 12, 2010 , together with all Riders to this document.

(B) "Borrower" is RICHARD WILLIAM ROGERS, AN UNMARRIED MAN

.

Borrower is the trustor under this Security Instrument.

(C) "Lender" is TRISTAR FINANCIAL CORP.

. Lender is a CALIFORNIA CORPORATION organized and existing under the laws of CALIFORNIA . Lender's address is 1000 MAIN STREET, LOS ANGELES, CALIFORNIA 90025

.

(D) "Trustee" is FIRST TITLE COMPANY
412 EAST SIGNAL STREET, SUITE 409, LOS ANGELES, CALIFORNIA 90025

.

(E) "MERS" is Mortgage Electronic Registration Systems, Inc. MERS is a separate corporation that is acting solely as a nominee for Lender and Lender's successors and assigns. **MERS is the beneficiary under this Security Instrument.** MERS is organized and existing under the laws of Delaware, and has an address and telephone number of P.O. Box 2026, Flint, MI 48501-2026, tel. (888) 679-MERS.

(F) "Note" means the promissory note signed by Borrower and dated FEBRUARY 12, 2010 . The Note states that Borrower owes Lender TWO HUNDRED TWO THOUSAND AND 00/100 Dollars (U.S. $ 202,000.00) plus interest.

CALIFORNIA--Single Family--Fannie Mae/Freddie Mac UNIFORM INSTRUMENT - MERS
Form 3005 01/01 Page 1 of 14

Borrower has promised to pay this debt in regular Periodic Payments and to pay the debt in full not later than MARCH 1, 2040 .

(G) "Property" means the property that is described below under the heading "Transfer of Rights in the Property."

(H) "Loan" means the debt evidenced by the Note, plus interest, any prepayment charges and late charges due under the Note, and all sums due under this Security Instrument, plus interest.

(I) "Riders" means all Riders to this Security Instrument that are executed by Borrower. The following Riders are to be executed by Borrower [check box as applicable]:

- [ ] Adjustable Rate Rider
- [ ] Balloon Rider
- [ ] 1-4 Family Rider
- [x] Condominium Rider
- [ ] Planned Unit Development Rider
- [ ] Biweekly Payment Rider
- [ ] Second Home Rider
- [ ] Other(s) [specify]

(J) "Applicable Law" means all controlling applicable federal, state and local statutes, regulations, ordinances and administrative rules and orders (that have the effect of law) as well as all applicable final, non-appealable judicial opinions.

(K) "Community Association Dues, Fees, and Assessments" means all dues, fees, assessments and other charges that are imposed on Borrower or the Property by a condominium association, homeowners association or similar organization.

(L) "Electronic Funds Transfer" means any transfer of funds, other than a transaction originated by check, draft, or similar paper instrument, which is initiated through an electronic terminal, telephonic instrument, computer, or magnetic tape so as to order, instruct, or authorize a financial institution to debit or credit an account. Such term includes, but is not limited to, point-of-sale transfers, automated teller machine transactions, transfers initiated by telephone, wire transfers, and automated clearinghouse transfers.

(M) "Escrow Items" means those items that are described in Section 3.

(N) "Miscellaneous Proceeds" means any compensation, settlement, award of damages, or proceeds paid by any third party (other than insurance proceeds paid under the coverages described in Section 5) for: (i) damage to, or destruction of, the Property; (ii) condemnation or other taking of all or any part of the Property; (iii) conveyance in lieu of condemnation; or (iv) misrepresentations of, or omissions as to, the value and/or condition of the Property.

(O) "Mortgage Insurance" means insurance protecting Lender against the nonpayment of, or default on, the Loan.

(P) "Periodic Payment" means the regularly scheduled amount due for (i) principal and interest under the Note, plus (ii) any amounts under Section 3 of this Security Instrument.

(Q) "RESPA" means the Real Estate Settlement Procedures Act (12 U.S.C. §2601 et seq.) and its implementing regulation, Regulation X (24 C.F.R. Part 3500), as they might be amended from time to time, or any additional or successor legislation or regulation that governs the same subject matter. As used in this Security Instrument, "RESPA" refers to all requirements and restrictions that are imposed in regard to a "federally related mortgage loan" even if the Loan does not qualify as a "federally related mortgage loan" under RESPA.

(R) "Successor in Interest of Borrower" means any party that has taken title to the Property, whether or not that party has assumed Borrower's obligations under the Note and/or this Security Instrument.

TRANSFER OF RIGHTS IN THE PROPERTY

The beneficiary of this Security Instrument is MERS (solely as nominee for Lender and Lender's successors and assigns) and the successors and assigns of MERS. This Security Instrument secures to Lender: (i) the repayment of the Loan, and all renewals, extensions and modifications of the Note; and (ii) the performance of Borrower's covenants and agreements under this Security Instrument and the Note. For this purpose, Borrower irrevocably grants and conveys to Trustee, in trust, with power of sale, the following described property located in the COUNTY of LOS ANGELES :

[Type of Recording Jurisdiction] [Name of Recording Jurisdiction]

PARCEL 1: THAT PORTION OF LOT 1, OF TRACT NO. 4600, IN THE CITY OF LOS ANGELES, COUNTY OF LOS ANGELES, STATE OF CALIFORNIA, AS PER MAP RECORDED IN BOOK 1150 PAGE(S) 44 AND 45 OF MAPS, IN THE OFFICE OF THE COUNTY RECORDER OF SAID COUNTY, SHOWN AND DEFINED AS UNIT 13 ON THE CONDOMINIUM PLAN RECORDED ON JUNE 26, 1990 AS INSTRUMENT NO. 90-1136000, OFFICIAL RECORDS OF SAID COUNTY.
PARCEL 2: AN UNDIVIDED 1/40TH INTEREST IN AND TO LOT 1 OF SAID TRACT NO. 46000, EXCEPT THEREFROM THOSE PORTIONS SHOWN AND DEFINED AS UNITS 1 THROUGH 12, INCLUSIVE AND 14 THROUGH 41 INCLUSIVE.

A.P.N.: 2780-002-145

which currently has the address of 8624 OAKLAWN AVENUE, NO. 13 (CANOGA PARK AREA)

[Street]

LOS ANGELES , California 91304 ("Property Address"):

[City] [Zip Code]

TOGETHER WITH all the improvements now or hereafter erected on the property, and all easements, appurtenances, and fixtures now or hereafter a part of the property. All replacements and additions shall also be covered by this Security Instrument. All of the foregoing is referred to in this Security Instrument as the "Property." Borrower understands and agrees that MERS holds only legal title to the interests granted by Borrower in this Security Instrument, but, if necessary to comply with law or custom, MERS (as nominee for Lender and Lender's successors and assigns) has the right: to exercise any or all of those interests, including, but not limited to, the right to foreclose and sell the Property; and to take any action required of Lender including, but not limited to, releasing and canceling this Security Instrument.

BORROWER COVENANTS that Borrower is lawfully seised of the estate hereby conveyed and has the right to grant and convey the Property and that the Property is unencumbered, except for encumbrances of record. Borrower warrants and will defend generally the title to the Property against all claims and demands, subject to any encumbrances of record.

THIS SECURITY INSTRUMENT combines uniform covenants for national use and non-uniform covenants with limited variations by jurisdiction to constitute a uniform security instrument covering real property.

UNIFORM COVENANTS. Borrower and Lender covenant and agree as follows:

1. Payment of Principal, Interest, Escrow Items, Prepayment Charges, and Late Charges. Borrower shall pay when due the principal of, and interest on, the debt evidenced by the Note and any prepayment charges and late charges due under the Note. Borrower shall also pay funds for Escrow Items pursuant to Section 3. Payments due under the Note and this Security Instrument shall be made in U.S. currency. However, if any check or other instrument received by Lender as payment under the Note or this Security Instrument is returned to Lender unpaid, Lender may require that any or all subsequent payments due under the Note and this Security Instrument be made in one or more of the following forms, as selected by Lender: (a) cash; (b) money order; (c) certified check, bank check, treasurer's check or cashier's check, provided any such check is drawn upon an institution whose deposits are insured by a federal agency, instrumentality, or entity; or (d) Electronic Funds Transfer.

Payments are deemed received by Lender when received at the location designated in the Note or at such other location as may be designated by Lender in accordance with the notice provisions in Section 15. Lender may return any payment or partial payment if the payment or partial payments are insufficient to bring the Loan current. Lender may accept any payment or partial payment insufficient to bring the Loan current, without waiver of any rights hereunder or prejudice to its rights to refuse such payment or partial payments in the future, but Lender is not

CALIFORNIA--Single Family--Fannie Mae/Freddie Mac UNIFORM INSTRUMENT - MERS
Form 3005 01/01 Page 3 of 14

obligated to apply such payments at the time such payments are accepted. If each Periodic Payment is applied as of its scheduled due date, then Lender need not pay interest on unapplied funds. Lender may hold such unapplied funds until Borrower makes payment to bring the Loan current. If Borrower does not do so within a reasonable period of time, Lender shall either apply such funds or return them to Borrower. If not applied earlier, such funds will be applied to the outstanding principal balance under the Note immediately prior to foreclosure. No offset or claim which Borrower might have now or in the future against Lender shall relieve Borrower from making payments due under the Note and this Security Instrument or performing the covenants and agreements secured by this Security Instrument.

2. Application of Payments or Proceeds. Except as otherwise described in this Section 2, all payments accepted and applied by Lender shall be applied in the following order of priority: (a) interest due under the Note; (b) principal due under the Note; (c) amounts due under Section 3. Such payments shall be applied to each Periodic Payment in the order in which it became due. Any remaining amounts shall be applied first to late charges, second to any other amounts due under this Security Instrument, and then to reduce the principal balance of the Note.

If Lender receives a payment from Borrower for a delinquent Periodic Payment which includes a sufficient amount to pay any late charge due, the payment may be applied to the delinquent payment and the late charge. If more than one Periodic Payment is outstanding, Lender may apply any payment received from Borrower to the repayment of the Periodic Payments if, and to the extent that, each payment can be paid in full. To the extent that any excess exists after the payment is applied to the full payment of one or more Periodic Payments, such excess may be applied to any late charges due. Voluntary prepayments shall be applied first to any prepayment charges and then as described in the Note.

Any application of payments, insurance proceeds, or Miscellaneous Proceeds to principal due under the Note shall not extend or postpone the due date, or change the amount, of the Periodic Payments.

3. Funds for Escrow Items. Borrower shall pay to Lender on the day Periodic Payments are due under the Note, until the Note is paid in full, a sum (the "Funds") to provide for payment of amounts due for: (a) taxes and assessments and other items which can attain priority over this Security Instrument as a lien or encumbrance on the Property; (b) leasehold payments or ground rents on the Property, if any; (c) premiums for any and all insurance required by Lender under Section 5; and (d) Mortgage Insurance premiums, if any, or any sums payable by Borrower to Lender in lieu of the payment of Mortgage Insurance premiums in accordance with the provisions of Section 10. These items are called "Escrow Items." At origination or at any time during the term of the Loan, Lender may require that Community Association Dues, Fees, and Assessments, if any, be escrowed by Borrower, and such dues, fees and assessments shall be an Escrow Item. Borrower shall promptly furnish to Lender all notices of amounts to be paid under this Section. Borrower shall pay Lender the Funds for Escrow Items unless Lender waives Borrower's obligation to pay the Funds for any or all Escrow Items. Lender may waive Borrower's obligation to pay to Lender Funds for any or all Escrow Items at any time. Any such waiver may only be in writing. In the event of such waiver, Borrower shall pay directly, when and where payable, the amounts due for any Escrow Items for which payment of Funds has been waived by Lender and, if Lender requires, shall furnish to Lender receipts evidencing such payment within such time period as Lender may require. Borrower's obligation to make such payments and to provide receipts shall for all purposes be deemed to be a covenant and agreement contained in this Security Instrument, as the phrase "covenant and agreement" is used in Section 9. If Borrower is obligated to pay Escrow Items directly, pursuant to a waiver, and Borrower fails to pay the amount due for an Escrow Item, Lender may exercise its rights under Section 9 and pay such amount and Borrower shall then be obligated under Section 9 to repay to Lender any such amount. Lender may revoke the waiver as to any or all Escrow Items at any time by a notice given in accordance with Section 15 and, upon such revocation, Borrower shall pay to Lender all Funds, and in such amounts, that are then required under this Section 3.

Lender may, at any time, collect and hold Funds in an amount (a) sufficient to permit Lender to apply the Funds at the time specified under RESPA, and (b) not to exceed the maximum amount a lender can require under RESPA. Lender shall estimate the amount of Funds due on the basis of current data and reasonable estimates of expenditures of future Escrow Items or otherwise in accordance with Applicable Law.

The Funds shall be held in an institution whose deposits are insured by a federal agency, instrumentality, or entity (including Lender, if Lender is an institution whose deposits are so insured) or in any Federal Home Loan Bank. Lender shall apply the Funds to pay the Escrow Items no later than the time specified under RESPA. Lender

CALIFORNIA--Single Family--Fannie Mae/Freddie Mac UNIFORM INSTRUMENT - MERS
Form 3005 01/01 Page 4 of 14

shall not charge Borrower for holding and applying the Funds, annually analyzing the escrow account, or verifying the Escrow Items, unless Lender pays Borrower interest on the Funds and Applicable Law permits Lender to make such a charge. Unless an agreement is made in writing or Applicable Law requires interest to be paid on the Funds, Lender shall not be required to pay Borrower any interest or earnings on the Funds. Borrower and Lender can agree in writing, however, that interest shall be paid on the Funds. Lender shall give to Borrower, without charge, an annual accounting of the Funds as required by RESPA.

If there is a surplus of Funds held in escrow, as defined under RESPA, Lender shall account to Borrower for the excess funds in accordance with RESPA. If there is a shortage of Funds held in escrow, as defined under RESPA, Lender shall notify Borrower as required by RESPA, and Borrower shall pay to Lender the amount necessary to make up the shortage in accordance with RESPA, but in no more than 12 monthly payments. If there is a deficiency of Funds held in escrow, as defined under RESPA, Lender shall notify Borrower as required by RESPA, and Borrower shall pay to Lender the amount necessary to make up the deficiency in accordance with RESPA, but in no more than 12 monthly payments.

Upon payment in full of all sums secured by this Security Instrument, Lender shall promptly refund to Borrower any Funds held by Lender.

4. Charges; Liens. Borrower shall pay all taxes, assessments, charges, fines, and impositions attributable to the Property which can attain priority over this Security Instrument, leasehold payments or ground rents on the Property, if any, and Community Association Dues, Fees, and Assessments, if any. To the extent that these items are Escrow Items, Borrower shall pay them in the manner provided in Section 3.

Borrower shall promptly discharge any lien which has priority over this Security Instrument unless Borrower: (a) agrees in writing to the payment of the obligation secured by the lien in a manner acceptable to Lender, but only so long as Borrower is performing such agreement; (b) contests the lien in good faith by, or defends against enforcement of the lien in, legal proceedings which in Lender's opinion operate to prevent the enforcement of the lien while those proceedings are pending, but only until such proceedings are concluded; or (c) secures from the holder of the lien an agreement satisfactory to Lender subordinating the lien to this Security Instrument. If Lender determines that any part of the Property is subject to a lien which can attain priority over this Security Instrument, Lender may give Borrower a notice identifying the lien. Within 10 days of the date on which that notice is given, Borrower shall satisfy the lien or take one or more of the actions set forth above in this Section 4.

Lender may require Borrower to pay a one-time charge for a real estate tax verification and/or reporting service used by Lender in connection with this Loan.

5. Property Insurance. Borrower shall keep the improvements now existing or hereafter erected on the Property insured against loss by fire, hazards included within the term "extended coverage," and any other hazards including, but not limited to, earthquakes and floods, for which Lender requires insurance. This insurance shall be maintained in the amounts (including deductible levels) and for the periods that Lender requires. What Lender requires pursuant to the preceding sentences can change during the term of the Loan. The insurance carrier providing the insurance shall be chosen by Borrower subject to Lender's right to disapprove Borrower's choice, which right shall not be exercised unreasonably. Lender may require Borrower to pay, in connection with this Loan, either: (a) a one-time charge for flood zone determination, certification and tracking services; or (b) a one-time charge for flood zone determination and certification services and subsequent charges each time remappings or similar changes occur which reasonably might affect such determination or certification. Borrower shall also be responsible for the payment of any fees imposed by the Federal Emergency Management Agency in connection with the review of any flood zone determination resulting from an objection by Borrower.

If Borrower fails to maintain any of the coverages described above, Lender may obtain insurance coverage, at Lender's option and Borrower's expense. Lender is under no obligation to purchase any particular type or amount of coverage. Therefore, such coverage shall cover Lender, but might or might not protect Borrower, Borrower's equity in the Property, or the contents of the Property, against any risk, hazard or liability and might provide greater or lesser coverage than was previously in effect. Borrower acknowledges that the cost of the insurance coverage so obtained might significantly exceed the cost of insurance that Borrower could have obtained. Any amounts disbursed by Lender under this Section 5 shall become additional debt of Borrower secured by this Security Instrument. These amounts shall bear interest at the Note rate from the date of disbursement and shall be payable, with such interest, upon notice from Lender to Borrower requesting payment.

CALIFORNIA--Single Family--Fannie Mae/Freddie Mac UNIFORM INSTRUMENT - MERS
Form 3005 01/01 Page 5 of 14

All insurance policies required by Lender and renewals of such policies shall be subject to Lender' s right to disapprove such policies, shall include a standard mortgage clause, and shall name Lender as mortgagee and/or as an additional loss payee and Borrower further agrees to generally assign rights to insurance proceeds to the holder of the Note up to the amount of the outstanding loan balance. Lender shall have the right to hold the policies and renewal certificates. If Lender requires, Borrower shall promptly give to Lender all receipts of paid premiums and renewal notices. If Borrower obtains any form of insurance coverage, not otherwise required by Lender, for damage to, or destruction of, the Property, such policy shall include a standard mortgage clause and shall name Lender as mortgagee and/or as an additional loss payee and Borrower further agrees to generally assign rights to insurance proceeds to the holder of the Note up to the amount of the outstanding loan balance.

In the event of loss, Borrower shall give prompt notice to the insurance carrier and Lender. Lender may make proof of loss if not made promptly by Borrower. Unless Lender and Borrower otherwise agree in writing, any insurance proceeds, whether or not the underlying insurance was required by Lender, shall be applied to restoration or repair of the Property, if the restoration or repair is economically feasible and Lender's security is not lessened. During such repair and restoration period, Lender shall have the right to hold such insurance proceeds until Lender has had an opportunity to inspect such Property to ensure the work has been completed to Lender's satisfaction, provided that such inspection shall be undertaken promptly. Lender may disburse proceeds for the repairs and restoration in a single payment or in a series of progress payments as the work is completed. Unless an agreement is made in writing or Applicable Law requires interest to be paid on such insurance proceeds, Lender shall not be required to pay Borrower any interest or earnings on such proceeds. Fees for public adjusters, or other third parties, retained by Borrower shall not be paid out of the insurance proceeds and shall be the sole obligation of Borrower. If the restoration or repair is not economically feasible or Lender's security would be lessened, the insurance proceeds shall be applied to the sums secured by this Security Instrument, whether or not then due, with the excess, if any, paid to Borrower. Such insurance proceeds shall be applied in the order provided for in Section 2.

If Borrower abandons the Property, Lender may file, negotiate and settle any available insurance claim and related matters. If Borrower does not respond within 30 days to a notice from Lender that the insurance carrier has offered to settle a claim, then Lender may negotiate and settle the claim. The 30-day period will begin when the notice is given. In either event, or if Lender acquires the Property under Section 22 or otherwise, Borrower hereby assigns to Lender (a) Borrower's rights to any insurance proceeds in an amount not to exceed the amounts unpaid under the Note or this Security Instrument, and (b) any other of Borrower's rights (other than the right to any refund of unearned premiums paid by Borrower) under all insurance policies covering the Property, insofar as such rights are applicable to the coverage of the Property. Lender may use the insurance proceeds either to repair or restore the Property or to pay amounts unpaid under the Note or this Security Instrument, whether or not then due.

6. Occupancy. Borrower shall occupy, establish, and use the Property as Borrower's principal residence within 60 days after the execution of this Security Instrument and shall continue to occupy the Property as Borrower's principal residence for at least one year after the date of occupancy, unless Lender otherwise agrees in writing, which consent shall not be unreasonably withheld, or unless extenuating circumstances exist which are beyond Borrower's control.

7. Preservation, Maintenance and Protection of the Property; Inspections. Borrower shall not destroy, damage or impair the Property, allow the Property to deteriorate or commit waste on the Property. Whether or not Borrower is residing in the Property, Borrower shall maintain the Property in order to prevent the Property from deteriorating or decreasing in value due to its condition. Unless it is determined pursuant to Section 5 that repair or restoration is not economically feasible, Borrower shall promptly repair the Property if damaged to avoid further deterioration or damage. If insurance or condemnation proceeds are paid in connection with damage to, or the taking of, the Property, Borrower shall be responsible for repairing or restoring the Property only if Lender has released proceeds for such purposes. Lender may disburse proceeds for the repairs and restoration in a single payment or in a series of progress payments as the work is completed. If the insurance or condemnation proceeds are not sufficient to repair or restore the Property, Borrower is not relieved of Borrower's obligation for the completion of such repair or restoration.

Lender or its agent may make reasonable entries upon and inspections of the Property. If it has reasonable cause, Lender may inspect the interior of the improvements on the Property. Lender shall give Borrower notice at the time of or prior to such an interior inspection specifying such reasonable cause.

CALIFORNIA--Single Family--Fannie Mae/Freddie Mac UNIFORM INSTRUMENT - MERS
Form 3005 01/01 Page 6 of 14

8. Borrower's Loan Application. Borrower shall be in default if, during the Loan application process, Borrower or any persons or entities acting at the direction of Borrower or with Borrower's knowledge or consent gave materially false, misleading, or inaccurate information or statements to Lender (or failed to provide Lender with material information) in connection with the Loan. Material representations include, but are not limited to, representations concerning Borrower's occupancy of the Property as Borrower's principal residence.

9. Protection of Lender's Interest in the Property and Rights Under this Security Instrument. If (a) Borrower fails to perform the covenants and agreements contained in this Security Instrument, (b) there is a legal proceeding that might significantly affect Lender's interest in the Property and/or rights under this Security Instrument (such as a proceeding in bankruptcy, probate, for condemnation or forfeiture, for enforcement of a lien which may attain priority over this Security Instrument or to enforce laws or regulations), or (c) Borrower has abandoned the Property, then Lender may do and pay for whatever is reasonable or appropriate to protect Lender's interest in the Property and rights under this Security Instrument, including protecting and/or assessing the value of the Property, and securing and/or repairing the Property. Lender's actions can include, but are not limited to: (a) paying any sums secured by a lien which has priority over this Security Instrument; (b) appearing in court; and (c) paying reasonable attorneys' fees to protect its interest in the Property and/or rights under this Security Instrument, including its secured position in a bankruptcy proceeding. Securing the Property includes, but is not limited to, entering the Property to make repairs, change locks, replace or board up doors and windows, drain water from pipes, eliminate building or other code violations or dangerous conditions, and have utilities turned on or off. Although Lender may take action under this Section 9, Lender does not have to do so and is not under any duty or obligation to do so. It is agreed that Lender incurs no liability for not taking any or all actions authorized under this Section 9.

Any amounts disbursed by Lender under this Section 9 shall become additional debt of Borrower secured by this Security Instrument. These amounts shall bear interest at the Note rate from the date of disbursement and shall be payable, with such interest, upon notice from Lender to Borrower requesting payment.

If this Security Instrument is on a leasehold, Borrower shall comply with all the provisions of the lease. Borrower shall not surrender the leasehold estate and interests herein conveyed or terminate or cancel the ground lease. Borrower shall not, without the express written consent of Lender, alter or amend the ground lease. If Borrower acquires fee title to the Property, the leasehold and the fee title shall not merge unless Lender agrees to the merger in writing.

10. Mortgage Insurance. If Lender required Mortgage Insurance as a condition of making the Loan, Borrower shall pay the premiums required to maintain the Mortgage Insurance in effect. If, for any reason, the Mortgage Insurance coverage required by Lender ceases to be available from the mortgage insurer that previously provided such insurance and Borrower was required to make separately designated payments toward the premiums for Mortgage Insurance, Borrower shall pay the premiums required to obtain coverage substantially equivalent to the Mortgage Insurance previously in effect, at a cost substantially equivalent to the cost to Borrower of the Mortgage Insurance previously in effect, from an alternate mortgage insurer selected by Lender. If substantially equivalent Mortgage Insurance coverage is not available, Borrower shall continue to pay to Lender the amount of the separately designated payments that were due when the insurance coverage ceased to be in effect. Lender will accept, use and retain these payments as a non-refundable loss reserve in lieu of Mortgage Insurance. Such loss reserve shall be non-refundable, notwithstanding the fact that the Loan is ultimately paid in full, and Lender shall not be required to pay Borrower any interest or earnings on such loss reserve. Lender can no longer require loss reserve payments if Mortgage Insurance coverage (in the amount and for the period that Lender requires) provided by an insurer selected by Lender again becomes available, is obtained, and Lender requires separately designated payments toward the premiums for Mortgage Insurance. If Lender required Mortgage Insurance as a condition of making the Loan and Borrower was required to make separately designated payments toward the premiums for Mortgage Insurance, Borrower shall pay the premiums required to maintain Mortgage Insurance in effect, or to provide a non-refundable loss reserve, until Lender's requirement for Mortgage Insurance ends in accordance with any written agreement between Borrower and Lender providing for such termination or until termination is required by Applicable Law. Nothing in this Section 10 affects Borrower's obligation to pay interest at the rate provided in the Note.

Mortgage Insurance reimburses Lender (or any entity that purchases the Note) for certain losses it may incur if Borrower does not repay the Loan as agreed. Borrower is not a party to the Mortgage Insurance.

CALIFORNIA--Single Family--Fannie Mae/Freddie Mac UNIFORM INSTRUMENT - MERS
Form 3005 01/01 Page 7 of 14

Mortgage insurers evaluate their total risk on all such insurance in force from time to time, and may enter into agreements with other parties that share or modify their risk, or reduce losses. These agreements are on terms and conditions that are satisfactory to the mortgage insurer and the other party (or parties) to these agreements. These agreements may require the mortgage insurer to make payments using any source of funds that the mortgage insurer may have available (which may include funds obtained from Mortgage Insurance premiums).

As a result of these agreements, Lender, any purchaser of the Note, another insurer, any reinsurer, any other entity, or any affiliate of any of the foregoing, may receive (directly or indirectly) amounts that derive from (or might be characterized as) a portion of Borrower's payments for Mortgage Insurance, in exchange for sharing or modifying the mortgage insurer's risk, or reducing losses. If such agreement provides that an affiliate of Lender takes a share of the insurer's risk in exchange for a share of the premiums paid to the insurer, the arrangement is often termed "captive reinsurance." Further:

(a) Any such agreements will not affect the amounts that Borrower has agreed to pay for Mortgage Insurance, or any other terms of the Loan. Such agreements will not increase the amount Borrower will owe for Mortgage Insurance, and they will not entitle Borrower to any refund.

(b) Any such agreements will not affect the rights Borrower has - if any - with respect to the Mortgage Insurance under the Homeowners Protection Act of 1998 or any other law. These rights may include the right to receive certain disclosures, to request and obtain cancellation of the Mortgage Insurance, to have the Mortgage Insurance terminated automatically, and/or to receive a refund of any Mortgage Insurance premiums that were unearned at the time of such cancellation or termination.

11. Assignment of Miscellaneous Proceeds; Forfeiture. All Miscellaneous Proceeds are hereby assigned to and shall be paid to Lender.

If the Property is damaged, such Miscellaneous Proceeds shall be applied to restoration or repair of the Property, if the restoration or repair is economically feasible and Lender's security is not lessened. During such repair and restoration period, Lender shall have the right to hold such Miscellaneous Proceeds until Lender has had an opportunity to inspect such Property to ensure the work has been completed to Lender's satisfaction, provided that such inspection shall be undertaken promptly. Lender may pay for the repairs and restoration in a single disbursement or in a series of progress payments as the work is completed. Unless an agreement is made in writing or Applicable Law requires interest to be paid on such Miscellaneous Proceeds, Lender shall not be required to pay Borrower any interest or earnings on such Miscellaneous Proceeds. If the restoration or repair is not economically feasible or Lender's security would be lessened, the Miscellaneous Proceeds shall be applied to the sums secured by this Security Instrument, whether or not then due, with the excess, if any, paid to Borrower. Such Miscellaneous Proceeds shall be applied in the order provided for in Section 2.

In the event of a total taking, destruction, or loss in value of the Property, the Miscellaneous Proceeds shall be applied to the sums secured by this Security Instrument, whether or not then due, with the excess, if any, paid to Borrower.

In the event of a partial taking, destruction, or loss in value of the Property in which the fair market value of the Property immediately before the partial taking, destruction, or loss in value is equal to or greater than the amount of the sums secured by this Security Instrument immediately before the partial taking, destruction, or loss in value, unless Borrower and Lender otherwise agree in writing, the sums secured by this Security Instrument shall be reduced by the amount of the Miscellaneous Proceeds multiplied by the following fraction: (a) the total amount of the sums secured immediately before the partial taking, destruction, or loss in value divided by (b) the fair market value of the Property immediately before the partial taking, destruction, or loss in value. Any balance shall be paid to Borrower.

In the event of a partial taking, destruction, or loss in value of the Property in which the fair market value of the Property immediately before the partial taking, destruction, or loss in value is less than the amount of the sums secured immediately before the partial taking, destruction, or loss in value, unless Borrower and Lender otherwise agree in writing, the Miscellaneous Proceeds shall be applied to the sums secured by this Security Instrument whether or not the sums are then due.

If the Property is abandoned by Borrower, or if, after notice by Lender to Borrower that the Opposing Party (as defined in the next sentence) offers to make an award to settle a claim for damages, Borrower fails to respond to Lender within 30 days after the date the notice is given, Lender is authorized to collect and apply the Miscellaneous Proceeds either to restoration or repair of the Property or to the sums secured by this Security Instrument, whether or not then due. "Opposing Party" means the third party that owes Borrower Miscellaneous Proceeds or the party against whom Borrower has a right of action in regard to Miscellaneous Proceeds.

Borrower shall be in default if any action or proceeding, whether civil or criminal, is begun that, in Lender's judgment, could result in forfeiture of the Property or other material impairment of Lender's interest in the Property or rights under this Security Instrument. Borrower can cure such a default and, if acceleration has occurred, reinstate as provided in Section 19, by causing the action or proceeding to be dismissed with a ruling that, in Lender's judgment, precludes forfeiture of the Property or other material impairment of Lender's interest in the Property or rights under this Security Instrument. The proceeds of any award or claim for damages that are attributable to the impairment of Lender's interest in the Property are hereby assigned and shall be paid to Lender.

All Miscellaneous Proceeds that are not applied to restoration or repair of the Property shall be applied in the order provided for in Section 2.

12. Borrower Not Released; Forbearance By Lender Not a Waiver. Extension of the time for payment or modification of amortization of the sums secured by this Security Instrument granted by Lender to Borrower or any Successor in Interest of Borrower shall not operate to release the liability of Borrower or any Successors in Interest of Borrower. Lender shall not be required to commence proceedings against any Successor in Interest of Borrower or to refuse to extend time for payment or otherwise modify amortization of the sums secured by this Security Instrument by reason of any demand made by the original Borrower or any Successors in Interest of Borrower. Any forbearance by Lender in exercising any right or remedy including, without limitation, Lender's acceptance of payments from third persons, entities or Successors in Interest of Borrower or in amounts less than the amount then due, shall not be a waiver of or preclude the exercise of any right or remedy.

13. Joint and Several Liability; Co-signers; Successors and Assigns Bound. Borrower covenants and agrees that Borrower's obligations and liability shall be joint and several. However, any Borrower who co-signs this Security Instrument but does not execute the Note (a "co-signer"): (a) is co-signing this Security Instrument only to mortgage, grant and convey the co-signer's interest in the Property under the terms of this Security Instrument; (b) is not personally obligated to pay the sums secured by this Security Instrument; and (c) agrees that Lender and any other Borrower can agree to extend, modify, forbear or make any accommodations with regard to the terms of this Security Instrument or the Note without the co-signer's consent.

Subject to the provisions of Section 18, any Successor in Interest of Borrower who assumes Borrower's obligations under this Security Instrument in writing, and is approved by Lender, shall obtain all of Borrower's rights and benefits under this Security Instrument. Borrower shall not be released from Borrower's obligations and liability under this Security Instrument unless Lender agrees to such release in writing. The covenants and agreements of this Security Instrument shall bind (except as provided in Section 20) and benefit the successors and assigns of Lender.

14. Loan Charges. Lender may charge Borrower fees for services performed in connection with Borrower's default, for the purpose of protecting Lender's interest in the Property and rights under this Security Instrument, including, but not limited to, attorneys' fees, property inspection and valuation fees. In regard to any other fees, the absence of express authority in this Security Instrument to charge a specific fee to Borrower shall not be construed as a prohibition on the charging of such fee. Lender may not charge fees that are expressly prohibited by this Security Instrument or by Applicable Law.

If the Loan is subject to a law which sets maximum loan charges, and that law is finally interpreted so that the interest or other loan charges collected or to be collected in connection with the Loan exceed the permitted limits, then: (a) any such loan charge shall be reduced by the amount necessary to reduce the charge to the permitted limit; and (b) any sums already collected from Borrower which exceeded permitted limits will be refunded to Borrower. Lender may choose to make this refund by reducing the principal owed under the Note or by making a direct payment to Borrower. If a refund reduces principal, the reduction will be treated as a partial prepayment without any prepayment charge (whether or not a prepayment charge is provided for under the Note). Borrower's acceptance of any such refund made by direct payment to Borrower will constitute a waiver of any right of action Borrower might have arising out of such overcharge.

15. Notices. All notices given by Borrower or Lender in connection with this Security Instrument must be in writing. Any notice to Borrower in connection with this Security Instrument shall be deemed to have been given to Borrower when mailed by first class mail or when actually delivered to Borrower's notice address if sent by other means. Notice to any one Borrower shall constitute notice to all Borrowers unless Applicable Law expressly requires

CALIFORNIA--Single Family--Fannie Mae/Freddie Mac UNIFORM INSTRUMENT - MERS
Form 3005 01/01 Page 9 of 14

otherwise. The notice address shall be the Property Address unless Borrower has designated a substitute notice address by notice to Lender. Borrower shall promptly notify Lender of Borrower's change of address. If Lender specifies a procedure for reporting Borrower's change of address, then Borrower shall only report a change of address through that specified procedure. There may be only one designated notice address under this Security Instrument at any one time. Any notice to Lender shall be given by delivering it or by mailing it by first class mail to Lender's address stated herein unless Lender has designated another address by notice to Borrower. Any notice in connection with this Security Instrument shall not be deemed to have been given to Lender until actually received by Lender. If any notice required by this Security Instrument is also required under Applicable Law, the Applicable Law requirement will satisfy the corresponding requirement under this Security Instrument.

16. Governing Law; Severability; Rules of Construction. This Security Instrument shall be governed by federal law and the law of the jurisdiction in which the Property is located. All rights and obligations contained in this Security Instrument are subject to any requirements and limitations of Applicable Law. Applicable Law might explicitly or implicitly allow the parties to agree by contract ~~or it~~ might be silent, but such silence shall not be construed as a prohibition against agreement by contract. In the event that any provision or clause of this Security Instrument or the Note conflicts with Applicable Law, such conflict shall not affect other provisions of this Security Instrument or the Note which can be given effect without the conflicting provision.

As used in this Security Instrument: (a) words of the masculine gender shall mean and include corresponding neuter words or words of the feminine gender; (b) words in the singular shall mean and include the plural and vice versa; and (c) the word "may" gives sole discretion without any obligation to take any action.

17. Borrower's Copy. Borrower shall be given one copy of the Note and of this Security Instrument.

18. Transfer of the Property or a Beneficial Interest in Borrower. As used in this Section 18, "Interest in the Property" means any legal or beneficial interest in the Property, including, but not limited to, those beneficial interests transferred in a bond for deed, contract for deed, installment sales contract or escrow agreement, the intent of which is the transfer of title by Borrower at a future date to a purchaser.

If all or any part of the Property or any Interest in the Property is sold or transferred (or if Borrower is not a natural person and a beneficial interest in Borrower is sold or transferred) without Lender's prior written consent, Lender may require immediate payment in full of all sums secured by this Security Instrument. However, this option shall not be exercised by Lender if such exercise is prohibited by Applicable Law.

If Lender exercises this option, Lender shall give Borrower notice of acceleration. The notice shall provide a period of not less than 30 days from the date the notice is given in accordance with Section 15 within which Borrower must pay all sums secured by this Security Instrument. If Borrower fails to pay these sums prior to the expiration of this period, Lender may invoke any remedies permitted by this Security Instrument without further notice or demand on Borrower.

19. Borrower's Right to Reinstate After Acceleration. If Borrower meets certain conditions, Borrower shall have the right to have enforcement of this Security Instrument discontinued at any time prior to the earliest of: (a) five days before sale of the Property pursuant to any power of sale contained in this Security Instrument; (b) such other period as Applicable Law might specify for the termination of Borrower's right to reinstate; or (c) entry of a judgment enforcing this Security Instrument. Those conditions are that Borrower: (a) pays Lender all sums which then would be due under this Security Instrument and the Note as if no acceleration had occurred; (b) cures any default of any other covenants or agreements; (c) pays all expenses incurred in enforcing this Security Instrument, including, but not limited to, reasonable attorneys' fees, property inspection and valuation fees, and other fees incurred for the purpose of protecting Lender's interest in the Property and rights under this Security Instrument; and (d) takes such action as Lender may reasonably require to assure that Lender's interest in the Property and rights under this Security Instrument, and Borrower's obligation to pay the sums secured by this Security Instrument, shall continue unchanged. Lender may require that Borrower pay such reinstatement sums and expenses in one or more of the following forms, as selected by Lender: (a) cash; (b) money order; (c) certified check, bank check, treasurer's check or cashier's check, provided any such check is drawn upon an institution whose deposits are insured by a federal agency, instrumentality or entity; or (d) Electronic Funds Transfer. Upon reinstatement by Borrower, this Security Instrument and obligations secured hereby shall remain fully effective as if no acceleration had occurred. However, this right to reinstate shall not apply in the case of acceleration under Section 18.

CALIFORNIA--Single Family--Fannie Mae/Freddie Mac UNIFORM INSTRUMENT - MERS
Form 3005 01/01 Page 10 of 14

20. Sale of Note; Change of Loan Servicer; Notice of Grievance. The Note or a partial interest in the Note (together with this Security Instrument) can be sold one or more times without prior notice to Borrower. A sale might result in a change in the entity (known as the "Loan Servicer") that collects Periodic Payments due under the Note and this Security Instrument and performs other mortgage loan servicing obligations under the Note, this Security Instrument, and Applicable Law. There also might be one or more changes of the Loan Servicer unrelated to a sale of the Note. If there is a change of the Loan Servicer, Borrower will be given written notice of the change which will state the name and address of the new Loan Servicer, the address to which payments should be made and any other information RESPA requires in connection with a notice of transfer of servicing. If the Note is sold and thereafter the Loan is serviced by a Loan Servicer other than the purchaser of the Note, the mortgage loan servicing obligations to Borrower will remain with the Loan Servicer or be transferred to a successor Loan Servicer and are not assumed by the Note purchaser unless otherwise provided by the Note purchaser.

Neither Borrower nor Lender may commence, join, or be joined to any judicial action (as either an individual litigant or the member of a class) that arises from the other party's actions pursuant to this Security Instrument or that alleges that the other party has breached any provision of, or any duty owed by reason of, this Security Instrument, until such Borrower or Lender has notified the other party (with such notice given in compliance with the requirements of Section 15) of such alleged breach and afforded the other party hereto a reasonable period after the giving of such notice to take corrective action. If Applicable Law provides a time period which must elapse before certain action can be taken, that time period will be deemed to be reasonable for purposes of this paragraph. The notice of acceleration and opportunity to cure given to Borrower pursuant to Section 22 and the notice of acceleration given to Borrower pursuant to Section 18 shall be deemed to satisfy the notice and opportunity to take corrective action provisions of this Section 20.

21. Hazardous Substances. As used in this Section 21: (a) "Hazardous Substances" are those substances defined as toxic or hazardous substances, pollutants, or wastes by Environmental Law and the following substances: gasoline, kerosene, other flammable or toxic petroleum products, toxic pesticides and herbicides, volatile solvents, materials containing asbestos or formaldehyde, and radioactive materials; (b) "Environmental Law" means federal laws and laws of the jurisdiction where the Property is located that relate to health, safety or environmental protection; (c) "Environmental Cleanup" includes any response action, remedial action, or removal action, as defined in Environmental Law; and (d) an "Environmental Condition" means a condition that can cause, contribute to, or otherwise trigger an Environmental Cleanup.

Borrower shall not cause or permit the presence, use, disposal, storage, or release of any Hazardous Substances, or threaten to release any Hazardous Substances, on or in the Property. Borrower shall not do, nor allow anyone else to do, anything affecting the Property (a) that is in violation of any Environmental Law, (b) which creates an Environmental Condition, or (c) which, due to the presence, use, or release of a Hazardous Substance, creates a condition that adversely affects the value of the Property. The preceding two sentences shall not apply to the presence, use, or storage on the Property of small quantities of Hazardous Substances that are generally recognized to be appropriate to normal residential uses and to maintenance of the Property (including, but not limited to, hazardous substances in consumer products).

Borrower shall promptly give Lender written notice of (a) any investigation, claim, demand, lawsuit or other action by any governmental or regulatory agency or private party involving the Property and any Hazardous Substance or Environmental Law of which Borrower has actual knowledge, (b) any Environmental Condition, including but not limited to, any spilling, leaking, discharge, release or threat of release of any Hazardous Substance, and (c) any condition caused by the presence, use or release of a Hazardous Substance which adversely affects the value of the Property. If Borrower learns, or is notified by any governmental or regulatory authority, or any private party, that any removal or other remediation of any Hazardous Substance affecting the Property is necessary, Borrower shall promptly take all necessary remedial actions in accordance with Environmental Law. Nothing herein shall create any obligation on Lender for an Environmental Cleanup.

NON-UNIFORM COVENANTS. Borrower and Lender further covenant and agree as follows:

22. Acceleration; Remedies. Lender shall give notice to Borrower prior to acceleration following Borrower's breach of any covenant or agreement in this Security Instrument (but not prior to acceleration under Section 18 unless Applicable Law provides otherwise). The notice shall specify: (a) the default; (b) the action

CALIFORNIA--Single Family--Fannie Mae/Freddie Mac UNIFORM INSTRUMENT - MERS
Form 3005 01/01 Page 11 of 14

required to cure the default; (c) a date, not less than 30 days from the date the notice is given to Borrower, by which the default must be cured; and (d) that failure to cure the default on or before the date specified in the notice may result in acceleration of the sums secured by this Security Instrument and sale of the Property. The notice shall further inform Borrower of the right to reinstate after acceleration and the right to bring a court action to assert the non-existence of a default or any other defense of Borrower to acceleration and sale. If the default is not cured on or before the date specified in the notice, Lender at its option may require immediate payment in full of all sums secured by this Security Instrument without further demand and may invoke the power of sale and any other remedies permitted by Applicable Law. Lender shall be entitled to collect all expenses incurred in pursuing the remedies provided in this Section 22, including, but not limited to, reasonable attorneys' fees and costs of title evidence.

If Lender invokes the power of sale, Lender shall execute or cause Trustee to execute a written notice of the occurrence of an event of default and of Lender's election to cause the Property to be sold. Trustee shall cause this notice to be recorded in each county in which any part of the Property is located. Lender or Trustee shall mail copies of the notice as prescribed by Applicable Law to Borrower and to the other persons prescribed by Applicable Law. Trustee shall give public notice of sale to the persons and in the manner prescribed by Applicable Law. After the time required by Applicable Law, Trustee, without demand on Borrower, shall sell the Property at public auction to the highest bidder at the time and place and under the terms designated in the notice of sale in one or more parcels and in any order Trustee determines. Trustee may postpone sale of all or any parcel of the Property by public announcement at the time and place of any previously scheduled sale. Lender or its designee may purchase the Property at any sale.

Trustee shall deliver to the purchaser Trustee's deed conveying the Property without any covenant or warranty, expressed or implied. The recitals in the Trustee's deed shall be prima facie evidence of the truth of the statements made therein. Trustee shall apply the proceeds of the sale in the following order: (a) to all expenses of the sale, including, but not limited to, reasonable Trustee's and attorneys' fees; (b) to all sums secured by this Security Instrument; and (c) any excess to the person or persons legally entitled to it.

23. Reconveyance. Upon payment of all sums secured by this Security Instrument, Lender shall request Trustee to reconvey the Property and shall surrender this Security Instrument and all notes evidencing debt secured by this Security Instrument to Trustee. Trustee shall reconvey the Property without warranty to the person or persons legally entitled to it. Lender may charge such person or persons a reasonable fee for reconveying the Property, but only if the fee is paid to a third party (such as the Trustee) for services rendered and the charging of the fee is permitted under Applicable Law. If the fee charged does not exceed the fee set by Applicable Law, the fee is conclusively presumed to be reasonable.

24. Substitute Trustee. Lender, at its option, may from time to time appoint a successor trustee to any Trustee appointed hereunder by an instrument executed and acknowledged by Lender and recorded in the office of the Recorder of the county in which the Property is located. The instrument shall contain the name of the original Lender, Trustee and Borrower, the book and page where this Security Instrument is recorded and the name and address of the successor trustee. Without conveyance of the Property, the successor trustee shall succeed to all the title, powers and duties conferred upon the Trustee herein and by Applicable Law. This procedure for substitution of trustee shall govern to the exclusion of all other provisions for substitution.

25. Statement of Obligation Fee. Lender may collect a fee not to exceed the maximum amount permitted by Applicable Law for furnishing the statement of obligation as provided by Section 2943 of the Civil Code of California.

BY SIGNING BELOW, Borrower accepts and agrees to the terms and covenants contained in this Security Instrument and in any Rider executed by Borrower and recorded with it.

The undersigned Borrower requests that a copy of any Notice of Default and any Notice of Sale under this Security Instrument be mailed to Borrower at the address set forth above.

____________________ (Seal)
RICHARD WILLIAM ROGERS -Borrower

____________________ (Seal)
-Borrower

____________________ (Seal)
-Borrower

____________________ (Seal)
-Borrower

____________________ (Seal)
-Borrower

____________________ (Seal)
-Borrower

Witness:

____

Witness:

____

CALIFORNIA--Single Family--Fannie Mae/Freddie Mac UNIFORM INSTRUMENT - MERS
Form 3005 01/01 Page 13 of 14

[Space Below This Line For Acknowledgment]

State of California)
) ss.
County of LOS ANGELES)

On ____________ before me, ____________

personally appeared RICHARD WILLIAM ROGERS

____

____________,

who proved to me on the basis of satisfactory evidence to be the person(s) whose name(s) is/are subscribed to the within instrument and acknowledged to me that he/she/they executed the same in his/her/th eir authorized capacity(ies), and that by his/her/their signature(s) on the instrument the person(s), or the entity upon behalf of which the person(s) acted, executed the instrument.

I certify under PENALTY OF PERJURY under the laws of the State of California that the foregoing paragraph is true and correct.

WITNESS my hand and official seal.

____
NOTARY SIGNATURE

____
(Typed Name of Notary)

NOTARY SEAL

CALIFORNIA--Single Family--Fannie Mae/Freddie Mac UNIFORM INSTRUMENT - MERS
Form 3005 01/01 Page 14 of 14

Loan Number: 200911000

CONDOMINIUM RIDER

THIS CONDOMINIUM RIDER is made this 12th day of FEBRUARY, 2010 , and is incorporated into and shall be deemed to amend and supplement the Mortgage, Deed of Trust, or Security Deed (the "Security Instrument") of the same date given by the undersigned (the "Borrower") to secure Borrower's Note to TRISTAR FINANCIAL CORP., A CALIFORNIA CORPORATION
(the "Lender") of the same date and covering the Property described in the Security Instrument and located at:

8624 OAKLAWN AVENUE, NO. 13 (CANOGA PARK AREA), LOS ANGELES, CALIFORNIA 91304
[Property Address]

The Property includes a unit in, together with an undivided interest in the common elements of, a condominium project known as:

OAK CREEK CONDOMINIUMS
[Name of Condominium Project]

(the "Condominium Project"). If the owners association or other entity which acts for the Condominium Project (the "Owners Association") holds title to property for the benefit or use of its members or shareholders, the Property also includes Borrower's interest in the Owners Association and the uses, proceeds and benefits of Borrower's interest.

CONDOMINIUM COVENANTS. In addition to the covenants and agreements made in the Security Instrument, Borrower and Lender further covenant and agree as follows:

A. Condominium Obligations. Borrower shall perform all of Borrower's obligations under the Condominium Project's Constituent Documents. The "Constituent Documents" are the: (i) Declaration or any other document which creates the Condominium Project; (ii) by-laws; (iii) code of regulations; and (iv) other equivalent documents. Borrower shall promptly pay, when due, all dues and assessments imposed pursuant to the Constituent Documents.

B. Property Insurance. So long as the Owners Association maintains, with a generally accepted insurance carrier, a "master" or "blanket" policy on the Condominium Project which is satisfactory to Lender and which provides insurance coverage in the amounts (including deductible levels), for the periods, and against loss by fire, hazards included within the term "extended coverage," and any other hazards, including, but not limited to, earthquakes and floods, from which Lender requires insurance, then: (i) Lender waives the provision in Section 3 for the Periodic Payment to Lender of the yearly premium installments for property insurance on the Property; and (ii) Borrower's obligation under Section 5 to maintain property insurance coverage on the Property is deemed satisfied to the extent that the required coverage is provided by the Owners Association policy.

What Lender requires as a condition of this waiver can change during the term of the loan.

MULTISTATE CONDOMINIUM RIDER
Single Family--Fannie Mae/Freddie Mac UNIFORM INSTRUMENT
Form 3140 1/01 Page 1 of 3

Borrower shall give Lender prompt notice of any lapse in required property insurance coverage provided by the master or blanket policy.

In the event of a distribution of property insurance proceeds in lieu of restoration or repair following a loss to the Property, whether to the unit or to common elements, any proceeds payable to Borrower are hereby assigned and shall be paid to Lender for application to the sums secured by the Security Instrument, whether or not then due, with the excess, if any, paid to Borrower.

C. Public Liability Insurance. Borrower shall take such actions as may be reasonable to insure that the Owners Association maintains a public liability insurance policy acceptable in form, amount, and extent of coverage to Lender.

D. Condemnation. The proceeds of any award or claim for damages, direct or consequential, payable to Borrower in connection with any condemnation or other taking of all or any part of the Property, whether of the unit or of the common elements, or for any conveyance in lieu of condemnation, are hereby assigned and shall be paid to Lender. Such proceeds shall be applied by Lender to the sums secured by the Security Instrument as provided in Section 11.

E. Lender's Prior Consent. Borrower shall not, except after notice to Lender and with Lender's prior written consent, either partition or subdivide the Property or consent to: (i) the abandonment or termination of the Condominium Project, except for abandonment or termination required by law in the case of substantial destruction by fire or other casualty or in the case of a taking by condemnation or eminent domain; (ii) any amendment to any provision of the Constituent Documents if the provision is for the express benefit of Lender; (iii) termination of professional management and assumption of self-management of the Owners Association; or (iv) any action which would have the effect of rendering the public liability insurance coverage maintained by the Owners Association unacceptable to Lender.

F. Remedies. If Borrower does not pay condominium dues and assessments when due, then Lender may pay them. Any amounts disbursed by Lender under this paragraph F shall become additional debt of Borrower secured by the Security Instrument. Unless Borrower and Lender agree to other terms of payment, these amounts shall bear interest from the date of disbursement at the Note rate and shall be payable, with interest, upon notice from Lender to Borrower requesting payment.

MULTISTATE CONDOMINIUM RIDER
Single Family--Fannie Mae/Freddie Mac UNIFORM INSTRUMENT
Form 3140 1/01 Page 2 of 3

BY SIGNING BELOW, Borrower accepts and agrees to the terms and covenants contained in this Condominium Rider.

_______________ (Seal)
RICHARD WILLIAM ROGERS -Borrower

_______________ (Seal)
-Borrower

_______________ (Seal)
-Borrower

_______________ (Seal)
-Borrower

_______________ (Seal)
-Borrower

_______________ (Seal)
-Borrower

MULTISTATE CONDOMINIUM RIDER
Single Family--Fannie Mae/Freddie Mac UNIFORM INSTRUMENT
Form 3140 1/01 Page 3 of 3

IMPOUND AUTHORIZATION

Loan Number: 200911000

Date: FEBRUARY 12, 2010

Borrower: RICHARD WILLIAM ROGERS

Property 8624 OAKLAWN AVENUE, NO. 13 (CANOGA PARK AREA), LOS ANGELES, CALIFORNIA 91304
(Address) (City) (State) (Zip)

We understood that according to the provisions of the Security Instrument, TRISTAR FINANCIAL CORP.

may require us to make monthly payments in addition to our principal and interest payment so that a fund can be created and maintained to pay taxes, insurance premiums and other expenses relating to the security property. Impounds will be required in the following circumstances:

- where required by state or federal regulatory authority; or
- where a loan is made, guaranteed or insured by a state or federal governmental lending agency; or
- where the original principal amount of such a loan exceeds 80% of the sales price or appraised value whichever is lower; or
- as required by lender as a condition of the loan.

The lender will pay interest on the impound account as required by law. The obligations of the borrower and lender regarding impound accounts will be set forth in the Security Instrument. We also understand that the payment for taxes and insurance may vary from year to year.

PLEASE NOTE THAT ANY BORROWER WHO IS DELINQUENT IN THE PAYMENT OF THEIR REAL ESTATE TAXES, HAZARD AND/OR FLOOD INSURANCE PREMIUMS, MAY BE REQUIRED BY THE LENDER TO PAY IMPOUNDS.

☐ Yes ☒ No **IMPOUNDS REQUIRED BY LENDER**

The undersigned understand that the establishment of an impound account for payments of real property taxes, hazard and/or flood insurance and other related expenses is REQUIRED.

☒ Yes ☐ No **IMPOUNDS REQUESTED BY BORROWER**

The undersigned understand that the establishment of an impound account for the payment of real property taxes, hazard and/or flood insurance and other related expenses is NOT REQUIRED; however, requests that such an account be established.

Client Name RICHARD WILLIAM ROGERS Date | Client Name Date

Client Name Date | Client Name Date

Client Name Date | Client Name Date

Loan Number: 2200911000

CA IMPOUND ACCOUNT STATEMENT AND ELECTION FORM

You have applied for a mortgage loan on the above property from TRISTAR FINANCIAL CORP. ("Lender"). Your loan documents contain provisions which require you to pay property taxes, insurance premiums and other charges relating to the property when they become due. Lender requires borrowers to establish an escrow or impound account, unless otherwise required by law, to ensure payment of these sums in connection with their loans. California law (Cal Civ Cod 2954) requires that you be informed of the following:

1. If you intend to occupy the property, and the original principal balance of the loan is less than 90% of the purchase price (in the case of a purchase money transaction) or 90% of the appraised value (in non-purchase money transaction), you are not required to establish an impound account for the payment of property taxes, insurance premiums and other applicable charges related to the property as a condition of Lender making you a mortgage loan. However, if you wish, Lender will establish an impound account for you and collect impound account payments every month along with payments of principal and interest. If you do so, Lender will pay you 2% per annum simple interest on funds held in your impound account.

2. By making escrow payments to Lender each month, together with the regular monthly payments, borrowers are able to budget the costs of their required property taxes, insurance premiums and other charges over the entire year. Escrow accounts also help to ensure that funds are available to pay these items as they become due.

Your escrow account will be reviewed at least once a year. At the time of review, we will provide you with an escrow account statement detailing receipts and payments and explaining any changes in the amount of your escrow payments. If the escrow payments collected are not sufficient to pay the annual taxes, insurance premiums or other charges as they become due, you will be required to pay any amounts necessary to make up the shortfall.

3. If you do not establish an impound account with Lender, you will be responsible for the timely payment of all property taxes, hazard insurance premiums and any other applicable charges related to the property. You will be required to furnish Lender and any successor servicer, proof of payment of these sums as provided in your loan documents. Your failure to make two (2) consecutive tax installments on the property prior to the delinquency date of such installments will result in you being required to establish an impound account.

I/We elect to do the following regarding an impound account:

______ Establish an impound account with Lender which will provide for monthly payments of the property taxes, hazard insurance premiums and other applicable charges related to the property.

______ Pay all property taxes, insurance premiums and other applicable charges directly.

ACKNOWLEDGEMENT

I/We hereby acknowledge receipt of this Impound Account Statement and Election Form, and further acknowledge that I/we understand its provisions.

Signature RICHARD WILLIAM ROGERS Date	Signature Date
Signature Date	Signature Date
Signature Date	Signature Date

ESCROW WAIVER AGREEMENT
(Tax Only)

Date: FEBRUARY 12, 2010

Loan Number: 200911000

Borrower(s) Name: RICHARD WILLIAM ROGERS

Property Address: 8624 OAKLAWN AVENUE, NO. 13 (CANOGA PARK AREA), LOS ANGELES, CALIFORNIA 91304

SKYLINE FINANCIAL CORP. ,
its successors or assigns, hereby agrees to waive collection of real estate tax escrows (impounds) on the above referenced loan, subject to the following conditions:

1. The Borrower(s) will pay all property taxes as they become due and payable;
2. The Borrower(s) will remain owner occupant of the subject property; and
3. Copies of paid receipts for any and all taxes will be sent to SKYLINE FINANCIAL CORP. , its successors or assigns, upon payment of said items.

Should the Borrower(s) fail with any of the above conditions, or if the loan payments become more than thirty (30) days delinquent, TRISTAR FINANCIAL CORP. , its successors or assigns, may cancel this agreement.

We hereby acknowledge receipt of a copy of the above statement.

Borrower RICHARD WILLIAM ROGERS Date	Borrower Date
Borrower Date	Borrower Date
Borrower Date	Borrower Date

Real Estate Tax Bill Certification

Loan Number: 200911000
Govt/PMI Number:
Date: FEBRUARY 12, 2010
Lender: TRISTAR FINANCIAL CORP.

Borrower Name: RICHARD WILLIAM ROGERS

Property Address: 8624 OAKLAWN AVENUE, NO. 13 (CANOGA PARK AREA), LOS ANGELES, CALIFORNIA 91304

I/We the purchaser(s) of the captioned property, do hereby acknowledge and agree to the following:

- Lender will maintain a monthly escrow account for the purpose of paying Real Estate Taxes and Hazard Insurance on this property, if applicable;
- If this property is in a "Homeowner Area" (area in which all real estate tax bills are forwarded directly to the homeowner, rather than to the lender), that tax bill will be immediately forwarded by me/us to:

  First American Real Estate Tax Service
  Escrow Reporting DAL-07
  8435 Stemmons Freeway
  Dallas, TX 75247

- Should the taxing authority assess an interest penalty to Lender, for a late tax payment which was the result of my/our failure to promptly send the tax bill to the above address, that penalty will be paid (along with the regular tax bill) from my/our escrow account without further notification to me/us.

Borrower RICHARD WILLIAM ROGERS Date	Borrower Date
Borrower Date	Borrower Date
Borrower Date	Borrower Date

Loan Number: 200911000

INITIAL ESCROW ACCOUNT DISCLOSURE STATEMENT

Borrower Name(s) and Address:
RICHARD WILLIAM ROGERS
8624 OAKLAWN AVENUE, NO. 13 (CANOGA PARK AREA)
LOS ANGELES, CA 91304

Servicer's Name, Address, and Toll-Free Number:
TRISTAR FINANCIAL CORP.
1000 MAIN STREET
LOS ANGELES, CALIFORNIA 90025
(310)321-4567

THIS IS AN ESTIMATE OF ACTIVITY IN YOUR ESCROW ACCOUNT DURING THE COMING YEAR BASED ON PAYMENTS ANTICIPATED TO BE MADE FROM YOUR ACCOUNT.

YOUR [X] MONTHLY ☐ BIWEEKLY MORTGAGE PAYMENT FOR THE COMING YEAR WILL BE $ 1,413.44 OF WHICH $ 1,099.86 WILL BE FOR [X] PRINCIPAL AND INTEREST ☐ INTEREST ONLY, AND $ 313.58 WILL GO INTO YOUR ESCROW ACCOUNT.

Period	Payments to Escrow Account	Payments from Escrow Account	Description	Escrow Account Balance
			Initial Deposit:	$ 627.16
04/01/10	313.58			940.74
05/01/10	313.58			1,254.32
06/01/10	313.58			1,567.90
07/01/10	313.58			1,881.48
08/01/10	313.58			2,195.06
09/01/10	313.58			2,508.64
10/01/10	313.58			2,822.22
11/01/10	313.58	1,612.50	COUNTY TAX	1,523.30
12/01/10	313.58			1,836.88
01/01/11	313.58			2,150.46
02/01/11	313.58	538.00	HAZARD INSURANCE	1,926.04
03/01/11	313.58	1,612.50	COUNTY TAX	627.12

Cushion selected by servicer $ 627.16

Total disbursements $ 3,763.00

PLEASE KEEP THIS STATEMENT FOR COMPARISON WITH THE ACTUAL ACTIVITY IN YOUR ACCOUNT AT THE END OF THE ESCROW ACCOUNTING COMPUTATION YEAR.

Borrower RICHARD WILLIAM ROGERS Date

Borrower Date

Borrower Date

Borrower Date

Borrower Date

Borrower Date

Loan Number: 200911949

ADDRESS CERTIFICATION

MORTGAGOR: RICHARD WILLIAM ROGERS

I hereby certify that the above referenced mortgaged property is located at the address indicated below, and that the correct mailing address of the mortgagor is also indicated below:

The complete PROPERTY street address is as follows:

8624 OAKLAWN AVENUE, NO. 13 (CANOGA PARK AREA)
(Street)

LOS ANGELES
(City)

CALIFORNIA 91304
(State) (Zip Code)

The complete MAILING address is as follows:

8624 OAKLAWN AVENUE, NO. 13
(Street)

CANOGA PARK
(City)

CALIFORNIA 91304
(State) (Zip Code)

Certified By
Closing Agent: MARY LEE

If the MAILING ADDRESS is the same as the PROPERTY ADDRESS, please indicate "SAME ADDRESS" in the space allocated for the mailing address.

CERTIFICATE OF LOANS TO ONE BORROWER

Loan Number: 200911000

Borrower(s): RICHARD WILLIAM ROGERS

Property Address: 8624 OAKLAWN AVENUE, NO. 13 (CANOGA PARK AREA), LOS ANGELES, CALIFORNIA 91304

The undersigned Borrower hereby certifies and represents to TRISTAR FINANCIAL CORP. ("Lender") that the total of all loans made by said Lender to the undersigned Borrower, including the loan hereby applied for, and to all other persons and entities which are required to be included in computing said total is as follows:

(1) This loan $ 202,000.00

(2) Other loans applied for or made (if none, state "no exceptions"; if any, complete the information for each loan and/or loan application):

NAME OF BORROWER	LOAN NUMBER	LOAN AMOUNT
________	________	$ ________
________	________	$ ________
________	________	$ ________
________	________	$ ________

I/We understand that the persons and entities which are required to be included are as follows:

(1) Any person or entity that is, or that upon making of a loan will become, obligor on a loan on the security of real estate;

(2) Nominees of such obligor;

(3) All persons, trusts, partnerships, syndicates and corporations of which such obligor is a nominee or a beneficiary, partner, member, or record or beneficial stockholder owning ten percent or more of the capital stock, or a nominee of any of these persons;

(4) If such obligor is a trust, partnership, syndicate or corporation, all trusts, partnerships, syndicates and corporations of which any beneficiary, partner, member of record or beneficial stockholder owning ten percent or more of the capital stock, is also a beneficiary, partner, member of record or beneficial stockholder owning ten percent or more of the capital stock of such obligor and;

(5) Members of the immediate family of any borrower.

Each of the undersigned, including, where the borrower is a corporation or partnership, each of the persons executing this certificate on behalf of such corporation or partnership, hereby certifies under penalty of perjury that the foregoing is true and correct.

Executed at SOUTHERN ESCROW
1001 MAIN STREET, LOS ANGELES, CALIFORNIA 90025 .

____________________ ____________________
RICHARD WILLIAM ROGERS

____________________ ____________________

____________________ ____________________

HAZARD INSURANCE REQUIREMENTS

LENDER: TRISTAR FINANCIAL CORP.
1000 MAIN STREET
LOS ANGELES, CALIFORNIA 90025
TO: ESCROW OFFICER MARY LEE

Following are the minimum hazard insurance requirements for this company. Please complete and return this form as soon as the information is available.

ESCROW: SOUTHERN ESCROW
1001 MAIN STREET
LOS ANGELES, CALIFORNIA 90025

Date: FEBRUARY 12, 2010
Escrow No: ML-09876
Our Loan No: 200911000

1. Coverage shall provide at least Broad Form on one to four units, and at least "Vandalism & Malicious Mischief" over four units, with no deviation. Homeowner's policies must be equal to HO 2 form.

2. All forms and endorsements pertaining to the Company requirements must appear on the Declaration page of the policy.

3. Lender's Loss Payable Endorsement 438 BFU to be affixed in favor of:
   TRISTAR FINANCIAL CORP., ITS
   SUCCESSORS AND/OR ASSIGNS
   1000 MAIN STREET
   LOS ANGELES, CALIFORNIA 90025
   Loan Number 200911000

4. Our loan number must be shown on the policy and any subsequent endorsements.

5. Effective date of new policies, endorsements, and/or assignments shall be as of, or prior to, date of funding.

6. **HAZARD INSURANCE:** Collect the original policy from the borrower(s). The policy must be in effect as of settlement, with coverage equal to the lesser of the mortgage amount or the replacement value of the dwelling (appraised amount minus site value), or **80%** of the dwelling amount (appraised value minus site value) with the statement "100% replacement guaranteed". The loss payee should read Chase Manhattan Mortgage Corporation, its successors and/or Assigns as their interest may appear, P.O. Box 11740, Monroe, LA 71211-1740. The first year's premium is to be paid prior to closing and a paid receipt must be attached to the original policy. Insurance must be placed with a company having a rating of at least "B" for (Best's rating) or a "6" (Best's Financial Performance Rating), or better. **BINDERS ARE NOT ACCEPTABLE AS PROOF OF INSURANCE EXCEPT WHERE REQUIRED BY STATE LAW.** If the loan is for a condominium unit, a certified copy of the Master Policy and original unit certificate is required. **PLEASE SHOW THE FIRST YEAR'S HAZARD PREMIUM AS A POC ITEM ON THE HUD-1.** "For Refinances, evidence of insurance must reflect at least 60 days remaining on the policy. The maximum allowable deductible is the higher of $1,000 or 1% of the policy face amount."

7. **FLOOD INSURANCE:** If any portion of the dwelling is in a special flood zone, a flood insurance policy (or an application for a policy) paid for by the Borrower(s) is required. Flood insurance should generally be in the form of the standard policy issued by members of the National Flood Insurers Association. A copy of the paid receipt for at least one year's premium must be attached. Chase Manhattan Mortgage Corporation must be named as mortgagee in the manner specified above for hazard insurance. The policy must be in effect as of settlement, with coverage equal to the lesser of the mortgage amount **or** the overall value of the property minus the value of the land, subject to a maximum limitation of $250,000 in most cases (which is the maximum coverage availaible through the National Flood Insurance Program).

All policies, assignments, and/or endorsements, for completion of our loan escrow, are to be mailed to this lending office, attention Funding Department.

AN ACCEPTABLE POLICY, WITH ENDORSEMENTS AND/OR ASSIGNMENTS, MUST BE FORWARDED AND RECEIVED BY US BEFORE THE LOAN IS FUNDED, OR THE COMPANY MAY BE FORCED TO PLACE INTERIM COVERAGE AT AN ADDITIONAL COST TO THE BORROWER.

By:______________________________

Loan Number: 200911000

HAZARD INSURANCE DISCLOSURE

PURSUANT TO CALIFORNIA CIVIL CODE §2955.5

Date: FEBRUARY 12, 2010

Lender: TRISTAR FINANCIAL CORP.

Borrower(s): RICHARD WILLIAM ROGERS

Property Address: 8624 OAKLAWN AVENUE, NO. 13 (CANOGA PARK AREA), LOS ANGELES, CALIFORNIA 91304

NO LENDER SHALL REQUIRE A BORROWER, AS A CONDITION OF RECEIVING OR MAINTAINING A LOAN SECURED BY REAL PROPERTY, TO PROVIDE HAZARD INSURANCE COVERAGE AGAINST RISKS TO THE IMPROVEMENTS ON THAT REAL PROPERTY IN AN AMOUNT EXCEEDING THE REPLACEMENT VALUE OF THE IMPROVEMENTS ON THE PROPERTY.

THIS DISCLOSURE IS NEITHER A CONTRACT NOR A COMMITMENT TO LEND.

By signing below, I hereby acknowledge receipt of a true copy of this disclosure.

Borrower RICHARD WILLIAM ROGERS Date	Borrower Date
Borrower Date	Borrower Date
Borrower Date	Borrower Date

CALIFORNIA FINANCE LENDERS LAW STATEMENT OF LOAN

Date: FEBRUARY 12, 2010

Lender Name: TRISTAR FINANCIAL CORP.

Lender Address: 1000 MAIN STREET
LOS ANGELES, CALIFORNIA 90025

Lender's License Number:

Borrower Name(s): RICHARD WILLIAM ROGERS

Borrower Address: 8624 OAKLAWN AVENUE, NO. 13 (CANOGA PARK AREA)
LOS ANGELES, CALIFORNIA 91304

1. This loan is made pursuant to the California Finance Lenders Law, Division 9 (commencing with Section 22000) of the Finance Code. The above-named lender is a licensed finance lender, Department of Corporations California Finance Lenders License No. 4109703 .

FOR INFORMATION CONTACT THE DEPARTMENT OF CORPORATIONS, STATE OF CALIFORNIA.

2. The California Finance Lenders Law requires that a licensed finance lender obtain a signed statement from a borrower as to whether any person has performed any act as a broker in connection with the making of a loan.

   Has any person performed any act as a broker in connection with the making of your loan? ☐ Yes ☒ No

   If your answer is yes, please indicate below the name of the person who will receive payment for broker services and a statement of all sums paid or payable to such person:

   Broker Name:
   Broker Address:

   Broker CFL or DRE License No.:

   Please indicate all amounts paid or payable for broker services rendered:

3. Loan Information:

   Date of Loan: FEBRUARY 12, 2010 **Loan Amount:** $202,000.00

   APR: 5.343% **Loan Maturity Date:** MARCH 1, 2040

   Payment Schedule:

359	1,099.86	04/01/2010
1	1,103.09	03/01/2040

Security: You are giving a security interest in real property: ☐ you already own ☒ you are purchasing
Property Address: 8624 OAKLAWN AVENUE, NO. 13 (CANOGA PARK AREA)
LOS ANGELES, CALIFORNIA 91304

A full statement of (i) the actual amount of cash you receive and retain, (ii) any funds paid to third persons pursuant to your written instructions, and (iii) any fees, charges, costs, insurance premiums or other sums which have been paid or are to be paid by you or on your behalf at the time the loan is made, is set forth in the HUD-1 or HUD-1A settlement statement delivered to you at settlement.

4. You have the right to make payment in advance in any amount at any time.

By signing below, you acknowledge that you have received and read this disclosure.

Borrower RICHARD WILLIAM ROGERS Date	Borrower Date
Borrower Date	Borrower Date
Borrower Date	Borrower Date

Loan Number: 200911000

APPRAISAL DISCLOSURE

Lender: TRISTAR FINANCIAL CORP.
1000 MAIN STREET
LOS ANGELES, CALIFORNIA 90025

Date: FEBRUARY 12, 2010

Borrower Name(s): RICHARD WILLIAM ROGERS

Property Address: 8624 OAKLAWN AVENUE, NO. 13 (CANOGA PARK AREA)
LOS ANGELES, CALIFORNIA 91304

You have the right to a copy of the appraisal report used in connection with your application for credit. If you wish a copy, please write to us at the mailing address we have provided. We must hear from you no later than 90 days after we notify you about the action taken on your credit application or you withdraw your application.

Contact: Brad Donnelly

Lender/Broker: TRISTAR FINANCIAL CORP.

Address: 1000 MAIN STREET
LOS ANGELES, CALIFORNIA 90025

Telephone: (310)321-4567

In your letter, give us the following information:

LOAN OR APPLICATION NUMBER, IF KNOWN, DATE OF APPLICATION, NAME(S) OF LOAN APPLICANT(S), PROPERTY ADDRESS, AND YOUR CURRENT MAILING ADDRESS.

Borrower RICHARD WILLIAM ROGERS Date

Borrower Date

Borrower Date

Borrower Date

Borrower Date

Borrower Date

NOTICE OF RIGHT TO COPY OF APPRAISAL

Loan #: 200911000

You have the right to a copy of the appraisal report used in connection with your application for credit. If you wish a copy, please write to us at the mailing address [we have provided] [shown below:]

TRISTAR FINANCIAL CORP.
1000 MAIN STREET
LOS ANGELES, CALIFORNIA 90025

We must hear from you no later than 90 days after we notify you about the action taken on your credit application or you withdraw your application. [In your letter, please include your name, the property address and your application or loan number, if known. If you have not already paid an appraisal fee, you may be required to reimburse us for the cost of the appraisal (and any photocopy and postage costs) as a condition to receiving a copy of the appraisal report.]

Signature RICHARD WILLIAM ROGERS Date | Signature Date

Signature Date | Signature Date

Signature Date | Signature Date

ACKNOWLEDGMENT OF RECEIPT OF APPRAISAL REPORT
(Home Valuation Code of Conduct)

Loan Number: 200911000

Date: FEBRUARY 12, 2010

Lender: TRISTAR FINANCIAL CORP.

Borrower: RICHARD WILLIAM ROGERS

Property Address: 8624 OAKLAWN AVENUE, NO. 13 (CANOGA PARK AREA)
LOS ANGELES, CALIFORNIA 91304

I understand that I am entitled to a copy of any report concerning the value of the property securing this loan promptly upon completion at no additional cost to me, and, in any event, no less than three (3) days prior to the closing of the loan.

I hereby acknowledge receipt of the report concerning the value of the property securing this loan, at no additional cost to me, no less than three (3) days prior to the closing of my loan.

Borrower RICHARD WILLIAM ROGERS Date	Borrower Date
Borrower Date	Borrower Date
Borrower Date	Borrower Date

AUTOMATED VALUATION MODEL NOTICE

Loan Number: 200911000

Date: FEBRUARY 12, 2010

Lender: TRISTAR FINANCIAL CORP.

Borrower: RICHARD WILLIAM ROGERS

Property Address: 8624 OAKLAWN AVENUE, NO. 13 (CANOGA PARK AREA), LOS ANGELES, CALIFORNIA 91304

AN AUTOMATED VALUATION MODEL IS NOT AN APPRAISAL. IT IS A COMPUTERIZED PROPERTY VALUATION SYSTEM THAT IS USED TO DERIVE A REAL PROPERTY VALUE.

YOU HAVE THE RIGHT TO RECEIVE A COPY OF THE AUTOMATED VALUATION MODEL (AVM) RESULT USED IN CONNECTION WITH YOUR APPLICATION FOR CREDIT. IF YOU WISH TO RECEIVE A COPY OF THE AVM RESULT, PLEASE SEND YOUR WRITTEN REQUEST TO:

TRISTAR FINANCIAL CORP.
1000 MAIN STREET
LOS ANGELES, CALIFORNIA 90025

LENDER MUST RECEIVE YOUR REQUEST FOR A COPY OF THE AVM RESULT NO LATER THAN 90 DAYS AFTER LENDER PROVIDES NOTICE OF THE ACTION TAKEN ON YOUR APPLICATION OR A NOTICE OF INCOMPLETENESS, OR IN THE CASE OF A WITHDRAWN APPLICATION, 90 DAYS AFTER THE WITHDRAWAL. FURTHER NOTE THAT RELEASE OF THE COPY OF THE AVM RESULT MAY BE CONDITIONED UPON PAYMENT OF A FEE.

IN YOUR REQUEST, PLEASE INCLUDE THE FOLLOWING INFORMATION: YOUR NAME AND ADDRESS, THE PROPERTY ADDRESS (IF DIFFERENT FROM YOUR ADDRESS), AND YOUR LOAN OR APPLICATION NUMBER, IF YOU KNOW THEM.

Page 1 of 2

Each of the undersigned hereby acknowledges receipt of a copy of this Automated Valuation Model Notice.

Borrower RICHARD WILLIAM ROGERS Date	Borrower Date
Borrower Date	Borrower Date
Borrower Date	Borrower Date

Page 2 of 2

CONSUMER CREDIT SCORE DISCLOSURE

Loan Number: 200911000

Date: FEBRUARY 12, 2010

Lender/Broker: TRISTAR FINANCIAL CORP.

Borrower: RICHARD WILLIAM ROGERS

Property Address: 8624 OAKLAWN AVENUE, NO. 13 (CANOGA PARK AREA), LOS ANGELES, CALIFORNIA 91304

The following notice is required under federal law:

NOTICE TO THE HOME LOAN APPLICANT

In connection with your application for a home loan, the lender must disclose to you the score that a consumer reporting agency distributed to users and the lender used in connection with your home loan, and the key factors affecting your credit scores.

The credit score is a computer generated summary calculated at the time of the request and based on information that a consumer reporting agency or lender has on file. The scores are based on data about your credit history and payment patterns. Credit scores are important because they are used to assist the lender in determining whether you will obtain a loan. They may also be used to determine what interest rate you may be offered on the mortgage. Credit scores can change over time, depending on your conduct, how your credit history and payment patterns change, and how credit scoring technologies change.

Because the score is based on information in your credit history, it is very important that you review the credit-related information that is being furnished to make sure it is accurate. Credit records may vary from one company to another.

If you have questions about your credit score or the credit information that is furnished to you, contact the consumer reporting agency at the address and telephone number provided with this notice, or contact the lender, if the lender developed or generated the credit score. The consumer reporting agency plays no part in the decision to take any action on the loan application and is unable to provide you with specific reasons for the decision on a loan application.

If you have questions concerning the terms of the loan, contact the lender.

The following notice is required under California law:

NOTICE TO THE HOME LOAN APPLICANT

In connection with your application for a home loan, the lender must disclose to you the score that a credit bureau distributed to users and the lender used in connection with your home loan, and the key factors affecting your credit scores.

The credit score is a computer generated summary calculated at the time of the request and based on information a credit bureau or lender has on file. The scores are based on data about your credit history and payment patterns. Credit scores are important because they are used to assist the lender in determining whether you will obtain a loan. They may also be used to determine what interest rate you may be offered on the mortgage. Credit scores can change over time, depending on your conduct, how your credit history and payment patterns change, and how credit scoring technologies change.

Because the score is based on information in your credit history, it is very important that you review the credit-related information that is being furnished to make sure it is accurate. Credit records may vary from one company to another.

If you have questions about your credit score or the credit information that is furnished to you, contact the credit bureau at the address and telephone number provided with this notice, or contact the lender, if the lender developed or generated the credit score. The credit bureau plays no part in the decision to take any action on the loan application and is unable to provide you with specific reasons for the decision on a loan application.

If you have questions concerning the terms of the loan, contact the lender.

Lender/Broker Contact Information: TRISTAR FINANCIAL CORP.
1000 MAIN STREET
LOS ANGELES, CALIFORNIA 90025
(310)321-4567

By signing below, the undersigned hereby acknowledges receipt of a copy of this disclosure.

Borrower RICHARD WILLIAM ROGERS Date

Page 1

Loan Number: 200911000

Date: FEBRUARY 12, 2010

Lender: TRISTAR FINANCIAL CORP.

Borrower: RICHARD WILLIAM ROGERS

Property Address: 8624 OAKLAWN AVENUE, NO. 13 (CANOGA PARK AREA), LOS ANGELES, CALIFORNIA 91304

CREDIT SCORING INFORMATION

The following consumer reporting agency(ies)/credit bureau(s) provided a credit score that was used by the Lender:

[X] **Equifax Credit Information Services**
P.O. Box 740241
Atlanta, GA 30374
To order report: 1-800-685-1111
To report fraud: 1-800-525-6285
Web Site: www.equifax.com

Current/Most Recent Credit Score: 809 Credit Score Date: 12/23/2009 Credit Score Range: 300-850

Key Factors Adversely Affecting Your Credit Score:
PROPORTION OF LOAN BALANCES TO LOAN AMOUNTS IS TOO HIGH
AMOUNT OWED ON REVOLVING ACCOUNTS IS TOO HIGH

[X] **TransUnion Consumer Disclosure Center**
P.O. Box 1000
Chester, PA 19022
To order report: 1-800-888-4213
To report fraud: 1-800-916-8800
Web Site: www.transunion.com

Current/Most Recent Credit Score: 811 Credit Score Date: 12/23/2009 Credit Score Range: 300-850

Key Factors Adversely Affecting Your Credit Score:
LENGTH OF TIME ACCOUNTS HAVE BEEN ESTABLISHED
PROPORTION OF LOAN BALANCES TO LOAN AMOUNTS IS TOO HIGH
LENGTH OF TIME REVOLVING ACCOUNTS HAVE BEEN ESTABLISHED

[X] **Experian National Consumer Assistance Center**
P.O. Box 2002
Allen, TX 75013
To order report: 1-888-397-3742
To report fraud: 1-888-397-3742
Web Site: www.experian.com

Current/Most Recent Credit Score: 801 Credit Score Date: 12/23/2009 Credit Score Range: 340-820

Key Factors Adversely Affecting Your Credit Score:
AMOUNT OWED ON ACCOUNTS IS TOO HIGH
LENGTH OF TIME REVOLVING ACCOUNTS HAVE BEEN ESTABLISHED

[ ]

Current/Most Recent Credit Score: Credit Score Date: Credit Score Range:

Key Factors Adversely Affecting Your Credit Score:

Initials: ______

Page 2

Loan Number: 200911000

NOTICE CONCERNING THE FURNISHING OF NEGATIVE INFORMATION TO CONSUMER REPORTING AGENCY

Lender: TRISTAR FINANCIAL CORP.

Borrower: RICHARD WILLIAM ROGERS

Property Address: 8624 OAKLAWN AVENUE, NO. 13 (CANOGA PARK AREA), LOS ANGELES, CALIFORNIA 91304

WE MAY REPORT INFORMATION ABOUT YOUR ACCOUNT TO CREDIT BUREAUS.

LATE PAYMENTS, MISSED PAYMENTS, OR OTHER DEFAULTS ON YOUR ACCOUNT MAY BE REFLECTED IN YOUR CREDIT REPORT.

By signing below, the undersigned hereby acknowledge(s) receipt of a copy of this disclosure.

Borrower RICHARD WILLIAM ROGERS Date	Borrower Date
Borrower Date	Borrower Date
Borrower Date	Borrower Date

STATE OF CALIFORNIA
DEPARTMENT OF CORPORATIONS

COMPARISON OF SAMPLE MORTGAGE FEATURES: TYPICAL MORTGAGE TRANSACTION

Date: FEBRUARY 12, 2010

Loan Number: 200911000

Borrower(s): RICHARD WILLIAM ROGERS

Property Address: 8624 OAKLAWN AVENUE, NO. 13 (CANOGA PARK AREA), LOS ANGELES, CALIFORNIA 91304

(Note to borrower: The information below provides only an estimate and samples of loan payment and loan balance scenarios. Borrower should carefully review all loan documents to confirm the actual amount, rate and scenario of his or her loan.)

	Principal and Interest	Interest Only	5/1 ARM	Interest Only	Option Payment
PROPOSED LOAN AMOUNT $ 202,000.00 30 -YEAR TERM	Fixed Rate (5.125 %)	Fixed Rate (5.125 %) Interest Only for First 5 Years	Fixed Rate for First 5 Years; Adjustable Each Year After First 5 Years (Initial rate for 1 to 5 is 5.125 %; Maximum Rate is ____ %)	Interest Only and Fixed Rate for First 5 Years; Adjustable Rate Each Year After First 5 Years (Initial rate for 1 to 5 is 5.125); Maximum Rate is ____ %)	Adjustable Rate for Entire Term of the Mortgage (Rate in month 1 is 5.125 %; Rate in month 2 through year 5 is ____ %; Maximum Rate is ____ %)

Payment Scenarios

Minimum Monthly Payment Years 1-5 except as noted	$1,099.86 *	$ 862.71	$1,099.86	$ 862.71	$1,099.86 *** (1st year only)
Monthly Payment in Year 6 with no change in rates	$1,099.86	$1,220.34 **	$1,099.86	$1220.34	$
Monthly Payment in Year 6 with a 2% rise in rates	$1,099.86	$1220.34	$	$	$
Minimum Monthly Payment	$1,099.86	$ 862.71	$1,099.86	$ 862.71	$ 1,099.86
Your Gross Income	$7,100.00	$7,100.00	$7,100.00	$7,100.00	$ 7,100.00
Difference	$	$	$	$	$
Maximum Monthly Payment in Year 6 with a 5% rise in rates	$1,099.86	$1220.34	$	$	$
Your Gross Income	$9,230.00	$7,100.00	$7,100.00	$7,100.00	$7,100.00
Difference	$	$	$	$	$

Loan Balance Scenarios

How much will be owed after 5 years?	$	$	$	$	$
Has the loan balance been reduced after 5 years of payments?	Yes The loan balance was reduced by $	No The loan balance was not reduced	Yes The loan balance was reduced by $	No The loan balance was not reduced	No The loan balance **increased** by $

* **This illustrates an interest rate and payments that are fixed for life of the loan.**

** **This illustrates payments that are fixed after the first five years of the loan at a higher amount because they include both principal and interest.**

*** **This illustrates minimum monthly payments that are based on an interest rate that is in effect during the first month only. The payments required during the first year will not be sufficient to cover all of the interest that is due when the rate increased in the second month of the loan. Any unpaid interest amount will be added to the loan balance. Minimum payments for years 2-5 are based on the higher interest rate in effect at the time, subject to any contract limits on payment increases. Minimum payments will be recast (recalculated) after 5 years, or when the loan balance reaches a certain limit, to cover both principal and interest at the applicable rate.**

Loan Number: 200911000

STATE OF CALIFORNIA
DEPARTMENT OF CORPORATIONS
INSTRUCTIONAL GUIDE FOR COMPARISON OF SAMPLE MORTGAGE FEATURES: TYPICAL MORTGAGE TRANSACTION

	Principal and Interest	Interest Only	5/1 ARM	Interest Only	Option Payment	Proposed Loan Type of Loan: (25)
	Fully Amortizing	Fully Amortizing	Fully Amortizing	Fully Amortizing	Fully Amortizing	Type of Amortization: (26)
PROPOSED LOAN AMOUNT $ (1) (1) -YEAR TERM	Fixed Rate ((2) %)	Fixed Rate ((3) %) Interest Only for First 5 Years	Fixed Rate for First 5 Years; Adjustable Each Year After First 5 Years (Initial rate for 1 to 5 is (4) %; Maximum Rate is (4) %)	Interest Only and Fixed Rate for First 5 years; Adjustable Rate Each Year After First 5 Years (Initial rate for 1 to 5 is (4) %; Maximum Rate is (4) %)	Adjustable Rate for Entire Term of the Mortgage (Rate in month 1 is (5) %; Rate in month 2 through year 5 is (5) %; Maximum Rate is (5) %)	(26)
Payment Scenarios						
Minimum Monthly Payment Years 1 - 5 except as noted	$ (6) *	$ (7)	$ (8)	$ (7)	$ (9) *** (1st year only)	$ (26)
Monthly Payment in Year 6 with no change in rates	$ (6)	$ (10) **	$ (11)	$ (12)	$ (13)	$ (26)
Monthly Payment in Year 6 with a 2% rise in rates	$ (6)	$ (10)	$ (14)	$ (15)	$ (16)	$ (26)
Minimum Monthly Payment	$ (6)	$ (7)	$ (8)	$ (7)	$ (9)	$ (26)
Your Gross Income	$ (17)	$ (17)	$ (17)	$ (17)	$ (17)	$ (26)
Difference	$ (18)	$ (18)	$ (18)	$ (18)	$ (18)	$ (26)
Maximum Monthly Payment in Year 6 with a 5% rise in rates	$ (6)	$ (10)	$ (19)	$ (20)	$ (21)	$ (26)
Your Gross Income	$ (17)	$ (17)	$ (17)	$ (17)	$ (17)	$ (26)
Difference	$ (22)	$ (22)	$ (17)	$ (22)	$ (22)	$ (26)
Loan Balance Scenarios						
How much will be owed after 5 years	$ (23)	$ (23)	$ (23)	$ (23)	$ (23)	$ (26)
Has the loan balance been reduced after 5 years of payments?	**Yes** The loan balance was reduced by $ (24)	**No** The loan balance was not reduced	**Yes** The loan balance was reduced by $ (24)	**No** The loan balance was not reduced	**No** The loan balance **increased** by $ (24)	**No/Yes** The loan balance: **did not change/ increased/ decreased** by $ (26)

Page 1 of 2

Instructions:

(1) Proposed loan amount and term.
(2) Current interest rate for fixed rate loan.
(3) Current interest rate for fixed rate loan that is interest-only for first 5 years.
(4) Current fixed interest rate for first 5 years and maximum rate based on 5% maximum increase.
(5) Current initial interest rate for month 1; interest rate for month 2 through year 5 based on current fully-indexed interest rate; maximum rate based on 5% maximum increase.
(6) Fixed rate loan payment (see *).
(7) Interest-only payment based on fixed rate for first 5 years.
(8) P&I payment based on fixed rate for first 5 years.
(9) Minimum option payment based on month 1 rate for first year only (see ***).
(10) P&I payment for remaining term (see **).
(11) P&I payment for remaining term (same as #8).
(12) P&I payment for remaining term.
(13) P&I payment based on increased principal balance for remaining term.
(14) P&I payment for remaining term based on decreased principal balance at 2% increase in interest rate.
(15) P&I payment for remaining term based on original principal balance at 2% increase in interest rate.
(16) P&I payment for remaining term based on increased principal balance at 2% increase in interest rate.
(17) Borrower's gross income from loan application.
(18) Subtract minimum monthly payment from gross income.
(19) P&I payment for remaining term based on reduced principal balance at maximum interest rate.
(20) P&I payment for remaining term based on original principal balance at maximum interest rate.
(21) P&I payment for remaining term based on increased principal balance at maximum interest rate.
(22) Subtract maximum monthly payment from gross income.
(23) Calculate loan balance after 5 years based on minimum monthly payments for years 1 through 5.
(24) Calculate the amount the loan balance has increased or decreased after 5 years.
(25) Insert type of proposed loan product.
(26) Insert applicable information for each scenario.

* **This illustrates an interest rate and payments that are fixed for life of the loan.**

** **This illustrates payments that are fixed after the first five years of the loan at a higher amount because they include both principal and interest.**

*** **This illustrates minimum monthly payments that are based on an interest rate that is in effect during the first month only. The payments required during the first year will not be sufficient to covered all of the interest that is due when the rate increased in the second month of the loan. Any unpaid interest amount will be added to the loan balance. Minimum payments for years 2-5 are based on the higher interest rate in effect at the time, subject to any contract limits on payment increases. Minimum payments will be recast (recalculated) after 5 years, or when the loan balance reaches a certain limit, to cover both principal and interest at the applicable rate.**

When completing this form:

- Add or delete columns on the form to reflect only loan products offered by the lender.
- Complete the last column on the right side entitled "Proposed Loan" for a nontraditional or adjustable rate loan proposed by the lender to the borrower and not disclosed in any other column of the form.
- In accordance with Title 10, California Code of Regulations, Sections 1436 and 1950.314.8, ensure this form is delivered to the borrower within 3 business days of a receipt of a completed application for a nontraditional loan or an adjustable rate loan, or before the borrower becomes obligated on the note, whichever is earlier.

Page 2 of 2

Loan Number: 200911000

SIGNATURE AFFIDAVIT AND AKA STATEMENT

SIGNATURE AFFIDAVIT

I, RICHARD WILLIAM ROGERS ,
certify that this is my true and correct signature:

RICHARD WILLIAM ROGERS
Borrower

Sample Signature

AKA STATEMENT

I, RICHARD WILLIAM ROGERS ,
further certify that I am also known as:

Name Variation (Print)	Sample Signature (Variation)
RICHARD ROGERS	
RICHARD WILLIAM ROGERS	
RICHARD W. ROGERS	
RICH ROGERS	
RICH WILLIAM ROGERS	
RICH W. ROGERS	

State of CALIFORNIA

County of LOS ANGELES

Subscribed and sworn to (or affirmed) before me on this day of ,
by RICHARD WILLIAM ROGERS

,
proved to me on the basis of satisfactory evidence to be the person(s) who appeared before me.

Signature ____________________

(seal)

LOAN NUMBER: 200911949

NAME AFFIDAVIT

THIS IS TO CERTIFY THAT RICHARD WILLIAM ROGERS

IS ALSO KNOWN AS RICHARD ROGERS, RICHARD WILLIAM ROGERS, RICHARD W. ROGERS, RICH ROGERS, RICH WILLIAM ROGERS, RICH W. ROGERS

X ______________________________ PLEASE SIGN NAME AS APPEARS ON DOCUMENTS

State of CALIFORNIA

County of LOS ANGELES

Subscribed and sworn to (or affirmed) before me on this day of ,
by RICHARD WILLIAM ROGERS

,

proved to me on the basis of satisfactory evidence to be the person(s) who appeared before me.

Signature ______________________

(seal)

COMPLIANCE AGREEMENT

STATE OF CALIFORNIA)
) SS:
COUNTY OF LOS ANGELES)

Loan Number: 200911000

Seller(s):

Lender: TRISTAR FINANCIAL CORP.

Borrower(s): RICHARD WILLIAM ROGERS

Property: 8624 OAKLAWN AVENUE, NO. 13 (CANOGA PARK AREA), LOS ANGELES, CALIFORNIA 91304

The undersigned borrower(s) for and in consideration of the above referenced Lender this date funding the closing of this loan agrees, if requested by Lender or Closing Agent for Lender, to fully cooperate and adjust for clerical errors, any or all loan closing documentation if deemed necessary or desirable in the reasonable discretion of Lender to enable Lender to sell, convey, seek guaranty or market said loan to any entity, including but not limited to, an investor, Fannie Mae, Freddie Mac, Federal Housing Authority, the Department of Veterans Affairs or any municipal bonding authority.

The undersigned borrower(s) agree(s) to comply with all above noted requests by Lender or Closing Agent for Lender within 30 days from the date of mailing said requests. Borrower(s) agree(s) to assume all costs including, by way of illustration and not limitation, actual expenses, legal fees and marketing losses, for failing to comply with correction requests in such 30 day time period.

The undersigned borrower(s) do hereby so agree and covenant in order to assure that the loan documentation executed this date will conform and be acceptable in the market place in the instance of transfer, sale or conveyance by Lender or its interest in and to said loan documentation.

Dated effective FEBRUARY 12, 2010 .

______________________ ______________________
RICHARD WILLIAM ROGERS

______________________ ______________________

______________________ ______________________

State of California)
) ss.
County of LOS ANGELES)

On ______________ before me, ______________________

personally appeared RICHARD WILLIAM ROGERS

____

____,

who proved to me on the basis of satisfactory evidence to be the person(s) whose name(s) is/are subscribed to the within instrument and acknowledged to me that he/she/they executed the same in his/her/their authorized capacity(ies), and that by his/her/their signature(s) on the instrument the person(s), or the entity upon behalf of which the person(s) acted, executed the instrument.

I certify under PENALTY OF PERJURY under the laws of the State of California that the foregoing paragraph is true and correct.

WITNESS my hand and official seal.

____
NOTARY SIGNATURE

____
(Typed Name of Notary)

NOTARY SEAL

Loan Number: 200911000

Lender: TRISTAR FINANCIAL CORP.

DOCUMENT CORRECTION AGREEMENT

AGREEMENT TO CORRECT MISSTATED OR PROVIDE ADDITIONAL DOCUMENTATION OR FEES: In consideration of Lender disbursing funds for the closing of the Loan secured by the Property being encumbered, and regardless of the reason for any loss, misplacement, or inaccuracy in any Loan documentation, Borrower(s) agree as follows: If any document is lost, misplaced, misstated or inaccurately reflects the true and correct terms and conditions of the Loan, upon request of the Lender, Borrower(s) will comply with Lender's request to execute, acknowledge, initial and deliver to Lender any documentation Lender deems necessary to replace or correct the lost, misplaced, misstated or inaccurate document(s). If the original promissory note is replaced, the Lender hereby indemnifies the Borrower(s) against any loss associated with a demand on the original note. All documents Lender requests of Borrower(s) shall be referred to as "Replacement Documents." Borrower(s) agrees to deliver the Replacement Documents within ten (10) days after receipt by Borrower(s) of a written request for such replacement. Borrower(s) also agree that upon request Borrower(s) will supply additional amounts and/or pay to Lender any additional sum previously disclosed to Borrower(s) as a cost or fee associated with the Loan, which for whatever reason was not collected at closing.

REQUEST BY LENDER: Any request under this Agreement may be made by the Lender, (including assignees and persons acting on behalf of the Lender) or Settlement Agent, and shall be **prima facie** evidence of the necessity for same. A written statement addressed to Borrower(s) at the address indicated in the Loan documentation shall be considered conclusive evidence of the necessity for Replacement Documents.

FAILURE TO DELIVER REPLACEMENT DOCUMENTS CAN CONSTITUTE DEFAULT: If the Loan is to be guaranteed by the Department of Veterans Affairs ("VA") or insured by the Federal Housing Administration ("FHA"), Borrower(s) failure or refusal to comply with the terms of the correction request may constitute a default under the note and/or deed of trust, and may give Lender the option of declaring all sums secured by the loan documents immediately due and payable.

BORROWER LIABILITY: If Borrower(s) fails or refuses to execute, acknowledge, initial and deliver the Replacement Documents or provide the Additional Documents or Fees to Lender more than ten (10) days after being requested to do so by Lender, and understanding that Lender is relying on these representations, Borrower(s) agree(s) to be liable for any and all loss or damage which Lender reasonably sustains thereby, including, but not limited to all reasonable attorney's fees and costs incurred by Lender.

This agreement shall survive the closing of the Loan, and inure to the benefit of Lender's successors and assigns and be binding upon the heirs, devisees, personal representatives, successors and assigns of Borrower(s).

Applicant RICHARD WILLIAM ROGERS Date	Applicant Date
Applicant Date	Applicant Date
Applicant Date	Applicant Date

Date Prepared: February 12, 2010

LIMITED POWER OF ATTORNEY

The Undersigned hereby appoints Tristar Financial Corp. and/or its assignees, to be my attorney in fact/Agent (hereinafter referred to as Agent), to act for me only as to the matters stated below.

Loan Number: 200911000

Property Address: 8624 Oaklawn Avenue, No. 13 (Canoga Park Area), Los Angeles, CA 91304

Legal Description: REFER TO SECURITY INSTRUMENT

Document Date: February 12, 2010

Seller Name: Walter and Gerri Singletary

Borrower Name: Richard William Rogers

POWERS:

In the event a clerical or typographical error is discovered on any document pertaining to this transaction, my agent and/or assignees, is hereby authorized to correct any clerical or typographical error and to initial, sign, seal and deliver as my act, any instrument to which my agent determines to be necessary to effectuate the correction. Specifically, my agent may make a correction limited to the matters stated below on an original document, and is authorized to rerecord that original document where appropriate. The undersigned declares that any and all corrections made by my agent shall be as valid as if they had been initialed, signed and delivered by me personally. The undersigned ratifies whatsoever my said agent shall lawfully do or cause to be done in the correction of clerical and typographical errors as limited below.

LIMITATIONS:

My agent is authorized to correct clerical and typographical errors as to the names of the parties to this transaction; the legal description; county or street address of the real property which is the subject of this transaction; and the date of any document.

My agent is not authorized to make any changes or corrections as to the interest rate stated on the deed of trust or promissory notes; the amount of principal indebtedness stated on the deed of trust or promissory note; or the amount of consideration on the Deed.

This Power of Attorney is made of my own free will for the purpose of facilitating necessary corrections. The undersigned understands that signing this Power of Attorney is not mandatory.

____

Borrower: RICHARD WILLIAM ROGERS Date

Page 1 of 2

ACKNOWLEDGMENT

State of California)
County of Los Angeles)

On ______________________ before me, ____
(here insert name and title of the officer)

personally appeared

RICHARD WILLIAM ROGERS, who proved to me on the basis of satisfactory evidence to be the person(s) whose name(s) is/are subscribed to the within instrument and acknowledged to me that he/she/they executed the same in his/her/their authorized capacity(ies), and that by his/her/their signature(s) on the instrument the person(s), or the entity upon behalf of which the person(s) acted, executed the instrument.

I certify under PENALTY OF PERJURY under the laws of the State of California that the foregoing paragraph is true and correct.

WITNESS my hand and official seal.

Signature ____________________________ (Seal)

Page 2 of 2

FALSE STATEMENT/EMPLOYMENT/OCCUPANCY FORM
BORROWERS CERTIFICATION

Loan Number: 200911000

Case Number:

To: RICHARD WILLIAM ROGERS

Property Address: 8624 OAKLAWN AVENUE, NO. 13 (CANOGA PARK AREA), LOS ANGELES, CALIFORNIA 91304

ABOVE DEPONENTS, being duly sworn, depose and state as follows:

That the mortgagor is currently employed, or if the Residential Loan Application or FHA Form 2900 disclosed both dependents to be employed, they are both currently employed and that such current employment continues with the same employer as disclosed in the above mentioned forms. That the income from employment disclosed in the above forms has not changed.

That all debts or outstanding obligations as of the date of making application were fully disclosed in the above forms. That there have been no new debts or credit obligations incurred from the date of making application to this date.

That in no way has there been any monies borrowed nor any debt incurred to obtain or cover the closing costs for this mortgage nor the downpayment, if any, on the purchase price of the home covered by the above applications, and that the mortgagor has not paid in excess of $ 252,500.00 for the said property. (See HUD Warning below)

[X] That they either now occupy, or intend to occupy within a reasonable time after closing, as their home, the property, on which this mortgage is placed.

[ ] The property, on which this mortgage is placed, has been purchased as an investment property, and they do not intend to occupy.

That they inspected said property, and the improvements on said property exist in the same condition now as they did when the **RESIDENTIAL APPRAISAL REPORT, THE DEPARTMENT OF HOUSING AND URBAN DEVELOPMENT CONDITIONAL COMMITMENT** or the **VETERANS ADMINISTRATION CERTIFICATE OF VALUE** was issued.

HUD/VA WARNING

We are aware of and understand that if we fail to move into the property within 90 days, that we are subject to prosecution under Section 1010, Title 18, United States Code, Federal Housing Administration Transactions, and that we are liable to be fined not more than $5,000, or imprisoned not more than two years, or both. We are aware of and understand that other Federal Statutes provide severe penalties for any fraud or misrepresentation made for the purpose of influencing the issuance of any guaranty or insurance or the making of any loan by the Administrator of Veterans Affairs.

CONVENTIONAL WARNING

It is a federal crime punishable by fine or imprisonment, or both, to knowingly make any false statements concerning any of the facts in connection with an application for a conventional mortgage, as applicable under the provisions of Title 18, United States Code, Section 1014.

Borrower RICHARD WILLIAM ROGERS Date | Borrower Date

Borrower Date | Borrower Date

Borrower Date | Borrower Date

LoanNumber: 200911000

OCCUPANCY AND FINANCIAL STATUS AFFIDAVIT

STATE OF CALIFORNIA)
) ss:
COUNTY OF LOS ANGELES)

BEFORE ME, the undersigned authority duly authorized to take acknowledgements and administer oaths, personally appeared RICHARD WILLIAM ROGERS (the "Borrower"), who upon being duly sworn on oath, certified as follows:

1. **Material Inducement:** Borrower understands and agrees that the statements contained herein are given as a material inducement to TRISTAR FINANCIAL CORP. (the "Lender"), and Lender is relying upon such statements, to make a mortgage loan (the "Loan") to Borrower, repayment of which is secured by a Mortgage, Deed of Trust, Security Deed or other instrument of security (the "Security Instrument") on certain real property located at 8624 OAKLAWN AVENUE, NO. 13 (CANOGA PARK AREA), LOS ANGELES, CALIFORNIA 91304 (the "Property").

2. **Occupancy:** [check one box only]

[X] **Principal Residence.** Borrower either currently occupies and uses the Property as Borrower's principal residence, or Borrower will occupy and use the Property as Borrower's principal residence within 60 days after Borrower signs the Security Instrument. Borrower will continue to occupy and use the Property as Borrower's principal residence for at least one (1) year from the date that Borrower first occupies the Property. However, Borrower will not have to occupy and use the Property as Borrower's principal residence within the time frames set forth above if Lender agrees in writing that Borrower does not have to do so. Lender may not refuse to agree unless the refusal is reasonable. Borrower will also not have to occupy and use the Property as Borrower's principal residence within the time frames set forth above if extenuating circumstances exist which are beyond Borrower's control.

[ ] **Second Home.** Borrower will occupy, and will use, the Property as Borrower's second home. Borrower will keep the Property available for Borrower's exclusive use and enjoyment at all times, and will not subject the Property to any timesharing or other shared ownership arrangement or to any rental pool or agreement that requires Borrower either to rent the Property or give a management firm or any other person any control over the occupancy or use of the Property.

[ ] **Investment.** The Property is owned and held by Borrower as an investment property. Borrower does not now occupy or use the property, and has no present intention to occupy or use the Property in the future, either as Borrower's principal residence or second home. Borrower now occupies and uses other property or properties as Borrower's principal residence and/or second home.

3. **Financial Status:** Borrower understands that Lender is making the Loan based upon statements and representations contained in, or made in connection with, the residential mortgage loan application given by Borrower to Lender (the "Loan Application"). Borrower hereby certifies that the information provided by Borrower contained in, or made in connection with, the Loan Application related to Borrower's financial status (such as Borrower's employment, income, available cash, debts, expenses, credit obligations, and the like), has not changed significantly and that the such information accurately reflects Borrower's current financial status. Borrower certifies further that Borrower has not received a layoff notice or otherwise have knowledge of a pending layoff, and Borrower, to the best of Borrower's knowledge and belief, is unaware of any events or circumstances in the foreseeable future that would impair or have an adverse effect on Borrower's ability to fulfill Borrower's Loan obligations, including, but not limited to Borrower's obligation to make required periodic payments.

4. **False, Misleading or Inaccurate Statements:** Borrower understands that Borrower will be in default under the terms of the Security Instrument if, during the application process for the Loan, Borrower or any persons or entities acting at the direction of Borrower or with Borrower's knowledge or consent gave materially false, misleading or inaccurate information or statements to Lender (or failed to provide Lender with material information) in connection with the Loan, including, but not limited to, representations concerning Borrower's occupancy of the Property and Borrower's financial status. Borrower understands further that any intentional or negligent misrepresentation(s) of the information contained in, or made in connection with, the Loan Application may result in severe civil and/or criminal penalties, including, but not limited to, fine or imprisonment or both under the provisions of Title 18, United States Code, Section 1001, et seq. and liability for monetary damages to the Lender, its agents, successors and assigns, insurers and any other person who may suffer any loss due to reliance upon any misrepresentation(s) which Borrower has made on or in connection with the Loan Application.

Page 1 of 2

Loan Number: 200911000

Borrower RICHARD WILLIAM ROGERS	Date	Borrower	Date
Borrower	Date	Borrower	Date
Borrower	Date	Borrower	Date

State of CALIFORNIA
County of LOS ANGELES

Subscribed and sworn to (or affirmed) before me on this day of , by
RICHARD WILLIAM ROGERS ,
proved to me on the basis of satisfactory evidence to be the person(s) who appeared before me.

(seal) Signature ______________________________

Page 2 of 2

OCCUPANCY AFFIDAVIT

Loan Number: 200911000

Lender: TRISTAR FINANCIAL CORP.

Borrower(s): RICHARD WILLIAM ROGERS

Property Address: 8624 OAKLAWN AVENUE, NO. 13 (CANOGA PARK AREA), LOS ANGELES, CALIFORNIA 91304

I/We, the undersigned "Borrower(s)" certify that the following statements are true with regard to Owner Occupancy of the security property located at 8624 OAKLAWN AVENUE, NO. 13 (CANOGA PARK AREA), LOS ANGELES, CALIFORNIA 91304
for which this mortgage is obtained.

Please mark with an "X" the applicable property type for which this mortgage is being obtained and sign below to indicate compliance with the Lender's occupancy requirements.

[X] **PRIMARY**

__ The property for which this mortgage is being obtained is being purchased/refinanced as a primary home and I/we intend to occupy the aforementioned property within thirty (30) days of the loan closing, or on the day of .

__ The property for which this mortgage is being obtained is being purchased/refinanced as a primary home and I/we intend to use the property as a year-round residence.

[ ] **SECOND HOME**

__ The security property is being purchased as a second home and I/we intend to occupy the property for at least fourteen (14) days or more annually.

__ The security property is being purchased as a second home and will be used for my/our exclusive use and enjoyment and is not subject to a mandatory rental pool.

__ The security property is being purchased for second home and I/we do not intend to lease the property.

__ The security property is being purchased for second home and is suitable for year-round occupancy.

Borrower RICHARD WILLIAM ROGERS Date	Borrower Date
Borrower Date	Borrower Date
Borrower Date	Borrower Date

Loan Number: 200911000

Form **W-9**
(Rev. October 2007)
Department of the Treasury
Internal Revenue Service

Request for Taxpayer Identification Number and Certification

Give form to the requester. Do not send to the IRS.

Print or type
See Specific Instructions on page 2.

Name (as shown on your income tax return)
RICHARD WILLIAM ROGERS

Business name, if different from above

Check appropriate box: [X] Individual/Sole proprietor [ ] Corporation [ ] Partnership
[ ] Limited liability company. Enter the tax classification (D=disregarded entity, C=corporation, P=partnership ➤------
[ ] Other (see instructions) ➤

[ ] Exempt payee

Address (number, street, and apt. or suite no.)
8624 OAKLAWN AVENUE, NO. 13

Requester's name and address (optional)
TRISTAR FINANCIAL CORP.
1000 MAIN STREET,
LOS ANGELES, CALIFORNIA
90025

City, state, and ZIP code
CANOGA PARK, CALIFORNIA 91304

List account number(s) here (optional)
200911000

Part I Taxpayer Identification Number (TIN)

Enter your TIN in the appropriate box. The TIN provided must match the name given on Line 1 to avoid backup withholding. For individuals, this is your social security number (SSN). However, for a resident alien, sole proprietor, or disregarded entity, see the Part I instructions on page 3. For other entities, it is your employer identification number (EIN). If you do not have a number, see *How to get a TIN* on page 3.

Social security number
000-00-0000

or

Employer identification number

Note. If the account is in more than one name, see the chart on page 4 for guidelines on whose number to enter.

Part II Certification

Under penalties of perjury, I certify that:

1. The number shown on this form is my correct taxpayer identification number (or I am waiting for a number to be issued to me), and
2. I am not subject to backup withholding because: (a) I am exempt from backup withholding, or (b) I have not been notified by the Internal Revenue Service (IRS) that I am subject to backup withholding as a result of a failure to report all interest or dividends, or (c) the IRS has notified me that I am no longer subject to backup withholding, and
3. I am a U.S. citizen or other U.S. person (defined below).

Certification instructions. You must cross out item 2 above if you have been notified by the IRS that you are currently subject to backup withholding because you have failed to report all interest and dividends on your tax return. For real estate transactions, item 2 does not apply. For mortgage interest paid, acquisition or abandonment of secured property, cancellation of debt, contributions to an individual retirement arrangement (IRA), and generally, payments other than interest and dividends, you are not required to sign the Certification, but you must provide your correct TIN. (See the instructions on page 4.)

Sign Here | **Signature of U.S. person** | **Date**

General Instructions

Section references are to the Internal Revenue Code unless otherwise noted.

Purpose of Form

A person who is required to file an information return with the IRS, must obtain your correct taxpayer identification number (TIN) to report, for example, income paid to you, real estate transactions, mortgage interest you paid, acquisition or abandonment of secured property, cancellation of debt, or contributions you made to an IRA.

Use Form W-9 only if you are a U.S. person (including a resident alien), to provide your correct TIN to the person requesting it (the requester) and, when applicable, to:

1. Certify that the TIN you are giving is correct (or you are waiting for a number to be issued),
2. Certify that you are not subject to backup withholding, or
3. Claim exemption from backup withholding if you are a U.S. exempt payee. If applicable, you are also certifying that as a U.S. person, your allocable share of any partnership income from a U.S. trade or business is not subject to the withholding tax on foreign partners' share of effectively connected income.

Note. If a requester gives you a form other than Form W-9 to request your TIN, you must use the requester's form if it is substantially similar to this Form W-9.

Definition of a U.S. person. For federal tax purposes, you are considered a U.S. person if you are:

- An individual who is a U.S. citizen or U.S. resident alien,
- A partnership, corporation, company, or association created or organized in the United States or under the laws of the United States,
- An estate (other than a foreign estate) or
- A domestic trust (as defined in Regulations section 301.7701-7).

Special rules for partnerships. Partnerships that conduct a trade or business in the United States are generally required to pay a withholding tax on any foreign partners' share of income from such business. Further, in certain cases where a Form W-9 has not been received, a partnership is required to presume that a partner is a foreign person, and pay the withholding tax. Therefore, if you are a U.S. person that is a partner in a partnership conducting a trade or business in the United States, provide Form W-9 to the partnership to establish your U.S. status and avoid withholding on your share of partnership income.

Form **W-9** (Rev. 10-2007)

The person who gives Form W-9 to the partnership for purposes of establishing its U.S. status and avoiding withholding on its allocable share of net income from the partnership conducting a trade or business in the United States is in the following cases:

- The U.S. owner of a disregarded entity and not the entity,
- The U.S. grantor or other owner of a grantor trust and not the trust, and
- The U.S. trust (other than a grantor trust) and not the beneficiaries of the trust.

Foreign person. If you are a foreign person, do not use Form W-9. Instead, use the appropriate Form W-8 (see Publication 515, Withholding of Tax on Nonresident Aliens and Foreign Entities).

Nonresident alien who becomes a resident alien. Generally, only a nonresident alien individual may use the terms of a tax treaty to reduce or eliminate U.S. tax on certain types of income. However, most tax treaties contain a provision known as a "saving clause." Exceptions specified in the saving clause may permit an exemption from tax to continue for certain types of income even after the payee has otherwise become a U.S. resident alien for tax purposes.

If you are a U.S. resident alien who is relying on an exception contained in the saving clause of a tax treaty to claim an exemption from U.S. tax on certain types of income, you must attach a statement to Form W-9 that specifies the following five items:

1. The treaty country. Generally, this must be the same treaty under which you claimed exemption from tax as a nonresident alien.
2. The treaty article addressing the income.
3. The article number (or location) in the tax treaty that contains the saving clause and its exceptions.
4. The type and amount of income that qualifies for the exemption from tax.
5. Sufficient facts to justify the exemption from tax under the terms of the treaty article.

Example. Article 20 of the U.S.-China income tax treaty allows an exemption from tax for scholarship income received by a Chinese student temporarily present in the United States. Under U.S. law, this student will become a resident alien for tax purposes if his or her stay in the United States exceeds 5 calendar years. However, paragraph 2 of the first Protocol to the U.S.-China treaty (dated April 30, 1984) allows the provisions of Article 20 to continue to apply even after the Chinese student becomes a resident alien of the United States. A Chinese student who qualifies for this exception (under paragraph 2 of the first protocol) and is relying on this exception to claim an exemption from tax on his or her scholarship or fellowship income would attach to Form W-9 a statement that includes the information described above to support that exemption.

If you are a nonresident alien or a foreign entity not subject to backup withholding, give the requester the appropriate completed Form W-8.

What is backup withholding? Persons making certain payments to you must under certain conditions withhold and pay to the IRS 28% of such payments. This is called "backup withholding." Payments that may be subject to backup withholding include interest, tax-exempt interest, dividends, broker and barter exchange transactions, rents, royalties, nonemployee pay, and certain payments from fishing boat operators. Real estate transactions are not subject to backup withholding.

You will not be subject to backup withholding on payments you receive if you give the requester your correct TIN, make the proper certifications, and report all your taxable interest and dividends on your tax return.

Payments you receive will be subject to backup withholding if:

1. You do not furnish your TIN to the requester,
2. You do not certify your TIN when required (see the Part II instructions on page 3 for details),
3. The IRS tells the requester that you furnished an incorrect TIN,
4. The IRS tells you that you are subject to backup withholding because you did not report all your interest and dividends on your tax return (for reportable interest and dividends only), or
5. You do not certify to the requester that you are not subject to backup withholding under 4 above (for reportable interest and dividend accounts opened after 1983 only).

Certain payees and payments are exempt from backup withholding. See the instructions below and the separate Instructions for the Requester of Form W-9.

Also see *Special rules for partnerships* on page 1.

Penalties

Failure to furnish TIN. If you fail to furnish your correct TIN to a requester, you are subject to a penalty of $50 for each such failure unless your failure is due to reasonable cause and not to willful neglect.

Civil penalty for false information withrespect to withholding. If you make a false statement with no reasonable basis that results in no backup withholding, you are subject to a $500 penalty.

Criminal penalty for falsifying information. Willfully falsifying certifications or affirmations may subject you to criminal penalties including fines and/or imprisonment.

Misuse of TINs. If the requester discloses or uses TINs in violation of federal law, the requester may be subject to civil and criminal penalties.

Specific Instructions

Name

If you are an individual, you must generally enter the name shown on your income tax return. However, if you have changed your last name, for instance, due to marriage without informing the Social Security Administration of the name change, enter your first name, the last name shown on your social security card, and your new last name.

If the account is in joint names, list first, and then circle, the name of the person or entity whose number you entered in Part I of the form.

Sole proprietor. Enter your individual name as shown on your income tax return on the "Name" line. You may enter your business, trade, or "doing business as (DBA)" name on the "Business name" line.

Limited liability company (LLC). Check the "Limited liability company" box only and enter the appropriate code for the tax classification ("D" for disregarded entity, "C" for corporation, "P" for partnership) in the space provided.

For a single-member LLC (including a foreign LLC with a domestic owner) that is disregarded as an entity separate from its owner under Regulations section 301.7701-3, enter the owner's name on the "Name" line. Enter the LLC's name on the "Business name" line.

For an LLC classified as a partnership or a corporation, enter the LLC's name on the "Name" line and any business, trade, or DBA name on the "Business name" line.

Other entities. Enter your business name as shown on required federal tax documents on the "Name" line. This name should match the name shown on the charter or other legal document creating the entity. You may enter any business, trade, or DBA name on the "Business name" line.

Note. You are requested to check the appropriate box for your status (individual/sole proprietor, corporation, etc.).

Exempt Payee

If you are exempt from backup withholding, enter your name as described above and check the appropriate box for your status, then

Form W-9 (Rev. 10-2007) Page **3**

check the "Exempt payee" box in the line following the business name, sign and date the form.

Generally, individuals (including sole proprietors) are not exempt from backup withholding. Corporations are exempt from backup withholding for certain payments, such as interest and dividends.

Note. If you are exempt from backup withholding, you should still complete this form to avoid possible erroneous backup withholding.

The following payees are exempt from backup withholding:

1. An organization exempt from tax under section 501(a), any IRA, or a custodial account under section 403(b)(7) if the account satisfies the requirements of section 401(f)(2),
2. The United States or any of its agencies or instrumentalities,
3. A state, the District of Columbia, a possession of the United States, or any of their political subdivisions or instrumentalities,
4. A foreign government or any of its political subdivisions, agencies, or instrumentalities, or
5. An international organization or any of its agencies or instrumentalities.

Other payees that may be exempt from backup withholding include:

6. A corporation,
7. A foreign central bank of issue,
8. A dealer in securities or commodities required to register in the United States, the District of Columbia, or a possession of the United States,
9. A futures commission merchant registered with the Commodity Futures Trading Commission,
10. A real estate investment trust,
11. An entity registered at all times during the tax year under the Investment Company Act of 1940,
12. A common trust fund operated by a bank under section 584(a),
13. A financial institution,
14. A middleman known in the investment community as a nominee or custodian, or
15. A trust exempt from tax under section 664 or described in section 4947.

The chart below shows types of payments that may be exempt from backup withholding. The chart applies to the exempt payees listed above, 1 through 15.

IF the payment is for . . .	THEN the payment is exempt for. . .
Interest and dividend payments	All exempt payees except for 9
Broker transactions	Exempt payees 1 through 13. Also, a person registered under the Investment Advisers Act of 1940 who regularly acts as a broker
Barter exchange transactions and patronage dividends	Exempt payees 1 through 5
Payments over $600 required to be reported and direct sales over $5,000 [1]	Generally, exempt payees 1 through 7 [2]

[1] See Form 1099-MISC, Miscellaneous Income, and its instructions.

[2] However, the following payments made to a corporation (including gross proceeds paid to an attorney under section 6045(f), even if the attorney is a corporation) and reportable on Form 1099-MISC are not exempt from backup withholding: medical and health care payments, attorneys' fees, and payments for services paid by a federal executive agency.

Part I. Taxpayer Identification Number (TIN)

Enter your TIN in the appropriate box. If you are a resident alien and you do not have and are not eligible to get an SSN, your TIN is your IRS individual taxpayer identification number (ITIN). Enter it in the social security number box. If you do not have an ITIN, see *How to get a TIN* below.

If you are a sole proprietor and you have an EIN, you may enter either your SSN or EIN. However, the IRS prefers that you use your SSN.

If you are a single-member LLC that is disregarded as an entity separate from its owner (see *Limited liability company (LLC)* on page 2), enter the owner's SSN (or EIN, if the owner has one). Do not enter the disregarded entity's EIN. If the LLC is classified as a corporation or partnership, enter the entity's EIN.

Note. See the chart on page 4 for further clarification of name and TIN combinations.

How to get a TIN. If you do not have a TIN, apply for one immediately. To apply for an SSN, get Form SS-5, Application for a Social Security Card, from your local Social Security Administration office or get this form online at *www.ssa.gov.* You may also get this form by calling 1-800-772-1213. Use Form W-7, Application for IRS Individual Taxpayer Identification Number, to apply for an ITIN, or Form SS-4, Application for Employer Identification Number, to apply for an EIN. You can apply for an EIN online by accessing the IRS website at *www.irs.gov/businesses* and clicking on Employer Identification Number (EIN) under Starting a Business. You can get Forms W-7 and SS-4 from the IRS by visiting *www.irs.gov* or by calling 1-800-TAX-FORM (1-800-829-3676).

If you are asked to complete Form W-9 but do not have a TIN, write "Applied For" in the space for the TIN, sign and date the form, and give it to the requester. For interest and dividend payments, and certain payments made with respect to readily tradable instruments, generally you will have 60 days to get a TIN and give it to the requester before you are subject to backup withholding on payments. The 60-day rule does not apply to other types of payments. You will be subject to backup withholding on all such payments until you provide your TIN to the requester.

Note. Entering "Applied For" means that you have already applied for a TIN or that you intend to apply for one soon.

Caution: *A disregarded domestic entity that has a foreign owner must use the appropriate Form W-8.*

Part II. Certification

To establish to the withholding agent that you are a U.S. person, or resident alien, sign Form W-9. You may be requested to sign by the withholding agent even if items 1, 4, and 5 below indicate otherwise.

For a joint account, only the person whose TIN is shown in Part I should sign (when required). Exempt payees, see *Exempt Payee* on page 2.

Signature requirements. Complete the certification as indicated in 1 through 5 below.

1. Interest, dividend, and barter exchange accounts opened before 1984 and broker accounts considered active during 1983. You must give your correct TIN, but you do not have to sign the certification.

2. Interest, dividend, broker, and barter exchange accounts opened after 1983 and broker accounts considered inactive during 1983. You must sign the certification or backup withholding will apply. If you are subject to backup withholding and you are merely providing your correct TIN to the requester, you must cross out item 2 in the certification before signing the form.

Form **W-9** (Rev. 10-2007)

Form W-9 (Rev. 10-2007) Page **4**

3. Real estate transactions. You must sign the certification. You may cross out item 2 of the certification.

4. Other payments. You must give your correct TIN, but you do not have to sign the certification unless you have been notified that you have previously given an incorrect TIN. "Other payments" include payments made in the course of the requester's trade or business for rents, royalties, goods (other than bills for merchandise), medical and health care services (including payments to corporations), payments to a nonemployee for services, payments to certain fishing boat crew members and fishermen, and gross proceeds paid to attorneys (including payments to corporations).

5. Mortgage interest paid by you, acquisition or abandonment of secured property, cancellation of debt, qualified tuition program payments (under section 529), IRA, Coverdell ESA, Archer MSA or HSA contributions or distributions, and pension distributions. You must give your correct TIN, but you do not have to sign the certification.

What Name and Number To Give the Requester

For this type of account:	Give name and SSN of:
1. Individual	The individual
2. Two or more individuals (joint account)	The actual owner of the account or, if combined funds, the first individual on the account [1]
3. Custodian account of a minor (Uniform Gift to Minors Act)	The minor [2]
4. a. The usual revocable savings trust (grantor is also trustee)	The grantor-trustee [1]
b. So-called trust account that is not a legal or valid trust under state law	The actual owner [1]
5. Sole proprietorship or disregarded entity owned by an individual	The owner [3]
For this type of account:	**Give name and EIN of:**
6. Disregarded entity not owned by an individual	The owner [3]
7. A valid trust, estate, or pension trust	Legal entity [4]
8. Corporate or LLC electing corporate status on Form 8832	The corporation
9. Association, club, religious, charitable, educational, or other tax-exempt organization	The organization
10. Partnership or multi-member LLC	The partnership
11. A broker or registered nominee	The broker or nominee
12. Account with the Department of Agriculture in the name of a public entity (such as a state or local government, school district, or prison) that receives agricultural program payments	The public entity

[1] List first and circle the name of the person whose number you furnish. If only one person on a joint account has an SSN, that person's number must be furnished.

[2] Circle the minor's name and furnish the minor's SSN.

[3] You must show your individual name and you may also enter your business or "DBA" name on the second name line. You may use either your SSN or EIN (if you have one), but the IRS encourages you to use your SSN.

[4] List first and circle the name of the trust, estate, or pension trust. (Do not furnish the TIN of the personal representative or trustee unless the legal entity itself is not designated in the account title.) Also see *Special rules for partnerships* on page 1.

Note. If no name is circled when more than one name is listed, the number will be considered to be that of the first name listed.

Secure Your Tax Records from Identity Theft

Identity theft occurs when someone uses your personal information such as your name, social security number (SSN), or other identifying information, without your permission, to commit fraud or other crimes. An identity thief may use your SSN to get a job or may file a tax return using your SSN to receive a refund.

To reduce your risk:

- Protect your SSN,
- Ensure your employer is protecting your SSN, and
- Be careful when choosing a tax preparer.

Call the IRS at 1-800-829-1040 if you think your identity has been used inappropriately for tax purposes.

Victims of identity theft who are experiencing economic harm or a system problem, or are seeking help in resolving tax problems that have not been resolved through normal channels, may be eligible for Taxpayer Advocate Service (TAS) assistance. You can reach TAS by calling the TAS toll-free case intake line at 1-877-777-4778 or TTY/TDD 1-800-829-4059.

Protect yourself from suspicious emails or phishing schemes. Phishing is the creation and use of email and websites designed to mimic legitimate business emails and websites. The most common act is sending an email to a user falsely claiming to be an established legitimate enterprise in an attempt to scam the user into surrendering private information that will be used for identity theft.

The IRS does not initiate contacts with taxpayers via emails. Also, the IRS does not request personal detailed information through email or ask taxpayers for the PIN numbers, passwords, or similar secret access information for their credit card, bank, or other financial accounts.

If you receive an unsolicited email claiming to be from the IRS, forward this message to *phishing@irs.gov.* You may also report misuse of the IRS name, logo, or other IRS personal property to the Treasury Inspector General for Tax Administration at 1-800-366-4484. You can forward suspicious emails to the Federal Trade Commission at: *spam@uce.gov* or contact them at *www.consumer.goc/idtheft* or 1-877-IDTHEFT (438-4338).

Visit the IRS website at *www.irs.gov* to learn more about identity theft and how to reduce your risk.

Privacy Act Notice

Section 6109 of the Internal Revenue Code requires you to provide your correct TIN to persons who must file information returns with the IRS to report interest, dividends, and certain other income paid to you, mortgage interest you paid, the acquisition or abandonment of secured property, cancellation of debt, or contributions you made to an IRA, or Archer MSA or HSA. The IRS uses the numbers for identification purposes and to help verify the accuracy of your tax return. The IRS may also provide this information to the Department of Justice for civil and criminal litigation, and to cities, states, the District of Columbia, and U.S. possessions to carry out their tax laws. We may also disclose this information to other countries under a tax treaty, to federal and state agencies to enforce federal nontax criminal laws, or to federal law enforcement and intelligence agencies to combat terrorism.

You must provide your TIN whether or not you are required to file a tax return. Payers must generally withhold 28% of taxable interest, dividend, and certain other payments to a payee who does not give a TIN to a payer. Certain penalties may also apply.

Form **W-9** (Rev. 10-2007)

Loan Number: 200911000

Form **4506-T**

(Rev. January 2010)

Department of the Treasury
Internal Revenue Service

Request for Transcript of Tax Return

Request may be rejected if the form is incomplete or illegible.

OMB No. 1545-1872

Tip: Use Form 4506-T to order a transcript or other return information free of charge. See the product list below. You can also call 1-800-829-1040 to order a transcript. If you need a copy of your return, use **Form 4506, Request for Copy of Tax Return.** There is a fee to get a copy of your return.

1a Name shown on tax return. If a joint return, enter the name shown first.
RICHARD WILLIAM ROGERS

1b **First social security number on tax return or employer identification number (see instructions)**
000-00-0000

2a If a joint return, enter spouse's name shown on tax return.

2b **Second social security number if joint tax return**

3 Current name, address (including apt., room, or suite no.), city, state, and ZIP code
RICHARD WILLIAM ROGERS
8624 OAKLAWN AVENUE, NO. 13, CANOGA PARK, CALIFORNIA 91304

4 Previous address shown on the last return filed if different from line 3

5 If the transcript or tax information is to be mailed to a third party (such as a mortgage company), enter the third party's name, address, and telephone number. The IRS has no control over what the third party does with the tax information.
TRISTAR FINANCIAL CORP., ITS SUCCESSORS AND/OR ASSIGNS

Caution: *If the transcript is being mailed to a third party, ensure that you have filled in line 6 and line 9 before signing. Sign and date the form once you have filled in these lines. Completing these steps helps to protect your privacy.*

6 **Transcript requested.** Enter the tax form number here (1040, 1065, 1120, etc.) and check the appropriate box below. Enter only one tax form number per request. ▶ 1040, 1099 AND W-2

a **Return Transcript,** which includes most of the line items of a tax return as filed with the IRS. A tax return transcript does not reflect changes made to the account after the return is processed. Transcripts are only available for the following returns: Form 1040 series, Form 1065, Form 1120, Form 1120A, Form 1120H, Form 1120L, and Form 1120S. Return transcripts are available for the current year and returns processed during the prior 3 processing years. Most requests will be processed within 10 business days . . . . . [X]

b **Account Transcript,** which contains information on the financial status of the account, such as payments made on the account, penalty assessments, and adjustments made by you or the IRS after the return was filed. Return information is limited to items such as tax liability and estimated tax payments. Account transcripts are available for most returns. Most requests will be processed within 30 calendar days . . ☐

c **Record of Account,** which is a combination of line item information and later adjustments to the account. Available for current year and 3 prior tax years. Most requests will be processed within 30 calendar days . . . . . ☐

7 **Verification of Nonfiling,** which is proof from the IRS that you **did not** file a return for the year. Current year requests are only available after June 15th. There are no availability restrictions on prior year requests. Most requests will be processed within 10 business days . . . . . . ☐

8 **Form W-2, Form 1099 series, Form 1098 series, or Form 5498 series transcript.** The IRS can provide a transcript that includes data from these information returns. State or local information is not included with the Form W-2 information. The IRS may be able to provide this transcript information for up to 10 years. Information for the current year is generally not available until the year after it is filed with the IRS. For example, W-2 information for 2007, filed in 2008, will not be available from the IRS until 2009. If you need W-2 information for retirement purposes, you should contact the Social Security Administration at 1-800-772-1213. Most requests will be processed within 45 days . . . . ☐

Caution: *If you need a copy of Form W-2 or Form 1099, you should first contact the payer. To get a copy of the Form W-2 or Form 1099 filed with your return, you must use Form 4506 and request a copy of your return, which includes all attachments.*

9 **Year or period requested.** Enter the ending date of the year or period, using the mm/dd/yyyy format. If you are requesting more than four years or periods, you must attach another Form 4506-T. For requests relating to quarterly tax returns, such as Form 941, you must enter each quarter or tax period separately.

12/31/2007 12/31/2008 ________ ________

Signature of taxpayer(s). I declare that I am either the taxpayer whose name is shown on line 1a or 2a, or a person authorized to obtain the tax information requested. If the request applies to a joint return, **either** husband or wife must sign. If signed by a corporate officer, partner, guardian, tax matters partner, executor, receiver, administrator, trustee, or party other than the taxpayer, I certify that I have the authority to execute Form 4506-T on behalf of the taxpayer.
Note: *For transcripts being sent to a third party, this form must be received within 120 days of signature date.*

Telephone number of taxpayer on line 1a or 2a
(818)739-4000

Sign Here

Signature (see instructions) Date

Title (if line 1a above is a corporation, partnership, estate, or trust)

Spouse's signature Date

For Privacy Act and Paperwork Reduction Act Notice, see page 2.
Cat. No. 37667N

Form **4506-T** (Rev. 1-2010)

Page 1 of 2

Loan Number: 200911000

General Instructions

Purpose of form. Use Form 4506-T to request tax return information. You can also designate a third party to receive the information. See line 5.

Tip. Use Form 4506, Request for Copy of Tax Return, to request copies of tax returns.

Where to file. Mail or fax Form 4506-T to the address below for the state you lived in, or the state your business was in, when that return was filed. There are two address charts: one for individual transcripts (Form 1040 series and Form W-2) and one for all other transcripts.

If you are requesting more than one transcript or other product and the chart below shows two different RAIVS teams, send your request to the team based on the address of your most recent return.

Automated transcript request. You can call 1-800-829-1040 to order a transcript through the automated self-help system. Follow prompts for "questions about your tax account" to order a tax return transcript.

Chart for individual transcripts (Form 1040 series and Form W-2)

If you filed an individual return and lived in:	Mail or fax to the "Internal Revenue Service" at:
Florida, Georgia North Carolina, South Carolina	RAIVS Team P.O. Box 47-421 Stop 91 Doraville, GA 30362 770-455-2335
Alabama, Kentucky, Louisiana, Mississippi, Tennessee, Texas, a foreign country, or A.P.O. or F.P.O. address	RAIVS Team Stop 6716 AUSC Austin, TX 73301 512-460-2272
Alaska, Arizona, California, Colorado, Hawaii, Idaho, Illinois, Indiana, Iowa, Kansas, Michigan, Minnesota, Montana, Nebraska, Nevada, New Mexico, North Dakota, Oklahoma, Oregon, South Dakota, Utah, Washington, Wisconsin, Wyoming	RAIVS Team Stop 37106 Fresno, CA 93888 559-456-5876
Arkansas, Connecticut, Delaware, District of Columbia, Maine, Maryland, Massachusetts, Missouri, New Hampshire, New Jersey, New York, Ohio, Pennsylvania, Rhode Island, Vermont, Virginia, West Virginia	RAIVS Team Stop 6705 P-6 Kansas City, MO 64999 816-292-6102

Chart for all other transcripts

If you lived in or your business was in:	Mail or fax to the "Internal Revenue Service" at:
Alabama, Alaska, Arizona, Arkansas, California, Colorado, Florida, Hawaii, Idaho, Iowa, Kansas, Louisiana, Minnesota, Mississippi, Missouri, Montana, Nebraska, Nevada, New Mexico, North Dakota, Oklahoma, Oregon, South Dakota, Tennessee, Texas, Utah, Washington, Wyoming, a foreign country, or A.P.O. or F.P.O.. address	RAIVS Team P.O. Box 9941 Mail Stop 6734 Ogden, UT 84409 801-620-6922
Connecticut, Delaware, District of Columbia, Georgia, Illinois, Indiana, Kentucky, Maine, Maryland, Massachusetts, Michigan, New Hampshire, New Jersey, New York, North Carolina, Ohio, Pennsylvania, Rhode Island, South Carolina, Vermont, Virginia, West Virginia, Wisconsin	RAIVS Team P.O. Box 145500 Stop 2800 F Cincinnati, OH 45250 859-669-3592

Line 1b. Enter your employer identification number (EIN) if your request relates to a business return. Otherwise, enter the first social security number (SSN) shown on the return. For example, if you are requesting Form 1040 that includes Schedule C (Form 1040), enter your SSN.

Line 6. Enter only one tax form number per request.

Signature and date. Form 4506-T must be signed and dated by the taxpayer listed on line 1a or 2a. If you completed line 5 requesting the information be sent to a third party, the IRS must receive Form 4506-T within 120 days of the date signed by the taxpayer or it will be rejected.

Individuals. Transcripts of jointly filed tax returns may be furnished to either spouse. Only one signature is required. Sign Form 4506-T exactly as your name appeared on the original return. If you changed your name, also sign your current name.

Corporations. Generally, Form 4506-T can be signed by: (1) an officer having legal authority to bind the corporation, (2) any person designated by the board of directors or other governing body, or (3) any officer or employee on written request by any principal officer and attested to by the secretary or other officer.

Partnerships. Generally, Form 4506-T can be signed by any person who was a member of the partnership during any part of the tax period requested on line 9.

All others. See Internal Revenue Code section 6103(e) if the taxpayer has died, is insolvent, is a dissolved corporation, or if a trustee, guardian, executor, receiver, or administrator is acting for the taxpayer.

Documentation. For entities other than individuals, you must attach the authorization document. For example, this could be the letter from the principal officer authorizing an employee of the corporation or the Letters Testamentary authorizing an individual to act for an estate.

Privacy Act and Paperwork Reduction Act Notice. We ask for the information on this form to establish your right to gain access to the requested tax information under the Internal Revenue Code. We need this information to properly identify the tax information and respond to your request. You are not required to request any transcript; if you do request a transcript, sections 6103 and 6109 and their regulations require you to provide this information, including your SSN or EIN. If you do not provide this information, we may not be able to process your request. Providing false or fraudulent information may subject you to penalties.

Routine uses of this information include giving it to the Department of Justice for civil and criminal litigation, and cities, states, and the District of Columbia for use in administering their tax laws. We may also disclose this information to other countries under a tax treaty, to federal and state agencies to enforce federal nontax criminal laws, or to federal law enforcement and intelligence agencies to combat terrorism.

You are not required to provide the information requested on a form that is subject to the Paperwork Reduction Act unless the form displays a valid OMB control number. Books or records relating to a form or its instructions must be retained as long as their contents may become material in the administration of any Internal Revenue law. Generally, tax returns and return information are confidential, as required by section 6103.

The time needed to complete and file Form 4506-T will vary depending on individual circumstances. The estimated average time is: **Learning about the law or the form,** 10 min.; **Preparing the form,** 12 min.; and **Copying, assembling, and sending the form to the IRS,** 20 min.

If you have comments concerning the accuracy of these time estimates or suggestions for making Form 4506-T simpler, we would be happy to hear from you. You can write to the Internal Revenue Service, Tax Products Coordinating Committee, SE:W:CAR:MP:T:T:SP, 1111 Constitution Ave. NW, IR-6526, Washington, DC 20224. Do not send the form to this address. Instead, see *Where to file* on this page.

For Privacy Act and Paperwork Reduction Act Notice, see page 2. Cat. No. 37667N

Form **4506-T** (Rev. 1-2010)

Page 2 of 2

TRISTAR FINANCIAL CORP.
1000 MAIN STREET
LOS ANGELES, CALIFORNIA 90025 Loan Number: 200911000

SERVICING DISCLOSURE STATEMENT

NOTICE TO FIRST LIEN MORTGAGE LOAN APPLICANTS
THE RIGHT TO COLLECT YOUR MORTGAGE LOAN PAYMENTS MAY BE TRANSFERRED

Date: FEBRUARY 12, 2010

You are applying for a mortgage loan covered by the Real Estate Settlement Procedures Act (RESPA) (12 U.S.C. 2601 et seq.). RESPA gives you certain rights under Federal law. This statement describes whether the servicing for this loan may be transferred to a different loan servicer. "Servicing" refers to collecting your principal, interest, and escrow payments, if any, as well as sending any monthly or annual statements, tracking account balances, and handling other aspects of your loan. You will be given advance notice before a transfer occurs.

Check the appropriate box under "Servicing Transfer Information."

SERVICING TRANSFER INFORMATION

☐ We may assign, sell, or transfer the servicing of your loan while the loan is outstanding.

or

☒ We do not service mortgage loans of the type for which you applied. We intend to assign, sell, or transfer the servicing of your mortgage loan before the first payment is due.

or

☐ The loan for which you have applied will be serviced at this financial institution and we do not intend to sell, transfer, or assign the servicing of the loan.

Loan Number: 200911000

NOTICE OF ASSIGNMENT, SALE OR TRANSFER OF SERVICING RIGHTS

You are hereby notified that the servicing of your mortgage loan, that is, the right to collect payments from you, is being assigned, sold or transferred from TRISTAR FINANCIAL CORP. to JPMORGAN CHASE BANK, N.A., P.O. BOX 8000, MONROE, LA 71211, effective APRIL 1, 2010.

The assignment, sale or transfer of the servicing of the mortgage loan does not affect any term or condition of the mortgage instruments, other than terms directly related to the servicing of your loan.

Except in limited circumstances, the law requires that your present servicer send you this notice at least 15 days before the effective date of transfer, or at closing. Your new servicer must also send you this notice no later than 15 days after this effective date or at closing. In this case, all necessary information is combined in this one notice.

Your present servicer is TRISTAR FINANCIAL CORP.
If you have any questions relating to the transfer of servicing from your present servicer call (310)321-4567 between 8:30 a.m. and 5:00p.m. on the following days: MONDAY - FRIDAY.
This is a ☐ toll-free or ☒ collect call number.

Your new servicer will be JPMORGAN CHASE BANK, N.A. C/O CHASE HOME FINANCE, LLC.
The business address for your new servicer is: P.O. BOX 79046, PHOENIX, ARIZONA 85062-9046.

The ☒ toll-free or ☐ collect call telephone number of your new servicer is (800)848-9136.
If you have any questions relating to the transfer of servicing to your new servicer call CUSTOMER RESEARCH at (800)848-9136 between 7:00 a.m. and 7:00 p.m. on the following days: MONDAY - FRIDAY.

The date that your present servicer will stop accepting payments from you is APRIL 1, 2010.
The date that your new servicer will start accepting payments from you is APRIL 1, 2010.
Send all payments due on or after that date to your new servicer.

You should also be aware of the following information, which is set out in more detail in Section 6 of the Real Estate Settlement Procedures Act (RESPA) (12 U.S.C. 2605):

During the 60-day period following the effective date of the transfer of the loan servicing, a loan payment received by your old servicer before its due date may not be treated by the new loan servicer as late, and a late fee may not be imposed on you.

Section 6 of RESPA (12 U.S.C. 2605) gives you certain consumer rights. If you send a "qualified written request" to your loan servicer concerning the servicing of your loan, your servicer must provide you with a written acknowledgment within 20 Business Days of receipt of your request. A "qualified written request" is a written correspondence, other than notice on a payment coupon or other payment medium supplied by the servicer, which includes your name and account number, and your reasons for the request. If you want to send a "qualified written request" regarding the servicing of your loan, it must be sent to this address:

JPMORGAN CHASE BANK, N.A. C/O CHASE HOME FINANCE, LLC
P.O. BOX 79046, PHOENIX, ARIZONA 85062-9046

Not later than 60 Business Days after receiving your request, your servicer must make any appropriate corrections to your account, and must provide you with a written clarification regarding any dispute. During this 60-Business Day period, your servicer may not provide information to a consumer reporting agency concerning any overdue payment related to such period or qualified written request. However, this does not prevent the servicer from initiating foreclosure if proper grounds exist under the mortgage documents.

A Business Day is a day on which the offices of the business entity are open to the public for carrying on substantially all of its business functions.

Section 6 of RESPA also provides for damages and costs for individuals or classes of individuals in circumstances where servicers are shown to have violated the requirements of that Section. You should seek legal advice if you believe your rights have been violated.

BORROWER ACKNOWLEDGMENT

I/We have read this disclosure form, and understand its contents, as evidenced by my/our loan signature(s) below.

Borrower RICHARD WILLIAM ROGERS Date	Borrower Date
Borrower Date	Borrower Date
Borrower Date	Borrower Date

Loan Number: 200911000

FEDERAL EQUAL CREDIT OPPORTUNITY ACT NOTICE

The Federal Equal Credit Opportunity Act prohibits creditors from discriminating against credit applicants on the basis of race, color, religion, national origin, sex, marital status, age (provided the applicant has the capacity to enter into a binding contract); because all or part of the applicant's income derives from any public assistance program; or because the applicant has in good faith exercised any right under the Consumer Credit Protection Act.

The Federal Agency that administers compliance with this law concerning this creditor is:

Federal Trade Commission
CRC-240
Washington, DC 20580

I/We acknowledge that I/we have received a copy of this notice.

RICHARD WILLIAM ROGERS Date ____________________ Date

____________________ Date ____________________ Date

____________________ Date ____________________ Date

Loan Number: 200911000

THE HOUSING FINANCIAL DISCRIMINATION ACT OF 1977
FAIR LENDING NOTICE

IT IS ILLEGAL TO DISCRIMINATE IN THE PROVISION OF OR IN THE AVAILABILITY OF FINANCIAL ASSISTANCE BECAUSE OF THE CONSIDERATION OF:

1. TRENDS, CHARACTERISTICS OR CONDITIONS IN THE NEIGHBORHOOD OR GEOGRAPHIC AREA SURROUNDING A HOUSING ACCOMMODATION, UNLESS THE FINANCIAL INSTITUTION CAN DEMONSTRATE IN THE PARTICULAR CASE THAT SUCH CONSIDERATION IS REQUIRED TO AVOID AN UNSAFE AND UNSOUND BUSINESS PRACTICE; OR

2. RACE, COLOR, RELIGION, SEX, MARITAL STATUS, DOMESTIC PARTNERSHIP, NATIONAL ORIGIN OR ANCESTRY.

IT IS ILLEGAL TO CONSIDER THE RACIAL, ETHNIC, RELIGIOUS OR NATIONAL ORIGIN COMPOSITION OF A NEIGHBORHOOD OR GEOGRAPHIC AREA SURROUNDING A HOUSING ACCOMMODATION OR WHETHER OR NOT SUCH COMPOSITION IS UNDERGOING CHANGE, OR IS EXPECTED TO UNDERGO CHANGE, IN APPRAISING A HOUSING ACCOMMODATION OR IN DETERMINING WHETHER OR NOT, OR UNDER WHAT TERMS AND CONDITIONS, TO PROVIDE FINANCIAL ASSISTANCE.

THESE PROVISIONS GOVERN FINANCIAL ASSISTANCE FOR THE PURPOSE OF THE PURCHASE, CONSTRUCTION, REHABILITATION OR REFINANCING OF ONE- TO FOUR-UNIT FAMILY RESIDENCES OCCUPIED BY THE OWNER AND FOR THE PURPOSE OF THE HOME IMPROVEMENT OF ANY ONE- TO FOUR-UNIT FAMILY RESIDENCE.

IF YOU HAVE QUESTIONS ABOUT YOUR RIGHTS, OR IF YOU WISH TO FILE A COMPLAINT, CONTACT THE MANAGEMENT OF THIS FINANCIAL INSTITUTION OR:

☐ **Department of Financial Institutions**
300 South Spring Street, Suite 15513
Los Angeles, CA 90013-1204
Tel: (213) 897-2085

☐ **Department of Financial Institutions**
45 Fremont Street, Suite 1700
San Francisco, CA 94105-2219
Tel: (415) 263-8500

☒ **Department of Real Estate**
320 W. 4th Street, Suite 350
Los Angeles, CA 90013-1105
(213) 620-2072

☒ **Department of Real Estate**
1515 Clay Street, Suite 702
Oakland, CA 94612-1462
(510) 622-2552

☐ **Department of Corporations**
320 West 4th Street, Suite 750
Los Angeles, CA 90013-2344
Tel: (213) 576-7500
(866) 275-2677 or 866 ASK CORP

☐ **Department of Corporations**
71 Stevenson Street, Suite 2100
San Francisco, CA 94105-2980
Tel: (415) 972-8559
(866) 275-2677 or 866 ASK CORP

Acknowledgement of Receipt:

I/We received a copy of this notice.

Borrower RICHARD WILLIAM ROGERS Date	Borrower Date
Borrower Date	Borrower Date
Borrower Date	Borrower Date

HOEPA/HMDA REQUIRED INFORMATION

Due to the recent amendments to Reg Z relating to higher priced mortgages for transactions secured by the consumer's principal dwelling, and HMDA requirements for rate spread reporting on all occupancy types, this form must be completed by the Correspondent on all loans delivered to Chase for funding on or after **October 1, 2009.**

Please complete the below, and submit with the closed loan file for funding:

Borrower's Last Name: ROGERS

Property Address: 8624 OAKLAWN AVENUE, NO. 13 (CANOGA PARK AREA), LOS ANGELES, CALIFORNIA 91304

Correspondent OR Chase Loan Number: 200911000

1. **Initial Application Date (as defined by your current policies and procedures)** JANUARY 20, 2010 .

   Note: If the initial application date is prior to October 1,2009 **and** the loan closed or will close prior to January 1, 2010 as indicated by the Note, there is no need to complete the remaining information on this form.

2. **Last date you (correspondent) locked the loan with the borrower** JANUARY 21, 2010 .

3. **If the loan is an ARM, list the initial index rate** %.

4. **If the loan is secured by the consumer's Principal Dwelling and is a Higher Priced Mortgage, please list the rate spread difference between the final APR and the and the Average Prime Offer Rate (APOR) as defined in Regulation Z.**
   Please refer to http://www.ffiec.gov/ratespread/default.aspx to access the FFIEC Rate Spread Calculator.

Any loan application delivered to Chase for funding on or after October 1, 2009 which does not contain this form with all required fields completed will be suspended until the completed form is received.

IMPORTANT REMINDERS: If the loan is secured by the consumer's principal dwelling and is a higher priced mortgage as defined in the amendments to Reg Z, you (Correspondent) must ensure all requirements have been met including, but not limited to the following: Repayment Ability, Income, and Asset verification, and for transactions closed on or after April 1,2010, an escrow account has been established (excluding co-ops).

The information contained in this form is not to be construed as legal advice, and is not meant to be used as a summary of the laws. If you have questions related to this or any other law, you are strongly encouraged to contact your Legal and Compliance Counsel for further guidance.

For additional information please refer to CB09-50.

Loan Number: 200911000

DISCLOSURE CONCERNING THE CHARGING OF PER DIEM INTEREST ON CALIFORNIA RESIDENTIAL MORTGAGE LOANS

You are about to close your California residential mortgage loan with a Residential Mortgage Lender licensed by the California Department of Corporations ("Lender"). Under California Law, Lender is authorized to begin charging interest on your loan at the note rate up to one day prior to the disbursement of the loan proceeds out of escrow. If a request to record the security instrument has been made, then the Lender is authorized to begin charging interest on your loan at the note rate up to one day prior to the disbursement of the loan proceeds to you or to a third party on your behalf.

However, if you elect disbursement of the loan proceeds to occur on a Monday or on the day immediately following a Bank Holiday, interest on your loan may commence to accrue on the business day immediately preceding the day of disbursement. For instance, if you elect to close our loan on a Monday, interest may begin to accrue on Friday, (the immediately preceding business day). The maximum amount of additional interest that may be charged to you prior to the disbursement date will be three days. Be aware that it may be possible to avoid this additional [per diem interest charge by requesting the disbursement of the loan proceeds on a day immediately following a business day.

I HAVE READ THE FOREGOING DISCLOSURE AND UNDERSTAND THAT I MAY BE CHARGED A HIGHER AMOUNT OF INTEREST IF I CHOOSE DISBURSEMENT OF MY LOAN PROCEEDS TO OCCUR ON A MONDAY OR ON A BUSINESS DAY IMMEDIATELY FOLLOWING A BANK HOLIDAY.

☐ I elect disbursement of my loan proceeds to occur on any day BUT a Monday or on a business day immediately following a Bank Holiday in order to avoid incurring interest charges beyond 24 hours prior to loan closing.

☐ I elect disbursement of my loan proceeds to occur on ____________ which is a Monday or a business day immediately following a Bank Holiday and agree to pay additional interest in the amount of $ ____________ to close my loan on this day.

ACKNOWLEDGEMENT

I/We acknowledge that we have received this Disclosure and further that I/we understand its provisions.

Borrower RICHARD WILLIAM ROGERS Date	Borrower Date
Borrower Date	Borrower Date
Borrower Date	Borrower Date

Loan Number: 200911000

CALIFORNIA DOMESTIC PARTNERSHIP ADDENDUM TO UNIFORM RESIDENTIAL LOAN APPLICATION

Date: FEBRUARY 12, 2010

Provided by: TRISTAR FINANCIAL CORP.

Borrower: RICHARD WILLIAM ROGERS

Property Address: 8624 OAKLAWN AVENUE, NO. 13 (CANOGA PARK AREA), LOS ANGELES, CALIFORNIA 91304

On and after January 1, 2005, California law extends the same rights, protections, benefits, and duties of marriage to persons registered as domestic partners in the State of California. Thus, a non-borrowing domestic partner whose domestic partnership is registered in California will be presumed to have a community property interest in the real property of the borrowing domestic partner that will secure repayment of this loan transaction regardless of whether the non-borrowing partner holds, or will hold, legal title to that property.

Furthermore, a legal union of two persons of the same sex, other than marriage, that is validly formed in another jurisdiction and that is substantially equivalent to a domestic partnership under California law is recognized as a valid domestic partnership in California regardless of whether it bears the name domestic partnership.

Accordingly, if you, as the Borrower, indicate that you are involved in a domestic partnership registered with the State of California or part of a legal union formed in another jurisdiction, the Lender will require that your domestic partner also sign the deed of trust or other security instrument (and perhaps other related loan documents) that secures repayment of this loan.

You should consult an attorney for specific legal advice regarding community property rights and for specific legal advice regarding rights, protections, benefits, and duties under California law.

The undersigned Borrower hereby represents to Lender and to Lender's actual or potential agents, brokers, processors, attorneys, insurers, servicers, successors and assigns, the following:

Please check all of those statements below that apply.

- ☐ I am not involved in a domestic partnership in California or in any other jurisdiction recognizing a domestic partnership or civil union.
- ☐ I do not have a pending termination or judgment of dissolution or nullity of a domestic partnership or civil union.
- ☐ I have registered a domestic partnership with the State of California. The Lender may request that you provide a Certificate of Domestic Partnership issued by the California Secretary of State.
- ☐ I am involved in a domestic partnership or civil union formed in a jurisdiction outside the State of California.

If you have registered a domestic partnership in California or formed a domestic partnership or civil union in another jurisdiction, please provide the name of your domestic partner in the space provided below:

Name: ______________________________

____

Borrower RICHARD WILLIAM ROGERS Date

TAX INFORMATION SHEET

Loan Number: 200911900

Borrower(s) Name(s): RICHARD WILLIAM ROGERS

Street Address: 8624 OAKLAWN AVENUE, NO. 13 (CANOGA PARK AREA), LOS ANGELES, CALIFORNIA 91304

New Construction? (Y/N) ______

ESCROW FOR TAXES? (Y/N) N PAYMENT FREQUENCY ______

Please indicate below, the name(s) of the municipality to which taxes are payable.

COUNTY (if any) ______

Taxes paid through: (MM/YY) ______

Address: ______

Last Amount paid or Estimated Amount of next disbursement: ______

Next tax payment due: (MM/YY) ______

Property Identification Number (i.e. parcel number): ______

CITY, TOWNSHIP OR BOROUGH (if any) ______

Taxes paid through: (MM/YY) ______

Address: ______

Last Amount paid or Estimated Amount of next disbursement: ______

Next tax payment due: (MM/YY) ______

Property Identification Number (i.e. parcel number): ______

SCHOOL (if any) ______

Taxes paid through: (MM/YY) ______

Address: ______

Last Amount paid or Estimated Amount of next disbursement: ______

Next tax payment due: (MM/YY) ______

Property Identification Number (i.e. parcel number): ______

Other (Assessments, etc.) ______

Taxes paid through: (MM/YY) ______

Address: ______

Last Amount paid or Estimated Amount of next disbursement: ______

Next tax payment due: (MM/YY) ______

Property Identification Number (i.e. parcel number): ______

TAX BILLS DUE WITHIN 30 DAYS OF CHASE'S PURCHASE OF THE LOAN MUST BE PAID BY THE CLOSING AGENT. FAILURE TO PAY TAXES DUE WITHIN 30 DAYS OF FUNDING WILL RESULT IN FUNDING DELAYS.

CLOSING AGENT: SOUTHERN ESCROW

ADDRESS: 1001 MAIN STREET, LOS ANGELES, CALIFORNIA 90025

PHONE NUMBER: (310) 321-9876 ESCROW/FILE #: ML-09876

BY: ______

______ ______

DATE NAME/TITLE

800-649-1362

Loan Number: 200911000

Lender: TRISTAR FINANCIAL CORP.

CUSTOMER IDENTIFICATION VERIFICATION

IMPORTANT INFORMATION ABOUT PROCEDURES FOR OPENING A NEW ACCOUNT

To help the government fight the funding of terrorism and money laundering activities, Federal law requires all financial institutions to obtain, verify, and record information that identifies each person who opens an account. What this means for you: When you open an account, we will ask for your name, address, date of birth, and other information that will allow us to identify you. We may also ask to see your driver's license or other identifying documents.

INSTRUCTIONS TO INDIVIDUAL COMPLETING THIS VERIFICATION

The named individual must present at least two (2) forms of identifying documents for review; at least one (1) of the identifying documents must be a government-issued document bearing a photograph of the named individual. Other identifying documents not specifically listed below must, at a minimum, bear the individual's name. Examples of other acceptable identifying documents include: Current government-issued visa; Medicare card; student identification card; voter registration card; recent property tax or utility bill; most recent W-2 or signed federal or state tax returns; bank statements; and proof of car/house/renter's insurance coverage. Please contact the above-named Lender if you have any questions regarding the acceptability of any identifying document.

Borrower's Name: RICHARD WILLIAM ROGERS Date of Birth: MARCH 22, 1956

[X] Residential or [ ] Business Address:* 8624 OAKLAWN AVENUE, NO. 13 (CANOGA PARK AREA)
LOS ANGELES, CALIFORNIA 91304

Taxpayer Identification Number (SSN):** 000-00-0000

Identifying Documents	Place of Issuance	ID Number	Date of Birth	Issue/Expiration Date(s)	Photo?
[ ] State/Foreign Driver's License					[ ] Yes [ ] No
[ ] State/Foreign ID Card					[ ] Yes [ ] No
[ ] U.S./Foreign Passport					[ ] Yes [ ] No
[ ] Military ID					[ ] Yes [ ] No
[ ] Resident Alien Card					[ ] Yes [ ] No
[ ] Social Security Card					
[ ] Birth Certificate					
[ ] Other:					[ ] Yes [ ] No
[ ] Other:					[ ] Yes [ ] No

ADDITIONAL COMMENTS

(e.g., please note any discrepancies in the borrower's identifying documents): ______________________

CERTIFICATION

I, the undersigned, hereby certify that: (i) I have personally examined the identifying documents indicated above presented to me by the named individual, (ii) I have accurately recorded the information appearing in the identifying documents I examined, and (iii) except as may be indicated above, each of the indicated identifying documents appears to be genuine, the information contained in the identifying documents is consistent in all respects with the information provided by the named individual, and, where applicable, the photograph appears to be that of the named individual.

____
Signature Date

____
Name and Title

*For an individual without a residential or business address, provide an APO or FPO box number, or the residential or business address of next of kin or another contact person.
**For non-U.S. persons without a tax identification number, provide a passport number and country of issuance; an alien identification card number, or the number and country of issuance of any other government-issued document evidencing nationality or residence and bearing a photograph or similar safeguard.

REQUEST FOR CHANGE TO INSURANCE POLICY

Date: FEBRUARY 12, 2010

Loan Number: 200911000

Phone Number: (310) 321-4567

Policy Number:

PLEASE MAKE THE CHANGES REQUESTED BELOW:

☒ Correct Mortgagee Clause to read:
CHASE HOME FINANCE, LLC
ITS SUCCESSORS AND/OR ASSIGNS
P.O. BOX 47020
DORAVILLE, GEORGIA 30362
Loan Number: 200911949

☐ Change Property Address to:

☐ Change Insured's Name(s) to:

☐ Please increase the amount of coverage to $

☐ Other:

Please send the endorsement(s) directly to
CHASE HOME FINANCE, LLC
ITS SUCCESSORS AND/OR ASSIGNS
P.O. BOX 47020
DORAVILLE, GEORGIA 30362
Loan Number: 200911000

Sincerely,
TRISTAR FINANCIAL CORP.

INSURED: RICHARD WILLIAM ROGERS

PROPERTY: 8624 OAKLAWN AVENUE, NO. 13
(CANOGA PARK AREA)
LOS ANGELES, CALIFORNIA 91304

____
Brad Donnelly

REQUEST FOR CHANGE TO FLOOD CERTIFICATION

Loan Number: 200911000

Date: FEBRUARY 12, 2010

Policy Number:

Phone Number: (310)321-4567

PLEASE MAKE THE CHANGES REQUESTED BELOW:

[X] Correct Mortgagee Clause to read:
CHASE HOME FINANCE, LLC
ITS SUCCESSORS AND/OR ASSIGNS
P.O. BOX 47020, DORAVILLE, GEORGIA 30362

☐ Change Property Address to: ____________________

☐ Change insured's Name(s) to: ____________________

☐ Please increase the amount of coverage to $

☐ Other: ____________________

Please send the endorsement(s) directly to CHASE HOME FINANCE, LLC ITS SUCCESSORS AND/OR ASSIGNS P.O. BOX 47020, DORAVILLE, GEORGIA 30362

Sincerely,
TRISTAR FINANCIAL CORP.

INSURED: RICHARD WILLIAM ROGERS

PROPERTY: 8624 OAKLAWN AVENUE, NO. 13 (CANOGA PARK AREA), LOS ANGELES, CALIFORNIA 91304

____
Loan Representative
Brad Donnelly

CHASE PRIVACY POLICY

Loan Number: 200911000

For over 200 years, respecting and protecting customer privacy has been vital to our business. By explaining our Privacy Policy to you, we trust that you will better understand how we keep our customer information private and secure while using it to serve you better.

The Privacy Policy explains the following:

- Protecting the confidentiality of our customer information
- Who is covered by the Privacy Policy
- The types of information we have about you and where it comes from
- The types of information Chase shares, why and with whom
- Opting out—how to instruct us not to share certain information about you or not to contact you

Protecting the Confidentiality of Customer Information

We take our responsibility to protect the privacy and confidentiality of customer information very seriously. We maintain physical, electronic and procedural safeguards that comply with federal standards to store and secure information about you from unauthorized access, alteration and destruction. Our control policies, for example, authorize access to customer information only by individuals who need access to do their work.

From time to time, we enter into agreements with other companies to provide services to us or make products and services available to you. Under these agreements, the companies may receive information about you but they must safeguard this information and they may not use it for any other purposes.

Who is Covered by the Privacy Policy

We provide our Privacy Policy to customers when they open a new account and annually after that. If we change our privacy policies to permit us to share additional information we have about you, as described below, or to permit disclosures to additional types of parties, you will be notified in advance.

This Privacy Policy applies to consumers who are customers or former customers of the Chase family of companies in the United States. Customers of certain Chase businesses, such as Private Banking, will be separately notified of the specific privacy policies that are applicable to those businesses. Similarly, Chase customers who receive information from Chase or transact business with Chase through the Internet are covered by the privacy policies posted on the websites they visit. For example, the Chase Online Consumer Information Practices as well as this Policy may be found at www.Chase.com.

The Chase family of companies include financial services companies owned by Chase that may provide products and services to you. For example, you may have a checking account with The Chase Manhattan Bank, a mortgage from Chase Manhattan Mortgage Corporation, MasterCard® and Visa® credit cards through Chase Manhattan Bank USA, N.A. and other services and products from those companies as well as from Chase Manhattan Automotive Finance Corporation and Chase Investment Services Corporation.

Information We Have About You

Chase receives information about you from various sources, including information from:

- your requests or applications for Chase products or services, such as your income in a loan application
- your transactions with us, our family of companies or others, such as your account balance with Chase or mortgage information from Chase or from others
- consumer reporting agencies (credit bureaus), such as your credit history

Information Chase Shares

Chase shares information it has about you, as described above, to give you superior customer service, provide convenient access to our services and make a wider range of products available to you. We share this information in the following ways:

Sharing Information for Legal and Routine Business Reasons and for Joint Marketing. We may disclose information we have about you as permitted by law. For example, we may share information with regulatory authorities and law enforcement officials; provide information to protect against fraud; report account activity to credit bureaus; share information with your consent and give account information to check and statement printers and other service providers who work for us. We may also share information we have about you, as described above, with firms Chase hires to market Chase products and services or with financial institutions not within the Chase family of companies with whom we have joint marketing agreements to provide you with offers of their financial products and services. For example, we may share information about you with an insurance firm in order that you may receive offers concerning various insurance products.

Sharing Information among the Chase Family of Companies. The Chase family of companies offers a wide array of financial products and services such as loans, deposits, investments and insurance. We may share information we have about you, as described above, such as identification, application and credit bureau information, and transaction and account balance information among the Chase family of companies. Some of the benefits to you of this sharing may include account upgrades based on our more complete knowledge of your total Chase relationship, improved customer service and responsiveness and detection of unusual behavior to help prevent unauthorized transactions or fraud. You may, however, instruct us not to share some of this information among the Chase family of companies for purposes described in choice # 1 on the accompanying Opt Out Form. If you opt out, we may continue to share other information among the Chase family of companies, including identification information (such as name and address) and information regarding your transactions or experiences with us (such as account balance and payment history), as well as survey or similar information from others.

Special Notice to Customers with accounts involving Program "Partners" and to Credit Card and Auto Finance Customers

Program "Partner" Accounts: You may choose to participate in a program where Chase "partners" with a prominent company, such as an airline, gasoline company or financial institution outside the Chase family of companies. When you choose to participate in a program like this, the name or logo of the program "partner" is prominently displayed on the program materials or websites. These programs may combine Chase products or services with those of other companies to give you a distinctive service or other benefits. For example, you may have a credit card from Chase offering you frequent flyer miles or do business with a bank that has arranged for Chase to issue credit cards to its customers. We share information we have about you, as described above, with these program "partners". Our "partners" use that information for purposes related to the "partner" program, for example to service your account, administer the program and update their records. Our "partners" may also use that information for marketing purposes unrelated to the program. You may, however, instruct us not to share personally identifiable information about you with our partners for marketing purposes unrelated to the "partner" program as described in choice # 2a on the accompanying Opt Out Form.

Credit Card Customers: Chase periodically reviews its own information regarding its customers, their credit card accounts and transactions to select customers to receive special offers from companies outside the Chase family of companies with whom we have marketing relationships and who offer non-financial products and services. These offers, which we believe will be of interest to you, may be for products or services such as travel programs, magazine subscriptions, dental or legal services, or gardening, sewing and pet clubs. Information provided to companies making these offers is limited to name, address and telephone number. You may, however, instruct us not to share this information about you with companies outside the Chase family of companies for these marketing purposes as described in choice # 2b on the accompanying Opt Out Form.

Auto Finance Customers: Chase may share your name, address, telephone number and account payoff information with an automobile dealership outside the Chase family of companies from which you purchased or leased a vehicle. This information sharing enables the dealership to contact you with offers for the lease or sale of another vehicle. You may, however, instruct us not to share this information about you with your auto dealership for these marketing purposes as described in choice # 2c on the accompanying Opt Out Form.

Please note: If you opt out under 2a, 2b, or 2c, we may continue to share as described above in "Sharing Information for Legal and Routine Business Reasons and for Joint Marketing" and in "Sharing Information among the Chase Family of Companies."

Opting Out

Your Right To Opt Out. You may instruct us not to share information about you, as described in this Privacy Policy.

How To Opt Out: To opt out, simply complete and follow the directions to call or otherwise notify us on the accompanying Opt Out Form.

The Chase Family of Companies are subsidiaries of J.P. Morgan Chase & Co.

OPT OUT FORM

We may share information about you among the Chase family of companies and/or outside the Chase family of companies. Chase offers you the Opt Out Choices listed below concerning this sharing of information, as well as the choice not to be contacted by mail or by telephone. If you decide that you want to choose any or all of these options, please complete the appropriate opt-out section(s) below. Please include your identifying information and notify us as follows:

By telephone: call us at 1-866-887-9769

You do not need to notify us if you have already opted out as described below or you have decided not to opt out. It may take up to four to six weeks to process your request. If you have multiple Chase accounts, we will follow these instructions for your consumer accounts covered by this Policy. If at a later time you wish to change these opt out instructions, please contact Chase at 1-866-887-9769.

Note: If you opt out, you may still receive offers with your account statements, when you contact us and in connection with the maintenance and servicing of your account relationship.

Opt Out Choices Regarding Information Chase May Share About You:

1. Sharing among the Chase Family of Companies as described in our Privacy Policy: Please do not share among the Chase family of companies (a) information from me or from others to determine my eligibility for products or (b) information from credit bureau reports for marketing purposes. Note: Restricting our sharing of this information may prevent you from receiving product offers from the Chase family of companies which may be of interest to you and meet your financial needs. [ ]

2. Sharing with Program "Partners" (2a) and companies making special offers to Chase Credit Card (2b) and Chase Auto Finance (2c) Customers as described in our Privacy Policy. Please do not share personally identifiable information about me:

a. with Program "Partners" for marketing purposes unrelated to the "partner" program; [ ]
b. with companies so they can make special offers of non-financial products and services to Chase Credit Card customers; and/or [ ]
c. with an auto dealer from which I purchased a vehicle so that the auto dealer may offer me another vehicle. [ ]

Note for Joint Accounts: Your opt out choices will also apply to other individuals who are joint account holders. If these individuals have separate accounts, your opt out will not apply to those separate accounts.

Opt Out Choices Regarding How Chase May Contact You

3. Please do not contact me with offers of products and services by mail. [ ]

4. Please do not contact me with offers of products and services by telephone. [ ]

RICHARD WILLIAM ROGERS
Name

8624 OAKLAWN AVENUE, NO. 13 (CANOGA PARK AREA)
Address

LOS ANGELES — CALIFORNIA — 91304
City — State — Zip Code

____
Signature — Date

______________________________ ______________________________
Account Type (e.g., Mortgage, Card, Auto, Checking, etc.) — Account Number

ADDITIONAL LOAN DOCUMENTS

The following documents are also regularly seen in loan packages and are provided for the reader's benefit. Samples of each document discussed in this section appear beginning on page 247.

Affiliated Business Arrangement Disclosure (Page 247)

1. The Affiliated Business Arrangement Disclosure is required whenever a settlement service provider involved in a RESPA-covered transaction refers the consumer to a provider with whom the referring party has an ownership or other interest.

2. The referring party must provide the Affiliated Business Arrangement Disclosure at or before the time of referral. This document describes the business arrangement that exists between the two providers and gives the borrower an estimate of the second provider's charges.

3. Except in cases where a lender refers a borrower to an attorney, credit reporting agency or real estate appraiser to represent the lender's interest in the transaction, the referring party may not require the consumer to use the particular provider being referred.

Additional Riders to Security Instrument (Pages 248–253)

1. The Condominium Rider (pages 185–187) included in the sample set of loan documents was previously described.

2. The following additional riders used in residential mortgage loan transactions are illustrated in the pages that follow:

   a. Adjustable-Rate Rider

   b. Balloon Rider

   c. Biweekly Payment Rider

IRS Form 8821 (Tax Information Authorization) (Pages 254–257)

1. This document increasingly is being used by lenders as a replacement for the IRS Form 4506-T Request for Copy of Transcript of Tax Return (pages 223–224) discussed earlier in this chapter. IRS Form 8821 allows entities to request returns from multiple tax years with one form.

2. To properly execute the form, the borrower must do the following:

   a. Verify his or her name, address and Social Security number.

   b. Read the instructions on page 2 and check the box on line 4. By checking this box, the borrower authorizes the IRS to issue the borrower's tax returns only to the lender. Supplemental correspondence and communications, which the borrower may not want the lender to see, will not be provided with the returns.

   c. Sign, date and print his or her name to complete the form.

Notice of Right to Cancel (Page 258)

1. If the loan includes a rescission option, the Notice of Right to Cancel gives the borrower three (3) business days to cancel the loan. A loan will have a rescission option if the transaction results in a mortgage or lien on the property.

2. There are three important dates referred to in the Notice of Right to Cancel:

   a. Document preparation date: the date the document was drafted

   b. Transaction date: the date the document was signed

c. End of rescission period date: the termination date of the borrower's right to cancel the loan

3. Some lenders calculate the rescission period. Other lenders, not knowing the exact date the documents will be signed, rely upon the Notary Signing Agent to complete the form at the signing.

4. A Notary Signing Agent calculates the rescission date as follows:

   a. From the signing date, the Agent should count three (3) business days after the signing date. The rescission period ends at midnight on the third business day following the signing.

   b. A "business day" includes any day of the week except Sunday and the following federal legal holidays: New Year's Day, Martin Luther King Jr. Day, Presidents' Day, Memorial Day, Independence Day, Labor Day, Columbus Day, Veterans Day, Thanksgiving Day and Christmas Day. For example, if a signing took place on a Friday, then Saturday is counted as the first business day. Since Sunday is not counted, Tuesday is the third business day.

   c. The Notary Signing Agent should ask the borrower to enter the proper dates into the Notice of Right to Cancel.

5. Since the Notice of Right to Cancel contains more than one signature space, the Notary Signing Agent must understand where to have the borrower sign the form at the signing appointment. On the sample Notice of Right to Cancel, there are two signature spaces; some forms may contain a third signature space. The three possible signature spaces are as follows:

   a. Borrower's Acknowledgment: This is where the borrower signs at the loan signing appointment. On the sample document, the signature line with the borrower's name printed underneath indicates this. However, many versions of the Notice of Right to Cancel do not contain the typed borrower name under the line where the borrower must sign.

b. Right to Cancel: This is where the borrower signs should he or she wish to exercise the right to cancel the loan before the rescission period ends. IMPORTANT: The borrower does not sign on this line at the loan signing appointment. Only if a borrower wishes to exercise the right to rescind the loan will the borrower sign in this space.

c. Confirmation Certificate: This is where the borrower confirms, subsequent to the conclusion of the rescission period, that he or she has not exercised the right to rescind the loan. Many times the borrower will sign a separate Customer's Statement of Non-Rescission (page 269) after the rescission period has ended, in which case this third signature space will not appear on the Notice of Right to Cancel. IMPORTANT: If this signature space does appear on the Notice of Right to Cancel, the borrower does not sign on this line at the loan signing appointment.

FNMA 1009 Affidavit (Page 259)

1. In the Federal National Mortgage Association (FNMA) 1009 Affidavit, also known as the Affidavit of Purchaser and Vendor, the buyer and seller in a purchase transaction must certify that the financial terms, liens and occupancy conditions set forth in the document are true.

2. The FNMA 1009 Affidavit is used to induce the lender to make or purchase the first mortgage and to induce the mortgage insurer, if any, to insure the loan.

3. The document is notarized with a jurat for both buyer (purchaser) and seller (vendor).

Mortgagor's Affidavit (Pages 260–261)

1. The purpose of the Mortgagor's Affidavit is to induce the mortgagee to make a mortgage loan that is secured by a first mortgage loan on the subject property.

2. In the Mortgagor's Affidavit, the borrower states that there have been no substantial changes to the borrower's financial condition, ownership status or the physical condition of the property.

3. The Mortgagor's Affidavit typically is notarized with a jurat.

Statement of Information (Page 262)

1. In the Statement of Information, a borrower is asked to provide personal, residential, occupational and marital status information.

2. Title companies use the information in this form to search the property title during escrow to ensure that there are no tax liens, judgments, bankruptcies or other matters that would affect the loan.

Addendums to the Note (Pages 263–267)

1. In a manner similar to a rider that modifies the terms of the Deed of Trust (Mortgage), an Addendum to the Note adds or deletes provisions to the Note (pages 167–169).

2. Common addenda include the following:

    a. Balloon Note Addendum

    b. Construction Loan Addendum

    c. Fixed-Rate Conversion Option Addendum

3. The following sample Note addenda are illustrated:

   a. Addendum to Adjustable-Rate Note (Fixed-Rate Conversion Option)
   b. Affordable Merit Rate Addendum to Note

   c. 3-Year Prepayment Penalty Addendum to Note

   d. Timely Payment Rewards Addendum to Note

Demand/Payoff Statement (Page 268)

1. The Demand/Payoff Statement is a document issued by the borrower's current mortgage holder that itemizes the costs to satisfy (pay off) the existing loan, including the outstanding principal balance, interest, late fees (if applicable) and other miscellaneous charges.

2. In a typical refinance transaction, the closing agent will disburse funds to pay off the current mortgagee once the new loan is funded.

3. Different versions of the Demand/Payoff Statement may require a borrower's signature or initials or may be unsigned.

Customer's Statement of Non-Rescission (Page 269)

1. In some loan document packages, a Statement of Non-Rescission will accompany the Notice of Right to Cancel. The Statement of Non-Rescission is required by a lender to confirm that a borrower has not exercised the option to rescind the loan under the three-day rescission rule. Some lenders will not fund the loan until they receive proof of non-rescission by the borrower.

2. Under no circumstances should the Statement of Non-Rescission be signed at the closing table. It should only be signed after the

three-day rescission period has elapsed and the borrower has not exercised the right to rescind.

3. When a Statement of Non-Rescission is present in the loan document package, the Notary Signing Agent should contact the contracting company to inquire how to handle this document at the signing. One possible option might be to hand the document to the borrower at the signing appointment with instructions to sign and date the form after the third business day and then fax the document or deliver it via overnight delivery to the closing agent. However, the Agent should receive exact instructions from the contracting company prior to the signing appointment.

Loan Modification Agreement (Pages 270–271)

1. The U.S. Department of Housing and Urban Development (HUD) defines a loan modification as a permanent change in one or more of the terms of a home mortgage loan that allows the loan to be reinstated and that results in a payment the borrower can afford. Lenders use a loan modification in an attempt to avoid foreclosure by negotiating with the borrower more favorable terms that allow a borrower to stay in the home.

2. In a loan modification, the existing Note and Deed of Trust (Mortgage) remain in place, but are modified through a Loan Modification Agreement that adjusts the interest rate, extends the loan period or adds the arrears and fees back onto the principal of the loan to be repaid over time.

3. While loan modifications are chiefly used to mitigate losses due to defaults and foreclosures, there have been cases where a borrower has renegotiated the terms and payments of a mortgage with a loan modification instead of refinancing the loan. In this type of transaction, the borrower is spared from paying the loan origination

and closing costs of a refinance loan and having to re-execute the myriad documents involved in such a transaction. The lender retains a customer who otherwise might refinance the loan with a competitor and keeps the loan on its books. Notary Signing Agents have reported being asked to handle assignments involving a loan modification agreement, because these agreements often require notarization and borrowers appreciate the convenience of having an Agent come to their homes to execute the agreement. In such assignments, the actual loan modification document may be the only form signed.

4. The sample Loan Modification Agreement is notarized with an acknowledgment.

AFFILIATED BUSINESS ARRANGEMENT DISCLOSURE NOTICE

TO:_________________________________ DATE:________________

PROPERTY: ____

This is to give notice that Test Lender has a business relationship with ABC Title Security Agency of Arizona. The majority shareholder of ABC Title Security Agency of Arizona is also the majority shareholder of Test Lender.

Set forth below is an estimate of the charges by ABC Title Security Agency of Arizona for the refinance of an average loan of $100,000 for the following settlement services:

ESCROW FEE:	$150
TITLE INSURANCE:	$355
RECONVEYANCE FEE:	$ 75

You are not required to use ABC Title Security Agency of Arizona as a condition for settlement of your loan on the subject property. You are free to check with other settlement service providers to determine that you are receiving the best services and the best rate for these services.

ACKNOWLEDGMENT
I/We have read this disclosure form and understand that Test Lender is referring me/us to purchase the above-described settlement services and may receive a financial or other benefit as the result of this referral.

______________________ ______________________
Borrower Date Borrower Date

______________________ ______________________
Borrower Date Borrower Date

ADJUSTABLE RATE RIDER

(1 Year Treasury Index–Rate Caps)

THIS ADJUSTABLE RATE RIDER is made this _________ day of __________________________, ______, and is incorporated into and shall be deemed to amend and supplement the Mortgage, Deed of Trust, or Security Deed (the "Security Instrument") of the same date given by the undersigned (the "Borrower") to secure Borrower's Adjustable Rate Note (the "Note") to ____ (the "Lender") of the same date and covering the property described in the Security Instrument and located at:

____

[Property Address]

THE NOTE CONTAINS PROVISIONS ALLOWING FOR CHANGES IN THE INTEREST RATE AND THE MONTHLY PAYMENT. THE NOTE LIMITS THE AMOUNT THE BORROWER'S INTEREST RATE CAN CHANGE AT ANY ONE TIME AND THE MAXIMUM RATE THE BORROWER MUST PAY.

ADDITIONAL COVENANTS. In addition to the covenants and agreements made in the Security Instrument, Borrower and Lender further covenant and agree as follows:

A. INTEREST RATE AND MONTHLY PAYMENT CHANGES

The Note provides for an initial interest rate of _________ %. The Note provides for changes in the interest rate and the monthly payments as follows:

4. INTEREST RATE AND MONTHLY PAYMENT CHANGES

(A) Change Dates

The interest rate I will pay may change on the first day of ____________________, ______, and on that day every 12th month thereafter. Each date on which my interest rate could change is called a "Change Date."

(B) The Index

Beginning with the first Change Date, my interest rate will be based on an Index. The "Index" is the weekly average yield on United States Treasury securities adjusted to a constant maturity of one year, as made available by the Federal Reserve Board. The most recent Index figure available as of the date 45 days before each Change Date is called the "Current Index."

If the Index is no longer available, the Note Holder will choose a new index which is based upon comparable information. The Note Holder will give me notice of this choice.

(C) Calculation of Changes

Before each Change Date, the Note Holder will calculate my new interest rate by adding ________________ percentage points (__________ %) to the Current Index. The Note Holder will then round the result of this addition to the nearest one-eighth of one percentage point (0.125%). Subject to the limits stated in Section 4(D) below, this rounded amount will be my new interest rate until the next Change Date.

The Note Holder will then determine the amount of the monthly payment that would be sufficient to repay the unpaid principal that I am expected to owe at the Change Date in full on the maturity date at my new interest rate in substantially equal payments. The result of this calculation will be the new amount of my monthly payment.

(D) Limits on Interest Rate Changes

The interest rate I am required to pay at the first Change Date will not be greater than _____________% or less than ________ %. Thereafter, my interest rate will never be increased or decreased on any single Change Date by more than one percentage point (1.0%) from the rate of interest I have been paying for the preceding 12 months. My interest rate will never be greater than _________ %.

(E) Effective Date of Changes

My new interest rate will become effective on each Change Date. I will pay the amount of my new monthly payment beginning on the first monthly payment date after the Change Date until the amount of my monthly payment changes again.

(F) Notice of Changes

The Note Holder will deliver or mail to me a notice of any changes in my interest rate and the amount

MULTISTATE ADJUSTABLE RATE RIDER–ARM 5-1 –Single Family–**Fannie Mae/Freddie Mac UNIFORM INSTRUMENT** **Form 3108 1/01** *(Page 1 of 2 pages)*

of my monthly payment before the effective date of any change. The notice will include information required by law to be given to me and also the title and telephone number of a person who will answer any question I may have regarding the notice.

B. TRANSFER OF THE PROPERTY OR A BENEFICIAL INTEREST IN BORROWER

Section 18 of the Security Instrument is amended to read as follows:

Transfer of the Property or a Beneficial Interest in Borrower. As used in this Section 18, "Interest in the Property" means any legal or beneficial interest in the Property, including, but not limited to, those beneficial interests transferred in a bond for deed, contract for deed, installment sales contract or escrow agreement, the intent of which is the transfer of title by Borrower at a future date to a purchaser.

If all or any part of the Property or any Interest in the Property is sold or transferred (or if Borrower is not a natural person and a beneficial interest in Borrower is sold or transferred) without Lender's prior written consent, Lender may require immediate payment in full of all sums secured by this Security Instrument. However, this option shall not be exercised by Lender if such exercise is prohibited by Applicable Law. Lender also shall not exercise this option if: (a) Borrower causes to be submitted to Lender information required by Lender to evaluate the intended transferee as if a new loan were being made to the transferee; and (b) Lender reasonably determines that Lender's security will not be impaired by the loan assumption and that the risk of a breach of any covenant or agreement in this Security Instrument is acceptable to Lender.

To the extent permitted by Applicable Law, Lender may charge a reasonable fee as a condition to Lender's consent to the loan assumption. Lender may also require the transferee to sign an assumption agreement that is acceptable to Lender and that obligates the transferee to keep all the promises and agreements made in the Note and in this Security Instrument. Borrower will continue to be obligated under the Note and this Security Instrument unless Lender releases Borrower in writing.

If Lender exercises the option to require immediate payment in full, Lender shall give Borrower notice of acceleration. The notice shall provide a period of not less than 30 days from the date the notice is given in accordance with Section 15 within which Borrower must pay all sums secured by this Security Instrument. If Borrower fails to pay these sums prior to the expiration of this period, Lender may invoke any remedies permitted by this Security Instrument without further notice or demand on Borrower.

BY SIGNING BELOW, Borrower accepts and agrees to the terms and covenants contained in this Adjustable Rate Rider.

_______________________________________(Seal)
-Borrower

_______________________________________(Seal)
-Borrower

MULTISTATE ADJUSTABLE RATE RIDER–ARM 5-1 –Single Family–**Fannie Mae/Freddie Mac UNIFORM INSTRUMENT** **Form 3108 1/01** *(Page 1 of 2 pages)*

BALLOON RIDER
(CONDITIONAL RIGHT TO REFINANCE)

THIS BALLOON RIDER is made this ____ day of _______________, ____, and is incorporated into and shall be deemed to amend and supplement the Mortgage, Deed of Trust, or Security Deed (the "Security Instrument") of the same date given by the undersigned ("Borrower") to secure Borrower's Note to ____________________________ ("Lender") of the same date and covering the property described in the Security Instrument and located at:

____

[Property Address]

The interest rate stated on the Note is called the "Note Rate." The date of the Note is called the "Note Date." I understand Lender may transfer the Note, Security Instrument, and this Rider. Lender or anyone who takes the Note, the Security Instrument, and this Rider by transfer and who is entitled to receive payments under the Note is called the "Note Holder."

ADDITIONAL COVENANTS. In addition to the covenants and agreements in the Security Instrument, Borrower and Lender further covenant and agree as follows (despite anything to the contrary contained in the Security Instrument or the Note):

1. CONDITIONAL RIGHT TO REFINANCE

At the Maturity Date of the Note and Security Instrument (the "Maturity Date"), I will be able to obtain a new loan ("New Loan") with a new Maturity Date of ___________________, ____, and with an interest rate equal to the "New Note Rate" determined in accordance with Section 3 below if all the conditions provided in Section 2 and 5 below are met (the "Conditional Refinancing Option"). If those conditions are not met, I understand that the Note Holder is under no obligation to refinance or modify the Note, or to extend the Maturity Date, and that I will have to repay the Note from my own resources or find a lender willing to lend me the money to repay the Note.

2. CONDITIONS TO OPTION

If I want to exercise the Conditional Refinancing Option at maturity, certain conditions must be met as of the Maturity Date. These conditions are: (a) I must still be the owner of the property subject to the Security Instrument (the "Property"); (b) I must be current in my monthly payments and cannot have been more than 30 days late on any of the 12 scheduled monthly payments immediately preceding the Maturity Date; (c) the New Note Rate cannot be more than five percentage points above the Note Rate; and (d) I must make a written request to the Note Holder as provided in Section 5 below.

3. CALCULATING THE NEW NOTE RATE

The New Note Rate will be a fixed rate of interest equal to Fannie Mae's required net yield for 30-year fixed-rate mortgages subject to a 60-day mandatory delivery commitment, plus one-half of one percentage point (0.5%), rounded to the nearest one-eighth of one percentage point (0.125%) (the "New Note Rate"). The required net yield shall be the applicable net yield in effect on the date and time of day that the Note Holder receives notice of my election to exercise the Conditional Refinancing Option. If this required net yield is not available, the Note Holder will determine the New Note Rate by using comparable information.

4. CALCULATING THE NEW PAYMENT AMOUNT

Provided the New Note Rate as calculated in Section 3 above is not greater than five percentage points above the Note Rate and all other conditions required in Section 2 above are satisfied, the Note Holder will determine the amount of the monthly payment that will be sufficient to repay in full (a) the unpaid principal, plus (b) accrued but unpaid interest, plus (c) all other sums I will owe under the Note and Security Instrument on the Maturity Date (assuming my monthly payments then are current, as required under Section 2 above), over the term

MULTISTATE BALLOON RIDER—Single Family—**Fannie Mae Uniform Instrument** **Form 3180 1/01 (rev. 9/01) (page 1 of 2)**

of the New Note at the New Note Rate in equal monthly payments. The result of this calculation will be the amount of my new principal and interest payment every month until the New Note is fully paid.

5. EXERCISING THE CONDITIONAL REFINANCING OPTION

The Note Holder will notify me at least 60 calendar days in advance of the Maturity Date and advise me of the principal, accrued but unpaid interest, and all other sums I am expected to owe on the Maturity Date. The Note Holder also will advise me that I may exercise the Conditional Refinancing Option if the conditions in Section 2 above are met. Th e Note Holder will provide my payment record information, together with the name, title, and address of the person representing the Note Holder that I must notify in order to exercise the Conditional Refinancing Option. If I meet the conditions of Section 2 above, I may exercise the Conditional Refinancing Option by notifying the Note Holder no later than 45 calendar days prior to the Maturity Date. The Note Holder will calculate the fixed New Note Rate based upon Fannie Mae's applicable published required net yield in effect on the date and time of day notification is received by the Note Holder and as calculated in Section 3 above. I will then have 30 calendar days to provide the Note Holder with acceptable proof of my required ownership. Before the Maturity Date, the Note Holder will advise me of the new interest rate (the New Note Rate), new monthly payment amount, and a date, time, and place at which I must appear to sign any documents required to complete the required refinancing. I understand the Note Holder will charge me a $250 processing fee and the costs associated with updating the title insurance policy, if any.

BY SIGNING BELOW, Borrower accepts and agrees to the terms and covenants contained in this Balloon Rider.

....(Seal) Borrower	....(Seal) Borrower
....(Seal) Borrower	[Sign Orig inal On ly]

Form 3180 1/01 (rev. 9/01) (page 2 of 2)

BIWEEKLY PAYMENT RIDER
(Fixed Rate)

THIS BIWEEKLY PAYMENT RIDER is made this ____ day of ________________, ____, and is incorporated into and shall be deemed to amend and supplement the Mortgage, Deed of Trust, or Security Deed (the "Security Instrument") of the same date given by the undersigned ("Borrower") to secure Borrower's Note (the "Note") to ____ ("Lender" of the same date and covering the property described in the Security Instrument and located at:

____

[Property Address]

ADDITIONAL COVENANTS. In addition to the covenants and agreements made in the Security Instrument, Borrower and Lender further covenant and agree as follows:

A. BIWEEKLY PAYMENTS

The Note provides for Borrower's biweekly loan payments, and the termination of Borrower's right to make the Biweekly Payments, as follows:

3. PAYMENTS

(A) Time and Place of Payments

I will pay principal and interest by making a payment every 14 days (the "Biweekly Payments"), beginning on ____________________, ____. I will make the Biweekly Payments every 14 days until I have paid all of the principal and interest and any other charges described below that I may owe under this Note. M y biweekly or any monthly payments will be applied to interest before Principal.

I will make my biweekly or any monthly payments at ____ or at a different place if required by the Note Holder.

(B) Amount of Biweekly Payments

My Biweekly Payment will be in the amount of U.S. $________________.

(C) Manner of Payment

My Biweekly Payments will be made by an automatic deduction from an account I will maintain with the Note Holder, or with a different entity specified by the Note Holder. I will keep sufficient funds in the account to pay the full amount of each Biweekly Payment on the date it is due.

I understand that the Note Holder, or an entity acting for the Note Holder, may deduct the amount of my Biweekly Payment from the account to pay the Note Holder for each Biweekly Payment on the date it is due until I have paid all amounts owed under this Note.

4. TERM

If I make all my Biweekly Payments on time, and pay all other amounts owed under this Note, I will repay my loan in full on ____________________, ____. If, on ____________________, ____, *[insert applicable 15-, 20- or 30-year maturity date based on a monthly repayment schedule]* I still owe amounts under this Note, I will pay those amounts in full on that date, which is called the "Maturity Date."

MULTISTATE BIWEEKLY PAYMENT RIDER (Fixed Rate) -- Single Family -- **Fannie Mae Uniform Instrument** **Form 3177 1/01** ***(page 1 of 2)***

5. *[omitted]*

6. *[omitted]*

7. BORROWER'S FAILURE TO PAY AS REQUIRED

(A) Late Charge for Overdue Payments

If the Note Holder has not received the full amount of any biweekly or monthly payment by the end of __________ calendar days after the date it is due, I will pay a late charge to the Note Holder. The amount of the charge will be __________% of my overdue payment of principal and interest. I will pay this late charge promptly but only once on each late payment.

(B) Default

If I do not pay the full amount of each biweekly or monthly payment on the date it is due, I will be in default. I also will be in default if I do not maintain the account I am required to maintain under Section 3(C) above.

(C) Termination of Biweekly Payments

If I am in default for three consecutive Biweekly Payments, the Note Holder may terminate my right to make Biweekly Payments under this Note. If the Note Holder terminates my Biweekly Payments, I will instead pay all amounts owed under this Note by making one payment each month on the first day of the month.

The Note Holder will determine the amount of my monthly payment by calculating the amount that would be sufficient to repay all amounts owed under this Note in full on the Maturity Date in substantially equal payments. Beginning with the first day of the month after the month in which I am given notice of termination, I will pay the new amount as my monthly payment until the Maturity Date.

B. BIWEEKLY PAYMENT AMENDMENTS TO THE SECURITY INSTRUMENT

1. Until Borrower's right to make Biweekly Payments is terminated under the conditions stated in Section A of this Biweekly Payment Rider, the Security Instrument is amended as follows:

(a) The word "monthly" is changed to "biweekly" in the Security Instrument wherever "monthly" appears.

(b) In Uniform Covenant 3 of the Security Instrument ("Funds for Escrow Items"), "12" is changed to "26."

2. If Lender terminates Borrower's right to make Biweekly Payments under the conditions stated in Section A of this Biweekly Payment Rider, the amendments to the Security Instrument contained in Section B1 above shall then cease to be in effect, and the provisions of the Security Instrument shall instead be in effect without the amendments stated in this Biweekly Payment Rider.

BY SIGNING BELOW, Borrower accepts and agrees to the terms and covenants contained in this Biweekly Payment Rider.

.... (Seal)
-Borrower

.... (Seal)
-Borrower

Form 3177 1/01 ***(page 2 of 2)***

Form **8821** (Rev. August 2008) Department of the Treasury Internal Revenue Service

Tax Information Authorization

▶ **Do not sign this form unless all applicable lines have been completed.**

▶ **Do not use this form to request a copy or transcript of your tax return. Instead, use Form 4506 or Form 4506-T.**

OMB No. 1545-1165

For IRS Use Only
Received by:
Name
Telephone ( )
Function
Date / /

1 Taxpayer information. Taxpayer(s) must sign and date this form on line 7.

Taxpayer name(s) and address (type or print)	**Social security number(s)**	**Employer identification number**
	Daytime telephone number ( )	Plan number (if applicable)

2 Appointee. If you wish to name more than one appointee, attach a list to this form.

Name and address

CAF No.
Telephone No.
Fax No.
Check if new: Address ☐ Telephone No. ☐ Fax No. ☐

3 Tax matters. The appointee is authorized to inspect and/or receive confidential tax information in any office of the IRS for the tax matters listed on this line. Do not use Form 8821 to request copies of tax returns.

(a) Type of Tax (Income, Employment, Excise, etc.) or Civil Penalty	**(b)** Tax Form Number (1040, 941, 720, etc.)	**(c)** Year(s) or Period(s) (see the instructions for line 3)	**(d)** Specific Tax Matters (see instr.)

4 Specific use not recorded on Centralized Authorization File (CAF). If the tax information authorization is for a specific use not recorded on CAF, check this box. See the instructions on page 4. If you check this box, skip lines 5 and 6 . ▶ ☐

5 Disclosure of tax information (you **must** check a box on line 5a or 5b unless the box on line 4 is checked):

a If you want copies of tax information, notices, and other written communications sent to the appointee on an ongoing basis, check this box . . . . . ▶ ☐

b If you do not want any copies of notices or communications sent to your appointee, check this box . . . . ▶ ☐

6 Retention/revocation of tax information authorizations. This tax information authorization automatically revokes all prior authorizations for the same tax matters you listed on line 3 above unless you checked the box on line 4. If you do not want to revoke a prior tax information authorization, you **must** attach a copy of any authorizations you want to remain in effect **and** check this box . . . . . ▶ ☐

To revoke this tax information authorization, see the instructions on page 4.

7 Signature of taxpayer(s). If a tax matter applies to a joint return, **either** husband or wife must sign. If signed by a corporate officer, partner, guardian, executor, receiver, administrator, trustee, or party other than the taxpayer, I certify that I have the authority to execute this form with respect to the tax matters/periods on line 3 above.

▶ **IF NOT SIGNED AND DATED, THIS TAX INFORMATION AUTHORIZATION WILL BE RETURNED.**

▶ **DO NOT SIGN THIS FORM IF IT IS BLANK OR INCOMPLETE.**

Signature Date

Print Name Title (if applicable)

☐☐☐☐☐ PIN number for electronic signature

Signature Date

Print Name Title (if applicable)

☐☐☐☐☐ PIN number for electronic signature

For Privacy Act and Paperwork Reduction Act Notice, see page 4. Cat. No. 11596P Form **8821** (Rev. 8-2008)

Form 8821 (Rev. 8-2008) Page **2**

General Instructions

Section references are to the Internal Revenue Code unless otherwise noted.

Purpose of Form

Form 8821 authorizes any individual, corporation, firm, organization, or partnership you designate to inspect and/or receive your confidential information in any office of the IRS for the type of tax and the years or periods you list on Form 8821. You may file your own tax information authorization without using Form 8821, but it must include all the information that is requested on Form 8821.

Form 8821 does not authorize your appointee to advocate your position with respect to the federal tax laws; to execute waivers, consents, or closing agreements; or to otherwise represent you before the IRS. If you want to authorize an individual to represent you, use Form 2848, Power of Attorney and Declaration of Representative.

Use Form 4506, Request for Copy of Tax Return, to get a copy of your tax return.

Use Form 4506-T, Request for Transcript of Tax Return, to order: (a) transcript of tax account information and (b) Form W-2 and Form 1099 series information.

Use Form 56, Notice Concerning Fiduciary Relationship, to notify the IRS of the existence of a fiduciary relationship. A fiduciary (trustee, executor, administrator, receiver, or guardian) stands in the position of a taxpayer and acts as the taxpayer. Therefore, a fiduciary does not act as an appointee and should not file Form 8821. If a fiduciary wishes to authorize an appointee to inspect and/or receive confidential tax information on behalf of the fiduciary, Form 8821 must be filed and signed by the fiduciary acting in the position of the taxpayer.

When To File

Form 8821 must be received by the IRS within 60 days of the date it was signed and dated by the taxpayer.

Where To File Chart

IF you live in . . .	THEN use this address . . .	Fax Number*
Alabama, Arkansas, Connecticut, Delaware, District of Columbia, Florida, Georgia, Illinois, Indiana, Kentucky, Louisiana, Maine, Maryland, Massachusetts, Michigan, Mississippi, New Hampshire, New Jersey, New York, North Carolina, Ohio, Pennsylvania, Rhode Island, South Carolina, Tennessee, Vermont, Virginia, or West Virginia	Internal Revenue Service Memphis Accounts Management Center PO Box 268, Stop 8423 Memphis, TN 38101-0268	901-546-4115
Alaska, Arizona, California, Colorado, Hawaii, Idaho, Iowa, Kansas, Minnesota, Missouri, Montana, Nebraska, Nevada, New Mexico, North Dakota, Oklahoma, Oregon, South Dakota, Texas, Utah, Washington, Wisconsin, or Wyoming	Internal Revenue Service 1973 N. Rulon White Blvd. MS 6737 Ogden, UT 84404	801-620-4249
All APO and FPO addresses, American Samoa, nonpermanent residents of Guam or the Virgin Islands**, Puerto Rico (or if excluding income under section 933), a foreign country, U.S. citizens and those filing Form 2555, 2555-EZ, or 4563.	Internal Revenue Service International CAF DP: SW-311 11601 Roosevelt Blvd. Philadelphia, PA 19255	215-516-1017

*These numbers may change without notice.

**Permanent residents of Guam should use Department of Taxation, Government of Guam, P.O. Box 23607, GMF, GU 96921; permanent residents of the Virgin Islands should use: V.I. Bureau of Internal Revenue, 9601 Estate Thomas Charlotte Amalie, St. Thomas, V.I. 00802.

Form 8821 (Rev. 8-2008) Page **3**

Where To File

Generally, mail or fax Form 8821 directly to the IRS. See the *Where To File Chart* on page 2. Exceptions are listed below.

If Form 8821 is for a specific tax matter, mail or fax it to the office handling that matter. For more information, see the instructions for line 4.

Your representative may be able to file Form 8821 electronically with the IRS from the IRS website. For more information, go to *www.irs.gov*. Under the *Tax Professionals* tab, click on *e-services–Online Tools for Tax Professionals*. If you complete Form 8821 for electronic signature authorization, do not file a Form 8821 with the IRS. Instead, give it to your appointee, who will retain the document.

Revocation of an Existing Tax Information Authorization

If you want to revoke an existing tax information authorization and do not want to name a new appointee, send a copy of the previously executed tax information authorization to the IRS, using the *Where To File Chart* on page 2. The copy of the tax information authorization must have a current signature and date of the taxpayer under the original signature on line 7. Write "REVOKE" across the top of Form 8821. If you do not have a copy of the tax information authorization you want to revoke, send a statement to the IRS. The statement of revocation or withdrawal must indicate that the authority of the appointee is revoked, list the tax matters and periods, and must be signed and dated by the taxpayer or representative. If the taxpayer is revoking, list the name and address of each recognized appointee whose authority is revoked. When the taxpayer is completely revoking authority, the form should state "remove all years/periods" instead of listing the specific tax matters, years, or periods. If the appointee is withdrawing, list the name, TIN, and address (if known) of the taxpayer.

To revoke a specific use tax information authorization, send the tax information authorization or statement of revocation to the IRS office handling your case, using the above instructions.

Taxpayer Identification Numbers (TINs)

TINs are used to identify taxpayer information with corresponding tax returns. It is important that you furnish correct names, social security numbers (SSNs), individual taxpayer identification numbers (ITINs), or employer identification numbers (EINs) so that the IRS can respond to your request.

Partnership Items

Sections 6221-6234 authorize a Tax Matters Partner to perform certain acts on behalf of an affected partnership. Rules governing the use of Form 8821 do not replace any provisions of these sections.

Representative Address Change

If the representative's address has changed, a new Form 8821 is not required. The representative can send a written notification that includes the new information and their signature to the location where the Form 8821 was filed.

Specific Instructions

Line 1. Taxpayer Information

Individuals. Enter your name, TIN, and your street address in the space provided. Do not enter your appointee's address or post office box. If a joint return is used, also enter your spouse's name and TIN. Also enter your EIN if applicable.

Corporations, partnerships, or associations. Enter the name, EIN, and business address.

Employee plan or exempt organization. Enter the name, address, and EIN of the plan sponsor or exempt organization, and the plan name and three-digit plan number.

Trust. Enter the name, title, and address of the trustee, and the name and EIN of the trust.

Estate. Enter the name, title, and address of the decedent's executor/personal representative, and the name and identification number of the estate. The identification number for an estate includes both the EIN, if the estate has one, and the decedent's TIN.

Line 2. Appointee

Enter your appointee's full name. Use the identical full name on all submissions and correspondence. Enter the nine-digit CAF number for each appointee. If an appointee has a CAF number for any previously filed Form 8821 or power of attorney (Form 2848), use that number. If a CAF number has not been assigned, enter "NONE," and the IRS will issue one directly to your appointee. The IRS does not assign CAF numbers to requests for employee plans and exempt organizations.

If you want to name more than one appointee, indicate so on this line and attach a list of appointees to Form 8821.

Check the appropriate box to indicate if either the address, telephone number, or fax number is new since a CAF number was assigned.

Line 3. Tax Matters

Enter the type of tax, the tax form number, the years or periods, and the specific tax matter. Enter "Not applicable," in any of the columns that do not apply.

For example, you may list "Income, 1040" for calendar year "2006" and "Excise, 720" for "2006" (this covers all quarters in 2006). For multiple years or a series of inclusive periods, including quarterly periods, you may list 2004 through (thru or a hyphen) 2006. For example, "2004 thru 2006" or "2nd 2005-3rd 2006." For fiscal years, enter the ending year and month, using the YYYYMM format. Do not use a general reference such as "All years," "All periods," or "All taxes." Any tax information authorization with a general reference will be returned.

You may list the current year or period and any tax years or periods that have already ended as of the date you sign the tax information authorization. However, you may include on a tax information authorization only future tax periods that end no later than 3 years after the date the tax information authorization is received by the IRS. The 3 future periods are determined starting after December 31 of the year the tax information authorization is received by the IRS. You must enter the type of tax, the tax form number, and the future year(s) or period(s). If the matter relates to estate tax, enter the date of the decedent's death instead of the year or period.

Form 8821 (Rev. 8-2008) Page **4**

In **column (d),** enter any specific information you want the IRS to provide. Examples of column (d) information are: lien information, a balance due amount, a specific tax schedule, or a tax liability.

For requests regarding Form 8802, Application for United States Residency Certification, enter "Form 8802" in column (d) and check the specific use box on line 4. Also, enter the appointee's information as instructed on Form 8802.

Note. If the taxpayer is subject to penalties related to an individual retirement account (IRA) account (for example, a penalty for excess contributions) enter, "IRA civil penalty" on line 3, column a.

Line 4. Specific Use Not Recorded on CAF

Generally, the IRS records all tax information authorizations on the CAF system. However, authorizations relating to a specific issue are not recorded.

Check the box on line 4 if Form 8821 is filed for any of the following reasons: (a) requests to disclose information to loan companies or educational institutions, (b) requests to disclose information to federal or state agency investigators for background checks, (c) application for EIN, or (d) claims filed on Form 843, Claim for Refund and Request for Abatement. If you check the box on line 4, your appointee should mail or fax Form 8821 to the IRS office handling the matter. Otherwise, your appointee should bring a copy of Form 8821 to each appointment to inspect or receive information. A specific-use tax information authorization will not revoke any prior tax information authorizations.

Line 6. Retention/Revocation of Tax Information Authorizations

Check the box on this line and attach a copy of the tax information authorization you do not want to revoke. The filing of Form 8821 will not revoke any Form 2848 that is in effect.

Line 7. Signature of Taxpayer(s)

Individuals. You must sign and date the authorization. Either husband or wife must sign if Form 8821 applies to a joint return.

Corporations. Generally, Form 8821 can be signed by: (a) an officer having legal authority to bind the corporation, (b) any person designated by the board of directors or other governing body, (c) any officer or employee on written request by any principal officer and attested to by the secretary or other officer, and (d) any other person authorized to access information under section 6103(e).

Partnerships. Generally, Form 8821 can be signed by any person who was a member of the partnership during any part of the tax period covered by Form 8821. See *Partnership Items* on page 3.

All others. See section 6103(e) if the taxpayer has died, is insolvent, is a dissolved corporation, or if a trustee, guardian, executor, receiver, or administrator is acting for the taxpayer.

Privacy Act and Paperwork Reduction Act Notice

We ask for the information on this form to carry out the Internal Revenue laws of the United States. Form 8821 is provided by the IRS for your convenience and its use is voluntary. If you designate an appointee to inspect and/or receive confidential tax information, you are required by section 6103(c) to provide the information requested on Form 8821. Under section 6109, you must disclose your social security number (SSN), employer identification number (EIN), or individual taxpayer identification number (ITIN). If you do not provide all the information requested on this form, we may not be able to honor the authorization.

The IRS may provide this information to the Department of Justice for civil and criminal litigation, and to cities, states, the District of Columbia, and U.S. possessions to carry out their tax laws. We may also disclose this information to other countries under a tax treaty, to federal and state agencies to enforce federal nontax criminal laws, or to federal law enforcement and intelligence agencies to combat terrorism.

You are not required to provide the information requested on a form that is subject to the Paperwork Reduction Act unless the form displays a valid OMB control number. Books or records relating to a form or its instructions must be retained as long as their contents may become material in the administration of any Internal Revenue law.

The time needed to complete and file this form will vary depending on individual circumstances. The estimated average time is: **Recordkeeping,** 6 min.; **Learning about the law or the form,** 12 min.; **Preparing the form,** 24 min.; **Copying and sending the form to the IRS,** 20 min.

If you have comments concerning the accuracy of these time estimates or suggestions for making Form 8821 simpler, we would be happy to hear from you. You can write to Internal Revenue Service, Tax Products Coordinating Committee, SE:W:CAR:MP:T:T:SP, 1111 Constitution Ave. NW, IR-6526, Washington, DC 20224. **Do not** send Form 8821 to this address. Instead, see the *Where To File Chart* on page 2.

NOTICE OF RIGHT TO CANCEL

LENDER: Quest Mortgage Company

DATE: June 14, 2010
LOAN NO.: 0035671320 - 9551
TYPE: ADJUSTABLE RATE

BORROWER(S): JANE WEBBER
ADDRESS: 857 EAST 152ND STREET
CITY/STATE/ZIP: LOS ANGELES, CA 90002

PROPERTY: 857 EAST 152ND STREET
LOS ANGELES, CA 90002

You are entering into a transaction that will result in a mortgage/lien/security interest on your home. You have a legal right under federal law to cancel this transaction, without cost, within THREE BUSINESS DAYS from whichever of the following events occurs last:

1. The date of the transaction, which is [ENTER DOCUMENT SIGNING DATE] ______________________ ; or
2. The date you received your Truth in Lending disclosures; or
3. The date you received this notice of your right to cancel.

If you cancel the transaction, the mortgage/lien/security interest is also cancelled. Within 20 CALENDAR DAYS after we receive your notice, we must take the steps necessary to reflect the fact that the mortgage/lien/security interest on your home has been cancelled, and we must return to you any money or property you have given to us or anyone else in connection with this transaction.

You may keep any money or property we have given you until we have done the things mentioned above, but you must then offer to return the money or property. If it is impractical or unfair for you to return the property you must offer its reasonable value. You may offer to return the property at your home or at the location of the property. Money must be returned to the address below. If we do not take possession of the money or property within 20 CALENDAR DAYS of your offer, you may keep it without further obligation.

HOW TO CANCEL
If you decide to cancel this transaction, you may do so by notifying us in writing, at:

Quest Mortgage Company
5500 Town Rd, Suite 900
Orange, California 92868

ATTN: FUNDING
PHONE: (714) 479-0355
FAX: (714) 347-1555

You may use any written statement that is signed and dated by you and states your intention to cancel, or you may use this notice by dating and signing below. Keep one copy of this notice because it contains important information about your rights.

If you cancel by mail or telegram, you must send the notice no later than MIDNIGHT of [ENTER FINAL DATE TO CANCEL] ______________________

(or MIDNIGHT of the THIRD BUSINESS DAY following the latest of the three events listed above). If you send or deliver your written notice to cancel some other way, it must be delivered to the above address no later than that time.
I WISH TO CANCEL

______________________ SIGNATURE　　______________________ DATE

The undersigned each acknowledge receipt of two copies of this NOTICE OF RIGHT TO CANCEL and one copy of the Federal Truth in Lending Disclosure Statement, all given by lender in compliance with Truth in Lending Simplification and Reform Act of 1980 (Public Law 96-221).

Each borrower in this transaction has the right to cancel. The exercise of this right by one borrower shall be effective to all borrowers.

______________________ BORROWER/OWNER JANE WEBBER　Date　　______________________ BORROWER/OWNER　Date

______________________ BORROWER/OWNER　Date　　______________________ BORROWER/OWNER　Date

LENDER COPY

FEDERAL NATIONAL MORTGAGE ASSOCIATION
AFFIDAVIT OF PURCHASER AND VENDOR

I. PARTIES: (Name and address)

LN# 12345

Lender TEST LENDER
111 TEST STREET, STE. 111 TUSTIN, CA 92780
Mortgage Insurer PMI COMPANY
(If applicable) 345 INSURANCE WAY

Property Vendor SAMUEL SELLER AND SALLY SELLER

Property Purchaser BARRY B. BUYER AND BARBARA BUYER

II. PROPERTY ADDRESS OR LEGAL DESCRIPTION: (Attach supplemental sheet if necessary)
999 REAL PROPERTY DRIVE, MORTGAGETOWN, CA 92567

III. THE PURPOSE OF THE LOAN ON THIS PROPERTY IS:
[X] To purchase it from the above vendors - Total Purchase Price 150,000.00
[ ] To refinance outstanding debt.
[ ] Other (Explain)

IV. FINANCIAL TERMS:
First Mortgage Amount 100,000.00
Cash Equity (Not necessary for refinance) 50,000.00
Secondary Financing
Amount ______
Interest Rate ______ % Term ______ (mos)
Monthly Payment $ ______
Name and Address of Holder:
______
______
Other (Explain) ______
Total Purchase Price (Not necessary for refinance) 150,000.00

V. LIENS: If this loan exceeds 80% of the appraised value or the purchase price of the property described in Item II above, no lien or charge upon such property has been given or executed or has been contracted or agreed to be so given or executed by Property Purchaser to a ny person, including Property Vendor, except for (1) liens disclosed in Item IV hereof, or (2) liens or charges which will be discharged from the proceeds of the subject mortgage.

VI. OCCUPANCY: Purchaser is now actually occupying the property described in Item II above or in good faith intends to so occupy such property as the principal residence.

VII. INDUCEMENT: The certifications of this Affidavit are for the purpose of inducing the Lender named above or its assignees to make or purchase the first mortgage described by this Affidavit, and inducing the Mortgage Insurer, if any, to insure such loan. Those executing this Affidavit acknowledge that if this loan excees 80% of the value or purchase price of the property and is made by a Federal Savings and Loan Association, and/or is subsequently purchased by a Federal Savings and Loan Association, the certification of this Affidavit shall be used for the purpose of inducing a Federal Savings and Loan Association to enter into such transaction and that the provisions of Section 1014 of Title 18, United States Code, which provide in part "Whoever knowingly makes any false statement or report for the purpose of influencing in any way the action of... a Federal Savings and Loan Association... upon any application ...shall be fined not more than $5,000 or imprisoned not more than two years or both" are applicable to such transaction.

VIII. PROPERTY VENDOR: The PROPERTY VENDOR hereby certifies that to the extent PROPERTY VENDOR is a party, the Financial Terms, including Total Purchase Price, the Liens and Occupancy are as set forth in Items III, IV, and VI above, and hereby acknowledges the inducement purpose of this Affidavit as set forth in Item VII above, and certifies that certain of the prepaid expenses involved in the transaction (i.e. interest charges, real estate taxes, hazard insurance premiums, and private mortgage insurance renewal premiums) have not been paid by the vendor on behalf of the property purchaser.

______
SAMUEL SELLER
______
SALLY SELLER

Sworn to and subscribed before me ______
this ______ day of ______

Notary Public for ______
County, State of ______

Date ______

(Notorial Seal)

IX. PROPERTY PURCHASER: The PROPERTY PURCHASER hereby certifies that the Financial Terms, including Total Purchase Price, the Liens and Occupancy are as set forth in Items III, IV, and VI above, and hereby acknowledges the inducement purpose of this Affidavit as set forth in Item VII above.

______
BARRY B. BUYER
______
BARBARA BUYER

Sworn to and subscribed before me ______
this ______ day of ______

Notary Public for ______
County, State of ______

Date ______

(Notorial Seal)

X. LENDER: Lender, by execution hereby, represents that the aforementioned statements are true and correct to the best of its knowledge.
TEST LENDER
by ______ (Signature) ______ (Title)

Date

LENDER USE ONLY			
Value $	150,000.00	Percent of Loan	
Mortgage	100,000.00	to Value	67.00

This form should be executed by purchaser(s), vendor(s) and lender no later than the date on which any disbursement on the loan is made.

FNMA 1009 FOR CALIFORNIA

MORTGAGOR'S AFFIDAVIT

The following certification is made by the undersigned as an inducement to the State of Wisconsin, Department of Veterans Affairs, mortgagee, to make a mortgage loan in the amount of $____________ to be secured by a first mortgage loan on the subject property.

The undersigned, hereby depose and say that:

1. The subject property for said mortgage loan is located at ____ ____.

2. The purchase price or the cost of the subject property is $____________.

3. The accepted offer to purchase property and/or construction contract between me and the contractor submitted to the lender with my application for a loan is the only contract between me and the seller of the property and/or the contractor and no side deals or other terms, conditions, understandings, or agreements between me and the seller and/or contractor exist unless disclosed in this offer to purchase and/or construction contract.

4. I, or we, the mortgagor(s), have paid $____________ in cash representing the equity and closing costs needed to legally close the purchase or construction transaction.

5. No portion of the cash down payment, closing costs or moving costs were borrowed except from a government sponsored program approved by the Department or borrowed against our own assets. I h ave incurred no debts in this transaction except from the aforementioned sources and the loan from the Department.

6. I, or we, will not use the property as a recreational or vacation home, or rent the property to any other person (except for one unit of a two unit residence or two units of a three unit residence or three units of a four unit residence), or use or permit the use of more than 15% of the area of my unit of the residence in a trade or business, or use or permit the use of the land for agricultural or commercial purposes.

7. I presently occupy the property as my principal residence or that I will occupy the subject property as my principal residence (may not be more than 60 days after closing) on or before ____________________.
Further I, or we, intend to maintain the property as my, our, principal residence.

8. I have no present intent to lease, sell, assign or transfer any interest in the subject property to another, and have not entered into any agreements, understanding or other arrangement to lease, sell, assign or transfer the subject property.

9. If employed full-time on the date of application for the mortgage loan, I am now employed full-time, or that if employed part-time on the date of application for the mortgage loan, I am now employed part-time.

10. I do not foresee any circumstances in the immediate future that would impair my ability to meet the monthly mortgage loan payments.

11. I understand that in the event of any transfer of title to another party or of certain transfers of physical possession of the subject property to another party the entire balance of the loan may be declared due and payable at the option of the mortgagee. I ag ree to notify the mortgagee in advance of any contemplated sale, rental or any other transfer affecting the property. I further agree to notify the mortgagee immediately in the event I should vacate the property, and to keep the mortgagee informed of my current mailing address.

12. The proceeds of the mortgage loan are not being used, nor will they be used to acquire or replace an existing mortgage or debt for which I am liable or which was incurred on my behalf, other than construction period loans which have a term of 24 months or less, and that I do not now and have not previously had a mortgage loan on the subject property.

13. The subject property includes a complete dwelling unit. I, or we, ____________ (have/have not) entered into a contract or agreement to modify the subject property within six months after closing beyond its physical condition at closing. (If modifications are planned within six months after closing, please indicate the projected cost $____________.)

14. No part of the proceeds of the mortgage loan is being applied to purchase appliances, furniture or other personal property not permanently affixed to the subject property.

15. For the purposes of this affidavit, an ownership interest in the principal residence includes ordinary full ownership (fee simple), a joint tenancy, a tenancy in common, life estate, land contract, interest in a cooperative or condominium, or interest held in trust which will constitute a present ownership interest if held directly by the borrower(s) or either of them.

Mortgagor(s) must indicate (X) the appropriate choice.

☐ I, or we, have had no ownership interest in any principal residence during the three-year period preceding the date of this affidavit.

☐ During the three-year period preceding the date of this affidavit I, or we, have had an ownership interest in the principal residence located at:

____
(Street Address)

____
(City) (State) (Zip Code)

16. I have read and understand the LIMITATIONS set forth below.

STATE OF WISCONSIN)
) SS
COUNTY OF __________________________)

____
MORTGAGOR

Subscribed and sworn to before me this ________ day of
__________________________, __________

____

____
MORTGAGOR

Wisconsin Notary Public
My Commission (expires) (is) ______________________

The above affidavit is true and correct to the best of my knowledge.

____
Closing Agent

LIMITATIONS

Neither the State of Wisconsin, Department of Veterans Affairs, nor the lender has the legal authority to:

1. Act as the veteran's architect. It does not supervise all details of the housing accommodation the veteran buys. The authorized lender, however, will make periodic inspections prior to disbursement of funds.

2. Guarantee that the housing accommodation is free of defects, such as dry-rot, faulty plumbing, wiring, sewage disposal, or other defective conditions.

3. Act as the veteran's attorney. It cannot give the veteran legal services if the veteran encounters trouble in buying or constructing the housing accommodation. The veteran is, however, required to notify the department of any such conditions in order that it may be aware of any problem that is encountered.

Neither the department nor the lender can compel a builder or seller to remedy defects or otherwise compel him to live up to his contract with the veteran, except by refusing to advance funds, if appropriate.

The department cannot guarantee that the veteran will be completely satisfied with the property or that the veteran can resell it at the price paid.

The amount of the annual taxes is determined by the local assessor. The department cannot change this. The veteran may determine the assessment and ratio by contacting the local assessor. If the veteran wishes to contest the amount of the property tax, he/she must file an appeal with the Board of Review. There is a time limit for filing. The local assessor can provide information and forms.

ESCROW NO.: **STATEMENT OF INFORMATION** TITLE NO:

MY FULL NAME

First Name ________ Full Middle Name – If none, indicate ________ Last Name ________

Birthplace ________ Year of Birth ________

I have lived continuously in the U.S.A. since ________

If married, complete the following:
Full Name of Wife/Husband ________
First Name ________ Full Middle Name – If none, indicate ________ Last Name ________

Birthplace ________ Year of Birth ________

SHE/HE has lived continuously in the U.S.A. since ________

We were married on ________ at ________

Wife's Maiden Name ________

Children's Name & DOB ________

My Social Security Number & Driver's License Number (State) ________

My Spouse's Social Security Number & Driver's License Number (State) ________

RESIDENCES DURING PAST 10 YEARS

Number and Street ________ City ________ FROM (Date) ________ TO (Date) ________

Number and Street ________ City ________ FROM (Date) ________ TO (Date) ________

OCCUPATIONS DURING PAST 10 YEARS
PURPOSE OF THIS FORM

Husband's ________
Firm Name ________ Location ________

Firm Name ________ Location ________

Husband's ________
Firm Name ________ Location ________

Firm Name ________

ANY FORMER MARRIAGE(S), IF ANY

If no former marriages, write "NONE" ________ Otherwise, please complete the following:

Name of former wife ________

Deceased [ ] Divorced [ ] When ________ Where ________

Name of Former Husband ________

Deceased [ ] Divorced [ ] When ________ Where ________

Date ________

The street address of the property in this transaction is ________
Indicate Street, Avenue or Drive

Home Phone ________

____
Signature

Business Phone ________

____
Signature (If married, both husband and wife must sign)

ADDENDUM TO ADJUSTABLE RATE NOTE

(Fixed Rate Conversion Option)

THIS ADDENDUM TO ADJUSTABLE RATE NOTE is made this ____ day of _______________, ____, and is incorporated into and shall be deemed to amend and supplement the Adjustable Rate Note made by the undersigned ("Borrower") to ____ ("Lender") and dated the same date as this Addendum (the "Note").

ADDITIONAL COVENANTS. In addition to the covenants and agreements made in the Note, Borrower and Lender further covenant and agree as follows:

A. FIXED INTEREST RATE OPTION

1. Option to Convert to Fixed Rate

I have a Conversion Option that I can exercise unless I am in default or this Section A1 will not permit me to do so. The "Conversion Option" is my option to convert the interest rate I am required to pay by the Note from an adjustable rate to the fixed rate calculated by the Note Holder under Section A2 below.

The conversion can only take place on (a) if the first Change Date is 21 months or less from the date of the Note, the third, fourth or fifth Change Date, or (b) if the first Change Date is more than 21 months from the date of the Note, the first, second or third Change Date. Each Change Date on which my interest rate can convert from an adjustable rate to a fixed rate also is called the "Conversion Date." **I can convert my interest rate only on one of the three Conversion Dates.**

If I want to exercise the Conversion Option, I must first meet certain conditions. Those conditions are that: (i) I must give the Note Holder notice that I want to do so at least 15 days before the next Conversion Date; (ii) on the Conversion Date, I must not be in default under the Note or the Security Instrument; (iii) by a date specified by the Note Holder, I must pay the Note Holder a conversion fee of U.S. $________________; and (iv) I must sign and give the Note Holder any documents the Note Holder requires to effect the conversion.

2. Calculation of Fixed Rate

My new, fixed interest rate will be determined by the Note Holder based on Fannie Mae's required net yield as of a date and time of day specified by the Note Holder for: (i) if the original term of the Note is greater than 15 years, 30-year fixed rate mortgages covered by applicable 60-day mandatory delivery commitments, plus five-eighths of one percentage point (0.625%), rounded to the nearest one-eighth of one percentage point (0.125%); or (ii) if the original term of the Note is 15 years or less, 15-year fixed rate mortgages covered by applicable 60-day mandatory delivery commitments, plus five-eighths of one percentage point (0.625%), rounded to the nearest one-eighth of one percentage point (0.125%). If this required net yield cannot be determined because the applicable commitments are not available, the Note Holder will determine my interest rate by using comparable information. My new rate calculated under this Section A2 will not be greater than the Maximum Rate stated in the Note.

3. New Payment Amount and Effective Date

If I am permitted to exercise the Conversion Option, the Note Holder will determine the amount of the monthly payment that would be sufficient to repay the unpaid principal I am expected to owe on the Conversion Date in full on the Maturity Date of the Note at my new fixed interest rate in substantially equal payments. The result of this calculation will be the new amount of my monthly payment. Beginning with my first monthly payment after the Conversion Date, I will pay the new amount as my monthly payment until the Maturity Date of the Note.

B. TRANSFER OF THE PROPERTY OR A BENEFICIAL INTEREST IN BORROWER

If my interest rate is converted to a fixed rate, some of the conditions under which I may be required to make immediate payment in full of all amounts I owe under the Note, which are described in the section of the Note captioned "Uniform Secured Note," shall cease to be in effect. Instead, some of these conditions will read as follows:

> **Transfer of the Property or a Beneficial Interest in Borrower.** As used in this Section 18, "Interest in the Property" means any legal or beneficial interest in the Property, including, but not limited to, those beneficial interests transferred in a bond for deed, contract for deed, installment sales contract or escrow agreement, the intent of which is the transfer of title by Borrower at a future date to a purchaser.
>
> If all or any part of the Property or any Interest in the Property is sold or transferred (or if Borrower is not a natural person and a beneficial interest in Borrower is sold or transferred) without Lender's prior written consent, Lender may require immediate payment in full of all sums secured by this Security Instrument. However, this option shall not be exercised by Lender if such exercise is prohibited by Applicable Law.
>
> If Lender exercises this option, Lender shall give Borrower notice of acceleration. The notice shall provide a period of not less than 30 days from the date the notice is given in accordance with Section 15 within which Borrower must pay all sums secured by this Security

FIXED RATE OPTION ADDENDUM (NOTE)—Single Family—**Fannie Mae Uniform Instrument** **Form 3256 1/01** ***(page 1 of 2)***

Instrument. If Borrower fails to pay these sums prior to the expiration of this period, Lender may invoke any remedies permitted by this Security Instrument without further notice or demand on Borrower.

BY SIGNING BELOW, Borrower accepts and agrees to the terms and covenants contained in this Addendum To Adjustable Rate Note.

.... (Seal)
-Borrower

.... (Seal)
-Borrower

.... (Seal)
-Borrower

[Sign Original Only]

Form 3256 1/01 ***(page 2 of 2)***

AFFORDABLE MERIT RATE ADDENDUM TO NOTE

THIS AFFORDABLE MERIT RATE ADDENDUM TO NOTE is made this ____________________, __________, and is incorporated into and shall be deemed to amend and supplement the Note made by the undersigned (the "Borrower") in favor of ____ ____ (the "Lender") and dated the same date as this Addendum (the "Note"). The Note is secured by a security instrument, as modified or amended, in favor of the Lender dated the __________ day of ______________________________, __________ (the "Security Instrument").

ADDITIONAL COVENANTS. In addition to the covenants and agreements made in the Note, Borrower and Lender further covenant and agree as follows:

1. AFFORDABLE MERIT RATE REDUCTION

Borrower has agreed to pay the rate of interest set forth in Section 2 of the Note (the "Note Rate") until the full amount of principal has been paid. However, if on either the second, third or fourth anniversary of the first payment date (the "Anniversary Date") Borrower has demonstrated a Good Payment History, Lender agrees to decrease the Note Rate by one percentage point. Borrower will be deemed to have demonstrated a "Good Payment History" if Borrower: (a) has made each of the most recent 24 consecutive monthly payments under the Note and Security Instrument before the next payment was due; and (b) has not had a Ninety-Day Delinquency under the Note and Security Instrument. A "Ninety-Day Delinquency" shall be defined for this purpose as any monthly payment which has not been made in full on the date due and remains unpaid, wholly or partially, three months or more from that due date; for example, the monthly payment due on February 1, is not made and is still unpaid on May 1. If Borrower demonstrates a Good Payment History, Lender will notify Borrower in writing that the Note Rate has decreased. The new Note Rate will take effect on the first day of the month following the earliest Anniversary Date on which the Borrower has demonstrated a Good Payment History ("Rate Reduction Date"). Beginning with Borrower's first monthly payment after the Rate Reduction Date, Borrower will pay the new amount as the monthly payment until the Maturity Date. Lender will decrease Borrower's Note Rate only one time during the term of the loan, provided Borrower demonstrates a Good Payment History on either the second, third or fourth Anniversary Date.

BY SIGNING BELOW, Borrower accepts and agrees to the terms and provisions contained in this Affordable Merit Rate Addendum to Note.

____ (Seal)
- Borrower

____ (Seal)
- Borrower

____ (Seal)
- Borrower

[Sign Original Only]

MULTISTATE AFFORDABLE MERIT RATE ADDENDUM TO NOTE--Single Family--**Freddie Mac UNIFORM INSTRUMENT** **Form 3294 4/00**
(page 1 of 1 pages)

3 YEAR PREPAYMENT PENALTY
ADDENDUM TO NOTE

This Addendum is attached to and made part of that Note (the "Note") dated ______________________ by and between ("Borrower(s)"), and ("Lender" or "Note Holder"). To the extent that this Addendum conflicts with the Note, this Addendum shall control. Unless specifically defined otherwise, all capitalized terms shall have the meanings set forth in the Note.

1. The paragraph of the Note entitled "Borrower's Right to Prepay," is hereby deleted and replaced with the following:

BORROWER'S RIGHT TO PREPAY

(A) Prepayment
I have the right to make payments of principal at any time before they are due. A "prepayment" is a payment of principal before it is due.

(B) Partial or Full Prepayments
I may make partial prepayments or a full prepayment. A "partial prepayment" is any amount paid in a month that is greater than the interest due in such month. A "full prepayment" is a payment of the entire unpaid principal balance.

(C) Prepayment Penalty
If I make a full prepayment during the first three (3) years of the Permanent Phase of the Loan, I will pay a prepayment penalty according to the schedule below. If I make a partial prepayment during the first three (3) years of the Permanent Phase of the Loan, I will pay a prepayment penalty according to the schedule below if the total of all partial prepayments I have made during any 12-month period exceeds 20% of the original loan amount set forth in the Note (the "20% Threshold"). The partial prepayment penalty will apply only to that portion of the total of all such partial prepayment amounts that exceed the 20% Threshold.

(D) Prepayment Penalty Schedule
The prepayment penalty shall be an amount equal to the following percentage of the prepayment I pay on the date of prepayment:

First Three Years of the Permanent Phase (1st month through the 36th month): 2%

(E) Notice
When I make a full or partial prepayment, I will tell the Note Holder in writing that I am doing so. I may not designate a payment as a prepayment if I have not made all the monthly payments due under this Note.

(F) Effect of a Partial Prepayment
The Note Holder will use my prepayments to reduce my unpaid principal balance after deducting any prepayment penalty assessed, any applicable fees and amounts past due, and any accrued and unpaid interest. If I make a partial prepayment, there will be no change in my monthly payment due date.

2. Other than as expressly set forth in this Addendum, the Note remains in full force and effect, according to its terms.

______________________________ Date ______________________________ Date

______________________________ Date ______________________________ Date

TIMELY PAYMENT REWARDS ADDENDUM TO NOTE

THIS TIMELY PAYMENT REWARDS ADDENDUM TO NOTE is made this _____ day of _____________, _____, and is incorporated into and shall be deemed to amend and supplement the Note made by the undersigned ("Borrower"), in favor of ____ ("Lender") and dated the same date as this Addendum (the "Note"). The Note is secured by a security instrument, as modified or amended, in favor of Lender dated the _____ day of _______________, _____ (the "Security Instrument").

ADDITIONAL COVENANTS. In addition to the covenants and agreements made in the Note, Borrower and Lender further covenant and agree as follows:

1. **TIMELY PAYMENT REWARDS RATE REDUCTION**
Borrower has agreed to pay the rate of interest set forth in Section 2 of the Note (the "Note Rate") until the full amount of principal has been paid. However, if on any one of the second, third, or fourth anniversaries of the scheduled due date of the first full installment payment due under the Note (each, an "Anniversary Date") Borrower has demonstrated a Good Payment History, Lender agrees to decrease the Note Rate by ________________ percentage point (_.__%). Borrower will be deemed to have demonstrated a "Good Payment History" if Borrower: (a) has made each of the most recent 24 consecutive monthly payments under the Note and Security Instrument before the date the next payment was due; and (b) has never been late by 3 months or more in making any monthly payments due under the Note. If Borrower demonstrates a Good Payment History, the new Note Rate will take effect on the earliest Anniversary Date on which Borrower has demonstrated a Good Payment History ("Rate Reduction Date"). Beginning with Borrower's first monthly payment after the Rate Reduction Date, Borrower will pay the new amount as the monthly payment until the Maturity Date. Lender will decrease Borrower's Note Rate only one time during the term of the loan, provided Borrower demonstrates a Good Payment History on any one of the second, third, or fourth Anniversary Dates.

BY SIGNING BELOW, Borrower accepts and agrees to the terms and covenants contained in this Timely Payment Rewards Addendum to Note.

____(Seal)
-Borrower

____(Seal)
-Borrower

MULTISTATE TIMELY PAYMENT REWARDS ADDENDUM TO NOTE -- Single Family -- **Fannie Mae UNIFORM INSTRUMENT Form 1410 4/01**

WAUSAU CITY BANK
DEMAND/PAYOFF STATEMENT
1/13/2007

To: Craig Daemler
Craig Daemler

RE: Loan NO. 0098765789
Craig Daemler

1220 Sesame Pl.
Los Angeles, CA 90045

45 Rosetown Place
El Sereno, CA 90032
Loan Type – Conventional

****

* PAYOFF FIGURES MUST BE VERIFIED WITHIN 24 HOURS PRIOR TO *
* PAYOFF. THE TOTAL AMOUNT NECESSARY TO PAY OFF THE LOAN IS *
* SUBJECT TO FINAL VERIFICATION FROM THE NOTEHOLDER. WE *
* RESERVE THE RIGHT TO ADJUST THESE FIGURES AND REFUSE ANY *
* FUNDS THAT ARE NOT SUFFICIENT TO PAY OFF THE LOAN IN *
* FULL. (THIS INLCUDES, BUT IS NOT LIMITED TO, DISHONORED *
* PAYMENTS, DISBURSEMENTS OR ADJUSTMENTS MADE BETWEEN *
* THE DATE OF THIS DEMAND/PAYOFF STATEMENT AND THE RECEIPT *
* OF THE PAYOFF FUNDS.) FOR SAME DAY CREDIT, PAYOFF FUNDS *
* MUST BE RECEIVED BY 3:00 PM CST MONDAY THROUGH FRIDAY. *
******PLEASE CALL (800)272-4740 TO VERIFY AMOUNTS****** *

The following amounts are required to pay this loan in full on 01/02/2006. The next scheduled payment due on this loan is the 01/02/2006 payment.

Current total unpaid Principal Balance	$	240179.94
Interest to 11/01/2006 at 07.250%	$	1546.50
TOTAL TO PAY LOAN IN FULL ON 01/03/2006	$	241726.50

IF NOT PAID IN FULL BY 01/02/2006, ADD DAILY INTEREST (PER DIEM)	$	47.71

The following amounts are additional loan servicing fees that are due and owing to Washington Mutual relating to this transaction:

PAYOFF STATEMENT FEE	$	30.00
RECORDING FEE	$	9.00
TOTAL AMOUNT DUE TO WASAU CITY BANK	$	241765.44

CUSTOMER'S STATEMENT OF NON-RESCISSION

Creditor:	Hunter Financial Group, Inc., dba, AmericaFirst Mortgage 7171 West Headline Dr. Arcadia, CA 91006
Property Address:	10987 Renault Drive Arcadia, CA 91006
Date of Closing:	January 30, 2006
Loan Number:	NAL138901

In order to induce lender to disburse the proceeds of the loan transaction referenced above, the undersigned represent and warrant that **three (3) business days have elapsed** since the date of such transaction and the undersigned have not exercised their right to cancel the transaction.

____________________________ Date

____________________________ Date

Note: All individuals having the Right to Cancel must sign.

____________________ [Space Above This Line For Recording Data] ____________________

LOAN MODIFICATION AGREEMENT
(Providing for Adjustable Interest Rate)

This Loan Modification Agreement ("Agreement"), made this ____ day of ________________, ______, between ________________________________ ("Borrower") and __________________________ ("Lender"), amends and supplements (1) the Mortgage, Deed of Trust, or Security Deed (the "Security Instrument") dated ______________________ and recorded in Book or Liber _____________, at page(s) ______________, of the _________________________ Records of ____,
(Name of Records) (County and State, or other jurisdiction)
and (2) the adjustable rate note (the "Note"), bearing the same date as, and secured by, the Security Instrument, which covers the real and personal property described in the Security Instrument and defined therein as the "Property", located at

____,
(Property Address)

the real property described being set forth as follows:

THE NOTE CONTAINS PROVISIONS ALLOWING FOR CHANGES IN THE INTEREST RATE AND THE MONTHLY PAYMENT. THE NOTE LIMITS THE AMOUNT THE BORROWER'S INTEREST RATE CAN CHANGE AT ANY ONE TIME AND THE MAXIMUM RATE THE BORROWER MUST PAY.

In consideration of the mutual promises and agreements exchanged, the parties hereto agree as follows (notwithstanding anything to the contrary contained in the Note or Security Instrument):

1. As of ________________________, the amount payable under the Note and the Security Instrument (the "Unpaid Principal Balance") is U.S. $________________, consisting of the unpaid amount(s) loaned to Borrower by Lender plus any interest and other amounts capitalized.

2. Borrower promises to pay the Unpaid Principal Balance, plus interest, to the order of Lender. Interest will be charged on the Unpaid Principal Balance at the yearly rate of _________%, from _________________, ______. The interest rate Borrower will pay may change in accordance with the terms of the Note. Borrower promises to make monthly payments of principal and interest of U.S. $____________________, beginning on the ____ day of ________________, ______. The amount of Borrower's monthly payments may change in accordance with the terms of the Note. Borrower will continue to make monthly payments on the same day of each succeeding month until principal and interest are paid in full, except that, if not sooner paid, the final payment of principal and interest shall be due and payable on the ____ day of ________________, ______, which is the present or extended Maturity Date.

3. If on the Maturity Date, Borrower still owes amounts under the Note and the Security Instrument, as amended by this Agreement, Borrower will pay these amounts in full on the Maturity Date.

4. Borrower understands and agrees that

   (a) All the rights and remedies, stipulations, and conditions contained in the Security Instrument relating to default in the making of payments under the Security Instrument shall also apply to default in the making of the modified payments hereunder.

LOAN MODIFICATION AGREEMENT—Single Family—**Fannie Mae Uniform Instrument** **Form 3161 6/06** ***(page 1 of 2)***

(b) All covenants, agreements, stipulations, and conditions in the Note and Security Instrument shall be and remain in full force and effect, except as herein modified, and none of the Borrower's obligations or liabilities under the Note and Security Instrument shall be diminished or released by any provisions hereof, nor shall this Agreement in any way impair, diminish, or affect any of Lender's rights under or remedies on the Note and Security Instrument, whether such rights or remedies arise thereunder or by operation of law. Also, all rights of recourse to which Lender is presently entitled against any property or any other persons in any way obligated for, or liable on, the Note and Security Instrument are expressly reserved by Lender.

(c) Borrower has no right of set-off or counterclaim, or any defense to the obligations of the Note or Security Instrument.

(d) Nothing in this Agreement shall be understood or construed to be a satisfaction or release in whole or in part of the Note and Security Instrument.

(e) All costs and expenses incurred by Lender in connection with this Agreement, including recording fees, title examination, and attorney's fees, shall be paid by the Borrower and shall be secured by the Security Instrument, unless stipulated otherwise by Lender.

(f) Borrower agrees to make and execute such other documents or papers as may be necessary or required to effectuate the terms and conditions of this Agreement which, if approved and accepted by Lender, shall bind and inure to the heirs, executors, administrators, and assigns of the Borrower.

______________________________ (Seal)
-Lender

______________________________ (Seal)
-Borrower

By: ______________________________

______________________________ (Seal)
-Borrower

______________________ [Space Below This Line for Acknowledgements] ______________________

LOAN MODIFICATION AGREEMENT—Single Family—**Fannie Mae Uniform Instrument** **Form 3161 6/06** ***(page 2 of 2)***

LISTS OF ADDITIONAL LOAN AND REAL ESTATE DOCUMENTS

The Notary Signing Agent may encounter additional forms or variations of the documents described and illustrated in this chapter. Lists of these forms appear on the following pages and are grouped as documents that must be signed, dated and/or initialed, that must be notarized and that ask the borrower to provide additional information.

Loan Documents Signed, Dated and/or Initialed

1. Addendum to Residential Loan Application
2. Aggregate Analysis Trial Balance
3. Aggregate Escrow Accounting Disclosure
4. Agreement for the Arbitration of Disputes
5. Authorization to Reverify
6. Automatic Drafting Authorization
7. Billing Rights
8. Borrower Credit Program Disclosure
9. Borrower's Disbursement Authorization
10. Borrower's Income Certification
11. Commitment Letter
12. Consumer Credit Score Disclosure Conditions
13. Fire Insurance Authorization
14. Flood Insurance Authorization
15. Home Equity Line of Credit and Promissory Note
16. Insurance Information Sheet
17. Inter Vivos Revocable Trust as Borrower Acknowledgment
18. Inter Vivos Revocable Trust Rider
19. Interest Rate and Loan Fee Policy
20. Lead Paint Disclosure
21. Loan Conditions
22. Loan Disbursement Summary
23. Loan Review Agreement

24. Non-Impound Notice
25. Overnight Fee Statement
26. Provider of Service Schedule
27. Request and Authorization for Lender's Loss Payable Endorsement
28. Request for Loss Payable Endorsement
29. Security Instrument Cover Sheet
30. State Application Disclosure
31. Terms of Your Loan
32. Verification of Important Loan Information

Loan and Real Estate Documents Notarized

Unless noted, all documents must be notarized with an acknowledgment.

1. Affidavit of Death of Spouse
2. Affidavit of Death of Spouse (jurat)
3. Affidavit of Continuous Marriage
4. Affidavit of Death of Joint Tenant
5. Affidavit of Death of Spouse Survivorship
6. Affidavit of No Debts/Liens
7. Affidavit of Payment of Taxes (jurat)
8. Affidavit of Settlement Agent
9. Affidavit to Affirm Conveyance
10. Assignment of Ownership Documents
11. Assignment of Proprietary Lease
12. Assignment — General Request for Special Notice
13. Borrower's Affidavit
14. Certification of Trust
15. Claim of Lien
16. Corporate Quitclaim Deed
17. Corporation Assignment Deed of Trust
18. Deceased Joint Tenancy Affidavit
19. Declaration of Abandonment of Declared Homestead
20. Estoppel Affidavit (By Individual Giving Deed in Lieu of Foreclosure) — Full Reconveyance

21. Grant Deed
22. Homestead Declaration
23. Homestead Waiver
24. Interspousal Transfer Grant Deed
25. Interspousal Transfer Grant Deed Community Property with Right of Survivorship
26. Joint Tenancy Grant Deed
27. Long Form All-Inclusive Deed of Trust and Assignment of Rents
28. Long Form Deed of Trust and Assignment of Rents
29. Long Form Security — Land Contract
30. Mortgagor's Affidavit for Master Home Equity Loan Policy and Certificate Program (oath)
31. Notice of Termination of "Right of First Refusal"
32. Occupancy Affidavit and Financial Disclosure Status Conditions
33. Partial Reconveyance
34. Quitclaim Deed
35. Release of Claim of Mechanics Lien
36. Request for Notice
37. Revocation of Power of Attorney
38. Section 255 Affidavit
39. Security Deed
40. Short Form Deed of Trust and Assignment of Rents (Individual)
41. Signature Statement Acceptance of Terms and Conditions
42. Special Power of Attorney as to Real Property
43. Specific Release of Lien
44. Special Warranty Deed
45. Subordination Agreement (Form A) — Existing Deed of Trust to New Deed of Trust
46. Subordination Agreement (Form B) — New Deed of Trust to New Deed of Trust
47. Subordination Agreement — Existing Deed of Trust to Additional Advance
48. Subordination Agreement — Lease to Deed of Trust

49. Substitution of Trustee
50. Substitution of Trustee and Full Reconveyance
51. Warranty Deed

Documents Completed by Borrower

The Statement of Information previously discussed in this chapter is one document in a loan package that asks the borrower to provide additional information. Two additional forms included in some loan packages that must be completed by the borrower during the signing appointment are listed below.

1. Nearest Living Relative
2. Property Locator ■

CHAPTER 5 TEST

True/False Questions

1. By signing the Borrower's Certification & Authorization, the borrower authorizes the lender to disclose the information contained in the loan application to any investor looking to purchase the loan.

2. The PATRIOT Act CIP is a commonly notarized form.

3. The legal description of the subject property may be found on the Note.

4. A Notary Signing Agent may explain the assumption provision contained in the Truth in Lending Disclosure Statement.

Multiple Choice Questions

(Choose the Best Answer)

1. At a loan signing when there is a discrepancy between the HUD-1 Settlement Statement and the Good Faith Estimate of settlement charges, which of the following documents contains the most accurate figures?
   a) The Good Faith Estimate
   b) The HUD-1 Settlement Statement
   c) The Loan Signing Prep Sheet
   d) The Instructions to Escrow

2. The Servicing Disclosure Statement does which of the following?
   a) Discloses that the borrower's impound account will be transferred to another servicer
   b) Discloses that the loan will be assigned, sold or transferred to another servicer
   c) Discloses that the closing agent will service the loan beyond the closing
   d) All of the above

3. Which of the following documents discloses the amount of prepaid finance charges for a loan?
   a) The Note
   b) The Biweekly Payment Rider
   c) The Mortgagor's Affidavit
   d) The Itemization of Amount Financed

4. Which of the following questions may a Notary Signing Agent answer without engaging in the unauthorized practice of law?
   a) "When will my loan close?"
   b) "Why does my loan not contain an assumption option?"
   c) "Where can I find the payment schedule for my loan?"
   d) "Is my prepayment policy typical of other such policies?

See page 331 for correct responses.

CHAPTER 6

Closing Out the Assignment

In conducting a successful loan signing, the Notary Signing Agent meticulously prepares for the appointment, arrives at the appointment at the scheduled time, presents the documents to the borrower without offering legal advice, obtains the borrower's signatures or initials on particular documents, notarizes the applicable forms and, before leaving the borrower's home, checks the documents to ensure that all needed signatures, dates and initials have been collected.

A Notary Signing Agent's responsibilities are not fulfilled once the appointment has concluded and the documents are signed. To finish the assignment, the Agent must attend to some matters that are as important as the actual signing itself. If the Agent does not complete these tasks, then his or her effort in preparing for the appointment and carrying out the signing has been for nothing.

The Notary Signing Agent's handling of these wrap-up tasks is vital for helping close the transaction for at least three reasons:

1. The borrower, signing service (if applicable), lender and closing agent in the transaction are entirely dependent upon the Notary

Signing Agent's follow through. The borrower ultimately will care very little that the Agent arrived on time and the signing appointment went flawlessly if the Agent returns the papers late and causes the borrower's interest rate lock to expire. And it will matter little to the other stakeholders in the transaction that the signing occurred if the Agent's mishandling of the documents after the signing causes a delay that places the transaction at risk.

2. The Notary Signing Agent will want to wrap up the assignment properly if he or she wants repeat business in the future. The best advertising strategy is always to provide excellent service from beginning to end. No matter how diligent the Agent has been in fielding the assignment, contacting the borrower and confirming the appointment, communicating with all parties involved every step of the way and carrying through with the signing itself, all will be lost if the Agent does not finish the job to the satisfaction of the signing service, lender or title company.[1]

3. Tending to some essential assignment wrap-up steps will help the Notary Signing Agent manage his or her business. When the Agent invoices a client for services performed immediately following an appointment, collections can be tracked and late payments kept to a minimum. In addition, by keeping clear, consistent and detailed written records of business activity, the Agent can effectively prepare for tax filings.

ASSIGNMENT WRAP-UP PROCEDURES

Review the Documents

Before leaving the borrower's home or office, the Notary Signing Agent must review the signed papers for omitted signatures, initials and dates.

[1] The owner of one signing service informed the NNA® that her biggest complaint with Notary Signing Agents is that some Agents hold on to documents too long following the signing appointment.

After returning to his or her office or home and before shipping the completed package to the escrow or title company, the Notary Signing Agent should give the completed package a second review. This once-over provides the Agent a final opportunity to ensure that the package is in good order and ready for shipment. Even at this late hour, the Agent still may have the opportunity to return to the borrower's home or office to collect a missing signature that was not spotted earlier. In addition, during the final review, the Agent also may discover and correct an improperly completed or illegible notarial certificate before the title company and the county recorder see it.

The following true story illustrates why a final review is so necessary. The story is told by an officer in a signing service who hired a Notary Signing Agent to conduct an assignment.

> We received an order from one of our title insurance accounts for a signing. We filled the order with a Notary Signing Agent who has done approximately 40 signings for us. The Notary has always done an excellent job and we appreciate her work. She met with the borrower, obtained all signatures, and forwarded the documents directly to the title company as instructed. However, she forgot to notarize the Deed of Trust.
>
> The title company missed her omission and forwarded the Deed of Trust to the county recorder. The county recorder let the documents sit until late December before notifying the title company and the lender that it could not be recorded because it was not notarized.
>
> The lender demanded payment in the amount of $6,334.20 for lost interest from the title company. The title company paid the lender. The title company then demanded payment of $6,334.20 from us (the signing company). We paid the title company. We will now demand payment from the Notary of $6,334.20.
>
> The Notary is now faced with a very serious problem. In all probability, she cannot afford to pay this out of her pocket and will have to turn to her bonding company for payment. Her bonding company will probably pay and cancel her bond. We feel very bad that a good Notary Signing Agent is faced with this problem. She is one of the many good ones and she just made a mistake.
>
> All in all, a very unfortunate situation. I would bet there is not a Notary in this business who has not forgotten to notarize a document after a long hard day. In most instances, our experience has been that the title company catches the mistake and we are all given the opportunity to correct it.

Let this story serve as a reminder of why a review is needed. The Notary Signing Agent should welcome every opportunity to avoid a potentially costly mistake, since it is in the Agent's ultimate best interest to do so.

Communicate with the Client

A second procedure for closing out the assignment is to communicate with the signing service, lender or title company on the status of the assignment. A provision in many signing service independent contractor's agreements requires the Notary Signing Agent to phone, fax or complete an online form at the signing service's website to report when the assignment has been completed.[2] A few companies even stipulate that the communication be received by midmorning the day after a signing appointment. The conscientious Agent will find that keeping clients informed about completed assignments will foster good will and repeat business.

Clients also may request information about the signing appointment itself — whether any documents were not signed and if the borrower had specific questions or special requests (provide borrower's copies, for example).

Comply with Fax Requests

If the documents are date-sensitive or the timing for the closing is tight, the lender or title company may ask the Notary Signing Agent to fax certain documents before the package is shipped via overnight courier.

For example, the lender may request faxed copies of the Notice of Right to Cancel and signature pages of the Note and the Deed of Trust or Mortgage to begin processing the file.

Ship the Package

The Notary Signing Agent should ship the loan package the same day or the next day for evening appointments. In case the client does not provide return shipping materials, the Agent should stock shipping supplies from the major couriers, including air bills and shipping sleeves. The major couriers will provide these supplies as a courtesy.

---

[2] Some signing services also accept email communications.

Once the Notary Signing Agent completes the air bill and drops the package, the Agent should file the sender's copy of the air bill and provide the signing service, escrow firm or title company with the shipment tracking number for reference. In their fax-back assignment forms, most clients include a space for the Agent to include the name of the courier, tracking number and date the package was shipped.

Saturday shipments require special consideration. If a Notary Signing Agent receives a Friday evening assignment, the Agent should confirm that the escrow or title company expects the documents on Monday morning. Often this will be the case.

When the documents are due back on a Monday morning following a Friday evening or Saturday signing, the Notary Signing Agent should call or log on to the overnight courier's website to inquire about that courier's Saturday pick-up policy or for the location and hours of the walk-in location nearest to the Agent's home or office.[3] The Agent also should verify that the shipment will arrive at its destination on Monday morning.

Lenders typically are willing to pay an additional fee for Saturday pickup.

BILLING AND RECEIVABLES

Invoices

Earlier in this Course, it was noted that the Notary Signing Agent works as an independent contractor. As an independent contractor, the Agent is solely responsible for all billings and collections.

The Notary Signing Agent's first order of business following the shipment of documents should be to invoice the client for the Agent's services. Industry practice for submitting invoices varies by company and is often addressed in the particular company's independent contractor's agreement.

There are at least three methods for submitting invoices: a fax-back form, a Web form and a direct invoice.

[3] At the time of printing, contact information for the major couriers was as follows: FedEx: 800-463-3339 (800-GO-FEDEX); http://www.fedex.com. UPS: 800-742-5877 (800-PICK-UPS); http://www.ups.com. DHL: 800-225-5345 (800-CALL-DHL); http://www.dhl.com/en.html.

Many signing services design the initial assignment sheet to double as an invoice that the Notary Signing Agent completes and returns via fax. Where such a form is used, no additional invoice is required.

The basic information often required in a typical fax-back form includes the following:

1. Confirmation the Notary Signing Agent made the trip

2. Confirmation the borrower signed the documents and, if not, an explanation of why the borrower did not sign

3. Date of signing

4. Round-trip mileage

5. Return courier name

6. Shipment tracking number

7. Date the documents were shipped

8. Company and contact name where package was shipped

9. Additional comments

A second means for submitting an invoice is through completion of an online form at the contracting company's website. The online form may contain many of the items included in the fax-back form.

A direct invoice may be used in at least two different ways. First, the invoice may be used in a single signing where multiple charges are incurred. In the illustration on the next page, the form itemizes the flat fee for the assignment as well as extra fees for emailed documents and additional mileage.[4]

[4] The Notary Signing Agent always should insist that additional charges for emailed documents, mileage, borrower copies, additional faxes, etc. be specified on the written assignment sheet.

INVOICE

BILL TO:

INVOICE DATE: March 1, 2012
COMPANY / ORGANIZATION: Rocket Document Signing Co.
ADDRESS: 125 Market Street
CITY / STATE / ZIP: Any City, CA 91006
ATTENTION: Marci Cranson PHONE: 800.555.7777

REMIT TO:

NOTARY NAME: Larry Loan Signer
ADDRESS: 598 Walnut Avenue
CITY / STATE / ZIP: Any City, CA 91006
PAYMENT TERMS: Net 30 Days
PHONE: 626.123.4567 FAX: 626.987.6543

NOTARY SIGNING AGENT SERVICES

DATE	BORROWER(S)	ORDER #	DESCRIPTION	AMOUNT DUE
2/15/12	Walterson	67879098	Loan signing fee	$ 50.00
"	"	"	e-mail doc. fee	$ 35.00
"	"	"	Additional mileage fee	$ 10.00

TOTAL AMOUNT DUE $ 95.00

The second way in which a direct invoice may be used is to submit charges for multiple appointments. This type of invoice is shown below.

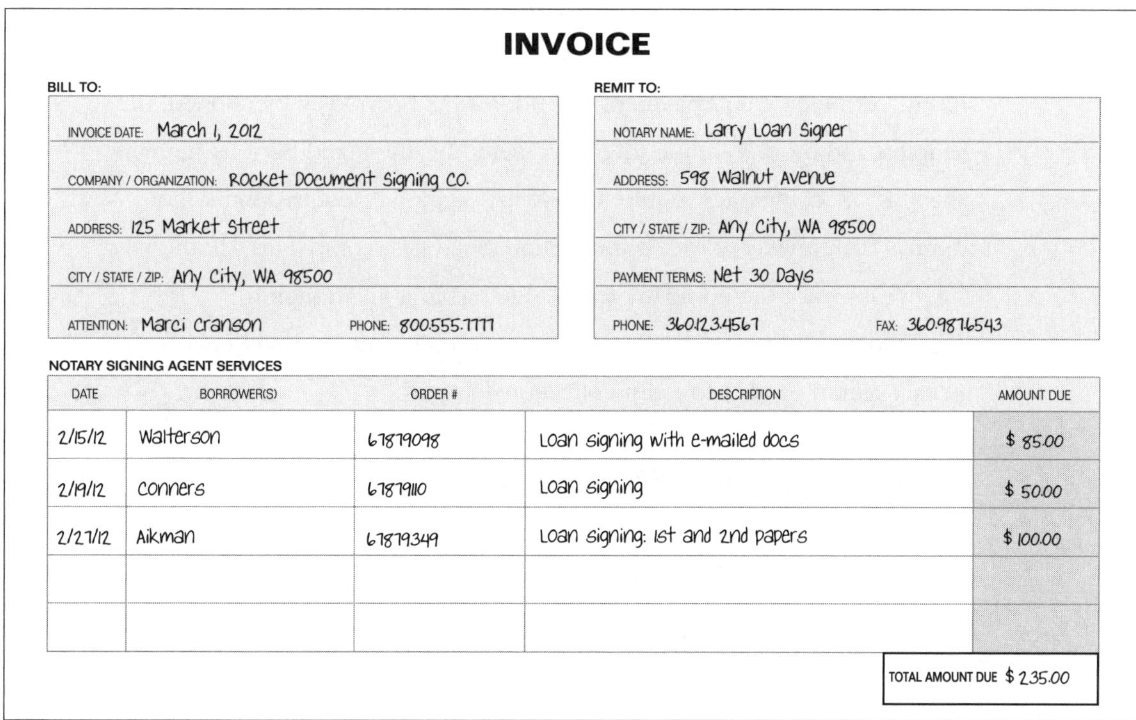

INVOICE

BILL TO:

INVOICE DATE: March 1, 2012
COMPANY / ORGANIZATION: Rocket Document Signing Co.
ADDRESS: 125 Market Street
CITY / STATE / ZIP: Any City, WA 98500
ATTENTION: Marci Cranson PHONE: 800.555.7777

REMIT TO:

NOTARY NAME: Larry Loan Signer
ADDRESS: 598 Walnut Avenue
CITY / STATE / ZIP: Any City, WA 98500
PAYMENT TERMS: Net 30 Days
PHONE: 360.123.4567 FAX: 360.987.6543

NOTARY SIGNING AGENT SERVICES

DATE	BORROWER(S)	ORDER #	DESCRIPTION	AMOUNT DUE
2/15/12	Walterson	67879098	Loan signing with e-mailed docs	$ 85.00
2/19/12	Conners	67879110	Loan signing	$ 50.00
2/27/12	Aikman	67879349	Loan signing: 1st and 2nd papers	$ 100.00

TOTAL AMOUNT DUE $ 235.00

Collections

Collecting on accounts is an important responsibility for any business owner. Collecting payments can be time-consuming and frustrating, but the process can be managed to ensure a positive cash flow and to guard against receivables becoming bad debts. The following steps will help the Notary Signing Agent get started.

1. Keep Detailed Records

Maintaining accurate records of all services performed and invoices submitted will help the Notary Signing Agent stay on top of receivables. The Agent has many options when it comes to keeping records.

Retaining a file of completed assignment sheets and outstanding invoices is one method. Pertinent entries in a record book or ledger are another.[5] Purchasing an accounting software program or creating a computer spreadsheet to track invoices and collections is yet another option. Each Agent must find and use the method that works best for him or her.

2. Follow the Company's Invoicing Policy

Each company — whether signing service, closing agency or lender — has its own billing and payment procedures. As previously mentioned, the simplest and most common invoicing method is the faxed-back assignment sheet. Some companies require the Notary Signing Agent to submit the Agent's own invoice for each transaction. Still other companies ask the Agent to invoice the company for all signings in a given month.

Finding and using an effective recordkeeping method will enable the Notary Signing Agent to keep collections current.

3. Understand the Payment Schedule

As with invoicing policies, payment policies also run the gamut from company to company. The major payment schedule policies in the loan signing industry are the following:

---

[5] See pages 297–302, where the NNA®'s Notary Signing Agent Log is discussed.

1. Payment upon close of the transaction

2. Payment every two weeks

3. Payment once a month

4. Payment when the company is paid

Notary Signing Agents should inquire about payment policies when submitting an application to a particular company or prior to accepting an assignment. Agents should refuse assignments from companies whose policies they deem unacceptable.

While contract clauses clearly can specify a particular company's payment policy, experience is often the only gauge in assessing a company's payment track record. The Notary Signing Agent will be able to assess the companies that remit payment according to their established policies after a few assignments. If a company is consistently late, the Notary Signing Agent may choose to terminate the contract with that company.

By serving only those clients who pay according to their stated policies, the Agent can effectively reduce outstanding receivables.

4. Proceed with Collections According to the Payment Schedule

The Notary Signing Agent should approach collections with a realistic understanding of the payment timetable. For example, a company with a 30-day payment policy may issue checks on the 15th day of each month and have a cut-off date on the 10th day of the month. Payment for an invoice submitted on the 11th of the month is not technically past due until the 15th day of the following month. When processing, handling and mail time are factored in, it is possible that a payment may not be received for 45 days after the invoice date.

The same once-per-month payment policy could actually work in the Notary Signing Agent's favor. If the Agent submitted an invoice on the cut-off day of the month, payment could be received within 30 days of the invoice date. As the two scenarios illustrate, the calendar will often affect when an Agent is paid. In the normal ebb and flow of monthly activity, the law of averages will be a factor, and the busy Agent can plan for a fairly steady cash flow.

Signing services report that one of the most unprofessional practices of Notary Signing Agents is the over-aggressive pursuit of collections that are not technically late. Having to research payments at the request of an inquiring Agent is a drain of resources that takes the company away from filling assignments. Some signing services have instituted policies to dock the pay of any Agent who pursues a payment that is not technically late.

The Notary Signing Agent should not bother a company for payment if it is operating within its stated payment policy.

5. Follow a Plan for Pursuing Collectables

The Notary Signing Agent should do the following:

1. **Set a time frame for starting collections for payments that are late:** For example, the Notary Signing Agent may decide to pursue collection if payment is not received within 45 days. By most standards, a payment 60 days past due is considered late. Agents should pay close attention to receivables and not let them go too long before starting collections.

2. **Establish clearly defined steps:** For example, an Agent may place a phone call on the 45th day to inquire about the status of a late payment, follow up with a polite letter if payment is not received after 10 days and follow up with a more strongly worded letter if payment is not received after 60 days. A company's failure to respond after these efforts may require the Agent to take additional steps, such as contacting the Better Business Bureau, retaining an attorney or taking the matter to small claims court.

3. **Document all phone conversations and correspondence**

6. Never Pursue the Borrower

If the chief complaint of signing services is that some Notary Signing Agents pursue payments that are not technically due, the most frequent complaint of Agents themselves is that some companies do not pay at all.

Although Notary Signing Agents have generated increased business from clients who operate outside the Agent's immediate area, the lack of a local presence has made it more problematic for Agents to collect payments when there is no convenient office to visit.

In order to protect themselves against nonpaying companies, some Notary Signing Agents have required a borrower to sign a collection letter at the loan signing appointment stating that, if the Agent is not paid by the lender or signing service, the borrower will pay the Agent. When the lender or signing service fails to pay within a certain period of time, the Agent pursues payment from the borrower.

Such a practice is problematic for at least two reasons:

1. The Notary Signing Agent has contracted to perform loan signing services for the contracting company, and the contracting company has agreed to pay the Agent for these services. The Notary Signing Agent has not entered into an agreement with the borrower, and the borrower does not directly pay the Agent. Thus, the Agent's complaint is not with the borrower but with the contracting company.

2. Under the federal RESPA statute, a Notary Signing Agent who attempts to collect from the borrower places the lender in direct violation of RESPA laws. Lenders could take legal action against Agents who follow this course of action.

It is far more effective to record the name and contact information of the closing agent and the lender in each transaction and use this information to secure payment from any delinquent signing service. For example, the Notary Signing Agent may contact the lender or closing agent to complain about a signing service that is late with payments. A lender or closing agent who receives repeated complaints about a signing service that does not pay its Agents eventually will cease doing business with that company.

Another strategy for determining whether a company is slow to pay or nonpaying is to require up-front payment for the first assignment from a new company. Some Notary Signing Agents set up a PayPal account (www.paypal.com) and require a company providing a first-time assignment to deposit the fee for the first assignment into their PayPal account prior to the signing as a condition of accepting the assignment.

Notary Signing Agents admittedly face collections challenges. There is no regulating authority that specifically addresses collection issues within the industry. The states do not require licensing for companies providing loan signing assignments, and there are no designated government agencies whose responsibility it is to police companies who do not pay Agents.

In an effort to assist Notary Signing Agents in procuring payment from delinquent accounts, the NNA® has joined forces with OldDebts.com to form an exclusive alliance for debt collection services. As a national leader in providing both flat fee and contingency fee debt collection, OldDebts.com uses extensive knowledge of the debt recovery process to recover unpaid collection accounts.

While collections can be a challenge, the good news is that most companies pay their Agents on time. With experience, the Notary Signing Agent will discover which companies are reputable and which are not. In the end, perhaps the most effective collections strategy is to sever relationships with the nonpaying companies at the earliest sign of trouble, before the unpaid invoices accumulate. Once again, the key is to keep on top of collections.

In the early days of the Notary Signing Agent's career, the number of signings the Agent performs for any one client likely will be small, and the Agent will have to forge relationships with many companies to obtain steady work. While it may be difficult to turn down assignments from a nonpaying client, the Agent who adopts this policy will limit losses, avoid expending time and effort pursuing collections and, most importantly, free up appointment times for the companies who do pay. Agents with many months of experience often will have built a business base with sound companies who have a solid payment track record and likely will not face a significant problem collecting on unpaid invoices.

TAX REPORTING

The matter of invoicing companies raises a related and important issue for Notary Signing Agents — taxes! Yes, Uncle Sam will want his share of the Agent's revenues, but the good news is that the Notary Signing Agent business provides tax benefits that are found in few other careers. In this section, the important details related to taxes and the important task of recordkeeping for taxes will be discussed.[6] The following pages cover tax reporting in general and should not be construed as specific advice. The Notary Signing Agent should consult with a tax professional to discuss individual tax issues.

IRS Form 1040 Schedule C or Schedule C-EZ

As an independent contractor, a Notary Signing Agent must declare all business related income on an IRS Form 1040 Schedule C ("Profit or Loss From Business") or Schedule C-EZ ("Net Profit From Business") and must include it with the Agent's personal tax return each year. If the Notary Signing Agent has been or is currently an employee, the Agent may never have filed a Schedule C or Schedule C-EZ.

Employees receive from their employers a W-2 form that itemizes their earnings for the year. Unlike an employee, the Notary Signing Agent will not receive a W-2 form. Instead, the Agent will receive an IRS Form 1099-MISC ("Miscellaneous Income"). Signing services and other clients from whom the Agent accepts assignments must complete and file with the IRS a 1099-MISC form for all Agents who earn more than $600 in any given

[6] While every effort has been made to ensure that the information included in the following section is consistent with tax laws, Notary Signing Agents should talk to a qualified tax preparer to discuss their individual tax situations. The tax implications of being a Notary Signing Agent are discussed in this chapter to underscore a tangible benefit of being a Notary Signing Agent. In addition to earning a part-time income, working flexible hours from home and being one's own boss, the tax laws favor Notaries and work to their benefit.

tax year. If an Agent completes signings with a number of companies, the Agent will receive a 1099-MISC form from each of these companies.

If a Notary Signing Agent's earnings with a company do not exceed the $600 minimum, a 1099-MISC form will not be issued. However, the IRS still requires Agents to declare all income earned from any client on a Schedule C or Schedule C-EZ.

The IRS Form 1040 Schedule C-EZ is a short version of Schedule C, which may be filed by Notary Signing Agents who meet the following criteria:

1. Had business expenses of $5,000 or less
2. Used the cash method of accounting
3. Did not have an inventory at any time during the year
4. Did not report a net loss
5. Operated only one business as a sole proprietor, qualified joint venture or statutory employee
6. Received no credit card or similar payments that included amounts not otherwise included in income
7. Had no employees during the year
8. Are not required to file IRS Form 4562 ("Depreciation and Amortization")
9. Did not deduct expenses for business use of a home
10. Did not have prior-year unallowed passive activity losses

The Notary Signing Agent should check with a tax preparer to determine if the Agent should file Schedule C-EZ.

SCHEDULE C (Form 1040)
Department of the Treasury
Internal Revenue Service (99)

Profit or Loss From Business
(Sole Proprietorship)
▸ **For information on Schedule C and its instructions, go to *www.irs.gov/schedulec***
▸ **Attach to Form 1040, 1040NR, or 1041; partnerships generally must file Form 1065.**

OMB No. 1545-0074
2011
Attachment Sequence No. **09**

Name of proprietor: LARRY LOAN SIGNER
Social security number (SSN): 000-00-0000

A Principal business or profession, including product or service (see instructions): NOTARY PUBLIC
B Enter code from instructions ▸

C Business name. If no separate business name, leave blank.: LARRY'S LOAN SIGNINGS
D Employer ID number (EIN), (see instr.)

E Business address (including suite or room no.) ▸ 22 OAK STREET, ANYTOWN, ANY STATE 99999
City, town or post office, state, and ZIP code

F Accounting method: **(1)** ☒ Cash **(2)** ☐ Accrual **(3)** ☐ Other (specify) ▸

G Did you "materially participate" in the operation of this business during 2011? If "No," see instructions for limit on losses . ☒ **Yes** ☐ **No**

H If you started or acquired this business during 2011, check here . . . ▸ ☐

I Did you make any payments in 2011 that would require you to file Form(s) 1099? (see instructions) . . . ☐ **Yes** ☐ **No**

J If "Yes," did you or will you file all required Forms 1099? . . . ☐ **Yes** ☐ **No**

Part I Income

1a	Merchant card and third party payments. For 2011, enter -0-	1a			
b	Gross receipts or sales not entered on line 1a (see instructions)	1b			12,500
c	Income reported to you on Form W-2 if the "Statutory Employee" box on that form was checked. **Caution.** See instr. before completing this line	1c			
d	**Total gross receipts.** Add lines 1a through 1c			1d	12,500
2	Returns and allowances plus any other adjustments (see instructions)			2	
3	Subtract line 2 from line 1d			3	
4	Cost of goods sold (from line 42)			4	
5	**Gross profit.** Subtract line 4 from line 3			5	12,500
6	Other income, including federal and state gasoline or fuel tax credit or refund (see instructions)			6	
7	**Gross income.** Add lines 5 and 6 ▸			7	

Part I of Schedule C, shown on the next page, is where the Notary Signing Agent records income from all invoices paid during the tax year.

Part II of Schedule C, shown on the next page, is where business expenses for the tax year are entered. Notary Signing Agents may deduct many expenses incurred in the operation of their business. Agents may find the following line-items in Part II of Schedule C to be of particular relevance:

1. **Line 8 ("Advertising"):** Here, the Agent would record the total amount spent for business cards, flyers, ads, promotional pens or any other method used to promote the Agent's business.

2. **Line 9 ("Car and truck expenses"):** Here, for example, the Agent would record all mileage expenses the Agent incurred in the performance of loan signings for the year.

3. **Line 10 ("Commissions and Fees"):** The Notary Signing Agent would record fees associated with the Notary commissioning, including application, Notary bond and filing fees.

4. **Line 15 ("Insurance other than health"):** If the Agent carries a Notary errors and omissions insurance policy, premiums paid on the policy may be entered in this line.
5. **Line 22 ("Supplies"):** The Notary Signing Agent would record costs for Notary supplies such as seals, certificates, journals, etc.

6. **Line 24a ("Travel"):** Here, amounts paid for tolls, parking or other travel expenses would be entered.

If the Notary Signing Agent incurs a business expense that cannot be categorized in one of the expense line-items listed on the front of Schedule C, then the Agent may list the expense on page 2 of the form and bring the amount of expense forward to Line 27a on page 1.

Part II Expenses — **Enter expenses for business use of your home only on line 30.**

8	Advertising	8	425	18	Office expense (see instructions)	18	
9	Car and truck expenses (see instructions)	9	1,356	19	Pension and profit-sharing plans .	19	
				20	Rent or lease (see instructions):		
10	Commissions and fees .	10		a	Vehicles, machinery, and equipment	20a	
11	Contract labor (see instructions)	11		b	Other business property . . .	20b	
12	Depletion	12		21	Repairs and maintenance . . .	21	
13	Depreciation and section 179 expense deduction (not included in Part III) (see instructions)	13		22	Supplies (not included in Part III) .	22	175
				23	Taxes and licenses	23	
				24	Travel, meals, and entertainment:		
14	Employee benefit programs (other than on line 19) . .	14		a	Travel	24a	80
				b	Deductible meals and entertainment (see instructions) .	24b	
15	Insurance (other than health)	15					
16	Interest:			25	Utilities	25	
a	Mortgage (paid to banks, etc.)	16a		26	Wages (less employment credits) .	26	
b	Other	16b		27a	Other expenses (from line 48) . .	27a	250
17	Legal and professional services	17		b	**Reserved for future use** . . .	27b	

28	**Total expenses** before expenses for business use of home. Add lines 8 through 27a . . . . . . ▶	28	2,786
29	Tentative profit or (loss). Subtract line 28 from line 7	29	9,714
30	Expenses for business use of your home. Attach **Form 8829.** Do **not** report such expenses elsewhere . .	30	
31	**Net profit or (loss).** Subtract line 30 from line 29. • If a profit, enter on both **Form 1040, line 12** (or **Form 1040NR, line 13**) and on **Schedule SE, line 2.** If you entered an amount on line 1c, see instr. Estates and trusts, enter on **Form 1041, line 3.** • If a loss, you **must** go to line 32.	31	
32	If you have a loss, check the box that describes your investment in this activity (see instructions). • If you checked 32a, enter the loss on both **Form 1040, line 12,** (or **Form 1040NR, line 13**) and on **Schedule SE, line 2.** If you entered an amount on line 1c, see the instructions for line 31. Estates and trusts, enter on **Form 1041, line 3.** • If you checked 32b, you **must** attach **Form 6198.** Your loss may be limited.	32a ☐ All investment is at risk. 32b ☐ Some investment is not at risk.	

For Paperwork Reduction Act Notice, see your tax return instructions. Cat. No. 11334P **Schedule C (Form 1040) 2011**

IRS Form 1040 Schedule SE

Notary Signing Agents also are responsible for paying self-employment taxes at the time of filing a personal tax return. Self-employment taxes are the equivalent of Social Security or FICA taxes for an employee. Tax laws require that persons who are in business for themselves pay self-employment taxes on all net earnings from self employment of $400 or more.

Once a Notary Signing Agent has determined the net profit from the Agent's signing business for the year by completing a Schedule C or Schedule C-EZ, the Agent must complete an IRS Form 1040 Schedule SE ("Self- Employment Tax") and pay 13.3 percent of net self-employment earnings. The maximum amount of self-employment earnings on which self-employment taxes must be paid is $106,800 for 2011. The maximum amount subject to self-employment taxes adjusts each year.

This law has potential benefits for Notary Signing Agents, because fees received for services performed as a Notary Public are not subject to self-employment taxes. The 2011 "Instructions for Schedule SE (Form 1040)" contain the following statement:

> 2. Fees received for services performed as a notary public. If you had no other income subject to SE tax, enter "Exempt-Notary" on Form 1040, Line 56. Do not file Schedule SE. However, if you had other earnings of $400 or more subject to SE tax, enter "Exempt-Notary" and the amount of your net profit as a notary public from Schedule C or Schedule C-EZ on the dotted line to the left of Schedule SE, line 3. Subtract that amount from the total of lines 1a, 1b, and 2, and enter the result on line 3.

These instructions address two possible scenarios. A Notary whose net earnings comprise Notary fees exclusively would not file a Schedule SE. Instead, the Notary would write the words "Exempt-Notary" on Line 56 of Form 1040 and enter 0 (zero) in that line on the form, since no self-employment taxes are due.

However, a portion of most Notary Signing Agents' net earnings is not directly attributable to Notary fees. A typical loan document signing fee may cover notarization, travel and general Notary Signing Agent or courier services. Any additional fee, unlike Notary fees, is subject to self-employment taxes. The Notary Signing Agent would complete a Schedule SE and follow the instructions cited above.

These instructions specifically state that the Notary Signing Agent would complete a Schedule C or Schedule C-EZ to arrive at the Agent's net profit. The net profit recorded in Part II of Schedule C, line 31, or Part II of Schedule C-EZ, line 3, would be entered into Part I of Schedule SE, line 2.

An example of the relevant portion of Schedule SE, completed according to the instructions for Schedule SE given above, appears in the illustration below.

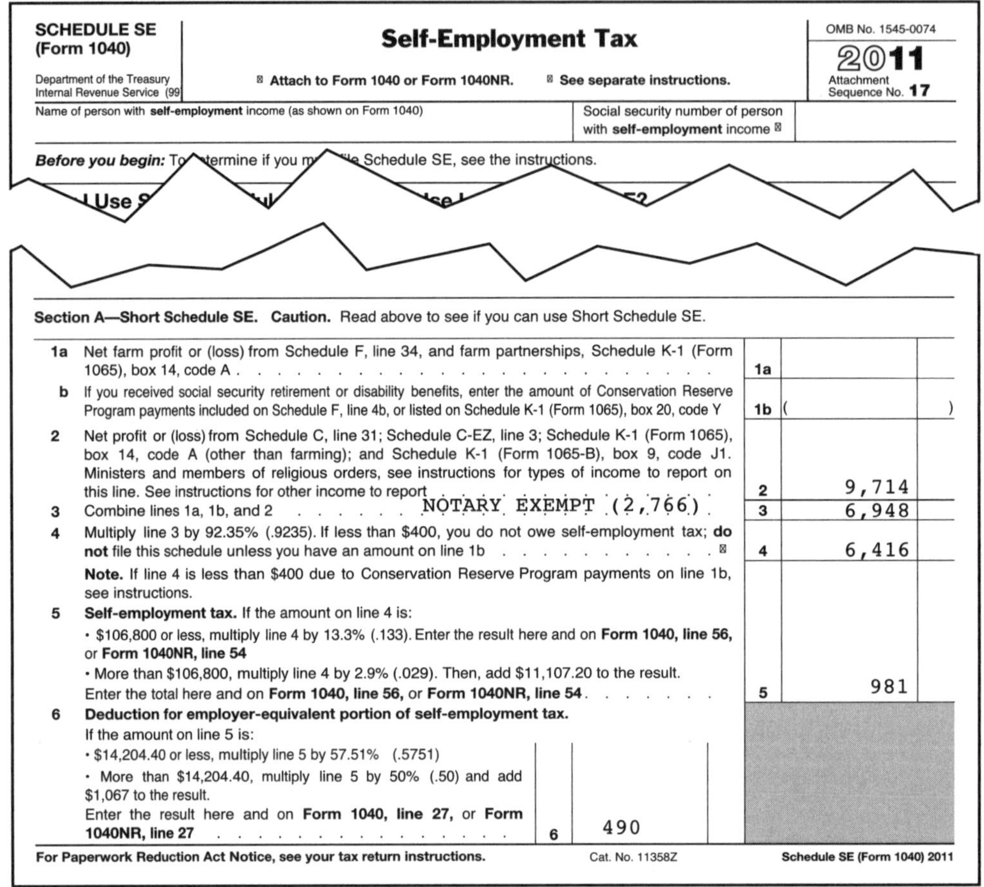

SCHEDULE SE (Form 1040) — **Self-Employment Tax** — OMB No. 1545-0074 — **2011**

Department of the Treasury Internal Revenue Service (99) — ▸ Attach to Form 1040 or Form 1040NR. ▸ See separate instructions. — Attachment Sequence No. **17**

Name of person with **self-employment** income (as shown on Form 1040) — Social security number of person with **self-employment** income ▸

Before you begin: To determine if you m... Schedule SE, see the instructions.

Section A—Short Schedule SE. Caution. Read above to see if you can use Short Schedule SE.

1a	Net farm profit or (loss) from Schedule F, line 34, and farm partnerships, Schedule K-1 (Form 1065), box 14, code A	**1a**	
b	If you received social security retirement or disability benefits, enter the amount of Conservation Reserve Program payments included on Schedule F, line 4b, or listed on Schedule K-1 (Form 1065), box 20, code Y	**1b**	( )
2	Net profit or (loss) from Schedule C, line 31; Schedule C-EZ, line 3; Schedule K-1 (Form 1065), box 14, code A (other than farming); and Schedule K-1 (Form 1065-B), box 9, code J1. Ministers and members of religious orders, see instructions for types of income to report on this line. See instructions for other income to report	**2**	9,714
3	Combine lines 1a, 1b, and 2 NOTARY EXEMPT (2,766)	**3**	6,948
4	Multiply line 3 by 92.35% (.9235). If less than $400, you do not owe self-employment tax; **do not** file this schedule unless you have an amount on line 1b ▸	**4**	6,416
	Note. If line 4 is less than $400 due to Conservation Reserve Program payments on line 1b, see instructions.		
5	**Self-employment tax.** If the amount on line 4 is: • $106,800 or less, multiply line 4 by 13.3% (.133). Enter the result here and on **Form 1040, line 56,** or **Form 1040NR, line 54** • More than $106,800, multiply line 4 by 2.9% (.029). Then, add $11,107.20 to the result. Enter the total here and on **Form 1040, line 56,** or **Form 1040NR, line 54**	**5**	981
6	**Deduction for employer-equivalent portion of self-employment tax.** If the amount on line 5 is: • $14,204.40 or less, multiply line 5 by 57.51% (.5751) • More than $14,204.40, multiply line 5 by 50% (.50) and add $1,067 to the result. Enter the result here and on **Form 1040, line 27,** or **Form 1040NR, line 27** — **6** 490		

For Paperwork Reduction Act Notice, see your tax return instructions. Cat. No. 11358Z **Schedule SE (Form 1040) 2011**

While the U.S. tax code exempts fees earned as a Notary Public from self-employment taxes, it is unclear whether Notary Signing Agents can benefit from this exemption. Many in the Notary Signing Agent profession believe Notary Signing Agents can legitimately claim an exemption for at least part of the signing fee.

But, as discussed earlier in this Course, a loan signing assignment does not correspond to a typical notarial transaction in which the person requesting notarial services pays the Notary for services rendered. Calling a portion of the Notary Signing Agent fee a Notary fee is problematic, because the Agent is not directly compensated by the borrower for notarizations performed on the loan documents, even though the borrower may indirectly pay the fee through loan application fees, points on the loan, the loan interest rate, a broker's fee, etc. Equally challenging is determining how much of a Notary Signing Agent fee could legitimately be claimed, since the notarizations comprise such a small part of the Agent's overall duties and may vary by assignment.

Further, claiming the exemption reserved for Notary fees could expose the Notary Signing Agent commissioned in the states of Nevada, Nebraska and North Carolina to regulation under state Notary fee laws. Statutes in these states restrict the fees a Notary Public may charge, and a Notary Signing Agent could be cited for misconduct for charging a fee other than the per signature fee for the notarial act.

While it is unclear whether Notary Signing Agents can claim the exemption for loan signing fees, the Agent could claim the exemption for fees received in notarizing signatures on corporate documents, powers of attorney, insurance forms or related items. This fee would be exempt from self-employment taxes since it was paid by the document signer to the Notary directly.

In light of the complexity of U.S. income tax laws on this particular point, the NNA® recommends that Agents seek specific guidance on completing Schedule SE from their accountant or professional tax advisor.

Paying Estimated Taxes

Federal and state income taxes must be paid on income earned or received. For an employee, amounts for federal and state income taxes are withheld from the employee's paycheck. Self-employed individuals, such as the Notary Signing Agent, typically must make quarterly estimated tax payments directly to the IRS and the state taxing commission if certain conditions apply.[7]

[7] For information about estimated tax payments and filing Form 1040 Schedule ES ("Estimated Tax for Individuals"), the Notary Signing Agent should consult his or her tax preparer for specific guidance or should log on to the Internal Revenue Service website, http://www.irs.gov.

NOTARY SIGNING AGENT LOG

To retain clear and sufficient documentation of business activity, a recordkeeping system is essential. A Notary Signing Agent may track business activity with software designed for the purpose or manually through the use of a record book or log.

On pages 300 and 301, a Notary Signing Agent Log is illustrated to help the Agent keep records for business and tax purposes. The Log contains five headings to organize the information recorded for each signing.

1. Loan signing appointment information
2. Notarizations
3. Invoice information
4. Fee itemization and tax reporting
5. Notes

Loan Signing Appointment Information

The Loan Signing Appointment Information section of the Notary Signing Agent Log contains seven columns of basic information about the signing appointment.

1. **Signing Date:** This is the date the Notary Signing Agent performed the signing. The Agent enters the date of the signing itself, not the date the assignment was received or the date when the Agent was paid.

2. **Borrower Last Name(s):** The Agent enters the surname(s) of the borrower(s) in this line.

3. **Signing Location(s):** The Notary Signing Agent records the name of the city where the signing took place. As a Notary, the Agent is

restricted to acting in cities and towns within the state that issued the Notary commission.

4. **Assigned By:** The Notary Signing Agent enters the name of the company that provided the assignment. The Agent then may use the information recorded in this column to invoice the company after the signing is complete and thus keep track of collections.

5. **Mileage (Start):** To claim mileage expenses for the business use of a car on Schedule C or Schedule C-EZ, the IRS requires that a written mileage log be kept. The Notary Signing Agent may use this column to enter the odometer reading at the time the Agent leaves for the signing.

6. **Mileage (End):** The Notary Signing Agent enters the odometer reading upon finishing the trip.

7. **Total Mileage:** This figure represents the total round-trip mileage for the assignment. In the illustration of a page from a Notary Signing Agent Log shown on pages 300 and 301 , the total miles for the ten signings reported on the page have been calculated at the bottom of this column.

Notarizations

The Notarizations section in the Log is used to record information about the documents that the Notary Signing Agent notarized in each set of loan documents. Agents who choose to claim the exemption of Notary earnings from self-employment taxes will use this information to help them calculate the amount of the exemption that is attributable to their loan signings.

1. **Number of Documents:** The Notary Signing Agent records the number of documents in the package that require notarization.

2. **Number of Signatures:** The Notary Signing Agent records the total number of signatures notarized for the documents listed in the previous column. In cases where two borrowers sign, the Agent would multiply the number of documents times the number of borrowers to calculate the number of signatures notarized.

3. **Value of Notary Fees:** The Agent calculates this fee by totaling the number of signatures notarized on all documents in the loan package and multiplying by up to the maximum fee state law permits the Agent to charge for the given notarial act.

Invoice Information

The Invoice Information section in the Notary Signing Agent Log is where the Agent enters the invoice information for the loan signing, including the date the invoice was sent, the date payment was received and the invoice amount.

1	Loan Signing Appointment Information							Notarizations		
	Signing Date(s)	Borrower Last Name(s)	Signing Location(s)	Assigned By (Name of Company)	Mileage (Start)	Mileage (End)	Total Mileage	# of Docs	# of Sigs	Value of Notary Fees
1	01/05/12	Williams	Shelton	ABC Title Company	15241	15275	34	1	1	$5.00
2	01/07/12	Atwater	Mossyrock	Never Late Signings	15310	15375	65	3	3	$15.00
3	01/08/12	Murphy	McIntosh	Rocket Signing Co.	15812	15833	21	4	8	$20.00
4	01/15/12	Westmoreland	Tacoma	ABC Title Company	16001	16045	44	2	4	$10.00
5	01/18/12	Abramowitz	McIntosh	Never Late Signings	16273	16298	25	3	3	$15.00
6	01/19/12	Bryant	Shelton	CityFunding.com	16376	16411	35	4	4	$20.00
7	01/21/12	O'Neill	Shelton	Acme Signing, Inc.	16589	16620	31	2	4	$10.00
8	01/22/12	Jackson	Shelton	Rocket Signing Co.	16802	16832	30	4	8	$20.00
9	01/23/12	Gregorian	Chain Hill	Never Late Signings	16975	17002	27	4	8	$20.00
10	01/24/12	Walker-Ryan	McIntosh	Acme Signing, Inc.	17066	17089	23	3	6	$15.00
Total							353	30	49	$150.00

1. **Invoice Sent:** The Notary Signing Agent enters the date the Agent invoiced the company providing the assignment. As was discussed earlier in this chapter, with many companies this step is as simple as faxing back the assignment form with added information about the appointment and return shipment of documents.

2. **Invoice Paid:** The Notary Signing Agent records the date the Agent received payment. It is important that this date be recorded accurately, because the Agent will report on Schedule C or Schedule C-EZ only those revenues received during the tax year. When an Agent conducts December signings, for example, the Agent may not be paid until January of the following year. The January revenues would not be reported on the prior year's tax return.

3. **Invoice Amount:** The Agent enters the dollar amount received for the signing. Only actual revenues should be entered in this

Invoice Information			Fee Itemization and Tax Reporting				2
Invoice Sent	Invoice Paid	Invoice Amount	Gross Sale Schedule C	Mileage Expense Schedule C	Report on Schedule SE	Notes	
01/06/12	01/31/12	$125.00	$125.00	$15.13	$120.00		1
01/08/12	01/31/12	$ 75.00	$ 75.00	$28.93	$60.00	$25.00 e-mail doc. fee	2
01/09/12	02/01/12	$ 50.00	$ 50.00	$9.35	$30.00		3
01/16/12	02/15/12	$125.00	$125.00	$19.58	$115.00		4
01/19/12	02/28/12	$ 50.00	$ 50.00	$11.13	$35.00		5
01/20/12	03/01/12	$ 50.00	$ 50.00	$15.58	$30.00		6
01/22/12	02/15/12	$125.00	$125.00	$13.80	$115.00	1st and 2nd papers; $25.00 e-mail doc. fee	7
01/23/12	02/23/12	$ 50.00	$ 50.00	$13.36	$30.00		8
01/24/12	03/01/12	$ 50.00	$ 50.00	$12.02	$30.00		9
01/25/12	02/20/12	$ 50.00	$ 50.00	$10.25	$35.00		10
		$750.00	$750.00	$149.13	$600.00		

column. Amounts for business expenses or offsets for the value of notarizations should not be recorded in this column. In another column of the Log, mileage expenses for individual assignments will be recorded. For all other business expenses, the Notary Signing Agent should keep copies of all receipts and claim those expenses in Part II of IRS Form 1040 Schedule C or Schedule C-EZ.

Fee Itemization and Tax Reporting

The final section in the Notary Signing Agent Log is for recording information that will be used in figuring the various amounts the Agent reports on each of the federal tax schedules reviewed earlier.

1. **Gross Sale Schedule C:** Gross receipts or sales is the term used on line 1b of Schedule C and Schedule C-EZ, where the Notary Signing Agent records total revenues. In practical terms, the amount entered in the Gross Sale column is identical to the amount entered in the Invoice Amount column of the Log. It is repeated in this column as a reminder of where the amount will be reported at tax time.

2. **Mileage Expense Schedule C:** In the Total Mileage column of the Log, the Notary Signing Agent recorded the total miles driven for each signing performed. In the Mileage Expense column of the Log, the figure in the Total Mileage column is multiplied by the standard IRS per-mile rate for the business use of a car. The rate in 2012 is 55½¢ ($0.55.5) per mile. Most Agents will use the IRS figure to calculate mileage expenses, unless their state law has different requirements.

3. **Report on Schedule SE:** In this column Notary Signing Agents enter the amount they have earned from their loan signings that does not qualify for the exemption of Notary earnings from self-employment taxes. To calculate this figure, the number in the Value of Notary Fees column is deducted from the number in the Gross Sale column.

Notes

The final column of the Log is for recording any notes, including additional expenses incurred for the assignment that should be included on Schedule C or Schedule C-EZ. Examples could include payments for tolls, parking fees at the location of the signing, the cost of making copies of documents or even an amount paid for coffee or food at a coffee shop or restaurant where the signing assignment took place. Notary Signing Agents must keep all receipts in order to claim expenses on Schedule C or Schedule C-EZ.

RECORDING FEES IN THE NOTARY JOURNAL

Notary Signing Agents in some states have a statutory obligation to complete a journal entry and record the Notary fees received for each notarization. This requirement may give rise to the following question: What is an effective way to record Notary fees in a journal, given that a typical loan signing fee includes the fee for notarization and possibly other services as well? There is not always a direct correlation between the notarizations performed in a loan signing and the fee paid for that signing. A number of variables are involved, including the following:

1. The Agent is not typically paid for the number of notarizations performed for a particular loan signing. Most signing services and closing agents pay a standard fee for every signing appointment, but that fee is rendered for all services performed by the Notary Signing Agent in connection with the appointment, not just the notarizations.

2. The number of documents requiring notarization varies from signing to signing.

3. The number of borrowers signing the documents varies from signing to signing.

4. The borrower does not pay the signing services fee directly to the Notary Signing Agent at the signing appointment.

5. In assignments where a signing service hires the Notary Signing Agent to handle the signing, the service will keep a portion of the fee.

6. Notary fees vary by state. This is a particular issue for Notary Signing Agents who are commissioned in states that have the highest fees.[8]

Given these diverse factors, a Notary Signing Agent may choose to record $0.00 or "No fee charged" in the fee column in the Agent's official journal to reflect the fact that the signing fee received was not for notarizations performed on the documents but for the sum total of signing services provided.

If, on the other hand, the Notary Signing Agent provided notarial services outside of a loan signing context and was paid for the notarizations directly by the document signer when services were rendered, the Agent would record the exact fee for the notarizations in the fee column.

This recommendation for recording fees in the journal may raise a different question. In not recording fees for notarizations performed in connection with loan signings but for all other notarial services, is the Agent guilty of discrimination in charging nothing for notarizations performed in connection with a loan signing, when quite possibly in the next notarization the Notary may charge $10.00?[9]

[8] Several states allow Notaries to charge $10.00 per signature for most acts, and many allow them to charge $5.00. Until July 1, 2013, Illinois Notaries may charge $25 when they notarize signatures on most documents of conveyance for residential real property in Cook County.

[9] 42 USC § 1981. Equal rights under the law protect individuals from discrimination based on race in making and enforcing contracts, participating in lawsuits, giving evidence, etc. The United States Constitution, Amendment XIV, states: "No state shall make or enforce any law which shall abridge the privileges or immunities of the citizens of the United States ... [or] deprive any person of life, liberty, or property without due process of law, [or] deny to any person within its jurisdiction the equal protection of the laws."

The issue of discrimination is an important one for Notaries. As a public official, the Notary Public should serve all people equally and charge equal fees to all.[10] *The Notary Public Code of Professional Responsibility* addresses the impropriety of improperly assessing a Notary fee based upon personal bias.

The Notary Public Code of Professional Responsibility
Guiding Principle 1, Article B

I-B-1: Improper Assessment of Fee

The Notary shall not base the charging or waiving of a fee for performing a notarial act, or the amount of the fee, on the signer's race, nationality, ethnicity, citizenship, religion, politics, lifestyle, age, disability, gender or sexual orientation, or on agreement or disagreement with the statements or purpose of a lawful document.

Based upon this standard, would the Notary Signing Agent be in violation of discrimination laws by recording Notary fees as illustrated in the example? To be guilty of discrimination, an action must be discriminatory on its face or present a clear pattern of discrimination that is observable over a period of time. For example, if a review of the Agent's journal showed that all the signers with last names belonging to a particular ethnic group were charged the maximum fee while everyone else was not, then such evidence could qualify as discrimination.

In the illustration provided, there is no discrimination if the Notary Signing Agent can prove that it was the Agent's policy to record fees in a loan signing context in this fashion and that the policy was applied equally to all without personal bias. The evidence in the Agent's journal and the related invoices would provide evidence that the fee policy was nondiscriminatory and was applied consistently. ■

[10] See Chapter 1, "The Notary Signing Agent's Role," for a discussion of the nature of the Notary's public office.

CHAPTER 6 TEST

True/False Questions

1. The Notary Signing Agent should review the signed documents only after returning to the Agent's home or office and before shipping.

2. Generally each company — whether signing service, closing agency or lender — has the same billing and payment procedures.

Multiple Choice Questions

(Choose the Best Answer)

1. The Notary Signing Agent must pay self-employment taxes on what type of income?
   a) All qualifying self-employment earnings of $600 or more
   b) All qualifying self-employment earnings of $400 or more
   c) All Notary fees received
   d) None of the above

2. Thorough Notary Signing Agents find that keeping clients informed about completed assignments results in which of the following?
   a) It fosters good will and repeat business.
   b) It will be frowned upon by signing agencies and lenders.
   c) It intrudes on the borrower's privacy.
   d) It is only necessary for the first few assignments.

3. The Notary Signing Agent's first order of business following the shipment of documents to the escrow company should be to do which of the following?
   a) Contact the borrower to evaluate the borrower's signing experience
   b) Invoice the client for the Agent's service
   c) Schedule and prepare for upcoming assignments
   d) All of the above

See page 331 for correct responses.

CHAPTER 7

Notary Signing Agent Responsibility

WHAT IS PROFESSIONALISM?

Professionalism is easier to recognize than it is to define. If asked what professionalism means, many people would answer by describing a personal experience with a doctor, teacher, attorney, minister or plumber.

For example, many would describe as professional a plumber who gets the job done and who is also pleasant, courteous and properly groomed, shows up on time, demonstrates respect for a customer's home and only bills for the work performed.

A professional attorney would be described in a similarly positive way. Expertise in the law and keeping the client's priorities clearly in mind are baseline benchmarks expected of all attorneys. However, the qualities that make an attorney a true professional extend beyond expertise and effectiveness in the practice of law. They include returning phone calls promptly, treating each client's case as no less important than any other, being punctual with clients and the court, being honest and trustworthy, mentoring young lawyers and engaging in pro bono and community service.

From these descriptions we can work towards a definition of the term. In particular, there are two key elements of professionalism:

1. Performing the tasks or duties associated with a given profession with a high degree of knowledge and skill, thereby achieving the desired result

2. Exhibiting the attributes and ethics associated with a given profession while performing those tasks or duties

Both elements — results and style — are important. The Notary Signing Agent must strive both to produce good results and to present a professional image at all times. In the home loan industry, this is critically important not only to the personal fortunes of the individual Agent, but also to the future success of the Notary Signing Agent vocation as a whole.

As the mortgage finance industry has evolved in the past decade, technological and societal changes have resulted in a depersonalization of the home loan process. It is quite likely that, in the entire transaction, the appointment with the Notary Signing Agent may be the only face-to-face encounter the borrower has with a business professional. When one considers the personal and financial magnitude of a real estate transaction, this one face-to-face encounter between the Notary Signing Agent and the borrower becomes all the more important. In order to inspire the confidence of the borrower, the Agent not only must facilitate the problem-free signing of loan documents but also must be personable and presentable.

A lot rides on the face-to-face appointment at which a borrower signs documents in front of a Notary Signing Agent. If the borrower has suffered through a particularly trying experience in applying for a loan, a competent Agent who arrives on time, demonstrates skill in handling the appointment and is pleasant and courteous can help redeem what has otherwise been a difficult ordeal. The opposite is also true: A problem-free loan process could be jeopardized by an Agent's unprofessional conduct.

The Notary Signing Agent's dealings with lenders and their surrogates is typically also a faceless process that takes place via phone, fax and email. While Agents may not meet many of their clients in person, clients will evaluate Agents by their performance in conducting error-free signings and by other indicators of professional competence, such as responsiveness to calls, likeability over the phone and other "soft skills,"[1] quick turnaround on assignments and grammatical writing skills, to name but a few.

The strength of any company contracted to provide Notary Signing Agent services is found in the number of highly dependable Agents it has — Agents who get the job done right the first time and who demonstrate the highest standards of professional excellence. For these companies, the issue is simple: Agents who consistently display professionalism get the calls for repeat business; those who fall short of professionalism do not.

This chapter will discuss the qualities that borrowers and lenders expect of Notary Signing Agents. Information in this chapter is based on interviews with companies that hire Notary Signing Agents and on experiences in actual loan signings conducted by the NNA® staff.

GAINING KNOWLEDGE AND SHARING EXPERTISE

Notary Signing Agents must first of all obtain the credentials and knowledge necessary to conduct loan signings with skill and effectiveness. The Notary Signing Agent Training Course and Certification Examination are designed to impart the basic knowledge essential to this task and to credential Agents who have mastered these fundamentals with the respected designation of NNA® Certified and Background Screened Notary Signing Agent.

However, the Course and Examination are not a destination; they are the beginning of a journey. As Agents apply their new knowledge in the practice of their vocation, they will gain experience and expertise in their trade. In turn, this gain will uncover new areas for growth and learning, leading to progressively greater experience and expertise. This cycle is the healthy pattern of professional growth over the course of a career and should be each Agent's unending pursuit.

To grow as a professional, Agents must demonstrate an ongoing commitment to education and lifelong training in their chosen field.

[1] According to the online encyclopedia, Wikipedia, soft skills are "the cluster of personality traits, social graces, facility with language, personal habits, friendliness, and optimism that mark people to varying degrees. Soft skills complement hard skills …, which are the technical requirements of a job …" (http://en.wikipedia.org/wiki/Soft_skills).

Consider this excerpt from *The Notary Public Code of Professional Responsibility:*

The Notary Public Code of Professional Responsibility
Guiding Principle X, Article A

X-A-4: Continuing Education Essential
The Notary shall keep current on new laws and regulations and on any other developments that affect the performance of notarial acts in the Notary's jurisdiction.

Illustration: The Notary is asked to notarize a document by a stranger who presents a "green card" as proof of identity. When the Notary explains that such a card is not on the statutory list of acceptable IDs, the stranger claims to have no other IDs.

However, another Notary advises that a recent change to the state's Notary code now allows use of green cards to identify signers, and shows an announcement of the law change in a periodical from a professional organization for Notaries.

The Professional Choice: The Notary completes the notarization, resolving to subscribe to the publication in order to keep abreast of new laws affecting notarial duties.

The standard promotes the professional commitment of staying current with all new laws and rules applicable to performing notarial acts in the Agent's state.

Learning of new law changes leads to another important professional responsibility: Notary Signing Agents who gain knowledge must share it with others. *The Notary Public Code of Professional Responsibility* obliges Notaries to dispense any important news or knowledge of notarization they have acquired.[2] They can do this by contacting their Notary colleagues and by contacting companies and any other persons they regularly deal with who could be affected by a new law, to ensure they know about the change at the earliest possible date.

Staying current with changes in Notary laws is but one area in which an Agent must keep abreast. The truly professional Notary Signing Agent must also obtain training in matters specifically related to signing agent duties.

[2] *The Notary Public Code of Professional Responsibility*, Standard X-B-1, says: "The Notary shall freely provide notarial expertise to less experienced Notaries and step forward to offer needed corrective advice on the proper performance of notarial acts."

Practical experience in conducting loan signings will unearth many new subjects for study. A short list of such subjects might include the following:

1. New types of loan documents the Agent has encountered for the first time in actual signings

2. New loan programs and products being offered in the market

3. Practices in the title, lending and recording industries that would broaden the Agent's knowledge and provide insight into how the Agent might perform or market his or her duties more effectively

4. Appropriate "soft skills" in the areas of written and verbal communications, conflict management and customer service that would enhance the Agent's effectiveness in these areas

Over the course of months and years, experienced Notary Signing Agents can acquire a treasure trove of valuable knowledge that will make their services more marketable to lenders and more helpful to borrowers.

PROFESSIONAL TRAITS AND BEHAVIORS

A home loan document signing career is all about relationships — relationships with borrowers and with contracting clients. Expertise in notarization and signing agent principles and practices is critically important. Whether a Notary Signing Agent is considered truly professional, however, will depend upon the qualities and behaviors the Agent exhibits during the course of performing actual signings and in dealings with contracting companies.

The following sections of this chapter will explore ways in which Notary Signing Agents can project professionalism in all of their professional dealings.

Professional Conduct with Borrowers

Notary Signing Agents always must demonstrate professionalism in their interactions and dealings with borrowers. There are a number of professional practices that will help the Agent to achieve this goal.

1. Calendar Integrity

It is a basic professional courtesy to arrive at a scheduled appointment on time. Arriving on time tells borrowers that the Notary Signing Agent respects their time and is committed to the task at hand.

Promptness is the result of self-disciplined and careful planning. It demonstrates that a businessperson is competent and has organized his or her schedule wisely. For example, to arrive at an appointment at the scheduled time, an Agent must schedule earlier appointments with adequate signing and travel time, obtain clear driving instructions to the signing location and leave with enough time to make the drive.

Being late almost always demonstrates that a person is disorganized, a quality that does not take one far in the loan document signing business. On the other hand, virtually all borrowers will understand and accept tardiness due to unforeseen delays such as traffic accidents, provided the Agent calls to report the problem and gives the borrower an estimated time of arrival.

There is an important term that every Notary Signing Agent should embrace as a fundamental core value: calendar integrity. Calendar integrity refers to the practice of keeping appointments, arriving for appointments on time and, in general, maintaining one's personal schedule with honesty.

Calendar integrity goes beyond simply arriving on time for an assignment. There are a number of practical implications of calendar integrity that are applicable to Notary Signing Agents in their relationships with clients.

An Agent must always follow through with the terms of any appointment he or she has taken on. If an Agent has agreed to perform a signing at a certain rate of pay, the Agent should never cancel or reschedule the appointment solely because the Agent received another call for a more lucrative or more conveniently located appointment around the same time.

One signing service representative told the NNA® of experiences with Notary Signing Agents who would not attend a confirmed signing appointment in protest over fee disputes related to the signing. In one such case, an Agent took on an assignment at an agreed fee. The Agent then mapped the directions to the signing and discovered that the address for the appointment was outside the Agent's radius of travel for the accepted fee. When the Agent called the signing service to request an additional amount for the extra travel and was denied, the Agent responded by refusing to go to the signing. The borrower then notified the closing company that the Agent did not show.

Certainly Notary Signing Agents should be compensated fairly for their work. They also should feel free to refuse assignments in circumstances in which the fee does not adequately compensate them for their service and travel. However, under the circumstances described above, a true professional would have carried through with the assignment and in the future would ask for the zip code of the signing location during the initial phone call with the client, in order to determine whether an additional fee for travel might be appropriate. Then, the Agent could negotiate the higher fee or refuse the signing if the request for a larger fee were denied. Under no circumstances should a professional Agent ever hold a contracting company hostage by hijacking a signing over a fee dispute.

Notary Signing Agents not only should honor their commitments, they also should realistically schedule appointments. Agents must take into account the possibility of unforeseen contingencies such as documents or borrowers not arriving at the appointment on time, unplanned interruptions during a signing, traffic congestion and inclement weather. An Agent also should not schedule two consecutive appointments so closely that everything must go perfectly during the first appointment in order to make the second on time. For example, it would be unwise to schedule cross-town appointments in a sprawling major urban area an hour apart during peak traffic hours.

Notary Signing Agents must not think that tardiness will affect only those borrowers who are stranded while waiting for the Agent to arrive.

Being late for appointments can have a negative impact on an Agent's relationship with contracting companies if an aggravated borrower calls the closing agent or the signing service that hired the Agent to complain about the Agent's unprofessional lack of punctuality.

2. Attire

While there is no standard for dress in the industry, a Notary Signing Agent's attire should mirror the local custom in the real estate and title industry. A suit and tie may be appropriate when conducting a signing in the financial districts of Manhattan, Los Angeles or Chicago, but such apparel is not necessary in most signings. Business-casual attire is suitable for most occasions. For men, a button-down or other shirt with a collar and slacks typically will suffice. Women should wear either a dress or a blouse with a skirt or slacks.

Signing service representatives generally discourage Agents from wearing shorts, T-shirts and jeans that are faded, tattered or torn. Under no circumstances should sweatshirts, sweatpants, flip flop shoes or beach sandals be worn.

When in doubt, overdress. It is much easier to dress down on short notice than to dress up.

3. Guests

The Notary Signing Agent should never bring another adult, a child or a pet to a signing. Nothing could make a borrower more nervous than for other persons to attend the signing unannounced. The potential hazard to the child aside, leaving a child in the car during the signing must be avoided, even if the borrower never sees the child. Knowing the child is in the car may well distract the Agent from giving full attention to the signing.

This does not mean that, in rare teaching or mentoring situations, an experienced Notary Signing Agent may not bring a student Agent to quietly observe a closing or should not accompany a less experienced Agent to a closing to lend support. However, such happenings should occur with the previous knowledge and permission of both the lender or signing service and the borrower, and such arrangements should not be attempted when factors such as limited work space in the borrower's home or an unusually tight schedule might make it unfeasible.

4. Parking

Notary Signing Agents should park their cars on the street and not in the borrower's driveway. That way, the Agent's car won't leak fluids or break down in the driveway or block other vehicles during the signing. An exception might occur if, during the scheduling phone call, the borrower invites or directs the Agent to park in the borrower's driveway or on the property.

5. Etiquette

When the borrower answers the door, the Notary Signing Agent should greet the borrower and wait to be invited inside. The Agent's venue of operations is almost always the borrower's home, and the Agent is always the guest.

6. Organization

The Notary Signing Agent should carry all notarial equipment and loan papers in an attaché or briefcase. An Agent who arrives at a signing with disheveled loan papers under his or her arm sends the wrong message to the borrower about the Agent's competence. Instead, when the borrower sees the Agent pull out the loan documents, they should be neatly clamped together, preferably with a binder clip. Throughout the entire signing, everything the Agent does should communicate that he or she is organized and has the signing under control.

7. Cell Phones

Once inside the borrower's home, the Notary Signing Agent should turn off all cell phones or put them in silent mode. Even though being reachable by phone at all times is essential to receiving business, the Agent should not take phone calls once an appointment begins.

The only calls that the Agent should take are calls in response to questions that a borrower asks about the loan and that the Agent cannot or by law should not answer.

8. Soliciting Business

At the close of every loan signing assignment, Notary Signing Agents should give the borrower a business card so that the borrower can contact the Agent after the signing is completed if there is a need.

However, Agents should not directly make solicitations for any other type of business the Agent may offer, including slipping the borrower a business card for products or services other than notarial or signing agent services.

On the other hand, it is perfectly acceptable to offer notarial services for any other types of transactions that call for a Notary in the future and even to ask the borrower to recommend the Agent to his or her friends, family and neighbors.

9. Stressful Signings

Taking out a home loan can be a daunting financial undertaking for many people. For this and other reasons, Notary Signing Agents will on occasion face stressful situations at loan signings. In most cases, borrowers will not display significant emotion or other behavioral indicators of stress. But it is important that Agents understand that some degree of stress will always be present, even if it is concealed or masked.

In an insightful study published in 1967, Holmes and Rahe created a life stress scale that assigned life crisis units to 43 different life stress events.[3] The purpose of the scale was to explain how life events contribute to the stress people experience.

The highest stressor — death of a spouse — was assigned 100 life crisis units. A divorce ranked second with 73 points assigned. The lowest stress-causing event noted on the scale, a minor violation of the law, was assigned 11 life crisis units.

[3] Thomas Holmes and Richard Rahe, "Holmes-Rahe Social Readjustment Rating Scale, " *Journal of Psychosomatic Research* 11 (1967), pp. 213-218.

While a majority of the 43 events involve negative circumstances (such as a divorce, personal injury or illness or trouble with a boss), not all were negative in nature. Getting married ranked number 7 on the list, and the birth of a child was listed as number 14. Even a vacation and retirement — events which most people would consider desirable or positive — were identified as stressful life events.

Of interest to the work of Notary Signing Agents is the fact that Holmes and Rahe ranked taking out a mortgage over $100,000 as the 20th most stressful life event. A mortgage or loan under $30,000 was ranked 37th.

But this doesn't tell the whole story. While taking out a mortgage is stressful in itself, it typically occurs in concert with other stressors identified on the stress list, including changing a residence, transferring children to new schools, changes in work responsibilities and personal financial state and business readjustments.

Herein lies the important point: At the consummation of a loan transaction, a number of personal and family events may converge to produce high levels of personal stress that can affect how people behave at signings.

In addition to the stress of life events, a loan signing appointment may be stressful for reasons specifically linked to the loan transaction. Possible causes could include the following:

1. The application and qualification process for the loan may have been overly difficult and time consuming.

2. The borrower may have had an unpleasant experience with a pushy broker or loan agent.

3. The amount of closing costs for the loan may be greater than expected.

4. The borrower's ID card may be unacceptable to establish identity for the notarizations required in the loan document package.

5. The sheer number of documents in the loan document package to review and sign could be voluminous.

It thus should really come as no surprise when borrowers appear on edge at a signing or even when anger simmers or bubbles over. How can a Notary Signing Agent respond in the most professional manner at times like these?

The first and best advice is to stay calm. Agents must be the stabilizing influence in the room, remaining cool under fire. Calmness can be contagious.

When the Notary Signing Agent assumes a calm demeanor, the objective is to help the borrower see that the Agent is truly interested in the problem. Listening carefully will demonstrate attentiveness to the borrower and concern about what the borrower has to say. In many situations when anger is expressed, a person will say that he or she needed to let some steam off or to vent on someone. Attentive listening can help reduce this pressure.

It is important to tell the borrower what the Agent can do to resolve the situation. For example, let's imagine a borrower who has endured a particularly lengthy and difficult loan application process. The loan finally is approved, and a date is set for the signing. The Notary Signing Agent arrives at the appointment and begins the notarization process but discovers that the borrower's ID has expired.

This is too much for the borrower, who does not want to deal with yet another delay. At this point, the Agent must say, "Mr. Jones, I understand you are upset because I cannot accept your ID card, but state law requires that I accept only a valid, current ID. Here is what I can do to get us over this hurdle." The Agent then explains that he or she can accept an alternative ID, such as a U.S. passport, or the oaths of credible identifying witnesses who can vouch for the borrower's identity. Ultimately, the Agent asks for the borrower's help in working toward a positive solution to the problem.

The key is for the Notary Signing Agent to maintain control and to present as many options as possible for resolving the notarial issue. In the event that a solution cannot be found, the goal is for the Agent to remain helpful, positive and solution-driven.

When all options have been exhausted, the borrower may not be happy about the fact that the Agent must terminate the appointment until a later date when the identification issue is resolved. The Agent has, however, proposed all available solutions to solve the problem and save the signing, and he or she has been thoroughly professional in the way he or she has handled the situation.

Professional Conduct with Clients

Notary Signing Agents also must demonstrate professionalism in their interactions and dealings with contracting companies. Three specific professional practices will be discussed: status reporting, problem solving and recordkeeping.

1. Status Reporting

It is the nature of the signing agent business that sometimes documents or borrowers do not arrive on time, an auto accident causes major time delays or a sudden storm impedes safe travel. In times like these, the professional Agent must make every effort to apprise all parties of the changed arrival plans.

Keeping all parties to a loan transaction in the loop is absolutely essential to maintaining good working relationships. Contracting companies want to know at the earliest possible time that a signing was completed successfully or if there were unresolved issues. Agents should immediately contact the contracting company in the event that the borrower halts the signing, providing any and all reasons for the termination (e.g., the documents contained errors, the loan amount was misstated, the borrower had cold feet, etc.). It is best to make the call to the appropriate contact even before the Agent leaves the appointment, in the event that there is some action that can be taken immediately to address the borrower's concerns.

For assignments in which certain signed and notarized papers must be faxed immediately after the conclusion of a signing, Notary Signing Agents should promptly attend to the transmission upon arrival back at the office and should follow up with a phone call to ensure the transmission was received. For signings taking place during the business day with the expectation that the documents will be delivered to the shipping courier before close of business, the Agent must hand off the documents on time and inform any relying parties. Finally, it goes without saying that Agents must also promptly invoice clients according to the terms of the written agreement between the Agent and the company.

In short, Notary Signing Agents should ensure that all parties in the transaction know exactly what is going on at all times. It may seem at times that the extra phone call is an annoyance to the busy title officer or loan agent, but they do appreciate Agents who maintain clear and frequent contact regarding assignments.

2. Problem Solving

While Notary Signing Agents should always communicate with clients about the status of assignments, they should avoid burdening clients with phone calls in regard to routine notarial matters.

Representatives of contracting companies want to be kept in the loop, but they do not want to field phone calls from Agents for advice on whether it's okay to proceed if the borrower is on medication or whether a particular ID suffices as satisfactory evidence of identity. They expect Agents to handle these mundane notarial matters themselves.

Signing service, lender, escrow and title company representatives are busy people who juggle multiple files between all of the phone calls that are part of a typical business day. In an industry where every phone call is potentially urgent, closing agents and contracting company representatives expect Agents to be resourceful, to apply common and business sense to practical issues and to take responsibility for finding answers to their problems.

Before picking up the phone to call a company representative, Agents should explore other avenues to find a solution on their own within the allowed legal limits of their discretion. In truth, closing agents hire Notary Signing Agents to resolve problems at a signing so that they can focus on other matters attendant to closing loans.

Of course, the Notary cannot give legal advice or provide answers to legal questions, which is to say that there are some problems Notary Signing Agents cannot solve without help. In Chapter 5, care was taken to emphasize that, when it comes to a borrower asking specific questions about the terms of the loan or the provisions in a certain document, Agents must rely on others to provide the answer. However, even then Agents may still be able to suggest the right person for the borrower to contact to get an answer to the question.

When seeking help to answer a borrower's specific non-notarial questions, professional Agents should know whom the borrower may call for the answer without having to make several calls to find the right person. The best time to clarify this is during the initial phone call with the contracting company. The contracting company almost always will provide the phone number of the title or escrow officer assigned to the closing, and the Agent should place a friendly call to this important contact before the signing to confirm that the individual will be available to help should a problem arise.

Agents who are members of the NNA® can also call the members-only Information Services Hotline to ask notarial questions in a signing agent context during regular business hours. The NNA® counselors who field calls from Notary Signing Agents are trained to assist Agents with many questions related to loan signings.

Notwithstanding the fact that an Agent cannot answer specific legal and technical questions about the borrower's loan or give legal or financial advice, it is an important component of a Notary Signing Agent's professionalism to be able to solve any and every problem within the Agent's legitimate domain.

3. Recordkeeping

One call a client does not want to field is a call from a Notary Signing Agent requesting an investigation into a nonpayment when the client knows that the investigation will prove the client has already paid the Agent. Signing service representatives interviewed by the NNA® mentioned this as a particularly vexing problem that wastes precious time and resources and reflects poorly on the Agent.

All Notary Signing Agents must have efficient and effective procedures for invoicing clients, tracking payments and maintaining their books. While most Agents would rather spend as much time as possible conducting signings and as little time as possible attending to accounting matters, a failure to invest sufficient time in keeping orderly financial records could put the Agent on poor terms with contracting companies.

Inquiries into payments should only be initiated when there is a legitimate case to pursue. A needless phone call placed to discuss a payment that has already been made or that is not late demonstrates the Agent's lack of organizational skills and his or her disrespect for the contracting company's time.

Professional Conduct with Colleagues

Finally, Notary Signing Agents should aspire to maintain a professional relationship with industry professionals and other Notary Signing Agents through networking and mentoring.

1. Networking

Notary Signing Agents should seek out local groups of mortgage industry professionals, such as a local chapter of escrow agents, become a member and participate in regular meetings. Not only will Agents meet contacts at these meetings who can generate future business, they also will learn from these associations how to perform their jobs better. In addition, they can keep apprised of emerging issues affecting the mortgage finance field.

2. Mentoring

Finally, most major professions — law, medicine, the ministry, teaching — encourage practitioners to give back to the profession by nurturing up-and-coming colleagues. For example, the legal profession has a longstanding "young lawyers" program, in which seasoned attorneys take novices under their wings and help them get started.

Earlier in this chapter Standard X-B-1 of *The Notary Public Code of Professional Responsibility* was cited in the context of Notary Signing Agents informing others about new law changes that affect signing agent practices. Standard X-B-1 also can be applied in the present context of experienced Agents mentoring new Agents. Experienced Agents should volunteer to help new Agents get started in the business and should not view the fledgling Agent as competition. The *Code* Commentary to Standard X-B-1 provides keen insight and a helpful summary: "Standard X-B-1 suggests that, as a member of a professional group, the Notary is obligated to share his or her expertise with less experienced Notaries. As a professional, the Notary must realize that he or she has a responsibility to the group as a whole. Helping other members better serves the public and develops the *esprit de corps* shared by professionals."

NOTARY LIABILITY

A Notary Signing Agent's responsibility also extends to the notarization performed on documents in the loan package. The following discussion treats the most pertinent aspects of Notary liability that a Notary Signing Agent must understand.

This section will discuss the criminal, civil and administrative penalties that can occur whenever a Notary engages in misconduct. While Notary misconduct is defined in various ways by the states, four specific categories of misconduct will be discussed:

1. Engaging in exploitative or deceptive conduct

2. Improperly identifying a signer

3. Misrepresenting the Notary office

4. Engaging in the unauthorized practice of law

Exploitative or Deceptive Conduct

Many states have laws that prohibit exploitative or deceptive conduct by public officials. We will discuss several offenses that fall into this category, including falsifying notarial certificates, impersonating a Notary, exerting improper influence and knowingly overcharging fees.

1. Falsifying Notarial Certificates

Completing a certificate the Notary knows to be false is an act of Notary misconduct that is specifically mentioned in the Notary laws of many states.[4] Three of the most common ways that notarial certificates are falsified are by misrepresenting personal appearance, falsifying signer identification and falsifying the date of notarization.

2. Impersonating a Notary

A second type of exploitative or deceptive conduct is impersonating a Notary, an offense that is addressed in the Notary statutes of several states.[5] Because the Notary's basic function is that of detecting and deterring document fraud, harsh penalties may be imposed against a person who acts as a Notary without having been granted a Notary Public commission.

3. Improper Influence

A third type of misconduct involving exploitation or deception is the Notary exerting improper influence. The Notary is an impartial witness to important transactions. The Notary's impartiality would be severely compromised if he or she sought to influence a person to enter into or avoid a transaction requiring a notarial act.

---

[4] For example, California Government Code, Title 1, Division 7, Chapter, 3, § 6203; Georgia Code Annotated, Title 45, Chapter 17, § 45-17-8(d); Utah Code Annotated, Title 46, Chapter 1, § 46-1-9.

[5] California Government Code, Title 2, Division 1, Chapter 3, § 8227.1; Revised Code of Washington, Chapter 42, § 42.44.160.

4. Knowingly Overcharging Fees

A final exploitative and deceptive practice is knowingly overcharging Notary fees. The states have different penalties for overcharging fees. In Texas, for example, if a Notary charges more than the statutory maximum, his or her commission may be suspended or revoked by the Secretary of State. In Arizona, charging more than the maximum fees is a class 5 felony. The Texas and Arizona laws also state that if a Notary charges more than the maximum fees allowed by law, the Notary is liable to the person overcharged for four times the fee unlawfully demanded.[6]

Improperly Identifying Signers

The next category of Notary misconduct is the failure to properly identify document signers. The required degree of care a Notary Signing Agent must take to ensure that any person appearing before the Agent is the person he or she purports to be can be understood in light of an Idaho statute that reads, "Each notary public shall exercise reasonable care in the performance of his duties generally, and shall exercise a high degree of care in ascertaining the identity of any person whose identity is the subject of a notarial act."[7]

Misrepresentation

A third category of Notary misconduct is misrepresenting the Notary office. Care must be taken by Notaries not only to perform only authorized acts, but also to ensure they do not mislead members of the public into believing they possess greater or different powers than the law actually grants.

Unauthorized Practice of Law

A fourth category of misconduct is the unauthorized practice of law. When anyone practices law without first being qualified and admitted to the state Bar Association, he or she can be criminally charged with engaging in the unauthorized practice of law.

---

[6] Texas Government Code, Title 4, Chapter 406, § 406.009, and Title 6, Chapter 603, § 603.010; Arizona Revised Statutes, Title 38, Chapter 3, Article 2, § 38-413.
[7] Idaho Code, Title 51, Chapter 1, § 51-111(1).

1. Prescribing the Notarial Act

The Notary Public Code of Professional Responsibility says that it is improper for a nonattorney to decide the type of notarization for a given transaction. In most cases, documents contain preprinted acknowledgment or jurat wording to guide the Notary in the specific act to perform. When there is no preprinted certificate wording on the document, the Notary may not make a decision regarding the notarial act to perform unless the Notary is an attorney or qualified as an expert in a pertinent field.

In cases where the notarial certificate is absent from the document, the Notary may show the client a variety of different certificates — acknowledgment, jurat or any other form as state law prescribes — and allow the client to select which certificate the Notary will complete and attach to the document. If the client cannot decide, then the Notary must ask the client to contact the person or agency requesting the notarization for specific assistance in selecting the appropriate notarial act.[8]

2. Prescribing or Preparing Documents

A Notary may not determine or prepare a document in a given transaction. It is the *Code*'s position that, without the formal legal training of an attorney or of a professional trained or certified in a pertinent field, the Notary has limited powers apart from performing the notarial act. It is unethical for a Notary to make recommendations concerning or assist with the completion of specific documents to help a client fulfill a legal need, such as a document for entrance into a foreign country.[9]

[8] *The Notary Public Code of Professional Responsibility*, Guiding Principle VI, Article A, VI-A-1, says: "The Notary who is not an attorney, or a professional duly trained or certified in a pertinent field, shall not determine or prescribe the particular type of notarial act or notarial certificate required in a given transaction."

[9] *The Notary Public Code of Professional Responsibility*, Guiding Principle VI, Article B, VI-B-2, says: "The Notary who is not an attorney, or a professional duly trained or certified in a pertinent field, shall not prepare a document for another person or provide advice on how to fill out, draft or complete a document."

3. Providing Unauthorized Advice

The third *Code* standard broadens the prohibition against the unauthorized practice of law to include offering any form of legal assistance or advice, whether or not such assistance involves a document.

Members of the public, a friend or a family member may think that the Notary is qualified to answer legal questions, since the Notary functions in the legal environment as an impartial witness to the execution of a variety of legal documents. The Notary must remember at all times that, while a notarization can have a significant impact upon a legal transaction, the Notary's powers are limited to the proper execution of the notarial act.[10]

Penalties for Misconduct

Having considered the various offenses that constitute official misconduct, we move to a discussion of the penalties Notaries can incur for engaging in misconduct. Three distinct categories of penalties will be discussed: criminal, civil and administrative.

1. Criminal Penalties

Notaries may expose themselves to prosecution for a criminal offense. A criminal offense is a violation of law that the government deems to be injurious to individual persons or to the community at large.

Crimes are typically classified as felonies or misdemeanors. A felony is a more serious crime than a misdemeanor and carries a stiffer sentence. A person who commits a felony or misdemeanor must make restitution to the public for the offense, whether by serving a prison sentence, paying a fine or both.

[10] *The Notary Public Code of Professional Responsibility*, Guiding Principle VI, Article C, VI-C-1, says: "The Notary who is not an attorney, or a professional duly trained or certified in a pertinent field, shall not provide advice on how to act or proceed in a given legal matter that may or may not involve a notarial act."

2. Civil Penalties

A second penalty a Notary may incur for committing an act of negligence or misconduct is a civil penalty. A civil penalty is imposed when a Notary is found liable in a civil suit for having performed an act that financially harmed another person. It does not matter whether the act was intentional (misconduct) or unintentional (negligence). When found liable in a civil action, the Notary may be required to pay damages to the victim, the victim's attorney's fees and court costs and the Notary's own legal defense costs.

3. Administrative Penalties

A final penalty a Notary may incur is an administrative penalty. An administrative penalty is the action that a commissioning official may take against a Notary who engages in an act of misconduct or negligence. Administrative penalties include commission denial, suspension or revocation and administrative fines. ■

CHAPTER 7 TEST

True/False Questions

1. The two main elements of professionalism are (1) performing a task with a high degree of skill and knowledge and (2) doing so in an ethical fashion.

2. Keeping current with new laws and rules applicable to performing notarial acts in the Notary Signing Agent's state is an important professional commitment.

3. Arriving late to a signing demonstrates that the Notary Signing Agent is disorganized.

4. Scheduling appointments an hour apart is a good rule of thumb for keeping a signing on track and maximizing a Notary Signing Agent's time and income potential.

5. Improperly identifying a signer is not considered misconduct.

Multiple Choice Questions

(Choose the Best Answer)

1. A Notary Signing Agent's punctuality tells borrowers which of the following?
   a) The Agent will execute the documents quickly with few mistakes.
   b) The Agent respects their time and is committed to the task at hand.
   c) The documents will be returned to the escrow company in a timely manner.
   d) None of the above.

2. Notary Signing Agents should never bring which of the following to a signing?
   a) Child
   b) Pet
   c) Cell phone
   d) Both a and b

3. Notary Signing Agents should give the borrower a business card so the borrower can contact the Agent after the signing is completed if there is a need. Agents should not, however, do which of the following?
   a) Directly solicit borrowers for any type of business unrelated to signing agent services
   b) Seek to offer investment services
   c) Recommend alternative settlement agencies
   d) All of the above

4. When someone practices law without first being qualified and admitted to the state Bar Association, they are doing which of the following?
   a) Engaging in the unauthorized practice of law
   b) Providing a valuable service to the public
   c) Giving advice only on documents with which they are familiar
   d) None of the above

5. A Notary's knowing completion of a notarial certificate containing a false statement is which of the following?
   a) Acceptable if the signer agrees
   b) A criminal act
   c) Allowable if ordered by an employer
   d) Punishable only if intentional

See page 332 for correct responses.

APPENDIX 1

Answers for Chapter Test Questions

CHAPTER 1 TEST

Answers: 1. False. 2. True. 3. False. 1. D. 2. A. 3. C.

CHAPTER 2 TEST

Answers: 1. True. 2. True. 1. B. 2. D.

CHAPTER 3 TEST

Answers: 1. True. 2. False. 3. True. 4. False. 5. True. 1. A. 2. C. 3. A.

CHAPTER 4 TEST

Answers: 1. True. 2. True. 3. False. 4. True. 1. A. 2. A. 3. D.

CHAPTER 5 TEST

Answers: 1. True. 2. False. 3. False. 4. False 1. B. 2. B. 3. D 4. C.

CHAPTER 6 TEST

Answers: 1. False. 2. False 1. B. 2. A. 3. B.

CHAPTER 7 TEST

Answers: 1. True. 2. True. 3. True. 4. False 5. False 1. B. 2. D. 3. D. 4. A. 5. B.

APPENDIX 2

Questions for Further Learning

1. According to your state's Notary laws, what are three examples of an "unlawful" notarization? (For example, the signer fails to personally appear before the Notary for a notarial act.)

2. If your state's Notary laws do not prohibit the practice of notarizing for family members, what will be your policy regarding notarizing for your relatives?

3. Do your state's Notary statutes provide any guidance for serving as the Notary and a witness on the same document? In the absence of a clear-cut statute, how will you respond to a client who asks you to serve in both roles in the same transaction?

4. How will you determine which brand and model of laser printer you will purchase for your Notary Signing Agent business?

5. At some point in your Signing Agent career, you may be asked to conduct a signing that involves a property located in another state and to complete a notarial certificate originating from that state. May you complete acknowledgment and other notarial certificates from other states? Under what circumstances may you complete another state's certificate?

6. How do your state's Notary laws define "Notary misconduct"? What specific offenses, if any, are cited?

7. What other loan documents have you come across that are not covered in this Course? If you're online, search the Internet to learn more about the documents.

8. In Chapter 4, an illustration for arranging the workplace at a loan signing was suggested. What merits does this method have? Can you think of a better way to set up the table for a signing?

9. What type of collections policy will you use for your business? What time frames will you use and what specific steps will you take to collect overdue payments?

10. How will you keep business records of the loan signings you perform?

APPENDIX 3

Why Notary Signing Agents Must Be Background Screened

Introduction

As a result of the Gramm-Leach-Bliley Financial Services Modernization Act (GLBA), discussed in Chapter 2 in the context of ensuring customer privacy, Notary Signing Agents must now be background screened. This appendix will discuss the events which led the banking regulators who are responsible for enforcing the GLBA to require Notary Signing Agents to undergo background checks.

Gramm-Leach-Bliley Act

Any discussion of why Notary Signing Agents must undergo background screening must start with a review of the relevant provisions of the GLBA itself. They are as follows:

Gramm-Leach-Bliley Act
5 USC, Subchapter I, Sec. 6801-6809
Disclosure of Nonpublic Personal Information

Sec. 6801. Protection of nonpublic personal information

(a) Privacy obligation policy

It is the policy of the Congress that each financial institution has an affirmative and continuing obligation to respect the privacy of its customers and to protect the security and confidentiality of those customers' nonpublic personal information.

(b) Financial institutions safeguards

In furtherance of the policy in subsection (a) of this section, each agency or authority described in section 6805(a) of this title shall establish appropriate standards for the financial institutions subject to their jurisdiction relating to administrative, technical, and physical safeguards —

(1) to insure the security and confidentiality of customer records and information;

(2) to protect against any anticipated threats or hazards to the security or integrity of such records; and

(3) to protect against unauthorized access to or use of such records or information which could result in substantial harm or inconvenience to any customer.

As discussed in Chapter 1, the GLBA is a federal law enacted in 1999 that in part spawned the present opportunity for Notary Signing Agents to handle loan document signings. In Chapter 2, we discussed how the GLBA also aims to protect the privacy of customer information held by financial institutions. The background screening requirement flows out of these customer privacy protection rules.

However, it is important to state at the outset that the actual provisions of the federal law itself do not contain any requirement for background checks, either for employees of financial institutions or for anyone else. Many Notary Signing Agents have questioned and even dismissed the need for background screening on the grounds that there is no express stipulation in the law itself that imposes such a requirement.

Interagency Guidelines

As is the case with many federal laws, the law itself contains precious few details on how its provisions are to be applied in the real world. Instead, Congress authorizes the Agencies responsible for overseeing the GLBA to establish appropriate standards for the financial institutions subject to their jurisdiction. Section 6801(b), cited at the beginning of this Appendix, provides this authorization. These standards, which carry the same legal force as the provisions of the law itself, are where we must turn to understand the reasons why Notary Signing Agents must undergo background checks.

In 2001, the rules and standards designed to implement the GLBA were issued by the relevant Agencies as Interagency Guidelines. These guidelines are as follows:

Federal Register
Vol. 66, No. 22 (February 1, 2001)

Interagency Guidelines Establishing Standards for Safeguarding Customer Information and Rescission of Year 2000 Standards for Safety and Soundness; Final Rule

Table of Contents

I. Introduction
- A. Scope
- B. Preservation of Existing Authority
- C. Definitions

II. Standards for Safeguarding Customer Information
- A. Information Security Program
- B. Objectives

III. Development and Implementation of Customer Information Security Program
- A. Involve the Board of Directors
- B. Assess Risk
- C. Manage and Control Risk
- D. Oversee Service Provider Arrangements
- E. Adjust the Program
- F. Report to the Board
- G. Implement the Standards

I. Introduction

The Interagency Guidelines Establishing Standards for Safeguarding Customer Information (Guidelines) set forth standards pursuant to section 39 of the Federal Deposit Insurance Act (section 39, codified at 12 U.S.C. 1831p–1), and sections 501 and 505(b), codified at 15 U.S.C. 6801 and 6805(b), of the Gramm-Leach-Bliley Act. These Guidelines address standards for developing and implementing administrative, technical, and physical safeguards to protect the security, confidentiality, and integrity of customer information.

A. *Scope*. The Guidelines apply to customer information maintained by or on behalf of entities over which OTS has authority. For purposes of this appendix, these entities are savings associations whose deposits are FDIC-insured and any subsidiaries of such savings associations, except brokers, dealers, persons providing insurance, investment companies, and investment advisers. This appendix refers to such entities as "you."

B. *Preservation of Existing Authority.* Neither section 39 nor these Guidelines in any way limit OTS's authority to address unsafe or unsound practices, violations of law, unsafe or unsound conditions, or other practices. OTS may take action under section 39 and these Guidelines independently of, in conjunction with, or in addition to, any other enforcement action available to OTS.

C. *Definitions.*
   1. Except as modified in the Guidelines, or unless the context otherwise requires, the terms used in these Guidelines have the same meanings as set forth in sections 3 and 39 of the Federal Deposit Insurance Act (12 U.S.C. 1813 and 1831p–1).
   2. For purposes of the Guidelines, the following definitions apply:
      a. *Customer* means any of your customers as defined in § 573.3(h) of this chapter.
      b. *Customer information* means any record containing nonpublic personal information, as defined in § 573.3(n) of this chapter, about a customer, whether in paper, electronic, or other form, that you maintain or that is maintained on your behalf.
      c. *Customer information systems* means any methods used to access, collect, store, use, transmit, protect, or dispose of customer information.
      d. *Service provider* means any person or entity that maintains, processes, or otherwise is permitted access to customer information through its provision of services directly to you.

II. Standards for Safeguarding Customer Information

A. *Information Security Program.* You shall implement a comprehensive written information security program that includes administrative, technical, and physical safeguards appropriate to your size and complexity and the nature and scope of your activities. While all parts of your organization are not required to implement a uniform set of policies, all elements of your information security program must be coordinated.

B. *Objectives.* Your information security program shall be designed to:
   1. Ensure the security and confidentiality of customer information;
   2. Protect against any anticipated threats or hazards to the security or integrity of such information; and
   3. Protect against unauthorized access to or use of such information that could result in substantial harm or inconvenience to any customer.

III. Development and Implementation of Information Security Program

A. *Involve the Board of Directors.*

Your board of directors or an appropriate committee of the board shall:

1. Approve your written information security program; and
2. Oversee the development, implementation, and maintenance of your information security program, including assigning specific responsibility for its implementation and reviewing reports from management.

B. *Assess Risk.*

You shall:

1. Identify reasonably foreseeable internal and external threats that could result in unauthorized disclosure, misuse, alteration, or destruction of customer information or customer information systems.
2. Assess the likelihood and potential damage of these threats, taking into consideration the sensitivity of customer information.
3. Assess the sufficiency of policies, procedures, customer information systems, and other arrangements in place to control risks.

C. *Manage and Control Risk.*

You shall:

1. Design your information security program to control the identified risks, commensurate with the sensitivity of the information as well as the complexity and scope of your activities. You must consider whether the following security measures are appropriate for you and, if so, adopt those measures you conclude are appropriate:
    a. Access controls on customer information systems, including controls to authenticate and permit access only to authorized individuals and controls to prevent employees from providing customer information to unauthorized individuals who may seek to obtain this information through fraudulent means.
    b. Access restrictions at physical locations containing customer information, such as buildings, computer facilities, and records storage facilities to permit access only to authorized individuals;
    c. Encryption of electronic customer information, including while in transit or in storage on networks or systems to which unauthorized individuals may have access;
    d. Procedures designed to ensure that customer information system modifications are consistent with your information security program;
    e. Dual control procedures, segregation of duties, and employee background checks for employees with responsibilities for or access to customer information;

f. Monitoring systems and procedures to detect actual and attempted attacks on or intrusions into customer information systems;
g. Response programs that specify actions for you to take when you suspect or detect that unauthorized individuals have gained access to customer information systems, including appropriate reports to regulatory and law enforcement agencies; and
h. Measures to protect against destruction, loss, or damage of customer information due to potential environmental hazards, such as fire and water damage or technological failures.

2. Train staff to implement your information security program.
3. Regularly test the key controls, systems and procedures of the information security program. The frequency and nature of such tests should be determined by your risk assessment. Tests should be conducted or reviewed by independent third parties or staff independent of those that develop or maintain the security programs.

D. *Oversee Service Provider Arrangements.*
You shall:

1. Exercise appropriate due diligence in selecting your service providers;
2. Require your service providers by contract to implement appropriate measures designed to meet the objectives of these Guidelines; and
3. Where indicated by your risk assessment, monitor your service providers to confirm that they have satisfied their obligations as required by paragraph D.2. As part of this monitoring, you should review audits, summaries of test results, or other equivalent evaluations of your service providers.

E. *Adjust the Program.* You shall monitor, evaluate, and adjust, as appropriate, the information security program in light of any relevant changes in technology, the sensitivity of your customer information, internal or external threats to information, and your own changing business arrangements, such as mergers and acquisitions, alliances and joint ventures, outsourcing arrangements, and changes to customer information systems.

F. *Report to the Board.* You shall report to your board or an appropriate committee of the board at least annually. This report should describe the overall status of the information security program and your compliance with these Guidelines. The reports should discuss material matters related to your program, addressing issues such as: risk assessment; risk management and control decisions; service provider arrangements; results of testing; security breaches or violations and management's responses; and recommendations for changes in the information security program.

G. *Implement the Standards.*
1. Effective date. You must implement an information security program pursuant to these Guidelines by July 1, 2001.
2. Two-year grandfathering of agreements with service providers. Until July 1, 2003, a contract that you have entered into with a service provider to perform services for you or functions on your behalf satisfies the provisions of paragraph III.D., even if the contract does not include a requirement that the servicer maintain the security and confidentiality of customer information, as long as you entered into the contract on or before March 5, 2001.

As stated in section II.B., the three objectives of the Interagency Guidelines are as follows:

1. Ensure the security and confidentiality of customer information

2. Protect against any anticipated threats or hazards to the security or integrity of such information

3. Protect against unauthorized access to or use of such information that could possibly harm any customer

The Interagency Guidelines require all financial institutions governed under the GLBA to design and implement a comprehensive written information security program. This program must include administrative, technical and physical safeguards appropriate to the size and complexity and the nature and scope of the given institution's activities. The purpose of the security program is to manage and control the risk associated with the sensitive personal financial information of the customers of the financial institution (Guidelines, Sec. II.A. and Sec. III.C.1.).

Financial institutions must consider whether any of eight stated security measures are appropriate to the institution's business activities and, if so, adopt each as necessary. The most relevant security measure applicable to Notary Signing Agent background screenings is "dual control procedures, segregation of duties, and employee background checks for *employees with responsibilities for or access to customer information*" (emphasis added) (Guidelines, Sec. III.C.1.e.). We will return to the implications of this provision of the Interagency Guidelines later.

The Interagency Guidelines require financial institutions to exercise due diligence in selecting service providers (Guidelines, Sec. III.D.1.). Financial institutions in turn must require their service providers to implement the measures needed to meet the Interagency Guidelines (Guidelines, Sec. III.D.2.). As mentioned in Chapter 2, the Interagency Guidelines define a service provider as "any person or entity that maintains, processes, or otherwise is permitted access to customer information through its provision of services directly to [entities over which OTS has authority]" (Guidelines, Sec. I.C.2.d. [and Sec. I.A.]). Title insurance companies and signing services would be considered service providers.

The Preamble to the Interagency Guidelines specifies that, as part of its due diligence in selecting service providers, "a financial institution must determine that the service provider has adequate controls to ensure that the subservicer will protect the customer information in a way that meets the objectives of these Guidelines."[1] The Interagency Guidelines define a subservicer as "any person who has access to an institution's customer information through its provision of services to the service provider."[2] As we mentioned in Chapter 2, subservicers include Notary Signing Agents hired by title companies and signing services.

In short, any service provider with access to the personal financial information of a financial institution's customers must implement the security measures under the financial institution's information security program. In turn, every subservicer under contract with the service provider must do the same. The Interagency Guidelines therefore apply to any company or person in the chain of a lending transaction who handles sensitive personal financial information, beginning with the lending institution that originates the loan and concluding with the Notary Signing Agent who executes the signing.

---

[1] *Federal Register*, Vol. 66, No. 22 (February 1, 2001), p. 8624, also available on the website of the GPO, http://frwebgate.access.gpo.gov/cgi-bin/getdoc.cgi?dbname=2001_register&docid=01-1114-filed.pdf.

[2] *Federal Register*, Vol. 66, No. 22 (February 1, 2001), p. 8619 n. 8. See previous note for URL.

According to the Interagency Guidelines, a financial institution should monitor on an ongoing basis the security measures of its service providers (and, by implication, of its subservicers). These security measures include the following (Guidelines, Sec. III.D.3.):

1. Auditable records of a service provider

2. Summaries of test results

3. Training (to recognize, respond to and report unauthorized attempts to obtain customer information)

We now return to discuss more fully the measure of direct relevance to Notary Signing Agents mentioned earlier, that of a financial institution requiring background checks for employees with responsibility for or access to customer information (Guidelines, Sec. III.C.1.e.). This rule requires all employees of the financial institution who handle or have access to the personal financial information of customers to undergo a background screening.

While the final Interagency Guidelines became effective upon publication (February 1, 2001), in 2004-2005, federal bank regulators began to review the files of various lenders providing home mortgage loans to ensure they were compliant with GLBA provisions and the Interagency Guidelines. The regulators discovered that independent Notary Signing Agents were utilized for the closings of many mortgage finance loans. Regulators inquired if these Notaries were background screened in conformance with the Interagency Guidelines. Since independent Notary Signing Agents were not actual employees, the lenders under review did not believe the background screening rule applied to them. The bank regulators determined that, even though Notary Signing Agents were not lender employees, the background screening measure was relevant since the Agents were paid a fee as a subservicer in the lending transaction.

Thus, bank regulators interpreted the Guidelines as applicable to independent Notary Signing Agents who had access to the personal financial information of borrowers. Consequently, the lenders began to ask title companies and signing services providing Notary Signing Agents for closings to ensure that these Agents were background screened. Some lenders even informed companies that they would no longer use their services if they did not require their Agents to be screened. Affected companies began to modify their intake procedures to incorporate the requirement, and Agents began to comply.

NNA® Background Screening Program

In the meantime, Notary Signing Agents who underwent screening soon discovered that a separate background check and fee were required by each company.

Discussions ensued among several of the larger title companies and the NNA® over the applicability of the screening requirement to Notary Signing Agents. In response, the NNA® proposed to offer Agents a single, fully GLBA-compliant background screening service that would qualify them to work with any company offering loan signings. As a result, effective October 1, 2006, the Notary Signing Agent Certification program was retooled to require Agents to undergo a single background check from a trusted, third-party service as well as pass the Notary Signing Agent Certification Examination. A task force of major title information services companies, led by Stewart Title, First American Lenders Advantage and LandAmerica OneStop, signed on to accept the single background check offered through the NNA's Notary Signing Agent Certification program.The newly designed Notary Signing Agent Certification program accomplishes the following:

1. It creates a central directory of background screened Notary Signing Agents.

2. It eliminates the need for Agents to submit to multiple screenings when they work for any company in the group of firms that accounts for the overwhelming majority of loan closings in the country.

3. It allows Agents to pay for screening one time, saving them the money they would have to pay for multiple screenings.

4. It allows Agents to submit their personal identifying information once instead of multiple times, lessening the possibility that the Agent's own personal information could be compromised.

5. It enhances the Agent's professionalism, since it carries with it a check of the Agent's background and character.

6. It protects consumers by ensuring that only Notary Signing Agents of the highest caliber and character handle or have access to their personal financial information.

7. The background check provided by the NNA®'s trusted third-party service is fully auditable by GLBA bank regulators, if necessary, adding to the value of Notary Signing Agent Certification for lenders who must comply with the GLBA.

Conclusion

The requirement that Notary Signing Agents must obtain a background check in order to receive loan document signing assignments flows out of the privacy protection provisions of the Gramm-Leach-Bliley Act. The Interagency Guidelines, which implement the GLBA, specify that, in creating their information security program, financial institutions must consider whether one particular security measure directly relevant to Notary Signing Agents is appropriate to the institution's business activities. That security measure is the matter of background screenings for employees with responsibilities for or access to customer information.

As regulators began enforcing the GLBA and the Interagency Guidelines, they discovered from audits of lenders that independent Notaries were handling a significant number of loan signings. The regulators determined that Notary Signing Agents, as subservicers of service providers in a loan transaction, must be considered employees of the lender for the purposes of the background screening requirement under the Interagency Guidelines.

Several financial institutions regulated under the GLBA approached the NNA® for assistance in designing a single-solution background screening program that could be offered to Notary Signing Agents at a reasonable cost and that could be leveraged by Agents conducting business with multiple companies. As a result, in 2006, the NNA®'s background screening program was launched. ■

Glossary of Important Terms

A

Abstract: Summary of the public records of the title to a piece of property

Adjustable-Rate Mortgage (ARM): Mortgage in which the interest is adjusted at periodic intervals, based on an index; cf. Balloon Mortgage, Fixed-rate Mortgage, Step-rate Mortgage, Two-step Mortgage; see also Cap, Margin

Adjustment Interval: For a standard adjustable-rate mortgage, the time between changes in the interest rate charged

AKA: Abbreviation for "also known as"; otherwise named

Amortization: Literally, "to kill off"; the repayment of a mortgage loan by installments, with regular payments to cover the principal and interest

Annual Percentage Rate (APR): Cost of a Mortgage or Deed of Trust stated as a yearly rate, which includes items such as interest, mortgage insurance and loan origination fee and which often is higher than the interest rate for the loan

Appraisal: Determination of a property's fair market value, based on comparative analysis of recent sales information of similar properties in the immediate vicinity

Appraised Value: Property's fair market value, based on the appraisal of a qualified appraiser

Appraiser: Trained and often certified individual, qualified by education and experience to inspect a property and determine its fair market value

Assessed Value: Value placed on real property by a public tax assessor for property tax purposes

Assessment: Procedure or process for establishing an assessed value on real property

Attorney in Fact: Person, not necessarily an attorney, who is given authority by means of a power of attorney to sign or act on behalf of another individual; cf. Trustee; see also Proxy, Signature by Proxy

B

Backdate: Deceptive and sometimes illegal act of dating a document with a date before that of the actual signing; cf. Predate; see also Postdate

Background Screening: Under the Interagency Guidelines, one of eight suggested security measures which financial institutions must consider and adopt, as appropriate, in their information security program, which is designed to protect customers' personal financial information and which is a requirement for employees with responsibilities for or access to customer information

Balloon Mortgage: Mortgage, usually fixed-rate, that has smaller payments for a certain period of time and one large payment for the remaining principal at a specified date; cf. Adjustable-Rate Mortgage, Fixed-Rate Mortgage, Step-Rate Mortgage, Two-Step Mortgage

Business Day: For purposes of calculating a rescission period as defined under the Truth in Lending Act (TILA), any day of the week excluding Sundays and 10 federal holidays

C

Calendar Integrity: Practice of keeping appointments, arriving for appointments on time and, in general, maintaining one's personal schedule with honesty

Cap: Set percentage amount by which a standard adjustable-rate mortgage may be changed each adjustment interval; see also Index, Margin

Cash-Out Refinance: Refinance transaction in which the amount of money received from the new loan exceeds the total of the money needed to repay the existing loan; a loan transaction in which the borrower receives additional cash that can be used for any purpose

Clear Title: Title that is free of liens or disputed interests

Closing: Meeting at which a sale of a property is finalized by the buyer signing mortgage documents and paying closing or settlement costs; also called a settlement

Closing Agent: Individual or firm that represents a buyer and handles the closing or settlement of the loan and the legal transfer of title and ownership from the seller to the buyer in a real property transaction; also called a settlement agent

Closing Costs: Fees paid by the borrower when property is purchased or refinanced; also called settlement costs

Cloud on Title: Any conditions revealed by a title search that adversely affect the title to a property

Collateral: Property or funds pledged as security, or guarantee of repayment, for a loan

Collections: Process of claiming a payment is due for services provided and receiving payment

Community Property: Form of co-ownership in which property acquired during a marriage is owned jointly, regardless of which spouse paid for it; cf. Joint Tenancy, Tenancy in Common

Conforming Loan: Generally, mortgage loan that is under the maximum dollar amount of loans established by Fannie Mae and Freddie Mac; cf. Jumbo Loan

Conventional Mortgage: Mortgage that is neither insured by the Federal Housing Administration (FHA) nor guaranteed by the U.S. Department of Veterans Affairs (VA); cf. FHA Mortgage, VA Mortgage

Conversion: Right of a borrower to convert an adjustable-rate or balloon mortgage loan into a fixed-rate mortgage loan

Conveyance: Transfer of title to or ownership of property; also the document by which such transfer is effected

County Recorder: Official, called a County Auditor in some states, who registers (records) deeds and certain other documents into the public record; see also Recordable Document

Credit Report: Report documenting an individual's credit history and current credit standing, including late payments, defaults or bankruptcies

Customer Identification Program (CIP): Program, required of all financial institutions under the PATRIOT Act, to identify all new account holders, maintain account holder identification information and check this information against lists of known terrorist or terrorist agencies provided by the government

D

Deed: Legal document that conveys title to real property

Deed of Trust: Legal instrument, used in some states instead of a Mortgage, that pledges a property to the lender as security for payment of a debt

Default: Failure to meet legal obligations in an agreement, including failure to make the monthly payments on a mortgage loan

Direct Work: Loan document signing assignment received through a lender, broker or closing agent without going through a middleman; cf. Signing Service

Down Payment: Difference between the purchase price and the portion of that purchase price that is being financed

E

Escrow: In a real property transaction, funds held by an escrow company on behalf of the buyer and the seller until the transaction has been completed

Escrow Company: Neutral third party that handles all funds in a real estate transaction, paying the real estate broker's commission, any loans or liens against the property, real estate taxes and any other fees associated with the transaction and sending the balance of the money to the seller

F

Fair and Accurate Credit Transactions (FACT) Act of 2003: Federal law which enables consumers to request and obtain a free credit report once every twelve months from each of the three nationwide consumer credit reporting companies; also contains provisions to help reduce identity theft

Fair Market Value: Highest price a buyer, willing but not compelled to buy, would pay, and lowest price a seller, willing but not compelled to sell, would accept; cf. Appraised Value

Fannie Mae (Federal National Mortgage Corporation, or FNMC): Congressionally chartered, shareholder-owned corporation established to expand the secondary mortgage market, which increases the supply of money available to lenders for mortgage loans; see also Freddie Mac

Federal Housing Administration (FHA): Agency of the U.S. Department of Housing and Urban Development (HUD), whose main activity is insuring residential mortgages

Fee Simple: Term used to describe the most complete ownership that a person can have over a property

***Federal Register*:** Daily publication of the United States Government, which provides notice to the public of a federal government agency's proposed new or amended rules

FHA Mortgage: Mortgage that is insured by the Federal Housing Administration (FHA); cf. Conventional Loan, VA Mortgage

Finance Charge: Total dollar amount that a loan costs the borrower

First Mortgage: Mortgage that is the primary lien against a property; cf. Second Mortgage

Fixed-Rate Mortgage: Mortgage in which the interest rate does not change for the life of the loan; cf. Adjustable-Rate Mortgage, Balloon Mortgage, Step-Rate Mortgage, Two-Step Mortgage

Foreclosure: Act of enforcing payment of a debt secured by a Mortgage or Deed of Trust, by seizing and then selling the property

Freddie Mac (Federal Home Loan Mortgage Corporation, or FHLMC): Congressionally chartered, shareholder-owned corporation established to expand the secondary mortgage market, which increases the supply of money available to lenders for mortgage loans; see also Fannie Mae

FSBO: For sale by owner

G

Gramm-Leach-Bliley Financial Services Modernization Act (GLBA) of 1999: Federal law enacted to protect the privacy of customer information held by financial institutions; see also Information Security Program, Interagency Guidelines

Grantee: Person to whom an interest in real property is conveyed

Grantor: (1) Person conveying an interest in real property; (2) Creator of a trust; see also Trust Agreement

H

Hazard Insurance: Form of insurance that protects the insured from certain losses, such as those due to fire, vandalism, storms and certain other natural causes

Homestead: Legal form signed by the owner to exempt property used as a home from forced sale to settle a judgment

HUD: U.S. Department of Housing and Urban Development

HUD-1 Settlement Statement: Document that provides an itemized listing of the funds that are payable at closing; see also U.S. Department of Housing and Urban Development (HUD)

I

Impounds: That portion of a borrower's monthly payments held by the lender or servicer to pay for taxes, hazard insurance, mortgage insurance, lease payments and other items as they become due

Independent Contractor: Person who earns a livelihood other than as a salaried employee

Independent Contractor's Agreement: Agreement that defines the business relationship between a signing service or a closing agency and a Notary Signing Agent

Index: Published interest rate, not controlled by the lender, to which the interest rate on an adjustable-rate mortgage (ARM) is tied; see also Margin

Information Security Program: Main component of the Gramm-Leach-Bliley Financial Services Modernization Act (GLBA) that financial institutions must implement to ensure the privacy of the personal financial information of customers; see also Interagency Guidelines

Installment: Regular periodic mortgage payment that a borrower pays, usually monthly but sometimes biweekly, to a lender

Interagency Guidelines: Rules and standards implementing the Gramm-Leach-Bliley Financial Services Modernization Act (GLBA), jointly promulgated in 2001 by the Office of the Comptroller of the Currency (Department of the Treasury), the Board of Governors of the Federal Reserve System, the Federal Deposit Insurance Corporation, the Office of Thrift Supervision (Department of the Treasury), the National Credit Union Administration, the Securities and Exchange Commission and the Federal Trade Commission; see also Information Security Program

Interest Rate: Periodic charge, expressed as a percentage, for use of credit

Invoice: Itemized list of services a Notary Signing Agent renders to a closing agent, lender or signing service for payment of services

IRS Form 1040 Schedule C (or C-EZ): Attachment to an individual's federal income tax return in which the totals for income and expenses received from self-employment appear

IRS Form 1040 Schedule SE: Attachment to an individual's federal income tax return in which the individual figures the amount due for self-employment taxes

IRS Form 1099-MISC: Federal income tax form received by a Notary Signing Agent who has earned $600 or more from a closing agent, lender, or signing service for providing loan document signing services

J

Joint Tenancy: Form of co-ownership in which each tenant has an equal interest in and equal rights to the property, including the right of survivorship; cf. Community Property, Tenancy in Common

Jumbo Loan: Mortgage loan, also known as a nonconforming loan, that exceeds the maximum dollar amount of loans established by Fannie Mae and Freddie Mac; cf. Conforming Loan

L

Legal Description: Property description, recognized by law, sufficient to locate and identify the property without oral testimony

Lender: Bank, mortgage company or mortgage banker that originates a loan and lends money

Lien: Voluntary or involuntary encumbrance against property for money due

Line of Credit: Agreement by a financial institution to extend credit up to a certain amount for certain period of time to a specified borrower

Loan-to-Value Ratio: Relationship between the amount of the mortgage loan and the sales price or appraised value of the property, expressed as a percentage

Lock-in: Commitment, also known as a rate lock, typically issued by a lender to a borrower and guaranteeing a specified interest rate and certain number of points for a limited time

M

Margin: Amount, usually a percentage, which is added to the index to determine the interest rate for adjustable-rate mortgages

Maturity: Date on which the principal balance of a loan becomes due and payable

Mentoring: Professional commitment of an experienced Notary Signing Agent to offer advice, counsel and insight to a new or inexperienced Notary Signing Agent

Mortgage: Legal instrument, used in some states instead of a Deed of Trust, that pledges a property to the lender as security for payment of a debt

Mortgagee: In a real property transaction involving a Mortgage, lending entity to which borrower has pledged the property as security for payment of the debt

Mortgagor: Borrower who signs a Mortgage, pledging the property as security for payment of the debt; cf. Trustee

N

Networking: In a business context, the exchange of information and establishment of personal connections within a group of people that have a commercial relationship

Noncompetition Clause: Provision in an independent contractor's agreement that prohibits the Notary Signing Agent from engaging in certain unfair competition practices

Nonconforming Loan: Mortgage loan, also known as a jumbo loan, that exceeds the maximum dollar amount of loans established by Fannie Mae and Freddie Mac; cf. Conforming Loan

Notary Signing Agent: Notary who specializes in home loan document signings

Notice of Right to Cancel: Document in a loan document package that informs the borrower of the borrower's right to cancel (rescind) a loan within three business days following the signing of documents; see also Rescission Period, Right of Rescission

O

Origination Fee: Charge to the borrower that covers the costs of issuing the loan, usually stated as a percentage of the face value of the loan

P

Paid Outside of Closing (POC): Term that refers to loan and other fees in a home loan transaction that are paid outside of escrow

PATRIOT Act: Legislation to help protect Americans against acts of terrorism, enacted in 2001 following the 9/11 attacks and renewed in 2006, which amended the federal Bank Secrecy Act to require all financial institutions to establish a Customer Identification Program (CIP) for identifying new account holders, including borrowers of home loans, for whom Notary Signing Agents are often asked to sign CIP forms at loan signings

PITI: Components — principal, interest, taxes and insurance — of a monthly mortgage payment

Point: Fee or charge equal to one percent of the principal loan amount collected by the lender at the time the loan is made

Postdate: Deceptive and sometimes illegal act of dating a document with a date after that of the actual signing; see also Backdate, Predate

Power of Attorney: Document that gives an attorney in fact the authority to sign or act on behalf of another individual; cf. Trust Agreement

Prequalification: Process of determining how much money a prospective borrower will be eligible to borrow before he or she applies for a loan

Predate: Deceptive and sometimes illegal act of dating a document with a date before that of the actual signing; cf. Backdate; see also Postdate

Prepayment: Unscheduled payment of all or part of the outstanding principal of a mortgage loan before it is due

Prepayment Penalty: Fee that may be charged to a borrower who prepays the outstanding balance on a loan before it is due

Prime Rate: Interest rate banks charge to preferred customers

Principal: (1) Amount of debt, not counting interest, remaining on a loan; (2) Person who is a signer of and party to a document

Prior to Docs (PTD): List of conditions the borrower must meet before the lender will prepare the loan documents

Prior to Funding (PTF): List of conditions the borrower must meet before the lender will send funds to close the escrow

Private Mortgage Insurance (PMI): Insurance that protects the mortgage lender against financial loss resulting from a borrower defaulting on a Mortgage or Deed of Trust

Professionalism: Act of performing a task with a high degree of knowledge, skill and sound judgment and with integrity, excellence and the utmost personal character

Proration: Allocation of expenses, such as taxes, based on the number of days the property is owned during the month of closing

Proxy: Function of one who acts as a substitute for another; see also Attorney in Fact, Signature by Proxy, Trustee

Public Record: Any record open to the public for inspection; see also County Recorder, Recordable Document

R

Rate Lock: Commitment, also known as a lock-in, typically issued by a lender to a borrower and guaranteeing a specified interest rate and certain number of points for a limited time

Real Estate Agent: Person licensed to negotiate and transact the sale of real estate on behalf of the property owner

Real Estate Settlement Procedures Act (RESPA) of 1974: Statute aimed at making consumers more informed about real property settlement services and at eliminating certain abusive practices within the settlement services industry, which requires many of the disclosures that are signed at real estate closings overseen by Notary Signing Agents

Receivables: Amounts of money subject to call for payment

Reconveyance: In a real property transaction involving a Deed of Trust, trustee's act of returning title to the trustor (borrower) when the debt on the property has been paid in full

Recordable Document: Document that may be registered (recorded) with an official agency, such as a County Recorder

Recording: Registration by an official agency, such as a County Recorder, of the details of a properly executed deed, mortgage note or other legal instrument, making the document part of the public record

Refinancing: Process of paying off one loan with the proceeds from a new loan using the same property as security

Regulation Z: Official regulations implementing the Truth in Lending Act (TILA), which provide important guidelines for the disclosures required under the TILA and for calculating the rescission period which applies to many consumer home loans

Rescission Period: Three-day period following signature of loan documents during which customer may cancel (rescind) certain home loan transactions; see also Notice of Right to Cancel, Right of Rescission

Reverse Mortgage: Mortgage that allows elderly homeowners to convert the equity in their home into cash

Right of First Refusal: Provision in an agreement that requires a property owner to give another party the first opportunity to purchase or lease the property before it is offered to others

Right of Rescission: Defining provision of the Truth in Lending Act (TILA), a borrower's right to cancel (rescind) certain home loan transactions; see also Notice of Right to Cancel, Rescission Period

Right of Survivorship: In joint tenancy or community property ownership, right of survivors to acquire the interest of a deceased joint tenant or spouse; cf. Tenancy in Common

S

Second Mortgage: Mortgage that has a lien position subordinate to the first mortgage

Secondary Mortgage Market: Market for the buying and selling of existing mortgages

Secured Loan: Loan backed by collateral

Security: Property pledged as collateral for a loan

Service Provider: Under the Interagency Guidelines, any person or entity that maintains, processes or otherwise is permitted access to a financial institution's customer information, including title companies and signing services; cf. Subservicer

Settlement, Settlement Agent, Settlement Costs: See Closing, Closing Agent, Closing Costs

Signature by Proxy: Signature to a document that is made by a person acting in a representative capacity — such as an attorney in fact or trustee — on behalf of another person

Signing Service: Company that serves as a middleman between closing agents and Notary Signing Agents in setting up loan document signings; cf. Direct Work

Soft Skills: Interpersonal, business etiquette and negotiation skills, nontechnical behaviors, attitudes and social graces necessary to build trusting relationships with customers and clients

Solicitation: Offer for business made to a potential client, used in this chapter to refer primarily to the unprofessional act of entreating or petitioning a borrower for business unrelated to notarization at the close of a loan signing

Step-Rate Mortgage: Mortgage in which interest rate, and thus payments, increase according to a specified scheduled (e.g., seven years), after which the interest rate and payments remain constant for the remainder of the loan; cf. Adjustable-Rate Mortgage, Balloon Mortgage, Fixed-Rate Mortgage, Two-Step Mortgage

Stipulation: Condition that must be met for a home loan to close

Subservicer: Under the Interagency Guidelines, any person who has access to an institution's customer information through its provision of services to the service provider, including Notary Signing Agents

T

Tenancy in Common: Form of co-ownership in which each tenant has a separate interest in and separate rights to the property, with no right of survivorship; cf. Community Property, Joint Tenancy

Title: Written proof of the right to own property

Title Company: Company that specializes in examining and insuring titles to real property

Title Insurance: Insurance against loss resulting from defects of title to a specifically described parcel of real property

Title Search: Examination of city, town or county records to determine the legal ownership of real property and the outstanding liens and claims against that real property

Trust Agreement: Document, also called a Declaration of Trust, by which a grantor names the trustee and beneficiaries of the trust; cf. Power of Attorney

Trustee: Fiduciary that holds or controls property for the benefit of another, e.g., (1) in a real property transaction involving a Deed of Trust, entity (usually a title company) that holds the property in trust as security for payment of the debt to the lender; cf. Mortgagee; (2) in a Trust Agreement, individual authorized to manage the assets of the trust for the benefit of the grantor and his or her beneficiaries; cf. Attorney in Fact; see also Proxy, Signature by Proxy

Trustor: Borrower who signs a Deed of Trust, pledging the property as security for payment of the debt; cf. Mortgagor

Truth in Lending Act (TILA) of 1968: Federal consumer statute designed to strengthen extension of consumer credit by fostering the informed use of credit, particularly by means of defining several lending terms and requiring all lenders to use this common terminology

Two-Step Mortgage: Adjustable-rate mortgage (ARM) that has one interest rate for the first five or seven years of its term and a different interest rate for the remainder of the term; cf. Adjustable-Rate Mortgage, Balloon Mortgage, Fixed-Rate Mortgage, Step-Rate Mortgage; see also Margin

U

Underwriting: Process of evaluating a loan application, by analyzing the borrower's creditworthiness and the quality of the property itself, to determine the risk involved for the lender

Uniform Residential Loan Application: Standardized loan application widely used in the mortgage industry

U.S. Department of Housing and Urban Development (HUD): Government agency whose mission is to create quality affordable homes for all citizens

U.S. Department of Veterans Affairs (VA): Government agency whose mission is to provide patient care and federal benefits to veterans and their dependents

V

VA Mortgage: Mortgage guaranteed by the U.S. Department of Veterans Affairs (VA); cf. Conventional Loan, FHA Mortgage

Vesting: Method of taking title to real property

Course Index

3-Year Prepayment Penalty Addendum to Note ... 244
1040 Schedule C/C-EZ. *See* IRS Forms
1040 Schedule SE. *See* IRS Forms
1099-MISC. *See* IRS Forms
4506-T. *See* IRS Forms
8821. *See* IRS Forms

A

Accepting Assignments. *See* Assignments, Receiving and Accepting
Acknowledgment of Receipt of Appraisal Report ... 128
Acknowledgment of Receipt of Good Faith Estimate and Truth in Lending Act Disclosures ... 119
Addendums to Note ... 243–244
Addendum to Adjustable-Rate Note ... 244
Addendum to Closing Instructions ... 116
Address Certification ... 126
Adjustable-Rate Mortgage (ARM) ... 42
Adjustable-Rate Rider ... 239
Affidavit of Purchaser and Vendor ... 242–243
Affiliated Business Arrangement Disclosure ... 47, 49, 239
Affordable Merit Rate Addendum to Note ... 244
Allonge ... 121
Annual Percentage Rate (APR) ... 41–42, 105–106, 118
Answering Borrower Questions. *See* Unauthorized Practice of Law
Appointment Book ... 62
Appointment Procedures. *See* Executing the Loan Signing; *See* Problems at the Appointment
Appointments, Setting or Confirming ... 7, 75–76
Appraisal, Appraiser ... 11, 129
Appraisal Disclosure ... 128
Appraisal Report ... 128
Appraised Value ... 11
APR. *See* Annual Percentage Rate
Arranging the Workspace ... 85–86
Assignments, Closing ... 280–283
See also Loan Documents, Reviewing; *See also* Loan Documents, Returning

Assignments, Obtaining 63–73
See also Loan Documents, Knowledge of
Assignments, Receiving and Accepting 73–75
Attorney in Fact. See Signatures and Initials
Attorney-Only States........... 15
Automated Valuation Model Notice 129

B

Background Screening........... 1, 24, 335–346
Balloon Rider........... 239
Billing. See Invoicing
Biweekly Payment Rider........... 239
Borrower........... 9, 10, 17, 78, 90, 123, 275
See also Loan Documents, Borrower's Copies; See also Problems at the Appointment; See also ; See also Signatures and Initials; See also Unauthorized Practice of Law; See also Professional Conduct
Borrower's Certification & Authorization 119
Borrower's Closing Statement. See Closing or Settlement Statement
Borrower's Final Closing Statement........... 113
Business Day 39, 45, 46, 241
Business Expenses. See IRS Forms, 1040 Schedule C/C-EZ
Business Tools........... 59–63
See also individual items
Buyer. See Borrower; See Purchase Transaction
Buyer's Final Closing Statement .. 113

C

Calendar Integrity........... 312–313
California Domestic Partnership Addendum to Uniform Residential Loan Application........... 140
California Finance Lenders Law Statement of Loan........... 127
California Impound Account Statement and Election Form........... 124–125
Cell Phone 33, 34, 59, 315–316
Certificate of Loans to One Borrower........... 126–127
Certification. See Notary Signing Agent Certification Program
CIP Form. See Customer Identification Verification
Clients. See Closing Companies; See Direct Work; See Escrow Companies; See Lenders; See Mortgage Banker; See Mortgage Broker; See Signing Services; See Title Companies
Closing Assignments. See Assignments, Closing
Closing Companies........... 72
Closing or Settlement 12–14
Closing or Settlement Agent 7, 9, 11–15, 17, 113, 115, 116, 126, 140
Closing or Settlement Costs 50, 51, 96, 106, 113–114, 116–117
Closing or Settlement Statement........... 79, 113
See also HUD-1/1A Settlement Statement
Closing Script........... 49–50, 51
Collections 286–291
Commercial Loan........... 18
Comparison of Sample Mortgage Features: Typical Mortgage Transaction........... 130
Compliance Agreement........... 111, 131–132, 133
Condominium Rider..... 123–124, 239
Confirming Appointments. See Appointments, Setting or Confirming
Construction Loan 18
Consumer Credit Score Disclosure 129
Continuing Education........... 309–311
See also Notary Signing Agent Certification Program
Copies of Documents. See Loan Documents, Borrower's Copies
Correcting Loan Documents........... 92
Credible Witness. See Identification
Credit Report........... 10, 130
Customer Identification Program (CIP) 53–55, 141
Customer Identification Verification 54–55, 140–141
Customer's Statement of Non-Rescission........... 244–245

D

Dates
- Backdated Documents 88–89
- Date Formats 89
- Date-Sensitive Documents ... 81, 99
- Document Date......... 80–81, 87–91
- Mismatched Dates........... 80, 87, 89
- Notarization Date.................. 87, 89
- Postdated Documents................. 88
- Rescission Dates 45–46, 83, 90, 241
- Signature Date 82, 87

Deed of Trust (Mortgage) 67, 75, 87, 89, 97, 121, 121–123
- *See also* Riders to Security Instrument

Demand/Payoff Statement 244
Direct Work......................... 63, 71–73
Disclosure Concerning the Charging of Per Diem Interest on California Residential Loans 139
Discrimination....................... 304–305
Document Correction Agreement......................... 111, 132

E

Earnings. *See* IRS Forms, 1040 Schedule C/C-EZ
Education. *See* Continuing Education
Electronic Documents (eDocs). *See* Security, Electronic; *See* Loan Documents, Receiving
Equity Line of Credit. *See* Home Equity Line of Credit
Escrow Account.............................. 48
- *See also* California Impound Account Statement and Election Form; *See also* Escrow Waiver Agreement (Tax Only); *See also* Impound Authorization; *See also* Initial Escrow Account Disclosure Statement

Escrow Companies......................... 72
Escrow Waiver Agreement (Tax Only) 125
Estimated Taxes 297
Examination. *See* Notary Signing Agent Certification Program
Executing the Loan Signing 8, 85–94
- *See also* Problems at the Appointment

Expenses. *See* IRS Forms, 1040 Schedule C/C-EZ
Explaining Documents to Borrower. *See* Unauthorized Practice of Law

F

Fair and Accurate Credit Transactions (FACT) Act............. 25
False Statement/Employment/ Occupancy Form Borrowers Certification.............. 111, 133–134
Fannie Mae 1003. *See* Uniform Residential Loan Application
Faxing Documents. *See* Loan Documents, Returning
Fax Machine................................... 60
Federal Equal Credit Opportunity Act Notice.......................... 112, 138
Fees for Services
- Notary Public 51, 295, 299–300, 304, 304–305, 325
- Notary Signing Agent 9, 51, 64, 66, 66–69, 70, 73, 295–297, 303–305, 304–305, 313

Finance Charge 118
FNMA 1009 Affidavit 242–243
Foreclosure 122, 245

G

General Closing Instructions............... 114–115, 141
GLBA. *See* Gramm-Leach-Bliley Financial Services Modernization Act
Good Faith Estimate of Settlement Charges ... 49, 50, 114, 116–117, 119
Good Faith Estimate Providers of Services 117
Gramm-Leach-Bliley Financial Services Modernization Act (GLBA) 16, 22–26, 142, 335–346

H

Hardship 120
Hazard Insurance 115
Hazard Insurance Authorization and Requirements 127, 141
Hazard Insurance Disclosure 127
HELOC. *See* Home Equity Line of Credit

HOEPA/HMDA Required Information 138–139
Home Equity Conversion Mortgage 18
Home Equity Line of Credit (HELOC)..........................14, 17, 44
Homestead Protection 15
Housing Financial Discrimination Act Fair Lending Notice....112, 138
HUD. *See* U.S. Department of Housing and Urban Development
HUD-1/1A Settlement Statement............49–50, 51–52, 79, 84, 96, 106, 113–114, 120

I

Identification................29, 68, 76, 95, 318–319, 325
See also Customer Identification Verification
Impound Account. *See* Escrow Account
Impound Authorization................124
Income. *See* IRS Forms, 1040 Schedule C/C-EZ
Independent Contractor..................7
Independent Contractor's Agreement.......65–69, 71, 282, 283
Information Security Program. *See* Interagency Guidelines
Initial Escrow Account Disclosure Statement...............48, 49, 125–126
Initials. *See* Signatures and Initials
Instructions to Escrow.............79, 96
Interagency Guidelines 23–26, 336–344, 345–346
Interest Rate 16. *See also* Annual Percentage Rate
Invoicing........283–285, 286, 300–302
IRS Forms
1040 Schedule C/C-EZ (Profit and Loss from Business).................7, 291–294, 295, 299, 301, 302
1040 Schedule SE (Self-Employment Tax) 7, 294–297
1099-MISC (Miscellaneous Income)..................65, 291–292
4506-T (Request for Copy of Transcript of Tax Return)........... 136–137, 240
8821 (Tax Information Authorization) 240
W-9 (Request for Taxpayer Identification Number and Certification)...................65, 136
Itemization of Amount Financed....40, 120

J

Journal. *See* Notary Journal

K

Knowledge of Loan Documents........................103–104

L

Lender Instructions.........................79
Lenders...................9, 10–11, 72, 123
Liability. *See* Misconduct
Licensure States 15
Limited Power of Attorney.......... 111, 132–133
Loan Documents. *See also* individual document titles
Lists of Additional Documents.... 111, 272–275
Sample Document Descriptions 113–142, 239–246
Sample Document Overview...........................110–112
Sample Documents...............142, 246
Loan Documents, Borrower's Copies 83–84, 96
Loan Documents, Correcting 92
Loan Documents, Knowledge of 103–104
Loan Documents, Receiving 8, 25, 28, 32, 74, 78
Loan Documents, Returning 8, 29–30, 30–31, 74, 79, 84, 282–283, 320
Loan Documents, Reviewing
After the Appointment...... 281–282
At the Appointment......29, 98, 280
Before the Appointment...... 22, 44, 78–85
Loan Documents, Securing......26–32
Loan Modification Agreement.........................245–246
Loan Signing Prep Sheet..........79–81

M

Marketing Signing Agent Services. *See* Assignments, Obtaining
Mentoring ... 323
Mileage Log ... 61, 299
Misconduct ... 297, 323–328
Mortgage. *See* Deed of Trust
Mortgage Banker ... 72
Mortgage Broker ... 72
Mortgagee ... 123
Mortgagor ... 123
Mortgagor's Affidavit ... 243

N

Name Affidavit ... 111, 130–131
Name Discrepancies ... 90, 95
See also Identification
Networking ... 322
Noncompetition Clause ... 66
Notarial Supplies ... 61
Notary Journal ... 26, 27, 29, 31, 79, 96, 303–306
Notary Misconduct and Liability. *See* Misconduct
Notary Public. *See* Notary Signing Agent
Notary Public Code of Professional Responsibility ... 21–22, 305, 310, 323, 326–327
Notary Signing Agent. *See also* Fees for Services; *See also* Subservicer
As Notary Public ... 8, 18–19, 21–22, 55, 299–300
Definition and Duties ... 5, 7–9, 13–16, 17–18, 55
Precursors ... 6
Notary Signing Agent Certification Program ... 1–3, 309
Notary Signing Agent Log ... 62, 298–303
Notary Signing Agent Opportunity ... 16–17
Notary Signing Agent Pledge of Ethical Practice ... 110
Note ... 67, 75, 79, 84, 87, 89, 97, 105, 120–121
See also Addendums to Note
Notice Concerning the Furnishing of Negative Information to Consumer Reporting Agency ... 129–130
Notice of Assignment, Sale or Transfer of Servicing Rights ... 121, 137–138
Notice of Right to Cancel ... 43, 83, 84, 90, 97, 119, 240–242
Notice of Right to Copy of Appraisal ... 128

O

Occupancy Affidavit ... 111, 135–136
Occupancy and Financial Status Affidavit ... 111, 134–135
Office Tools ... 61
Opt-Out Option ... 142
Outsourcing ... 16

P

PATRIOT Act ... 52–54, 140–141
Payment Letter to Borrower .. 119–120
Payment Policies ... 70, 286–288
Penalties for Misconduct ... 327–328
Personal Data Assistant (PDA) ... 62
Power of Attorney ... 92–93
Prepayment Penalty ... 118
Prepayment Policy ... 105
Printer ... 62–63
Privacy Policy Disclosure ... 142
Privacy Protection ... 21–34
Problems at the Appointment
Borrower Will Not Sign ... 98–99
Stressful Signings ... 316–319
Professional Conduct
With Borrowers ... 312–319
With Clients ... 319–322
With Colleagues ... 322–323
Professionalism ... 307–309, 311
See also Continuing Education
Property Tax Information Certificate ... 13
Proxy. *See* Signatures and Initials
Purchase Transaction ... 10, 14, 18

R

Real Estate Settlement Procedures Act (RESPA) ... 46–55, 113–114, 116–117, 119, 125–126, 137–138, 239, 289–290
Real Estate Tax Bill Certification ... 125

Receiving Assignments. *See* Assignments, Receiving and Accepting
Receiving Documents. *See* Loan Documents, Receiving
Recordkeeping....................... 286–302
Refinance Transaction 10, 12, 14, 17, 44
Regulation Z 38–46
Request for Change to Flood Certification....................... 115, 141
Request for Change to Insurance Policy................................ 115, 141
Rescission...................... 12, 39, 42–46
See also Notice of Right to Cancel; *See also* Customer's Statement of Non-Rescission
RESPA. *See* Real Estate Settlement Procedures Act
Restrictive States 15
Returning Documents. *See* Loan Documents, Returning
Reverse Mortgage 18, 76
Reviewing Documents. *See* Loan Documents, Reviewing
Riders to Security Instrument................. 123–124, 239
Right of Rescission. *See* Rescission

S

Sale Transaction. *See* Purchase Transaction
Schedule C/C-EZ. *See* IRS Forms
Schedule SE. *See* IRS Forms
Secondary Mortgage Market 89
Second Mortgage................10, 14, 66
Security, Document 26–32
Security, Electronic 25
Security Instrument. *See* Deed of Trust (Mortgage)
Self-Employment Taxes. *See* IRS Forms, 1040 Schedule SE
Seller. *See* Purchase Transaction
Seller's Final Closing Statement ... 113
Service Providers 24, 342
Servicing Disclosure Statement..... 49, 137
Setting Appointments. *See* Appointments, Setting or Confirming
Setting the Table....................... 85–86
Settlement. *See* Closing or Settlement
Settlement Agent. *See* Closing or Settlement Agent
Settlement Costs. *See* Closing or Settlement Costs
Settlement Service Providers... 47–48, 117, 239
See also Service Providers
Settlement Statement. *See* HUD-1/1A Settlement Statement
Shipping Documents. *See* Loan Documents, Returning
Signature Affidavit & AKA Statement.................. 111, 130–131
Signatures and Initials 82
Attorney in Fact (Proxy)....... 92–94
Borrower 90, 91
Trustee..91
Signing Services.................... 7, 63–71
See also Service Providers
Smartphone....................................62
Soft Skills.............................. 309, 311
Solicitation .... 316. *See*
Specific Closing Instructions........ 115
Statement of Information 243
Stipulations 77, 79, 83, 96, 98
Subservicer...................... 24, 342, 346

T

Tax Deductions. *See* IRS Forms, 1040 Schedule C/C-EZ
Tax Information Sheet 140
Tax Reporting. *See* Estimated Taxes; *See* IRS Forms, 1040 Schedule C/C-EZ; *See* IRS Forms, 1040 Schedule SE
TILA. *See* Truth in Lending Act
Timely Payment Rewards Addendum to Note 244
Title Companies...................... 72, 123
See also Service Providers
Title Search 11
Training. *See* Continuing Education
Trustee.. 123
See also Signatures and Initials
Trustor.. 123
Truth in Lending Act (TILA).... 37–46, 117–119, 120, 240–242
Truth in Lending Disclosure Statement.......... 40–41, 42, 84, 105, 117–119

U

Unauthorized Practice of Law............ 79, 104–110, 325–327
Uniform Residential Loan Application (Fannie Mae 1003)...................10, 117
USA PATRIOT Act. *See* PATRIOT Act
U.S. Department of Housing and Urban Development (HUD)..................47–53
See also Real Estate Settlement Procedures Act (RESPA)

V

Vesting..97

W

W-9. *See* IRS Forms
Wrapping Up Assignments. *See* Assignments, Closing

ABOUT THE NNA®

The National Notary Association

Since 1957, the National Notary Association — a nonprofit educational organization — has served the nation's Notaries Public with a wide variety of instructional programs and services.

As the country's clearinghouse for information on Notary laws, customs and practices, the NNA educates Notaries through publications, seminars, webinars, online training, annual conferences, its website and the NNA Hotline that offers immediate answers to specific questions about notarization.

The Association is perhaps most widely known as the preeminent source of information for and about Notaries. NNA works include the following:

- *The National Notary*, a magazine for NNA members featuring how-to articles and practical tips on notarizing

- *Notary Bulletin*, an online newsletter that keeps NNA members and customers up to date on developments affecting Notaries, especially new state laws and regulations

- *Sorry, No Can Do!* series, four volumes that help Notaries explain to customers and bosses why some requests for notarizations are improper and cannot be accommodated

- *U.S. Notary Reference Manual*, an invaluable resource for any person relying upon the authenticity and correctness of legal documents

- *Notary Public Practices & Glossary*, a definitive reference book on notarial procedures and widely hailed as the Notary's bible

- State *Notary Law Primers*, short guidebooks that explain a state's Notary statutes in easy-to-understand language

- *The Notary Public Code of Professional Responsibility*, a comprehensive and detailed code of ethical and professional conduct for Notaries

- *The Model Notary Act*, prototype legislation conceived in 1973 and updated in 1984, 2002 and 2010 by an NNA-recruited panel of secretaries of state, legislators and attorneys, and regularly used by state legislatures in revising their Notary laws

- *Notary Signing Agent Training Course*, a manual covering every aspect of signing agent procedures that prepares candidates for the Notary Signing Agent Certification Examination developed by the NNA

- Public-service pamphlets informing the general public about the function of a Notary, including *What Is A Notary Public?* printed in English and Spanish

In addition, the NNA offers the highest quality professional supplies, including official seals and stamps, embossers, recordkeeping journals, jurat stamps, thumbprinting devices and notarial certificates.

Though dedicated primarily to educating and assisting Notaries, the NNA supports implementing effective Notary laws and informing the public about the Notary's vital role in modern society. ■

NOTES

NOTES

NOTES

NOTES

NOTES